SANDRA GUSTAFSON'S

GREAT SLEEPS
LONDON

FIFTH EDITION

CHRONICLE BOOKS
SAN FRANCISCO

Printed in the United States of America

FIFTH EDITION

ISSN: 1074-5033
ISBN: 0-8118-3299-6

Cover design: Ayako Akazawa
Book design: Words & Deeds
Typesetting: Jack Lanning
Series Editor: Jeff Campbell
Author photograph: Marv Summers

Distributed in Canada by
Raincoast Books
9050 Shaughnessy Street
Vancouver, B.C. V6P 6E5

10 9 8 7 6 5 4 3 2 1

Chronicle Books LLC
85 Second Street
San Francisco, California 94105

www.greateatsandsleeps.com
www.chroniclebooks.com

*With genuine thanks again to Marion Fujimoto,
a very special person in my life, and without whose
dedicated help and support I would not be able to
work and write without worry.*

Contents

To the Reader

Go where we may, rest where we will,
Eternal London haunts us still.

> —*Thomas Moore*, Rhymes on the Road, *c. 1820*

When a man is tired of London, he is tired of life; for there is
in London all that life can afford.

> —*Dr. Samuel Johnson*

The British hold a unique place in the hearts of Americans, for we are bound together and influenced in our daily lives by ancestral ties; shared language, laws, literature, customs, and traditions; and strong social and religious values. When we look back, most of us began our lifetime love affair with London as children, listening to nursery rhymes, singing songs, reading about the royal family, and pretending to be a part of it all. For many of us reared in the English-speaking world, a trip to London is like coming home.

Intriguing, invigorating, exciting, London is full of fascinating contrasts. Whether you are making your first or twentieth visit, whatever you are looking for is here: history, tradition, pomp and pageantry, the bright lights of the theater, wonderful music and famous art, fine shopping, and food from around the globe.

Central London has 7 million inhabitants, with another 5.5 million living on the outskirts and commuting into town. The city is host to more than 29 million visitors every year from more than forty countries, and the hotel occupancy rate reflects this: It runs at almost 90 percent. In fact, the number of available rooms is so inadequate that the London Tourist Board is shooting to have fifteen thousand additional rooms ready by 2004. To make Great Sleeping matters even worse, the cost of a London hotel room has increased by more than 60 percent over the last ten years and shows no signs of backsliding. London now has the unfortunate reputation for being one of the most expensive cities in the world to visit, listed in the top five with the highest per diem rates, right up there with Tokyo and ahead of New York.

Many of London's top hotels can easily charge more than $500 per night, with breakfast and VAT (at 17.5 percent) costing extra. The most expensive room in town, the Royal Suite at the Lanesborough on Hyde Park, will set you back a mere £4,400 *per night,* personalized business cards and stationery included, breakfast extra. At the other end of the spectrum, a campsite on the outskirts of town costs £6.

And even though travelers are learning that bigger hotels with fancy price tags are not necessarily better, the sad fact is that for many Americans, so-called budget accommodations in London are not low cost at all. The average London budget hotel runs from £60 to £100 per night for two and offers little in the way of Ye Olde English charm—even less when it comes to space. Travelers who want their money's worth must be creative and remember not to be intimidated by the first quoted price; always try to negotiate. To trim costs, look for weekend packages, off-season rates, and, in small places, offer to pay cash instead of using a credit card. If your stay will be a week or longer, negotiate to get the seventh night free. In many hotels, children sharing their parents' room sleep free or for half price. If you go in the summer, consider accommodations in centrally located college and university dormitories that open their doors to tourists when the students go home.

In small mum-and-pop operations, don't look for many frills, except on the lamp shades and curtains. Most have ten or twelve small rooms decorated in a combination of styles and colors. Usually the bathrooms are down the hall, but in an effort to please American guests, an airless portable unit has been wedged into a corner in some rooms, and the price increased to cover the "improvement." Despite these drawbacks and others, you will usually be treated as a welcome family guest by your hosts. The owner will call you by name, take your phone messages, and collect your mail. On your next visit, you won't have to tell him how to fix your bacon and eggs, and you will get your same room if you request it.

None of the listings in this or any of the books in the Great Eats/Great Sleeps series can be bought or solicited. I do *all* of the research and legwork, and for every edition, I personally check and recheck every hotel and shop listed. Nothing is ever automatically "in," whether it has been a tried-and-true listing or is a well-regarded newcomer. If I find it dirty, unfriendly, overpriced, or otherwise unacceptable, it is out, no matter how great it used to be, how cheap it is, how nice the owner is, or how many others praise it. Because I do all the hotel inspecting myself, I can offer candid, firsthand appraisals, telling you when to leave your expectations at the door, or when to get ready for a Big Splurge stay in a lovely hotel you will want to return to again and again.

My primary guidelines, of course, are value for money and cleanliness, followed by location and management attitude. All Great Sleeps in London, except for the campsites and one or two youth hostels, are within the Circle Line on the London Underground (the tube), which means you will never be more than a thirty-minute tube ride from your hotel into central London. There is no reason to stay far from the action just to save a few pounds. You will quickly spend the difference on extra tube and bus fares, not to mention valuable vacation time and energy spent commuting to all the places you want to see. Think about it . . . do you really want to leave your lodging early in the morning and not be able to go back and rest or freshen up for dinner because it takes too much time in transit? If you are a woman, do you want to curtail evenings at the theater or attending concerts or resort to expensive taxi fares because it is not safe to ride out to the "burbs" late at night on the tube, never mind the walk from the tube stop to the door of your Great Sleep in the dark? I also expect hotel management to be helpful and friendly. In budget Great Sleeps, you cannot expect uniformed porters to carry your bags to rooms vying for a spread in *Architectural Digest,* but you can expect and insist on a clean room in a hospitable place.

During my research in London, I visited hundreds of hotels and other accommodations, and the final selection includes everything from bunks in college dorms to campsites, to family-run B&Bs, to full-service apartments, rooms in private homes, and small, antique-filled, unforgettable boutique hotels. Some fall into the Big Splurge category, for those with higher expectations and more flexible budgets; others are utilitarian and businesslike; and still others are just plain cheap and cheerful. When looking at hotels, I tried to consider your needs and anticipate possible disasters. I have taken elevator rides that were short prison sentences and have felt as though I were on an Outward Bound course as I climbed twisting stairways and groped down gloomy hallways. I checked out the hall toilets, showers, and bathtubs; noted the condition of the shower curtains (if any); felt the toilet tissue (to see if it was No. 1 sandpaper, waxed, or soft); examined the towels; opened closets and dresser drawers; and bounced on beds and looked under them. I also checked on smoking versus nonsmoking policies. (Did the hotel have rooms or floors specifically set aside for nonsmokers, or did the policy consist of the maid opening the window and spraying the room an hour before a guest's arrival?) I dealt with rude owners, indifferent managers, and strange cleaning staff. I found dust balls under the beds, floods in the hallways, food hidden under mattresses, mice in the kitchens, and mold in many bathrooms. I walked more than 570 miles, wore out my shoes and an umbrella, and took notes seven days a week for three and a half months, rain or shine. Endurance was a necessity, not an option, but I loved every minute of it because my job *never* seems like work.

Longtime readers will no doubt notice that the name of the *Cheap Sleeps* series has changed, but it is important to note that this has not changed at all the spirit of the revised and updated fifth edition of *Great Sleeps London.* The purpose is exactly the same: to help you to find the best value for your money so you can spend it wisely. Whatever reason you have for visiting London, and whatever your budget may be, I hope *Great Sleeps London* will continue to hold the key for a more enjoyable stay and make it easier for you to plan the best possible trip.

Wherever your dreams may take you, if you remember to always travel with a smile, lots of patience, and above all a positive attitude, your trip will be successful. May your weather be fair, your time rewarding, and with *Great Sleeps London* in hand, your money well spent. If, at the end of your trip, you return home pleased and satisfied that it was good based on my recommendations, then I have accomplished my goal. Thank you for endorsing my efforts, and I wish you good luck and a safe and wonderful journey.

Tips for Great Sleeps in London

1. Know thyself. When booking a hotel room, what matters most to you? Cost only? A view? Smoking versus nonsmoking? Quiet? Closet space? Charm? Convenience? Type of bed? Bathroom facilities? Besides the budget, consider your interests, habits, physical condition and needs, and sense of aesthetics. Is the hotel room a retreat, or merely a place to take a fast shower and spend the night? In other words . . . what is *your* bottom line for acceptance?

2. Unless you are a nomadic backpacker who does not care where you lay your head, do not even consider arriving in London without confirmed hotel reservations. Why waste precious vacation time standing in lines at tourist offices or railway stations, hoping to land something in your price range, only to wind up spending more money for accommodations in a marginal location because nothing else is available?

3. The cheapest room will be one in the back of the hotel, without private facilities. No matter where it is situated, a room with a double bed and a shower will be smaller and will cost less than a room with twin beds and a bathtub.

4. In lower-priced hotels and B&Bs that offer rooms with and without private toilet and bathing facilities, you will save money and gain precious space if you reserve a room *without* a private toilet and shower or bathtub. Often these "private" bathrooms are little more than airless portable units squeezed into a corner of the room. In most cases, the hall facilities are far superior.

5. If you are susceptible to cold and visit London during the winter, ask whether your room will be heated continuously or if the central heating will be turned off at certain times during the day and night, leaving you in icy discomfort. One hotelier told me his simple policy on this: "I turn the heat on when I think it should be, not when you think it should be." Conversely, if you go in summer, a room facing the front of the hotel may have the best view, but if you open the window for air (most hotels do not have air-conditioning), you may get an overdose of noise, exhaust fumes, and dirt from passing traffic.

6. From a security standpoint, stay at least one floor above ground level.

7. To get the best hotel price, go in the off-season, from November through March.

8. You would be surprised at the discounts you can get if only you ask. For instance, ask that the price of breakfast be deducted from your room rate; inquire about special weekend or holiday rates; if your children share your room, do they stay free? If you stay a week or more in a small B&B or offer to pay in cash, you might get a price break, depending on the season. Booking on-line is often another way to cut hotel costs. If you reserve through a toll-free 800 number from the States, know that the operators are seldom authorized to grant discounts. While it always pays to ask if they can reserve special rate deals, you usually have to speak directly with the hotel to do that. Also, if one 800 operator says the hotel in question is fully booked, wait a while and call back. Cancellations happen as often as reservations.

9. Another way to save money is to find a package combining your airfare with your hotel stay.

10. *Always* inspect the room before you check in.

11. Upon arrival, review the rates and what they include. Don't wait until the end of your stay; checkout time is not when you want to discover the rates did not include the VAT (17.5 percent value-added tax) or those huge breakfasts you enjoyed every morning.

12. Be sure you understand the house rules. How late will someone be at the desk to let you in or to take telephone messages? When is checkout time, and can you store luggage in a safe place at the hotel if your flight leaves later in the day? If you have an early-morning flight, can you get a cup of tea or coffee and a roll before the hotel breakfast is served? Please also be aware that in many small B&Bs, towels are not changed daily, but only twice weekly, as the law demands.

13. When calling home, beware of using the hotel telephone before inquiring about their surcharges. Use your own phone card or buy an international calling card, available at most news kiosks and agents in London. Surcharges in hotels can run as high as 100 percent of the cost of the call. (See "Staying in Touch," page 33.)

14. Don't go uninsured. Check your homeowner's and health insurance coverage before you go to learn what is covered abroad, and what is not, and always seriously consider buying supplemental travel insurance. For more information, please see "Insurance," page 29, and "Health Matters," page 30.

15. Most hostels and university dorms have lockers or safes, and sometimes both. If you plan to stay in youth hostels or bunk in large dorm rooms in some of the college and university accommodations, invest in the best combination locks you can find both to store your luggage or backpack and to hold their zippers closed. Wear a money belt, leave nothing of value in your room (even if

you are just taking a quick shower down the hall), don't flash cash or jewelry, and lock up all valuables and important papers in the facility's safe.

16. Do your own laundry or take it to the neighborhood laundromat. Hotel laundry charges can ruin a budget with the cost of washing and ironing two shirts. If you wash clothes in your hotel room, please be considerate and do not let your things drip-dry onto the carpeting.

17. Never change money in a hotel, and try not to use the many Chequepoint or other exchange offices you will pass. The rates will not be in your favor. (See "Money Matters," page 25.)

18. If you receive unacceptable service at your hotel, complain to the owner or highest person in charge, not to the desk clerk, who has no authority to make changes and may not report your complaint to higher-ups for fear of losing his or her job. If the situation cannot be resolved to your satisfaction, report your problem to the London Tourist Board. Then let me know (see "Readers' Comments," page 343). I cannot be your go-between, but I want to know if an entry of mine does not live up to your expectations. I personally report all complaints and compliments to the management on my next visit to inspect that hotel.

One last recommendation: This has nothing to do with London, but I must tell you about it even though the hotel is a long way from the British capital. If I could figure out a way to do it, I would experience a bit of heaven on earth by moving permanently to Dunain Park Hotel, a lovely Georgian country home set amid six acres of beautiful gardens and rolling woodlands overlooking the Caledonian Canal, just outside Inverness in the heart of the Scottish Highlands. It is owned and personally run by Edward and Ann Nicoll, who are ably assisted by Alex at the desk and three important permanent guests: Laddie, Lassie, and Pepe, the three dogs who had the good sense to move in and be adopted by the Nicoll family. Ann is a noted gourmet cook, and every meal you enjoy here will reflect her talent and expertise. Edward is the official host, always on red alert to make sure everyone's needs are met. The hotel's overall excellence is reflected in its being awarded the prestigious César Award as the Scottish Country House of the Year for 2001.

Dunain Park looks and feels like the Nicolls's own home because it is, with their many lovely antiques, paintings, family photos, and collectibles lovingly displayed throughout. The bedrooms are all spacious and tastefully furnished, with comfortable sitting areas, cable television, views over the hills, and huge Italian-marble-lined baths. The formal dining room shines in the morning light as you gently ease in to a filling breakfast, cooked to your order. The eggs come from the next farm, and the warm scones, whole-meal toast, buttery croissants, jams, and marmalades are all homemade. In the evening this room serves as the stage set for Ann's exceptional dinners, featuring Angus beef, local produce, and a bountiful dessert buffet. Just one of her many lovely touches is the tray of coffee and homemade sweets set out in the sitting room for guests to help themselves to after dinner.

During the day, in addition to walking on the grounds, you can work off some of those delicious calories by doing laps in the heated indoor swimming pool or melting them off in the sauna. Only a brisk walk away is the charming town of Inverness, beautifully situated on the River Ness and the perfect starting point for exploring the Scottish Highlands, strolling the banks of Loch Ness, or just meandering around the town, appreciating its friendly atmosphere and local shops. Sports enthusiasts will find themselves close to twenty golf courses, as well as wonderful fishing holes and riding trails.

You can visit Dunain Park Hotel any time of year, but my favorite times to go are during the Christmas and New Year's holidays, when it is beautifully decorated and special meals are served; in the spring, when more than seven thousand bulbs are in full bloom in the garden; and in summer, when the days are long and the heather is on the hills. Whenever you go, please give them my warmest regards and don't forget to say hello to Laddie, Lassie, and Pepe as well. Dunain Park Hotel, Inverness, Scotland IV3 8JN; tel: 01463-230512; fax: 01463-224532; email: Dunainparkhotel@btinternet.com; Internet: www.dunainparkhotel.co.uk. All of the rates for the eleven rooms and two cottages are quoted on request and change according to the time of year. They are moderate when you see that they include dinner, bed, and breakfast in the winter, and in the summer, bed and breakfast with dinner optional. Special package rates are offered at Christmas, New Year's, and Easter.

General Information

The good traveler has the gift of surprise.
                    —*W. Somerset Maugham*

Be prepared.
                    —*Boy Scout motto*

When to Go

A vacation is what you take when you can no longer take what you've been taking.
                    —*Earl Wilson*

For most of us a trip to London is not a spur-of-the-moment decision. It is usually part of a carefully planned vacation anticipated for some time. If you are really serious about having the most economical trip possible, you must plan to go during the low season. Low season for both airline fares and hotel rates generally runs between November and March, with the week around the Christmas and New Year's holidays excepted. The weather can be cold, damp, and rainy, but on the plus side, tickets to your favorite show will be easier to get, and you will not have to face crowds in the museums. If you are a shopper, don't forget the January sales, when prices are slashed to their lowest point of the year.

High season runs from April to October, with the big influx from June through August. In August you will share your London vacation with fellow travelers from around the world but with very few Londoners, because most of them will have escaped to the country for their summer holidays. Also, during the summer, hotel prices will be at their peak. If there is a heat wave, you will swelter, because few hotels have any sort of air-conditioning other than a fan, if you are lucky enough to snag one of the few fans the hotel *may* have on hand. Fall is my favorite time in London. The weather is nice, the colors are magnificent, and the tourists are few. As Christmas approaches, London becomes a fairyland of lights, and the beautifully decorated stores are filled with tempting presents.

Holidays and Events

Public holidays in England—other than Christmas, New Year's, and Easter—are referred to as "bank holidays," because on those days the banks are closed. It used to be that everything else was closed as well, but now you will find major stores and many shops open for five or six hours. Museums have their own bank holiday schedules; call ahead to check on opening hours.

New Year's Day	January 1
Good Friday	Friday before Easter
Easter Sunday	Varies
Easter Monday	Monday after Easter
May Day bank holiday	First Monday in May
Spring bank holiday	Last Monday in May
Summer bank holiday	Last Monday in August
Christmas Day	December 25
Boxing Day	December 26

Events in London

The following calendar is a mere starting point. For detailed information on what is happening in London, consult the weekly guides *Time Out in London* or *What's On,* available at all London news kiosks. The London Tourist Board operates Visitorcall, giving daily updated telephone information on London's events, exhibitions, theater, concerts, sight-seeing, and more. Tel: 020 7971 0026; Internet: www.LondonTown.com.

January: Charles I Commemoration. The last Sunday in January marks the anniversary of the 1649 execution of King Charles I.

February: Gerrard Street in Chinatown celebrates Chinese New Year. Dates are based on the lunar calendar; Tel: 020 7439 3822.

March: The Easter Parade in Battersea Park includes floats and marching bands; wear your Easter bonnet and join the parade. The boat race between the eight-man rowing sculls of Cambridge and Oxford runs four miles along the Thames from Putney to Mortlake; Tel: 020 7379 3234.

April: The London Marathon Race, the world's largest, with more than thirty thousand participants running almost twenty-seven miles, takes place in late April; Tel: 020 7620 4117.

May: The Chelsea Flower Show, an international floral spectacle, defies description. For ticket information, write Shows Department, Royal Horticultural Society, Vincent Square, London SW1P 2PE; Tel: 020 7630 7422.

June: June is a busy month. The Derby takes place at Epsom Racecourse in Surrey (Tel: 01372 470 047), along with Royal Ascot, a four-day event in Berkshire that is as well known for its fashion attendees, glamorous outfits, and outrageous hats as it is for its actual horse races (Tel: 01344 622 211). Another June event (the second or third weekend of the month) is Trooping the Colour, the official birthday celebration of the queen, which represents the ultimate in pomp and pageantry. For tickets, you *must* apply in writing between January and the end of February, enclosing an International Reply Coupon. You can ask for free, unlimited tickets to the first rehearsal, pay around £10 to attend the second rehearsal, or pay £20 for the actual day of the event and be limited to three tickets. Tel: 020 7414 2279, 020 7414 2479. Send your application and International Reply Coupon to Headquarters, Household Division,

Horse Guards, Trooping the Colour, Whitehall SW1A 2AX. Also in June and into early July are the Wimbledon Lawn Tennis Championships (Tel: 020 8946 2244) and the Henley Royal Regatta (Tel: 01491 572 153).

July: Royal Tournament, at Earl's Court Exhibition Center, Warwick Road (Tel: 020 7244 0371) is a fabulous display of British athletic and military skills.

August: The Notting Hill Carnival, Ladbroke Grove, is the largest street festival in Europe (Tel: 020 8964 0544).

September: Chelsea Antiques Fair (Tel: 01444 482 514).

November: State Opening of Parliament (sometimes it's in late October). The ceremony is not open to the public, but you can stand on the parade route and see the royal procession (Tel: 020 7219 4272). The Lord Mayor's Procession and Show in the City is a colorful parade celebrating the inauguration of the new lord mayor, who rides in a gilded coach from Guildhall to the Royal Courts of Justice, usually on the second Saturday in November (Tel: 020 7606 3030). At the Remembrance Sunday Ceremony, the queen, the prime minister, and other VIPs lay wreaths and observe a moment of silence at the Cenotaph, commemorating those who died fighting for Britain in both world wars.

December: The lighting of the Christmas tree in Trafalgar Square (Tel: 020 7211 2109), as well as special lighting ceremonies in most of the main shopping areas of the city, are festive occasions. New Year's Eve Celebrations are centered on Trafalgar Square, and if you like ringing in the New Year squeezed into a crushing mob scene of half inebriated revelers, then, Happy New Year!

What to Bring

On a long journey, even a straw weighs heavy.
—*Spanish proverb*

There is no such thing as bad weather, only wrong clothing.
—*Old Estonian saying*

If you accept only one piece of advice from me on packing, let it be this: Travel light. Take half as many clothes as you think you will need and twice as much money. You will thank me. Porters are almost relics of the past, especially in airports and train stations. They don't exist at any of the B&Bs I know of, and most of the time, neither do elevators. Dragging heavy bags up and down stairs in tube stations is no fun. Keep in mind you are going to London, not Pluto, so you will be able to wash, throw out, or buy more of whatever you need while you are there.

Pack your bags with the weather in mind. Day after day, the weather reports on the radio and "telly" will be one or a combination of the following: fine but frosty; scattered clouds; possible showers interspersed with sunny periods; drizzle turning to heavy rain; blustery. British weather is generally mild, but impossible to predict. To be safe, never leave the hotel without an umbrella and sunglasses. For daily updates, call the twenty-four-hour Weathercall at 0891 500 401 (50p per minute; you can get national weather information at this number as well), or look on the Internet at www.weather.com. You also can call 020 7388 7575 for London weather information.

London's Average Daytime Temperatures, Hours of Sunshine, and Rainfall

	Jan.	Feb.	Mar.	Apr.	May	June	July	Aug.	Sept.	Oct.	Nov.	Dec.
Temp (°C/F)	6/43	6/43	8/46	10/50	13/55	16/61	19/66	19/66	16/61	13/55	9/48	7/45
Rainfall (inches)	1.8	1.2	1.7	1.5	1.9	1.8	1.8	1.7	1.6	2.2	1.8	1.5
Hours of Sunshine	2	2.5	3.3	5.3	6.3	6.2	6.7	6.6	5.0	3.5	2.3	1.5

We all know that comfortable, well-broken-in shoes are a must on everyone's list. So is an umbrella, the collapsible kind you can tuck into a purse or tote bag. Other essentials include sweaters for layering, a hat that can be rolled up or squashed in your luggage without losing shape, and a raincoat with a zip-out lining. London is a rather formal city, where you see men in the supermarkets on a Saturday afternoon or a Sunday properly dressed in a coat and tie. Short shorts, halter tops, baseball caps, and other vacation-resort-style clothing is inappropriate here, no matter how high the thermometer climbs in August.

Leave your diamonds, emeralds, gold bracelets, and other valuables at home. If you do bring something of value and are not wearing it, put it in the hotel safe. Don't hide it in your room because hotel thieves know about every hiding place you can think of, and probably some you cannot.

The following list of useful items is not exhaustive, but it is one compiled over the years by a veteran traveler.

- Calculator
- Electrical adapter kit
- Surge protector (for a computer)
- Moist towelettes and a bottle of antiseptic wash
- A bar or bottle of bath soap and shampoo
- Sunscreen and sunglasses
- Portable radio with earphones
- Pedometer to keep track of the number of miles you walk, so you can impress your friends when you return
- First-aid kit

- Sewing kit, with a pair of decent scissors
- Travel tool kit with Swiss Army knife, screwdriver, tape, stapler, packing tape, Scotch tape, string
- Rubber doorstop as a security measure
- Rubber sink for drip-dry laundries; clothesline with clothespins, or clothespins you can hang up; a small container of spot remover to use on tough stains before you wash your clothes in your room sink or bathtub. (However, don't pack laundry soap; it's cheap and readily available wherever you go.)
- Suction hook for the back of the bathroom or bedroom door
- Suction-cup magnifying mirror
- Alarm clock
- Flashlight
- Something to read
- Camera, and five more rolls of film than you think you will need
- Extra batteries
- And, if you are going to be away for a long time, a few photos in lightweight folding leather frames of the people you will miss the most

Disabled Travelers

London is better than some cities for the handicapped visitor, but it still has a long way to go. A few helpful telephone numbers and addresses are listed here. One of the best travel resources is on the Internet at www.access-able.com.

Disabled visitors to London should invest in the best book on the subject: *Access in London,* by Gordon Couch, William Forrester, and Justin Irwin. It is available free of charge (but a donation is welcome) from Access Project, 39 Bradley Gardens, W13 8HE; Tel: 020 7250 3222. It's also available for £7.95, including postage, from RADAR (Royal Association for Disability and Rehabilitation), 12 City Forum, 250 City Road, EC1V 8AF; Tel: 020 7250 3222.

For information on arts and entertainment, contact or visit Artsline: 54 Chalton Street, NW1; Tel: 020 7388 2227; Internet: www.dircon.co.uk/artsline; Tube: Euston; Open: Mon–Fri 9:30 A.M.–5:30 P.M.

DIAL (Disability Arts in London) produces a monthly magazine and organizes events in London: Diorama Arts Centre, 34 Osnaburgh Street, NW1; Tel: 020 7916 6351; Fax: 020 7916 5396; Email: dial@dial.dircon.co.uk; Internet: www.dial.dircon.co.uk; Open: Mon–Fri 10:30 A.M.–6:30 P.M.

Holiday Care Service offers help in finding accommodations for disabled visitors. Tel: 01293 774 535; Fax: 01293 784 647; Email: holiday.care@virgin.net; Internet: freespace.virgin.net/hol.care; Open: Mon–Fri 9 A.M.–5 P.M.

William Forrester, an experienced London guide who is himself disabled, leads tours for disabled visitors. Tel: 01483 575 401.

London Transport publishes a free booklet, *Access to the Underground,* that gives information on facilities for the disabled on the tube. Contact the London Transport Unit for the Disabled, 172 Buckingham Palace Road, SW1; Tel: 020 7918 3312; Fax: 020 7918 3876; Email: lt.udp@buses.co.uk. The booklet is also available from all LT ticket offices and information centers at Euston, King's Cross, Liverpool Street, Oxford Circus, Piccadilly Circus, St. James's Park, and Victoria Stations, and at Heathrow Airport.

Tripscope has information on transport for the elderly and handicapped; Tel: 020 8580 7021.

Students should contact Students with Disabilities: Chapter House, 18–20 Crucifix Lane, SE1; Tel: 0800 328 5050; Open: Mon–Fri 1:30–4:30 P.M.

Discounts

Museums

London's museums offer a visual banquet of delights—from Goya at the Royal Academy of Arts to Fabergé at the Victoria and Albert. There are more than three hundred museums, galleries, and collections in London, and many of them are now free, except for certain special exhibitions and events. There are four national museums that are always free to everyone, except for special exhibitions: the British Museum, Tate Britain, Tate Modern, and National Gallery. Many other museums have free admission for seniors over sixty, those with disabilities, and children under sixteen. The rest of us pay a standard £1 for entrance to the Natural History Museum, Science Museum, Victoria and Albert Museum, Imperial War Museum, National Maritime Museum in Greenwich, Apsley House, Theatre Museum, and more.

Among the smaller, specialist museums and collections that do not charge admission are: Bethnal Green Museum of Childhood, Bank of England Museum, Geffrye Museum, Serpentine Museum in Hyde Park, and the Wallace Collection.

Among the famous buildings that can be viewed free of charge are the Royal Courts of Justice, Central Criminal Court (Old Bailey), and Guildhall. For a listing of museum shops, please see page 318.

Seniors

Sometimes it pays to get older, especially if you are traveling. Significant savings are available to seniors as young as fifty. Interested? Read on.

Many airlines, including British Airways, offer special discounts on their regular airfares. British Airways also offers senior citizen discounts on a range of their tours within the country to those sixty or older, and to any companions traveling with them who are fifty or older.

Men who are sixty-five and women who are sixty qualify for some worthwhile discounts on train travel within the U.K. You may be able to save up to a third on some fares and pay half price for off-peak Cheap Day Return Tickets. You can purchase these and other train tickets in London at mainline railway stations: Victoria, Euston, Charing Cross, King's Cross, St. Pancras, or Waterloo. (See "Transportation," page 36, for more on British rail travel.)

Anyone over sixty is admitted free to all national museums. Very often seniors can get reduced entry tickets to many other London attractions and theaters, and at the movies. Always ask, and have your passport handy for proof; you never know where and when you will get lucky and get in for less. Usually these bargains are not advertised; *you must ask.*

Note: Senior citizens, unfortunately, are called old-age pensioners (OAPs) in Britain, so if the term *senior citizen* doesn't work, try OAP.

Students and Teachers

If you can prove you are a degree-seeking student in a secondary or postsecondary school and are over twelve, your best travel investment will be the International Student Identity Card (ISIC). With this card you will have access to more than eight thousand discounts on transportation, accommodations, and cultural events. You must always present the card to get the discount. Always ask about a discount even if none is mentioned. Because of bogus ISICs, many airlines and some other places now require other proof of student identity. To be on the safe side, carry with you a signed letter from your registrar attesting to your student status and stamped with the school seal, and carry your school ID card. If you buy your card in the States, you will get limited accident, medical, hospital, and medical evacuation insurance and access to a toll-free hot line for help in medical, legal, and financial emergencies abroad. When you apply for the card, ask for a copy of the International Student Identity Card Handbook, which lists some of the discounts by country. The card is valid from September to December of the following year, and the cost is around $22. The card is available from most student unions and student travel agencies (see "Budget Travel Organizations" below).

The International Teacher Identity Card (ITIC) offers similar discounts, including medical insurance. The cost is also around $22, and it can be ordered from the same travel organizations (see below).

If you are under twenty-six and not a student, you still can get some discounts. The Federation of International Youth Travel Organizations (FIYTO) issues a discount card to those under twenty-six who are not students. It is known as the GO 25 Card. It costs $22, is valid for one year, and offers many of the same discounts and benefits as the ISIC. Most of the budget travel organizations listed below sell the card. To apply, you will need proof of birth date and a passport-size photo.

Budget Travel Organizations

The budget travel companies on the following list offer discounted flights for students and young persons, rail passes, ISIC and ITIC discount cards, hostel memberships, travel guides, and general budget-travel know-how based on firsthand experience.

usitCAMPUS: Affiliated with Council Travel in the United States, this agency specializes in sending young people all over the world at minimal expense. The main office in London is at 52 Grosvenor Gardens, SW1; Tel: 0870 240 1010 (general information call center); Internet: www.usitworld.com or usitcampus.co.uk. Tube: Victoria; Open: Mon–Fri 9 A.M.–6 P.M., Sat 10 A.M.–4 P.M.

Other offices with generally the same hours are: YHA Adventure Shop, 14 Southampton Street, WC2; Tel: 020 7836 3343; YHA Adventure Shop, 174 Kensington High Street, W8; Tel: 020 7938 2188; South Bank University Students' Union, Keyworth Street, SE1; Tel: 020 7401 8666.

Council Travel: This full-service travel agency specializes in student, youth, and budget travel. It has more than fifty offices around the world and sells the ISIC, GO 25, and ITIC cards. The London office is at 28A Poland Street, W1; Tel: 0870 240 1010 (toll-free in the United States 800-2COUNCIL); Internet: www.counciltravel.com; Tube: Oxford Circus; Open: generally Mon–Fri 9 A.M.–6 P.M., Sat 10 A.M.–5 P.M.

Educational Travel Centre: This budget travel agency has a free pamphlet, *Taking Off,* covering general travel information; Tel: 800-747-5551; Internet: www.edtrav.com.

Theater and Concerts

Half-price tickets for theater performances and concerts are sold at the Half-Price Ticket Booth in the Clocktower Building by the south corner of Leicester Square. "What a deal!" you think. "All the top London shows and concerts for half price." *Wrong!* Yes, you can buy tickets for some of the hit shows and concerts, but not all on the top-ten hit parade by any means. Here is how the Half-Price Ticket Booth works: Drop by the kiosk on the south edge of the grassy part of Leicester Square and check out what's "on sale" for the day's matinee and evening shows. Tickets are sold in a limited number only for that day's performances and are restricted to four per person. There is a £2 service charge per ticket, you have no seat choice, and you cannot return the tickets or use your credit card. If you are willing to queue for up to an hour or more, pay cash, and hope for a good seat . . . good luck. Tel: 020 7831 0971; Tube: Leicester Square; Open: Tues–Sat noon–6:30 P.M. Tickets are sold for matinees until thirty minutes before the performance and beginning at 2 P.M. for evening performances. Sunday it's open for matinees only noon–3:30 P.M. Warning: Be wary of ticket touts around here who try to sell you front-row seats to Andrew Lloyd Webber's latest hit. These are bogus. There are other so-called discount ticket outlets in and around Leicester Square, but they are not cheap and are not part of the Half-Price Ticket Booth.

If you are being especially frugal and don't mind cutting it close, you can take your chances trying to snag a reduced-price standby ticket at the box office about an hour before curtain. If the show you want to see is sold out, don't always believe it. You can always queue for returned tickets ("returns") on the afternoon or evening before the performance, too. If you have an ISIC or are a senior citizen, you are sometimes eligible to buy tickets at the box offices of the top shows at reduced prices. Not all theaters participate in this, and some do it only for matinees, so call first. If you are a senior citizen but don't look it, bring along your passport as proof of age. Free West End theater guides are distributed by tourist offices and kept in most hotels. You can also check the daily papers for what's on or look in the weekly magazine *Time Out*.

If taking a chance on standby tickets or queuing for a theater ticket at the Half-Price Ticket Booth is not your idea of vacation fun, there are other ways to purchase theater and concert tickets. Remember that matinee performances are cheaper than evening shows, and seats for Monday to Thursday West End performances are usually cheaper than those for Friday and Saturday nights. The easiest, and costliest, way is to book before leaving home through Keith Prowse, 234 West 44th Street, New York, NY 10036; Tel: 212-398-1430 or 800-669-8687 (outside New York); Internet: www.keithprowse.com; Open: Mon–Fri 9 A.M.–8 P.M., Eastern Standard Time. Once in London, it is almost as expensive to buy tickets through a booking agent such as those in the basement of Harrods, or deal with your hotel concierge. Be forewarned that in addition to the full price of your ticket, agencies and concierges take a service charge, sometimes as high as 25 percent on *each* ticket, depending on the popularity of the show. Unless you are hell-bent on seeing a particular show and cost is no object, I suggest that you wait until you arrive in London and try your luck directly at the theater box office. This way you will at least save the booking fee.

When booking a seat, keep in mind the following locations: Stalls are the best, then the Dress Circle, Upper Circle, and finally the Balcony, often referred to as "the gods," meaning you are so far up you are almost in heaven.

Discount Cards

The LONDON for less card offers discounts from 20 to 70 percent at more than three hundred places in London, including selected museums and attractions, concerts, hotels, tours, car rental agencies, restaurants, and some shops. The card can be purchased at any London Tourist Information Centre, and the price is under £15. One discount card is valid for up to four people for up to eight consecutive days. Tel: 888-463-6753; Internet: www.for-less.com; Open: Mon–Fri 9 A.M.–4:30 P.M.

The London Pass provides free entry to more than forty attractions and free, unlimited use of public transportation. Participants include art galleries, museums, river cruises, historic sites and houses, cathedrals, guided tours, and more. The pass is valid for one, two, three, or six days and costs around $25, depending on its period of validity. It is issued with a hundred-page guide with maps and other useful information. Tel: 0870 242 9988; Internet: www.londonpass.com.

Tours

Gastro-Soho Tour

Jenny Linford, a recognized London food expert, leads this weekly two-hour tour through Soho's varied food shops. It is a fascinating glimpse into a part of ethnic London most visitors would never see on their own. For around £20 per person, including refreshments, Jenny will lead you through Chinatown, Italian delis, whiskey shops, European bakeries, and much more. If you are a foodie, you will love this. To book a tour, call Jenny and arrange your dates.

Telephone: 020 8440 0794

Credit Cards: None, cash only

Price: Around £20 per person

The Original London Walks

Veteran travelers know that the best way to see and understand a city is to walk. To put purpose in your steps, join one of the dozens of fascinating walks organized by the Original London Walks, the oldest and by far the best walking tour organization in the city. Its distinctive black-and-white brochures can be found in almost every hotel and in all the tourist offices. The walks last at least two hours, take place rain or shine, and run 365 days a year, including Christmas and Boxing Day. There is no need to book ahead . . . just show up at the appointed time and place, pay the modest fee, and get set for two of the most interesting hours you will spend in London. The range of interests covered is enormous; there are bound to be at least two or three tours to appeal to everyone. If you decide you want to take several walks, ask about the Discount Walkabout Card. The walk offerings are not restricted to London, but include full- and half-day trips outside the capital.

Telephone: 020 7624 3978

Recorded Information: 020 7794 1764

Fax: 020 7625 1932
Email: london@walks.com
Internet: www.walks.com
Credit cards: None, cash only
Price: £5 (£3.50 for senior citizens and full-time students under 30 with ID)

Tourist Offices and American Embassy

The British Tourist Authority has information on all parts of Britain, including books, maps, gifts, theater and hotel bookings, and a travel agency. The head U.S. office is at 551 Fifth Avenue, Suite 701, New York, NY 10176-0799; Tel: 212-986-2266 (executive offices), 212-986-2200 (brochures and travel information), 800-462-2748 (toll-free from the United States); Fax: 212-986-1188; Email: travelinfo@bta.org.uk; Internet: www.travelbritain.com.

In London, the Britain Visitor Center and English Tourist Center is at 1 Lower Regent Street, London SW1; Tel: 020 8846 9000; Internet: www.visitbritain.com; www.englishtourism.org.uk; Tube: Piccadilly Circus; Open: Mon–Fri 9 A.M.–6:30 P.M., Sat–Sun 10 A.M.–4 P.M.

The City of London Information Center dispenses information and advice, primarily on the city. Ask for the monthly *Diary of Events,* listing a wide variety of free entertainment in London. St. Paul's Churchyard, London EC4; Tel: 020 7606 3030, or 020 7332 3456; Internet: www.cityoflondon.gov.uk; Tube: St. Paul's; Open: Mon–Fri 9:30 A.M.–5 P.M., Sat until noon.

The Victoria Tourist Information Centre of the London Tourist Board is at Victoria Station Forecourt, London SW1; Tel: 020 7932 2000; Internet: www.londontown.com; Tube: Victoria; Open: Mon–Sat 8 A.M.–8 P.M., Sun until 6 P.M. Other offices are at Heathrow Airport, the Tower of London, Liverpool Street Station, and Waterloo. For the latest information on what's happening in London, call Visitorcall, a recorded service that is available twenty-four hours a day. For a free card listing all of the London Tourist Board's services, call 020 7971 0026.

The American Embassy is at 24 Grosvenor Square, London W1; Tel: 020 7499 9000; Tube: Bond Street; Consular hours: Mon–Fri 8:30 A.M.–5:30 P.M.

Money Matters

Nothing is certain in London but expense.

—William Shenstone, remark quoted in Isaac
D'Israeli, Curiosities of Literature, *1791–1834*

It doesn't seem to cost a lot of money to go away.

—Lewis Carroll, Alice in Wonderland

While cash never goes out of style, it isn't smart to travel with big wads of it. If you carry traveler's checks, charge on your credit cards, and use ATMs, you will have the money game down pat. Be sure to carry a few of your own personal checks. If you suddenly run out of money, you can use them to get cash advances, provided the credit cards you have allow that.

Always arrive in London with a few pounds in your pocket. True, you may pay something to get these pounds before you leave home, but it will be a welcome investment against getting off a long flight, waiting for baggage, and then having to hunt down an ATM (that works) or, worse yet, queuing at a currency exchange office with rates definitely *not* in your favor. Some U.S. banks can supply foreign currency if you order it ahead, but it is just as easy to contact one of the following companies that specialize in foreign currency orders shipped directly to your address. Warning: Don't wait for the last minute to arrange for currency to be sent; unfortunately, delays do occur.

American Express provides cash or traveler's checks in foreign currencies to its cardholders. If you have a green card, the commission on it is 1 percent. Gold and platinum cardholders pay no commission. Tel: 800-221-7282; Internet: www.americanexpress.com.

Capital Foreign Exchange, a division of Associated Foreign Exhange, offers U.S. and over one hundred foreign currency travelers checks, which can be shipped directly to you ($15 fee). Contact them at 825 14th Street NW, Washington, DC 20005; Tel: 888-842-0880; Internet: www.afex.com; Credit Cards: MC, V; Open: Mon–Fri: 9 A.M.–5:30 P.M.

Thomas Cook provides foreign cash or traveler's checks in U.S. dollars, which can be sent to your address or collected at a Thomas Cook office. It also issues foreign-denomination traveler's checks commission-free, which can be converted back to U.S. dollars at no additional charge. Other services include immediate wire transfer service, international drafts, cutting international currency checks, foreign check collection, and rechargeable worldwide phone cards ($10 to $40). Tel: 800-287-7362; Internet: www.us.thomascook.com.

Automated Teller Machines—ATMs

What did we ever do before ATMs? These electronic wonders of convenience are now available in Britain, provided your bank belongs to one of the London networks. Before you race to the nearest London ATM and punch in your stateside PIN (personal identification number), there are some things you should know. For openers, commissions and fees could cost you up to 10 percent of the transaction. Find out what rate your bank charges, because the transaction fee could cost you dearly if you do only small cash withdrawals. ATMs abroad may not always function, thanks to clogged computer lines, which means you will have to find another ATM or come back to that one. If your PIN is a word, learn its numeric equivalent, because some British ATM keypads show only numbers. Also, if your PIN is longer than three or four digits, it may not work. If your ATM card displays the Cirrus or Plus logo, you are in business, but call your bank for a listing of corresponding London banks to check on the usability of your PIN and for limits on the frequency and amount of withdrawals.

Often you can use a credit card in London ATMs, if your card company is tied in with a British bank. Check with the issuing bank and remember to have your card coded with a PIN. Because interest rates begin to accrue the minute of your withdrawal, consider this option carefully. It could cost you more than it is worth in interest and service fees.

Credit Cards

For the most part, I recommend using a credit card. The benefits are many. It is the safest way to spend because it eliminates carrying large sums of cash, which must be obtained by converting money. You have a record of your purchases, and best of all, your billing often is delayed by four to six weeks after your purchases, whereas if you pay cash, the money is gone immediately. With a credit card, the money stays in your bank account, hopefully drawing interest, until you need it to pay your final bill. Credit card companies get wholesale exchange rates, passing this along to their customers. They will give you their best rate on the day of processing your bill, not on the day of purchase, and that also can work to your advantage. Credit card currency-conversion fees can range from 1 to 5 percent, but in most cases, you still will be ahead of the game.

Furthermore, with American Express, MasterCard, and Visa, you can get an instant cash advance in local currency *if* your card is tied to your bank account. These three major credit cards also work in some ATMs. The cards will require a four-digit PIN; contact your credit card company for details on obtaining one.

Finally, MasterCard and Visa are known in the U.K. as EuroCard or Access and Carte Bleu or BarclayCard, respectively.

Heaven forbid your credit cards get lost or are stolen, but if they are, don't panic. Report the loss immediately to one of the following twenty-four-hour hot lines and then notify the police and inform your bank by phone and in writing.

In London:

American Express	01273 696933
	Toll-free: 0800 521 313
Diners Club	01252 513500
	Toll-free: 0800 460 800
MasterCard	01733 318950
	Toll-free: 0800 964 767
Visa	Both toll-free: 0800 891 725
	0800 895 082

Following are the U.S. numbers to call to report a theft or loss of your cards:

American Express	Toll-free: 800-233-5432
	Collect: 336-393-1111
	www.americanexpress.com
Diners Club	Toll-free: 800-234-6377
	collect: 702-797-5532
	www.diners-club.co.uk
MasterCard	Toll-free: 800-307-7309
	collect: 314-542-7111
	www.mastercard.com
Visa	Toll-free: 800-336-8472
	collect: 410-581-9994
	www.visa.com

Cash Advances

If you are an American Express, MasterCard, or Visa cardholder, you can get a cash advance in local currency if your card is tied to your bank account. Associated British banks will also give you cash advances as large as your remaining credit line. *Be careful,* however, because the interest begins the moment you touch the money, and it is usually prime plus 12.5 percent.

American Express cardholders can get fast money, without commission, by writing personal checks at an American Express office. The amount you can get depends on the type of card you have (green, gold, or platinum), and whether there are funds in your bank account to cover the check. For more information on this lifesaving service and more, contact American Express Global Assist at 800-333-2639.

MasterCard or Visa advances are available through banks displaying those card signs. There are additional costs for the advance ranging up to 10 percent.

For any Diners Club cardholder, a cash advance is easy. Just present the card and a picture ID at any Eurochange bank, and that's it.

Currency Exchange

One of the best rates for all currency conversions is at Marks & Spencer exchange offices. They charge no commission and are open all day Monday to Saturday until at least 6 P.M., and Sunday noon–6 P.M. Visit the Marks & Spencer at 458 Oxford Street, W1 (Tube: Bond Street, Marble Arch), or on King's Road, SW8 (Tube: Sloane Square).

Your next best rate of exchange will be at a London bank. Banking hours are Mon–Fri 9 A.M.–4 P.M. Banks are closed weekends, holidays, and often in the afternoon before a holiday and sometimes the day after. After banks, exchange rates go from bad to worse in this order: hotels, airports, and money changers. Chequepoint and other exchange businesses have offices throughout London. They have long hours, but their rates are *very* deceptive, even if they say they take no commission. The exchange rate may seem in your favor, but it never is. Someone is making money on the deal, and it is *not* you. Avoid these places unless you are desperate.

Traveler's Checks

In London, American Express traveler's checks are the most widely accepted, and they are cashed commission free at all American Express offices. Before leaving home, cardholders can order their traveler's checks by phone (800-221-7282). If you are a member of the Automobile Club of America, American Express traveler's checks are available free to you. Some banks and credit unions offer their customers traveler's checks of varying brands free, or for a service fee unless you maintain a certain balance. In London, Thomas Cook/MasterCard and Barclay's/Visa traveler's checks can be cashed commission free at any of their respective offices, but American Express has by far the most conveniently located offices throughout the city. For the office most convenient to you, consult the telephone directory; otherwise, use one of these central American Express office locations: 30–31 Haymarket (Tube: Piccadilly; this is the head office in London); 78 Brompton Road, almost across from Harrods (Tube: Knightsbridge); 102–104 Victoria Street (Tube: Victoria Station); 231-233 Regent Street (Tube: Oxford Circus); 40 Great Russell Street, near the British Museum (Tube: Russell Square). Offices are generally open Mon–Fri 9 A.M.–5:30 P.M., Sat 9 A.M.–noon. Call 020 7837 555 or 0800 521 313 for further information when in London. For lost or stolen American Express traveler's checks, call toll-free in the U.K. 0800 521 313, or collect in the U.S. 801-964-6665.

MasterCard traveler's checks can be cashed commission free at any Thomas Cook office in London. Call Thomas Cook in the United States at 800-287-7362, or toll-free in London 0800 964 767). The MasterCard toll-free number in England is 0800 622 102; in the United States it's 800-223-7373.

Visa traveler's checks issued from a Barclay's Bank can be cashed commission free at most Barclay's Banks in London. Visa's toll-free U.S. number is 800-227-6811; in London it's 0800 895 082.

Wiring Money to London

Having funds sent to you abroad can be complicated, costly, and fraught with peril. Consider this option only when every *other* possibility has been exhausted.

American Express has MoneyGram, MoneyFast, MoneySafe, and MoneyEasy, all relatively safe and sane ways to wire money. In the United States, the toll-free number is 800-926-9400; in the U.K., it's 0800 8971 8971.

For Western Union, call 0800 833 833 in London and be prepared to pay a commission of 10 percent.

Tipping

How much is too much, and what is enough? Americans are known as big tippers, but the British are funny sometimes about money, so you have to be careful not to overdo your tipping.

Hairdressers	10 to 15 percent of the bill; £1 to £2 for shampoo person
Hat and coat checkers in the theater	50p per item
Hotels	A tough call. If the owner is helping you with your bags, a tip will offend. If his or her son or an employee carries them, then a small gratuity of £1 per bag will be appreciated.
Porters	£1 to £1.50 per bag, depending on how heavy and how far it's carried
Restaurants	Tip *only* if the service is not included. The VAT will be included. If the service is not included, tip 12.5 percent; *never* tip the bartender at a pub.
Taxi drivers	10 to 15 percent or round off the amount
Washroom attendants	Leave 20p to 50p in their saucers, depending on what they do for you

Insurance

British law states that hotel cancellations less than forty-eight hours prior to arrival can result in a two-night room charge. If the room can be relet, this may not apply, but who wants to take a chance? If you have prepaid a large portion of your trip, especially if you have rented a flat and paid a big chunk in advance, you are crazy not to buy cancellation insurance. London hoteliers, apartment rental agencies, and serviced apartment owners and managers, especially independents, are merciless when it comes to refunds. Their policy is very simple: No refunds. Period.

Read through your homeowner's policy and see if it covers you in any way when you are traveling, and if it does not, again, consider adding a floater policy for the duration of your trip, especially if you are traveling with a laptop or other expensive equipment. If you are a premium credit card holder (for example, American Express Platinum), check to see what emergency coverages are offered to members.

There are many ways to purchase travel insurance: through travel agents, apartment rental agencies, and from specialized travel companies. Your travel agent or the American Automobile Association can advise you on companies that deal specifically in trip-cancellation insurance. My advice is to compare several policy plans before investing. A few of the major travel insurance companies are:

Access America   800-284-8300, www.accessamerica.com

C.S.A. Travel Protection   800-348-9505, www.csatravel.com

Safeware (insures laptops www.safeware.com
for an annual premium)

Wallach and Co.   800-237-6615, www.wallach.com

For information on health insurance, see the next section, "Health Matters."

Health Matters

No one plans on a medical crisis during a trip or wants to cut the trip short or abandon it altogether because of some emergency or sudden change of plans. Travel insurance is seldom a great bargain, but it does buy you protection and, just as important, peace of mind should these unfortunate circumstances happen to you.

Even though all British citizens are eligible for free medical care, visitors are not. Check with your health care plan to see what, if any, coverage you will have in London, and seriously consider taking out a supplemental policy to cover your trip. The small amount you spend in supplemental insurance will be nothing compared to a foreign medical emergency for which *you* pick up the tab. Check the small print on your existing U.S. policy. If it does cover you at all, you'll probably be required to pay out of pocket and then file for reimbursement when you get home. If you have a chronic health condition, you might need to get home in a hurry. If you are traveling with an elderly person who becomes ill, both of you would want to fly home together. Few U.S. medical policies will cover these types of evacuations.

If you need medical care while in London, you can seek twenty-four-hour emergency services or advice from the following:

Royal London Hospital	Whitechapel Road, E1; Tel: 020 7377 7000; Tube: Whitechapel
SOS Doctors	020 763 3332
Nurse Evaluators (advice and information)	020 0845 4647
Dental emergencies	020 7955 2186, Mon–Fri 8:45 A.M.– 3:30 P.M.

Should you need a pharmacy (chemist), try the following:

Bliss Chemist	5 Marble Arch W1; Tel: 020 7723 6116; Tube: Marble Arch; Open: daily 9 A.M.–midnight
Boots	302 Regent Street, W1; Tel: 020 7637 9418; Tube: Oxford Circus; Open: Mon–Fri 8 A.M.–7 P.M., Sat 9 A.M.–6 P.M.
Boots	Piccadilly Circus; Tel: 020 7734 6126; Tube: Piccadilly Circus; Open: Mon–Sat 8:30 A.M.–8 P.M., Sun noon–6 P.M.
Boots	75 Queensway; Tel: 020 7229 9266; Tube: Queensway or Bayswater; Open: Mon–Sat 9 A.M.–10 P.M., Sun 5–10 P.M.
Zafash Pharmacy	(the only 24-hour pharmacy) 233–235 Old Brompton Road, SW5; Tel: 020 7373 2798; Tube: Earl's Court

Emergency Number

For an ambulance, in case of fire, or to reach the police, call 999 (toll-free, including from pay phones).

Safety and Security

London is safer than many large cities, and violent crime is rare. Generally, assaults are in the nature of handbag snatchers and pickpockets along Oxford and Regent Streets, in Knightsbridge around Harrods, in crowded street markets such as Portobello Road and Petticoat Lane, and in the airports. The tube stations are also targeted areas, especially late at night. Thieves work in pairs: one creates a diversion, the other grabs your purse, wallet, or bags. If you follow the following basic, commonsense rules both in your hotel room and on the street, you should be safe:

1. Avoid hotels rooms below or on the ground level. Always use the deadbolt and chain, employ a rubber doorstop for further security, and never open the door to strangers.

2. Don't leave cameras, airline tickets, laptops, or other valuables lying around your room. Use the in-room safe, many of which are

now designed to accommodate a laptop, or the hotel safe. Lock your suitcases when you leave your room for the day, but don't leave valuables in them.

3. Put your money and valuables in a money belt worn *inside* your clothing, either around your waist or in a necklace money holder under your shirt. Never take more money than you will need for the day, and bring only one credit card.

4. If you are carrying a purse, wear it crosswise across your body, with the opening against your body. Don't put your wallet in your back pocket. Don't put either your purse or wallet on the table or counter while signing a credit card or looking over your bill.

5. Do not leave baggage unattended or out of sight. Do not leave belongings beside, under, or on the back of your chair. Put your purse in your lap, not between your feet.

6. Leave expensive jewelry and furs at home.

7. Don't travel alone or walk down dark streets or through parks of any size late at night.

8. Women alone should avoid the tube at night, carry a loud whistle, and not be afraid to use it.

9. Avoid crowds and be vigilant when standing in line to get on or off public transportation.

10. Photocopy your passport; leave a list of your credit card numbers and the serial numbers for computers and other expensive items with someone at home in case any are lost or stolen. Also make a note of the telephone numbers listed on the back of your credit card to call if you have a problem. For a lost passport, you have to prove who you are, and a photocopy will do the trick. While you are photocopying your passport, copy any other papers crucial to a safe and sane trip and return home (air and rail tickets, medical data, etc.). Also, take a copy of your prescriptions, plus a letter from your physician giving the generic names of the drugs you take. American brands may not be available.

11. Try to let someone know where you are going and when you will be back, especially late at night.

12. Call 999 in an emergency.

13. If you are a victim of a crime, report it to the police immediately, and get a police report to include when filing an insurance claim.

14. Finally . . . always look *right* when crossing the street.

Lost and Found

For lost or stolen items, report the loss or theft to police and then call the appropriate number from the following list:

Lost at the airport

Heathrow	020 8745 7727
Gatwick	01293 503162
London City	020 7646 0640 or 020 7646 0782
Luton	01582 423289
Stansted	01279 680 500
Lost on the bus or tube	020 7486 2496
Lost on railways	Lost property is held for seven days at the rail station where it was found, and then is taken to Waterloo Lost Property. Call the central number, and an operator will connect you with the appropriate station. 020 7928 5151
Lost on a taxi	020 7833 0996

Staying in Touch

Email and the Internet

Some hotels have Internet services available to their guests at a nominal fee, but most visitors should plan on going to a cyber café for their personal email and Internet use. I have not listed cyber cafés in this guide, since so many of them are here today, gone tomorrow, but they will not be difficult to find. My best advice is to ask at your hotel where you can find the nearest one—and surely there will be one within a five-minute walk. They're cheap, too.

easyEverything is the world's largest chain of Internet cafés. There are branches all over London, open seven days a week, twenty-four hours a day, with more than a hundred computers in each café. For peak and off-peak prices and maps to the café locations, visit www.easyEverything.com.

Regular Mail

Does anyone remember the letter carrier? If you are still using his or her services, allow seven to ten days for an airmail letter or postcard to reach its destination. The central telephone number for all post office inquiries is 0345 2233 44; Internet: www.postoffice.co.uk.

Receiving Mail: If, for some reason, you don't want mail to arrive for you at your hotel address in London, there are two other reliable alternatives. You can receive mail sent from home via *poste restante* at the Trafalgar Square Post Office, which will hold mail for one month. Have your correspondent write on the envelope your name, with the last name underlined or in capital letters, and the words *Poste Restante* and *Hold for*

30 days on the left side of the envelope, and send the mail to you at this address: Post Office, 24–28 William IV Street, London, WC2N 4DL. Be sure to bring a photo ID when you come to pick it up.

Or, you can pick up your mail at the American Express office at 30–31 Haymarket, London, SW1Y 4BS; Tel: 020 7484 9600; Tube: Piccadilly Circus. The envelope should be addressed to you, with your name in capital letters and *client letter service* boldly written on it. Mail will be held for thirty days free of charge for cardholders; others pay a small fee. After that, it is by arrangement and there will be a fee for everyone.

Sending Mail: Stamps are sold at all post offices, large supermarkets, and news agents.

Sending Packages: If you send packages, have everything sent airmail. Surface may be cheaper, but it takes up to nine weeks for surface parcels to reach their destination. Frankly speaking, though, sending packages from any place abroad can be a terrific headache. There are size and weight limitations, which are minor when you see how much the postage on a box will cost, even for surface mail. Try not to do it. Somehow, stuff it into your luggage and if necessary pay for an extra bag on the airline. Another option is to let the store mail it for you, and that way you save the VAT, but of course pay the postage. If that doesn't work, look in the telephone directory for parcel mailing services. I have used Mail Boxes, Etc. with great success sending items to other European addresses and to my own. One of the better franchises is at 28 Old Brompton Road, South Kensington, SW7; Tel: 020 7581 2825; Tube: South Kensington; Open Mon–Fri 8:30 A.M.–6:30 P.M., Sat 9 A.M.–noon (call before you go, because sometimes hours vary). Ask for Peter or John. They can pack and send, or you can pack and they can send.

Telephone

There are three kinds of public phones in Britain: those that accept BT (British Telecom) phone cards, those that accept BT phone cards *and* credit cards, and those that accept coins.

The coin-operated phone booths are few and far between and are an antiquated nightmare. They accept all but 1p coins and are inconvenient in that you have to have a pocketful of change, and the phones do not make change, so if you insert more than you use, tough luck.

BT phone cards are a much smarter way to go. You can buy them from post offices or news kiosks displaying the green-and-white phone card sign. These cards come in values of £2 and up and can be used to make a call around the corner or across the globe.

The credit card phone call is self-explanatory: the cost of the call is charged against your credit card account.

Calls Made within Britain: All telephone numbers in greater London have eight-digit numbers beginning with 7 and preceded by the central London area code: 020 7 (e.g., 020 7654 1234); suburban London numbers begin with 8 and are preceded by the same area code: 020 8 (e.g., 020 8765 1234). If you are in London and are dialing another number within the same area code, you need not use the 020 area code. If you are calling outside your area code or are someplace else in the country, perhaps in Manchester or Cornwall, you will need to use the 020 area code plus the eight-digit number. To dial a mobile phone (cell phone) you always need the full area code and number.

There is no such thing as a free call in Britain, other than toll-free and some operator information calls (the toll-free prefix is 0800). If you call only next door, you will pay for it. All calls fall into three rate periods: lowest, Mon–Fri 6 P.M.–8 A.M. and all day Sat and Sun; mid-range, Mon–Fri 8 A.M.–9 A.M. and 1–6 P.M.; and most expensive, Mon–Fri 9 A.M.–1 P.M.

Calling the U.K. from Abroad: The country code is 00 44. If you are calling London from outside the U.K., you omit the first 0 of the 020 code and dial 00 44 20 + the eight-digit London number (e.g., 00 44 20 7123 4567).

Calling Abroad from the U.K.: If you are calling the United States from London, dial 001+ area code + number (e.g., 001 313-123-4567). But please be forewarned: if you pick up the phone in your hotel and make an international call through the hotel operator, or just dial out yourself, you could be charged an astronomical 100-percent-plus surcharge. The cheapest way to simplify calling home and avoid the hotel surcharges is to buy a prepaid international telephone card, either before you leave or in London at most newsstands and post offices. They are surprisingly cheap and give you lots of gabbing time. Or, you can use the services of the long-distance carriers AT&T or MCI. To get a calling card, which you must have to call using one of these companies, call one of the following before you leave on your trip:

| AT&T USA Direct | 800-225-5288 |
| MCI Call USA | 800-444-4444 |

Operator Services: Dial the following numbers for these services:

Operator	100
London directory inquiries	192
International inquiries	153
International operator	155

If you cannot find what you need from other resources, check with Scoot (Tel: 0800 192 192; Internet: www.scoot.co.uk), a business directory service that provides telephone numbers and addresses by type, not name, throughout the U.K. The call and the information are free.

Talking Pages (Tel: 0800 600 900) is a twenty-four-hour free service that lists businesses in London and throughout the U.K.

Transportation
Getting to and from the Airports

Gatwick, Heathrow, London City, Luton, and Stansted airports all serve London. Heathrow is the world's busiest airport, with more than 60 million passengers traveling through it every year. Gatwick is an also-ran, with a mere 35 million passengers.

Gatwick: Farther out than Heathrow, Gatwick (Tel: 01293 535 353) has the Gatwick Express train into Victoria Station (Internet: www.gatwickexpress.co.uk), which is a breeze. It runs twenty-four hours, every day, every fifteen minutes, except between 12:30 A.M. and 5 A.M., when it runs every hour. Tickets cost around £12 one way, £22 return (valid for one month), are half-price for children under fifteen and free for children under five. The trip takes between thirty and forty-five minutes to Victoria Station, where you can either hail a cab or get on the tube.

Connex South Central runs the cheapest train ride between Gatwick and London Victoria. Their trip takes between thirty-three and forty-six minutes, runs every fifteen minutes most of the day and hourly at night, and costs less than £9.

Thameslink rail services run to Gatwick from King's Cross, Farringdon, Blackfriars, and London Bridge Stations. Jetline coaches run hourly from Victoria, Marble Arch, and Baker Street Stations. Taking a taxi from Gatwick is upwards of £75, plus tip and baggage fees.

If you are flying British Airways, departing passengers leave from Gatwick. Ticket holders can check in at Victoria Station, which eliminates dragging luggage from London to the airport. You must arrive at the British Airways check-in desk at least two hours before departure to get your seat assignment, check your baggage, and purchase Gatwick Express train tickets. Trains leave for the airport every fifteen minutes. Once there, you walk to your gate and board the plane. It's oh so convenient. For information, call the Gatwick number listed above.

Heathrow: In a cab from Heathrow (Tel: 0870 000 0123 or 020 8759 4321) to London, prepare to spend £55–70, plus a charge for each bag and a 10 to 15 percent tip. If there are several of you, it makes sense; otherwise, it is an expensive way to start your London sojourn.

One of the easiest alternatives is the Heathrow Express (Tel: 0845 600 1515; Internet: www.heathrowexpress.co.uk), the nonstop, high-speed rail link between Heathrow and Paddington Station. It runs 365 days a year, with trains leaving every fifteen minutes from 5:30 A.M. to 11:30 P.M. The trip takes about fifteen or twenty minutes each way. Children up to age fifteen travel free when accompanied by one adult with a ticket purchased *before* boarding, or pay half-fare if the ticket is purchased on board. Tickets cost £12 one way, £22 return. There are no senior discounts. When you return to Heathrow this way, most airlines have check-in desks operating at Paddington, allowing you to check in any time between 5 A.M. and 9 P.M. on the day you fly, up to two hours before flight departure if you have check-in luggage, or a mere hour ahead with carry-on luggage only. Whenever you check in, your baggage is tagged, and you never have to worry about it until you arrive at your destination. If you plan to turn in VAT forms, please allow time to do so at Heathrow, because as yet there are no facilities for this at Paddington.

If you don't take the Heathrow Express, another option is the Airbus to and from all four terminals (Tel: 08705 757 747 or 020 8400 6656; Internet: www.GoByCoach.com). Buses run daily every thirty minutes from 7 A.M. to 8:30 P.M. and drop you at central London locations. There's no need to book ahead, since you pay on board. Tickets cost £7 one way, £10 return.

There is also the Heathrow Airport shuttle, Hotelink (Tel: 01293 532244; Email: reservations@hotelink.co.uk; Internet: hotelink.co.uk), offering one-way or return door-to-door service for around £15 per person each way. The service operates daily with drive time, depending on the traffic.

The cheapest and slowest choice is to take the Piccadilly Line tube, which takes about one hour to reach central London and costs under £5 one way. Trains run from 5:30 A.M. to 11:30 P.M. and leave from Terminals 1, 2, 3, and 4.

London City Airport: The Airbus service goes to Liverpool Street Station from London City Airport (Tel: 020 7646 0088) every ten minutes, takes thirty minutes, and costs £6. A taxi takes forty minutes and costs around £23–25.

Luton: If you take a taxi to Luton (Tel: 01582 405100), it could cost more than your round-trip easyJet flight does! I know, because it happened to me on a day the trains and buses were on strike and I had to make my flight. Otherwise, there are better choices. The really cheap ride into London is on the Green Line coach service (Tel: 020 8668 7261), which runs from Victoria, Buckingham Palace Road, Marble Arch, and Baker Street Stations at forty minutes past the hour. The ride takes ninety-plus minutes and costs £8 one way, £12 return, half price if you are under fifteen, free for children under five. There is also Thameslink rail service (Tel: 08457 484 950), which takes you to and from King's Cross. The trains leave every ten minutes, take about forty minutes, and cost £10 one way.

Stansted: The best way to get from Stansted Airport (Tel: 01279 680 500) into London is to take the Stansted Express train (Tel: 08457 484 950) to Liverpool Street Station. The trip takes about forty-five minutes. Trains run every fifteen or thirty minutes, depending on the time of day. Tickets cost around £15 one way, half-price for those under fifteen. A taxi will be at least £60, plus tip and baggage fees.

The Tube and Buses

First a few facts and figures. The tube carries more than a billion passengers per year on a system so ancient that a spare part had to come from a museum. One-third of London workers commute on the tube, and nine out of ten visitors rely on it 364 days a year (it is closed on Christmas Day). The system breaks down every sixteen minutes, and one in twelve escalators is out of service at all times (usually the one you want to use). If you think the London Underground system is in bad shape, try the commuter trains, which are in chaotic disarray (see "Traveling Beyond London," page 41).

London Transport Travel Information (Tel: 020 7222 1234; Internet: www.londontransport.co.uk) is a twenty-four-hour information line for London bus and tube travel. If that is busy, and it always seems to be, you can get recorded information by calling 020 7222 1200. Their offices have information on London transportation via tube and bus, and they provide free maps and information for disabled travelers and on places of interest and guided tours. They are in the following locations: King's Cross, Liverpool Street, Oxford Circus, Piccadilly Circus, and St. James's Park Stations; at Heathrow Airport, Terminals 1, 2, and 3; and the National Rail stations Euston, Paddington, and Victoria. London Transport tickets and information are also available at Greenwich and Waterloo International. Office hours are generally daily 8 A.M.–5:30 P.M.

An essential investment if you will be in London for a day or two is the *A–Z London Street Map* (pronounced "a" to "zed"), available at bookstores and news kiosks. You can buy the map in regular or super-scale size, in book or foldout form, and it comes with an Underground map. This is a purchase that will never go out of style, will tell you more than you will ever need to know, and it will save you time and confusion when you don't know how to get from the Tate Britain to Buckingham Palace.

The cheapest and fastest way to get around London is to master the tube and bus systems. The tube will be faster, but the bus is much more scenic and fun. The view of London from the top of a red double-decker bus is unbeatable. Bus stops are marked with two kinds of signs: the compulsory stop, which has a white background, and the request stop, which is red. At the first, the bus will automatically stop; at the request stop, you have to flag it down. On a double-decker, the conductor will collect your fare from you. On the single-driver buses (no conductor), you will pay as you enter. To get off, ring the bell as you approach your stop. If you are not sure as to your stop, ask the driver to tell you. The most scenic bus routes in London are the following:

Bus 11:   The heart of London from King's Road to St. Paul's Cathedral

Bus 12:   From Bayswater to the Houses of Parliament and Westminster Bridge

Bus 19:   From Sloane Square to Piccadilly Circus, Bloomsbury to Islington

Bus 88:   Oxford Circus to the Tate Gallery

To save money on both the tube and the bus, buy a Travel Card, which allows you to ride for less money than you would spend for single-fare tickets. Depending on the type of card you buy, it will be good for one to thirty days and can be purchased at any tube station. Travel Cards are sold by zone. Most visitors need only a card for Zone 1, which is central London. You will need a passport-size color photo for the thirty-day Travel Card. Bring your own, or hope there is a photo booth in the tube station. If you are in London for only a few days but are planning limited tube rides within Zone 1, a carnet of ten tickets makes better cost-sense than purchasing individual tickets. If you travel into Zone 2 with any type of Zone 1 ticket and are caught, you will pay a £10 fine.

Taxi

Black cabs are as famous in London as red double-decker buses, but more expensive. The drivers are reliable, know their way around, and have strictly enforced codes of conduct. Many now have a no-smoking policy. Every licensed black cab has a "For Hire" sign and a white license plate on the back stating how many passengers it will carry. Drivers of black cabs must pass a complicated test called "The Knowledge" to prove they know where every street is and the shortest way to get to it. For 750 square miles, and for a 6-mile radius from the center of London, the driver has to know every street, building, club, hospital, police station . . . you name it. The qualification takes three years to achieve, and 30 percent of those who take it fail. Those who succeed receive a badge from the Public Carriage Office and can then buy or rent a cab and work as an independent contractor. Hotels and main tourist areas have taxi stands, but you can also flag one down. If the yellow "For Hire" sign is on, the cab is available. Many cabbies turn the sign off at night in order to pass up undesirable-looking fares, so it pays to flag at night even if the sign is off. To pay, you must get out of the cab (rain or shine) and pay through the window. Tip the cabbie from 10 to 15 percent, depending on your mood and his attitude and speed in getting you to your destination. There will be an extra charge for baggage. If you want to be assured of a taxi at a specific time, call a twenty-four-hour radio taxi. You will pay from the minute the driver gets the call, but you will avoid the worry of being late because you could not get a taxi during rush hour or at some odd hour. Radio Taxis (Tel: 020 7272 0272) and Dial a Cab (Tel: 020 7253 5000) are twenty-four-hour call services for black cabs.

Any complaints or inquiries about black cabs should be made to the Public Carriage Office, Tel: 020 7230 1631 or 020 720 1632; Open: Mon–Fri 9 A.M.–4 P.M. If you have a complaint, be sure you also have the number of the cab, which should be displayed both inside the cab and on the back plate. For lost property, call 020 7918 2000, Mon–Fri 9 A.M.– 4 P.M. If the items are found, it takes three working days to get them back.

Mini-cabs: Mini-cabs, sometimes called saloon cars, are not black cabs; they are ordinary cars available for hire by telephone. They cannot be hailed in the street because it is illegal. Over long distances, these cabs are usually cheaper than black taxis, but the drivers are unlicensed, untrained, and often uninsured, not to mention unreliable. If you do use one, always discuss price when you book and confirm it with the driver. Often, concierges use them if you ask for transportation to the airport. There is usually a kickback from the company to the concierge, but it is built into the price, and you will never know what it is. Addison Lee (Tel: 020 7387 8888), one of the more reliable mini-cab companies, is open twenty-four hours a day.

Car

In London! What for? Driving in London is hazardous to your health. It is a hair-raising experience and only for the very, very brave or foolish. The British drive on the opposite side of the road, which means having to retrain yourself to look in the opposite direction (and, obviously, to drive on the other side of the road). Parking is impossible. There is never any within walking distance of where you want to be, unless it is an expensive car park. The cost of petrol (gasoline) is sky-high. But if you insist, check with your airline for a fly-drive package. Otherwise, shop the major car rental companies carefully *before* you leave home, because rates and deals vary greatly. If you wait until you arrive to make rental arrangements, you will be very put off by the prices and all the tacked-on charges.

If you want the convenience and luxury of a car and driver at your disposal, contact Gordon Reynolds, a former police officer who is now a licensed London Taxi Driver. Gordon is great, and his services are available for airport pickup and drop-off, private tours, or any other driving needs you may have in and around London. Telephone and Fax: 020 8428 0986, Mobile phone: 083 1616 107.

Walking

One of the best ways to experience London is on foot. You can venture forth with the express purpose of wandering and seeing what you can along the way. Don't worry about getting lost; you can always jump on a bus or hail a cab if you get too far from your base. I think one of the best ways to learn about London is to go on a guided walking tour. On these tours you will be guided by well-informed leaders to any number of interesting places you would probably not discover on your own. You can peek into the haunts of Shakespeare, Dickens, and Sherlock Holmes. You can explore the inner workings of legal London and sit in on an actual trial at Old Bailey, go on a late-night pub crawl, or see where Jack the Ripper stalked his prey. You will probably see brochures on these walking tours at your hotel; please try to make enough time to go on at least one. For more information, see "Tours," page 23.

Traveling Beyond London

All of Britain is joined by rail links. The question now is . . . do you want to use this mode of transportation? Unfortunately, British Rail as we knew and loved it has been privatized. The railways are now run by independent train companies, which have turned train travel into what is truly a nightmare of long delays, late departures and arrivals, and dirty, unkempt trains, not to mention mechanically unsafe ones, in many instances. Just to prove my point, on a return trip at Christmastime from Inverness to London, my train was two hours late in leaving, during which time all passengers were advised to wait outside, in twenty-degree weather, beside the appropriate train track, because the train would be arriving any minute. Once on board, we encountered further delays along the way, and then we had engine failure, forcing those of us who had paid extra to have a straight-through trip to change twice (schlepping our own luggage because there were no porters), and after scrambling for any seat on the new train, we learned there would be no toilets in service because the train had run out of water! And never mind heat—there was none of that, either. This trip was so horrible that just before arrival into London (five hours late), train officials boarded the train and passed out vouchers for free trips on future journeys.

If you plan to do much train travel, by all means have a very flexible schedule that can withstand delays, cancellations, and interruptions. Quite frankly, until the situation has improved drastically, I would advise forgetting all about train travel in the U.K. Go by coach, or book a flight. The economy airline easyJet is cheap (especially if you book far enough in advance), reliable, on time, and safe. Overhead is kept to a minimum because there are no offices. Reservations are available only on-line at www.easyJet.com.

If you insist on taking the train, you can purchase tickets in London, but you *must* do it at one of the mainline rail stations, because rail tickets are no longer sold through travel agencies or from a central office in London. The special fares, deals, and prices each competing company has are numerous and well worth exploring. Why pay $300 for a seat you could have had for $35 had you booked seven days in advance? When trying to get these fares, dig in your heels; don't give up, and be prepared to encounter very surly and unhelpful ticket agents who are interested only in their next tea break, definitely not you and your train travel needs. It may pay to buy a discount travel card. For instance, foreigners with a Britrail card can get unlimited travel within a certain time frame. Flexipass cards are available only outside Britain. See www.britrail.com for more on the Flexipass.

If you are over sixty, it may pay to invest in a Senior Citizen Rail Card, which entitles you to ride the rails for a year for at least a third less than regular ticket prices. Travelers age sixteen to twenty-six can participate in a similar program. For these and other money-saving fares, restrictions always apply. For information on your particular trip, times, and prices call the National Rail Enquiry information line at 0345 484 950 or 0845 748 4950. The mainline railway stations in London are Charing Cross, Liverpool, Victoria, Waterloo, Euston, King's Cross, and Paddington. All have tube stops. Good Luck.

Eurostar trains (Tel: 01233 617575 or 0990 186186; Internet: www.eurostar.co.uk) leave Waterloo every hour for Paris (Gare du Nord) and Brussels (Gare du Midi). The trip lasts about three hours, and prebooking is advised.

Even riding the bus from one point to another in Britain is expensive, and it can seem to take forever. Travelers no longer have much choice of competing services. The two principal bus lines are National Express (Tel: 0990 808 080; Internet: www.GoByCoach.com), which goes to destinations all over England, Scotland, and Wales, and Eurolines (Tel: 01582 404 511), which goes to the continent.

Once you are out of the impossible London traffic mess, driving is easier. Traffic is not what it is in the States, drivers are actually courteous, and roads are well marked. If there are two or three in your group, driving may be more economical (and definitely much nicer) than buying separate train or bus tickets.

Time

On the last Sunday of March, the British clocks go forward one hour from Greenwich Mean Time (GMT) to British Summer Time (BST). On the last Sunday of October, the clocks revert to GMT. The number to dial in London for the time is 123.

Standards of Measure

England uses the metric system. Here are the equivalents:

1 inch = 2.54 centimeters	1 centimeter = 0.39 inches
1 mile = 1.61 kilometers	1 kilometer – 0.62 miles
1 foot = 0.30 meters	1 meter = 3.28 feet
1 yard = 0.91 meters	1 meter = 1.09 yards
1 ounce = 28 grams	1 gram = 0.04 ounces
1 pound = 0.45 kilograms	1 kilogram = 2.2 pounds
1 U.S. gallon = 3.79 liters	1 liter = 0.26 gallons

To convert Celsius to Fahrenheit, multiply by 1.8 and add 32. To convert Fahrenheit to Celsius, subtract 32 and multiply by .56.

How to Use Great Sleeps London

The advantage of a hotel is that it is a refuge from home life.
—*George Bernard Shaw*

I called down to the desk and said, "Is this room service?" The clerk said, "Yes." I said, "So, send up a room."
—*Words on a large modern art painting by Richard Prince, 1949–, displayed at the Royal Academy of Art, London, 2001*

Big Splurges

Hotels in the Big Splurge category are higher priced because of their amenities, ambience, service, and overall appeal, but they still represent the best values in their class. These are hotels to consider if your budget is more flexible, if you are celebrating a special occasion, or if you want better facilities but prefer a less formal atmosphere than at the big hotels, along with their intimidatingly high prices. All Big Splurges are marked with a dollar sign ($). See the index of Big Splurges, page 338, for a complete list.

Crowns and Stars

Hotels in Great Britain are not controlled by a government rating system, as they are in many other countries. The British Tourist Authority operates a voluntary registration and optional grading system of one to five crowns for all tourist accommodations, from the Ritz down to the grubbiest B&B, measuring level and range of services, food, and other qualities. Note the words *voluntary* and *optional*. Many good hotels refuse to take part in this classification system because it does not mean that quality, cleanliness, or value go along with the rated hotel. In fact, many hotels in London displaying two and three crowns are filthy, without redeeming decoration or friendly management. They may have the required number of lights by the bed, or the right number of toilets and showers in order to qualify for a certain number of crowns, but there it stops.

To confuse matters further, the English Tourism Council has joined forces with two automobile clubs, the AA and RAC, to create another voluntary rating scheme for hotels and guest accommodations. Their system uses stars and diamonds: one to five stars symbolize the quality, level of service, food, and range of services available in London hotels; one to five diamonds rate accommodations outside London.

A word to the wise is to consider the crowns, stars, and diamonds but not bank on them. *Great Sleeps London* ignores them altogether.

Reservations

Are reservations necessary? Absolutely! Confirmed reservations are essential to the success of any trip to London or any other world capital, if you want to be in charge of how much you spend. With the electronic age, it is easy to telephone, fax, or email reservation requests and in most cases to guarantee them with a credit card. In only a very few small budget hotels and B&Bs will you be asked to guarantee your room with an international money order in pounds (see "Deposits," page 45).

In this age of electronics, why anyone would resort to letter writing for reservation purposes is a mystery to me. Many hotels let reservation letters stack up and plan to deal with them later, when they have time, which is usually never. Transatlantic mail can take as long as two weeks one way, and if there is a strike, who knows how long the letter could be in transit? When you consider the entire cost of your trip against the cost, convenience, and speed of email, a fax, or a telephone call, the letter option is woefully inadequate, and I don't recommend it.

No matter how you make your reservation, the following points should be included in your inquiry:

1. The dates of stay, time of arrival (including flight number), and number of persons in your party. Tell the hotel you are a reader of *Great Sleeps London* because you might get a discount or a better room.

2. The size and type of room you need: double or twin beds, extra beds, adjoining rooms, nonsmoking, quiet, and so on.

3. Facilities needed: private toilet, shower and/or bathtub, or hall facilities if acceptable.

4. Location of room: with a view, on the street, at the back of the hotel.

5. The rates: Determine what the nightly rate will be and whether or not the VAT (value-added tax of 17.5 percent) is included, as well as what sort of breakfast the hotel serves. This is the time to negotiate any rate discounts.

6. The deposit required and the form of payment acceptable.

7. The hotel will undoubtedly ask you to send a fax (and keep a copy) confirming *your* end of the reservation. Be sure to note the date and time of your call, the name of the person with whom you spoke, and the particulars of your reservation, spelling out the rates, whether breakfast is included, and if so, what type and any discounts that may have been given. Take this with you, along with the hotel's confirmation.

8. *Important:* Request that the hotel send you a confirmation of your reservation with the amount of deposit, rates, and other particulars, and carry this with you to the registration desk when you check in. You will avoid a multitude of snafus when you arrive, such as having the desk clerk tell you that you have no reservation, or that it is "lost." Believe me, this happens more often than you would think.

9. Cancellation and refund policy.

Email and the Internet

Email is a quick way to nail down hotel reservations. You may not want to put your credit card number in an email message, but you can fax it after you have made your arrangements. Not all hotels will have an email or Internet address, but when they do, I have included this information.

Fax

This is another easy way to reserve a room. It is also the best way to confirm your reservations and to make sure that all parties get the details correct. When you make a reservation, ask for a confirmation fax from the hotel acknowledging all pertinent details. To send a fax message to London from the United States, dial 011-44 plus the hotel fax number, minus the first zero of the area code.

Telephone

When you consider the cost of a phone call to London, it is nothing in comparison to the cost of the trip, and the convenience is wonderful. It allows you to wheel and deal, sorting out the reservation so it is in your best interest. *Always* make the call during the hotel's weekday business hours (London is six hours ahead of Eastern Standard Time and nine hours ahead of Pacific Time). That way you'll avoid talking to a night clerk who has no authority to negotiate rates or to offer you a deal. Before calling, write down all your requests and questions. Be sure to ask for a confirmation fax from the hotel, and follow up your call with the same. To dial London direct from the United States, dial 011-44 plus the number of the hotel, minus the first zero of the area code.

Deposits

After accepting your reservation, most hotels require at least a one-night deposit, more if you are renting a flat. This is smart insurance for both parties. The easiest way to handle all deposits is with a credit card. If the hotel does not accept credit cards, and a few budget hotels still do not, there are other ways of sending the deposit, none of which are particularly convenient or without extra costs. Sending your personal check to these little establishments is not an option; they want the money in pounds sterling. Call American Express at 800-926-9400 for more information on sending a MoneyGram, which is a direct wire service to a bank or office in London that will accept them. Or, if you prefer sending a money order, call 800-999-9660 Mon–Fri 6:30 A.M.–6 P.M., Sat 7 A.M.–3 P.M., Mountain Time. The benefit here is not time, but you can mail it and save a hefty wiring fee. This service is available to anyone. Another company handling foreign money matters is Thomas Cook; call 800-287-7362.

Cancellations

If you need to cancel or to cut your stay short, for *any* reason, be prepared for some anxious moments when it comes to getting back any prepaid money. When you reserve a hotel room or flat, you are entering into a legally binding contract with the proprietor of the establishment. This means that if you have to cancel or leave early, the proprietor may be entitled to compensation if he or she cannot relet your room or flat. If a deposit has been paid, count on forfeiting it if you cancel at the last minute. This whole area has the potential for creating much tension, so know the hotel, B&B, or flat rental cancellation policy *before* you go, and before you tie up a big chunk of your vacation money.

The best way to circumvent this cancellation nightmare is to buy cancellation or trip-interruption insurance before you leave home. Some apartment-letting services also have cancellation policies you can take out. If you have only a one-night deposit invested, it is probably not worth it; but if you have a half-month deposit on a flat, it certainly is. (See "Insurance," page 29, for more information.)

Checking In/Checking Out

The lobby or reception area of a hotel is usually one of the most attractive parts of the building, both because first impressions are important, and because this is where the owner and manager spend their day. When you arrive at your hotel, ask to see your room. This is a normal and expected practice. After approving the accommodations, reconfirm the rate, making sure there are no hidden extras. This will prevent unpleasant surprises at checkout time.

In London, the hotel day begins and ends at noon. If you overstay (without prior arrangement), you will probably be charged the price of an extra day. If you leave earlier than your reservation ending date, you could be charged for the nights not stayed, and if you cancel altogether less than forty-eight hours before arrival, the law says you are liable to pay for two nights unless the room can be relet. These instances are rare, but they do happen, and you don't want to have these hassles. If your flight is leaving later in the afternoon, most hotels will keep your luggage in a safe place and let you use the lobby. If your flight arrives early in the morning, your room may not be ready for immediate occupancy. Most hotels will try their best to let you into your room as soon as possible, but if you absolutely must have the room early in the morning, you should consider booking it for the night before. You will pay for an unoccupied room, but it will be yours from the minute you arrive.

A word or two on terminology: A *double* is a room with a double bed for two people. A *twin-bedded* room has two twin beds. When booking, it is *vital* that you be specific about whether you would like a room for two with twin beds or a room for two with a double bed. If you ask for "a double room," you will get a room with a double bed.

Rates: Paying the Bill

All hotels in Britain are required by law to plainly display their minimum and maximum overnight rates. The price must include service, and it may or may not include the 17.5 percent VAT. Depending on the economy and the state of tourism, London hotel rates usually increase from 2 to 10 percent every year, around April. The rates quoted in *Great Sleeps London* were correct at press time, but please allow for the probability of a yearly increase.

When reserving, *always* ask for a discount and be ready to negotiate the rates. Many hotels offer low-season rates, and you would be surprised at the tremendous discounts the high-end hotels will give. All it takes is for *you* to *ask*. Many times, the hotel won't mention them unless you do. All rates given in *Great Sleeps London* are for the full price and do not reflect special discounts or discount time periods. Where discounts are available, they are noted. But, and this is important, even if no discounts are mentioned, that does not mean they will not be available.

Every hotel listing states which credit cards are accepted. In most Great Sleeps, a one-night deposit guaranteed by a credit card is required to secure your reservation. A few lower-priced hotels still refuse to take any sort of credit cards. They accept only cash up front in British pounds. The following abbreviations are used to denote which credit cards a hotel will accept:

American Express	AE
Diners Club	DC
MasterCard	MC
Visa	V

Hotel exchange rates are terrible, no matter what the front desk may claim. If you are paying your bill in cash, change your money into pounds *before* checkout time (see "Money Matters," page 25). No matter how you pay, be sure to go over your bill carefully and get a receipt marked "paid in full."

Breakfast

Almost all London hotels and B&Bs include either a Continental or an English breakfast in the cost of their rooms. If you are trying to save as much money as possible, ask that the cost of the breakfast—per person, per day—be deducted from your daily hotel rate. Unfortunately, London hoteliers are very reluctant to deduct breakfast, and many simply refuse because it is such a big moneymaker. However, sometimes in the low seasons, or for long stays, management will bend. This must be arranged *before* check-in. The hotel will probably not allow you to eat there one morning and somewhere else another. You will have to make up your mind and stick to it.

Actually, a proper English breakfast enables many to skip lunch and to save money that way. An English breakfast has many interpretations, anything from the addition of an egg and a slice of bacon to the regular Continental breakfast of toast or roll and marmalade to a full-blown meal of hot or cold cereal, eggs any style, meats, beans, toast, fried bread, mushrooms, tomatoes, and all the tea and coffee you can drink. Many hotels and B&Bs pride themselves on their generous home-cooked breakfasts, a tradition in England. The smaller hotels and B&Bs seldom vary their breakfast menus, so after two or three mornings of this cholesterol festival, many of us yearn for just a simple piece of fruit and a bagel.

Smoking/Nonsmoking Rooms

London hotels are showing trends of adding more nonsmoking rooms. If a hotel provides exclusive nonsmoking rooms, it is noted in the "Facilities and Services" section. The index has a list of hotels with rooms set aside exclusively for nonsmoking guests. Always ask for a nonsmoking room. This at least puts the hotel on notice to air out the room and spray it, and it gives you some clout if the room smells *overwhelmingly* like cigars, since you have specifically asked for a nonsmoking room. Some hotels try to accommodate these requests; others flat-out refuse.

Facilities and Services

Each listing gives the number of rooms in the hotel and whether they have private baths, and if so, how many. This information appears below the establishment's address. At the end of each listing, a brief summary describes hotel facilities and services. These may include air-conditioning, a bar, direct-dial phone, hair dryer, lift, data port, laundry service, minibar, parking, room service, satellite TV, pay-per-view movies or VCR, safe in the room or in the office (and if there is a charge), or exclusive nonsmoking rooms. The better the hotel, the more services offered, and usually the higher its room rates. Check each listing for those amenities you consider essential for a comfortable stay. For a complete list of hotels with nonsmoking rooms, see page 338.

Nearest Tourist Attractions

Each hotel listing tells you the nearest tourist attractions that are within a reasonable walking distance.

Transportation

The closest tube stops are given with each hotel listing. That is not to say that taking the bus might not be a better way for you to get where you want to go. It is beyond the scope of *Great Sleeps London* to give the bus routes, but you can get free bus maps from London Transport Travel Information offices, found in major tube stations and at Heathrow Airport. When in doubt, just ask at the hotel desk. (See "Transportation," page 36, for more information on public transportation.)

Maps

Every postal code covered in *Great Sleeps London* has a corresponding map showing all of the hotels and Great Chic shopping establishments within that area. Each hotel's map key number is repeated in the text; it appears in parentheses to the right of the hotel name. Establishments outside the boundaries of these maps are unnumbered.

The maps in *Great Sleeps London* are meant to help you locate all the hotels and shops in the book; they are not meant to replace detailed street maps to guide you as you travel about the city. If you're going to be in London even for a couple of days, it pays to pick up a copy of the *A–Z London Street Map* (pronounced "a" to "zed"), the most comprehensive map of the city you can get. It includes a tube map.

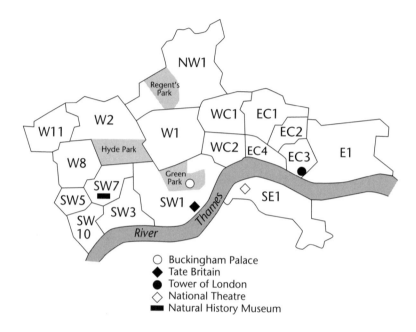

NW1

Regent's Park

W11　W2

W8　Hyde Park　W1　WC1　EC1

EC2

WC2　EC4　EC3　E1

Green Park ○

SW7　SW1 ◆　Thames　SE1 ◇

SW5

SW3

SW 10　River

○ Buckingham Palace
◆ Tate Britain
● Tower of London
◇ National Theatre
▬ Natural History Museum

HOTEL LISTINGS BY POSTAL CODE

London is far more difficult to see properly than any other place. London is a riddle.
> —*G. K. Chesterton,* All Things Considered, *1908*

London is chaos incorporated.
> —*George Mikes,* Down with Everybody, *1951*

London is one of the largest cities in the world. Covering more than 610 square miles, with 7 million inhabitants in the metropolitan area, it is twice the size of Paris or New York City. Originally, London was a collection of small villages. In a sense, it still is, each "village" having its own unique character and atmosphere.

One of the great allures of visiting London is that you can never see it all. There is always one more pub, a special museum, or a historic street or neighborhood left to explore. It is beyond the scope of *Great Sleeps London* to go into detail about all of the sight-seeing possibilities that await you. The following sketches of the highlights, organized by postal code, are designed to give you a quick idea of what is around your hotel. For an in-depth description of what to see in London, the green Michelin *Tourist Guide to London* is a classic.

As Paris is divided into arrondissements, London is divided into postal codes. You will see them included in all street addresses and on most street signs. Knowing one postal code from another is important when booking your hotel accommodations. The letters, which stand for compass directions with reference to the central district, start with W1 and then are divided into WC and EC for West Central and East Central, NW and SW for North West and South West, and so on. All districts bordering on the central districts are numbered with a one (1) and continue to increase in number as they get farther from the center. If you see W8, you know you are not in the heart of Piccadilly in the West End; SE10 tells you the address is well into the tourist boonies. All hotel and shop listings in *Great Sleeps London* provide the postal code and are arranged accordingly. This system parallels the arrangement of the restaurants in *Great Eats London.* If you are staying in SW1 and are trying to decide where to eat dinner close to your hotel, refer to the SW1 section in *Great Eats London* for a listing of nearby restaurants.

W1

The West End

I like to walk down Bond Street, thinking of all the things I don't want.

—*Logan Pearsall Smith,*
Afterthoughts, *1931*

The postal code West One (W1) corresponds to the West End, the area filled with department stores, theaters, shops, pubs, restaurants, and nightlife.

Elegant Mayfair and St. James's, which are west of Regent Street and north of Piccadilly, are characterized by gentlemen's clubs, expensive shops, plush hotels, royal residences, and parks. The tailoring standards of the world are defined on Savile Row, and the finest (and most expensive) shopping is found along Jermyn, South Molton, and New and Old Bond Streets. St. James's Park and Green Park offer good views of Buckingham Palace. If you see the royal standard (flag) flying at Buckingham Palace, you will know the queen is in residence.

Piccadilly is London's equivalent of Times Square, with incessant traffic, crowds, bright lights, noise, and general confusion for the uninitiated. Piccadilly Circus isn't actually a circus anymore, but it seems like one, with six traffic-clogged main roads spiraling from it.

The word *Soho* comes from the hunting call "so-ho." Its use as a place name seems to be associated with the area's former popularity as a location for fox and hare hunting. Today, Soho is full of character and characters, and the type of hunting has changed dramatically. For centuries this area has been home to immigrants and refugees, who opened a cosmopolitan mix of shops, restaurants, bars, pubs, and sleazy sex and strip joints. Bustling by day and exciting by night, this is London's center of entertainment and nightlife of all types. Here are the West End theaters, a great selection of cinemas, hundreds of restaurants and clubs catering to every taste and budget, and Chinatown, which hums until the wee hours, drawing many after-theater diners and other night owls.

Marylebone is a residential area with many lovely squares. Doctors' offices line Harley Street, and all Sherlock Holmes fans know about 221B Baker Street.

TOURIST ATTRACTIONS
Mayfair, Marylebone, Piccadilly Circus, Marble Arch, Soho, Wellington Arch, Royal Academy of Arts, Spencer House, Regent Street, Oxford Street, St. James's Church

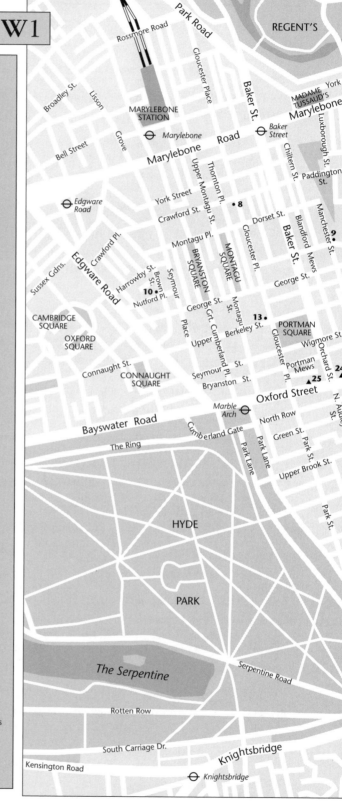

W1

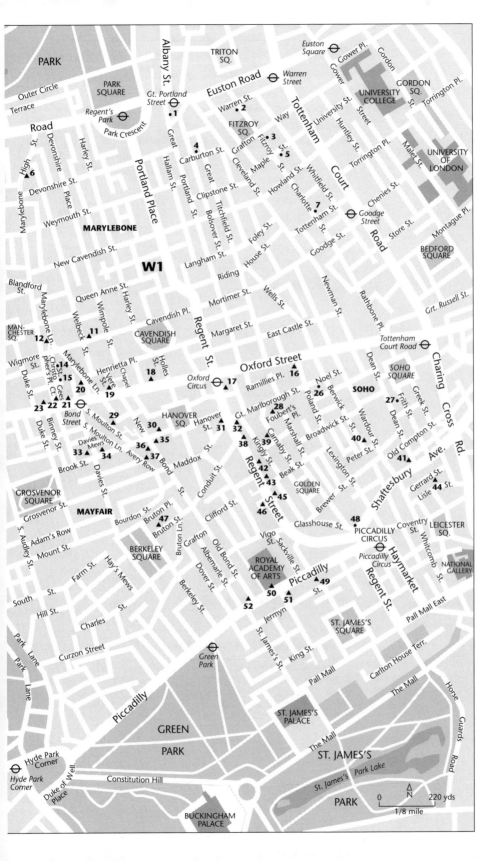

Few visitors know that 27 Wimpole Street was the residence of Henry Higgins in the film *My Fair Lady,* or that Charles Dickens wrote *David Copperfield* and *The Old Curiosity Shop* while living at 1 Devonshire Place. While you are in Marylebone (pronounced MAR-lee-bun), you will be able to visit the Planetarium and stand in the interminable queue for Madame Tussaud's Wax Museum.

The Marble Arch was originally built as the entrance to Buckingham Palace, but it was too small. It was moved to its current location in 1851 and has been a landmark ever since.

HOTELS IN W1

OTHER OPTIONS

Apartment Rentals

Hostels

Student Dormitories

Student-Only Accommodations

YMCAs

($) indicates a Big Splurge

GEORGIAN HOTEL (8)
87 Gloucester Place, W1
Tube: Baker Street

19 rooms, all with shower or bath and toilet

For one of the best Great Sleeping values near Baker Street and within walking distance of Oxford Street and Regent's Park, the Georgian Hotel receives my vote of confidence. It is obvious from first glance that owners Sam Popat and Nick Damji continue to spend time, money, and effort to maintain the consistently high standards of their spotless hotel. The identically decorated bedrooms, which are repainted yearly, are done in gold, green, and blue. Good lighting, luggage racks, and individually controlled central heating add to their allure. So do new beds every three years, double-glazed windows where possible (it is a listed building, and some things cannot be altered), and a London information packet. The bathrooms are exceptionally nice, with heated towel racks and collapsible laundry lines, so handy for those quick overnight drying needs. However, note that only nine of the rooms, which include the triples and family rooms, have an in-room bathroom; the other ten have their own adjacent private bathrooms, which are equally as nice. The only drawbacks are the ground-floor rooms, which open directly onto the street, and some of the back rooms, which face a wall. Naturally, these back rooms are quiet, and the opposing wall has been painted and potted plants positioned in an effort to break the monotonous view. Best bets, in my opinion, are street-side rooms from the second floor up, especially No. 5, which has two floor-to-ceiling windows, twin beds, and a corner area for stashing luggage, or No. 19 on the back, with twin beds, a view, and its own private bathroom just next to it.

The breakfast room, also decorated in golds and greens, has a mirrored section that gives the room depth. Your morning breakfast buffet includes ham, cheese, hard-boiled eggs, fruit juices, yogurt, cereals, toast, jam, and coffee or tea.

A final bonus point that really puts this hotel at the top of its class is that it has a lift to all floors.

FACILITIES AND SERVICES: Central heat, direct-dial phones, hair dryer and iron available, lift, room safe large enough for a laptop, TV, tea and coffeemakers, fax for guests and will accept incoming emails, desk open for reservations 7 A.M.–10:30 P.M.

TELEPHONE
020 7935 2211/7486 3151

FAX
020 7486 7535

EMAIL
info@georgianhotel.demon.co.uk

INTERNET
www.londoncentralhotel.com

CREDIT CARDS
AE, MC, V

RATES
Single £80, double £95–100, triple £105, family room for four £130

BREAKFAST
English breakfast buffet included

NEAREST TOURIST ATTRACTIONS: Regent's Park, Madame Tussaud's

HART HOUSE HOTEL (13)
51 Gloucester Place, W1
Tube: Baker Street, Marble Arch
16 rooms, all with shower or bath and toilet

TELEPHONE
020 7935 2288
FAX
020 7935 8516
EMAIL
reservations@harthouse.co.uk
INTERNET
www.harthouse.co.uk
CREDIT CARDS
AE, MC, V
RATES
Single £70, double £105, triple £130, quad £150,
BREAKFAST
English breakfast buffet included

Hart House is a sixteen-room bed-and-breakfast hotel superbly run by Andrew Bowden, who took it over from his parents about twenty years ago. The building was part of an original terrace of Georgian mansions occupied by French nobility during the French Revolution.

Everything in the conveniently located hotel is always very clean and in perfect order, thanks to a committed redecorating schedule. In addition, most of the rooms have that hard-to-find commodity in London: *space.* Number 7 is a front-facing triple with a large bath and shower and two floor-to-ceiling windows. On the back of the hotel, No. 9, a spacious triple, has a new bathroom and an interesting view over the apartments beyond. Number 8 has a window overlooking a small balcony, and No. 11 is sunny perch for a solo traveler. All of the rooms are nicely fitted with coordinated fabrics and furniture that includes an armoire, desk, comfortable chair, and chest of drawers. The lower-floor breakfast room has three skylights and a coal-burning fireplace, making it a cheerful spot for guests to enjoy the traditional English breakfast included in the price of a room. Large tables set with blue-and-white china encourage sharing and getting to know the other guests. Andrew Bowden's outgoing hospitality and reasonable rates make this a favorite, so get your reservation as soon as you know your London dates.

FACILITIES AND SERVICES: Central heat, direct-dial phones, hair dryer, no lift, office safe, TV, tea and coffee-makers, desk open for reservations 7:30 A.M.–10:30 P.M.

NEAREST TOURIST ATTRACTIONS: West End theaters, shopping, Hyde Park, Regent's Park

HAZLITT'S ($, 27)
6 Frith Street, W1
Tube: Tottenham Court Road
23 rooms, all with shower or bath and toilet

TELEPHONE
020 7434 1771
FAX
020 7439 1524
EMAIL
reservations@hazlitts.co.uk

There is no question about it: Hazlitt's is one of London's best small hotels. The combination of history, charm, and character, along with the hotel's unique surroundings and personal service, all in a super location, have made it a standout from the moment it opened its doors in 1986. It is on the edge of Soho, within interesting and easy walking distance of more than thirty West End theaters, twenty cinemas, the Royal Opera House, and dozens of restaurants in every price category (see *Great Eats London)*. Named for the great English essayist and critic William Hazlitt, who boarded here, wrote his last essay here, and died here, the hotel occupies three Georgian townhouses built in 1718. All twenty-three rooms are named after the eighteenth- and early-nineteenth-century residents of or visitors to the original houses. Many celebrities of our own day have stayed here, and it is especially popular among authors. Traditionally, guests who have had a recent work published leave a signed copy of their latest book in a special cabinet in the sitting room.

The entire hotel is a study in tasteful decorating, dominated by a sensational collection of more than two thousand original prints hung throughout the hotel, including in all of the guest bathrooms. The individually decorated bedrooms have high ceilings and comfortable beds, many of which are four-posters with snowy white Egyptian cotton duvet coverings. Six rooms on the top floor have air-conditioning. Most of the classic bathrooms have original Victorian claw-footed bathtubs and brass faucet hardware, lovingly polished by a full-time staff member solely employed for this purpose.

The ground-floor Baron Willoughby Suite is magnificent, with a massive four-poster bed, marble fireplace, and another tiny fireplace in the bathroom, leather-tufted chesterfield, and corner cabinet with a display of antique plates, teacups, and teapots. The Earl of St. Albans has a half-canopy bed, mirrored armoire, and a beautiful collection of bird prints hung in the bathroom. Another beautiful collection of framed prints of water animals and a larger bathroom highlight the top-floor Mary Baker Room, which also has a sweet corner fireplace and an impressively carved headboard on its four-poster bed. For those requiring as much space as possible, consider the Jonathan Swift Room, with its three-hundred-year-old bed frame; the Prussian President Room, with a walk-in closet and an extra sofa bed; or the William Duncombe Room, which has a fireplace discovered a few years ago during a renovation project, a marvelous, massive double bed, and a five-drawer dresser. Even the bathroom is special, thanks to its pitched,

INTERNET
www.hazlittshotel.com

CREDIT CARDS
AE, DC, MC, V

RATES
Single £165, double £225, suite £330; all rates subject to VAT of 17.5 percent

BREAKFAST
Continental breakfast only, £10 extra per person, served in the room or in one of the sitting rooms

beamed ceiling with a skylight. Single guests are not expected to do penance in uninteresting surroundings, especially in the burgundy-colored Charles Lamb Room, with a carved headboard, leather-topped writing desk, and small fireplace framed by a pair of busts sculpted by the owner's grandfather. The Sir William Ross Room is also perfect for a single. Although it doesn't have a view, it does have the advantage of more space and a marble washstand in the bathroom.

It is the nature of old buildings that nothing is perfect. The management asks guests, "Please be kind to the furniture, and if it is not being kind to you, let us know and we will attend to it." Because the original character of the buildings has been kept, some floors may lean a little and there might be a ray or two of light under the doorway, and there is no elevator. However, the hotel has succeeded beautifully in maintaining the comfort of twentieth-century life without sacrificing the historical spirit of its surroundings for its grateful and contented guests.

NOTE: See page 167 for the Gore, and page 178 for the Rookery, two other outstanding hotels under the same ownership.

FACILITIES AND SERVICES: Air-conditioning in 6 top-floor rooms, central heat, direct-dial phones, hair dryer, laundry service, room safe, satellite TV, data ports, room service for light meals, no lift, 24-hour desk

NEAREST TOURIST ATTRACTIONS: Soho, West End theaters, Royal Opera House

IVANHOE SUITE HOTEL/PENSION (15)
1 St. Christopher's Place, W1
Tube: Bond Street
7 rooms, all with shower or bath and toilet

A Great Sleep in London continues to be the seven-room Ivanhoe Suite Hotel/Pension. Situated on a pedestrian walkway, this hotel consists of attractive singles and doubles, each with its own sitting area and tiled bathroom with stall showers. At street level on St. Christopher's Place, there is a hidden security system whereby guests view the front door below when someone rings their private doorbell. The white-glove test will never be necessary, as the rooms are nothing short of antiseptically clean and tidy. I like No. 4, which would accommodate two nicely; it's done in soft peach with blue accents and has a view onto St. Christopher's Place

TELEPHONE
020 7935 1047

FAX
020 7724 0563

INTERNET
www.scoot.co.uk/
ivanhoe_suite_hotel

CREDIT CARDS
AE, DC, MC, V

RATES
Single £70, double £85, triple £100

BREAKFAST
Continental breakfast included and served in the room

and the metal fountain. I also like the similar No. 6, a sunny double with a large closet, plenty of shelf space in a nice bathroom, and an interesting view of the square below. Another of my favorites is the bright No. 3, large enough for three people. For shoppers, this hotel is settled in an area that almost qualifies as Mecca. Besides the interesting boutiques along St. Christopher's Place, you are only minutes from New and Old Bond Streets and all the temptations of their elegant shops. Good restaurants and typical pubs are also only minutes away (see *Great Eats London*).

FACILITIES AND SERVICES: Electric heat, fans in all rooms, direct-dial phones, hair dryer, laundry service, minibar, office safe, cable TV, radio, room clocks, individual security for each room, trouser press, tea and coffeemakers, office open 7:30 A.M.–midnight; no lift

NEAREST TOURIST ATTRACTIONS: Shopping, Wallace Collection, Hyde Park

POSTHOUSE LEISURE BREAKS

For one of the better hotel values in the capital, schedule your visit around one of the Posthouse Leisure Breaks. These offer excellent package plans not only for London visitors but for those of you traveling elsewhere in the U.K. where there are Posthouse hotels. In London, the Great Sleeping deals can range from a simple room upgrade to five nights for the price of four; midweek, weekend, or holiday stays that include dinner, bed, and breakfast; and Theatre Breaks tickets to all the top West End shows, the opera and ballet, rock concerts, or the Chelsea Flower Show. Dinner vouchers, travel cards, and free (or greatly reduced) rates for children sharing their parents' room are usually part of the plans. In some cases you can use your dinner voucher at another participating hotel or restaurant, or have lunch or afternoon tea instead. A full English breakfast is often included. A minimum stay of two consecutive nights is required, and other restrictions apply. For complete details and a price breakdown, contact the numbers listed here and ask for the magazine that details all of their offers.

Hotels participating in the London Posthouse Leisure Breaks are the Posthouse Bloomsbury, WC1 (page 112); the Posthouse Kensington, W8 (page 86); and the Posthouse Regent's Park, W1, described below.

TELEPHONE
0345 40 40 40; 800-225-5843 (toll-free from the U.S.)

FAX
01384 486159 (U.K.); 602-735-7296 (U.S.)

INTERNET
www.posthouse-hotels.com

CREDIT CARDS
AE, DC, MC, V

POSTHOUSE REGENT'S PARK (4)
Carburton Street, W1
Tube: Great Portland Street, Regent's Park
333 rooms, all with shower or bath and toilet

TELEPHONE
0870 400 9111; 800-225-5843
(toll-free from the U.S.)
FAX
020 7387 2806
EMAIL
meetings-regentspark@forte-
hotels.com
INTERNET
www.posthouse-hotels.com
CREDIT CARDS
AE, DC, MC, V
RATES
Singles from £95, doubles
from £120
BREAKFAST
English breakfast £13.95

Once you get past the truly ugly gray cement-block exterior, reminiscent of Eastern Bloc architecture before the collapse of the Berlin Wall, this massive chain hotel offers a uniformly contemporary haven about five minutes from the West End. The hotel participates in the Posthouse Leisure Breaks, which are described above.

FACILITIES AND SERVICES: Bar, central heat, direct-dial phones with voice mail in some, hair dryer, laundry service, lift, minibar, data port in superior rooms, parking, restaurant, 24-hour room service, office safe, tea and coffeemakers, trouser press, satellite TV, conference rooms and business services for guests

NEAREST TOURIST ATTRACTIONS: West End, Regent's Park, Madame Tussaud's, Planetarium

REGENT PALACE HOTEL (48)
Piccadilly Circus, W1
Tube: Piccadilly Circus
910 rooms, 120 with shower or bath and toilet

TELEPHONE
0870 400 8703
FAX
020 7734 6435
INTERNET
www.forte-hotels.com
CREDIT CARDS
AE, DC, MC, V
RATES
Single £80, double £80–95
BREAKFAST
Prepackaged Continental
breakfast £5

The Regent Palace hotel used to be quite something in its heyday, but things have changed with the years, and it is now a giant sleeping factory where you are barely a number and hardly a name to the overworked and undertrained front desk staff. However, if you seek a dead-central location and low-priced (for London) accommodations, the Regent Palace, one of the largest hotels in London, may suit you just fine. Situated overlooking Eros and Piccadilly Circus, no hotel could be nearer the bright lights and bustle of London than this—steps away from theaters, nightclubs, restaurants, shops, tube and bus transportation, and several major museums. The 910 rooms, which are strung out along never-ending halls, are acceptably furnished in typical, dull-hotel style. If sleep is part of your nightly plan, avoid the rooms on the eighth and ninth floors, which are often filled with school groups. Only some of the doubles have private facilities; all of the other rooms have only a sink with hot and cold water. In my opinion, it does not make Great Sleeping sense for two people to pay one penny more to upgrade to a room with your own tight-fitting, airless, "phone booth" shower and toilet. The institutional hall facilities are large and remind me of what you would find in a health club or college dorm. A maid opens the door to the shower or bath on request and cleans it after each use. Save even more money and avoid eating breakfast here, especially the boxed editions that are made up who knows when and passed out every morning at a central distribution point in the bar.

FACILITIES AND SERVICES: Bars, central heat, direct-dial phones, hair dryers available, ironing rooms, laundry service, lift, office safe, some trouser presses, tea and coffeemakers, pay TV, 24-hour desk, nonsmoking floors available

NEAREST TOURIST ATTRACTIONS: Piccadilly Circus, West End, shopping

10 MANCHESTER STREET (9)
10 Manchester Street, W1
Tube: Baker Street, Bond Street

46 rooms, all with shower or bath and toilet

At 10 Manchester Street you will find no sign, no awning or flag flying over the main entrance, no red-carpeted stairs, and no hot-and-cold running valets. What you will find is a privately owned, handsome, discreet townhouse hotel in the heart of the West End, close to Marylebone High Street, fashionable Bond Street, and the magnificent Wallace Collection. The red brick 1919 hotel property offers quality accommodations with an eye toward the comfort and convenience of each guest. When you arrive, you will be offered complimentary coffee or tea in the main sitting lounge, attractively furnished in beige and brown. A glowing electric fireplace adds a further note of welcome. Breakfast is served in two dining rooms; it is a filling buffet that includes freshly squeezed orange juice and Starbucks special roast coffee. All of the rooms and suites are well laid out and have space to comfortably live. Each has a desk, cushioned chair, satellite television, CD player, plenty of natural light, good beds, and tiled bathrooms with dressing gowns and Escada toiletries. Special weekend rates throughout the year and winter promotions from January through March make 10 Manchester a notable Great Sleeping choice in London.

FACILITIES AND SERVICES: Direct-dial phones, tea and coffeemaking facilities, hair dryer, laundry service, lift, office safe, trouser press, TV with satellite hookup, CD player, 10 nonsmoking rooms, complimentary bottle of mineral water upon arrival

NEAREST TOURIST ATTRACTIONS: Oxford Street, Wallace Collection, Regent's Park

TELEPHONE
020 7486 6669

FAX
020 7224 0348

EMAIL
stay@10manchesterstreet.fsnet.co.uk

INTERNET
www.10manchesterstreet.com

CREDIT CARDS
AE, MC, V

RATES
Single or small double £132, double £165, suite £225; special weekend promotions and lower winter rates

BREAKFAST
Continental breakfast £5

W2

Paddington and Bayswater

TOURIST ATTRACTIONS
Hyde Park, Speaker's Corner,
Bayswater Road Art Exhibition,
Kensington Gardens

Paddington is a good choice if you are on a budget or traveling by car. It is close to Hyde Park, where you can jog or walk off some of those full English breakfasts and your children can play and expend some of their pent-up energy. If you have a car, parking can be a nightmare, but not if you stay in one of the hotels on Sussex Gardens, where free parking is often part of the deal. Restaurants in the area are budget conscious and seldom gourmet. Many of the hotels that line both sides of the busy Sussex Gardens are geared toward tourists spending one or two nights near Paddington Station; in short, they're dull. However, the competition is stiff, making hotel prices here among the lowest in London.

Transportation is superb. The area is served by four Underground lines—Metropolitan, Bakerloo, District, and Circle—and all the Great Sleeps in W2 are within walking distance of, or a short cab ride away from, Paddington Station, where the fast-rail link to Heathrow Airport runs every fifteen minutes between 5:30 A.M. and 11:30 P.M. and less than under thirty minutes either way. You can also check in for your flight at Paddington, which has desks for many airlines with full luggage check-in facilities. This means you will save the hassle of getting to and queuing at Heathrow with luggage in tow. If you have a late afternoon or evening flight, you can check your baggage, spend the day in London, then hop on the tube for Heathrow, all the while not worrying about luggage.

Bayswater lies north of Kensington Gardens and is known as a residential area of contrasts. It is home to many Indians, Pakistanis, and Arabs, budget hotels, and shops of all types. Queensway, its main thoroughfare, has the large Whiteleys of Bayswater indoor shopping mall, which houses stores, cafés, and cinemas, as well as the major chain shops and restaurants serving a multitude of ethnic and local foods. On Sunday, it is pleasant to walk along Bayswater Road, where artists and craftspeople display their works for sale (see Bayswater Road Art Exhibition, page 278).

HOTELS IN W2

OTHER OPTIONS

Apartment Rentals

YMCAs

($) indicates a Big Splurge

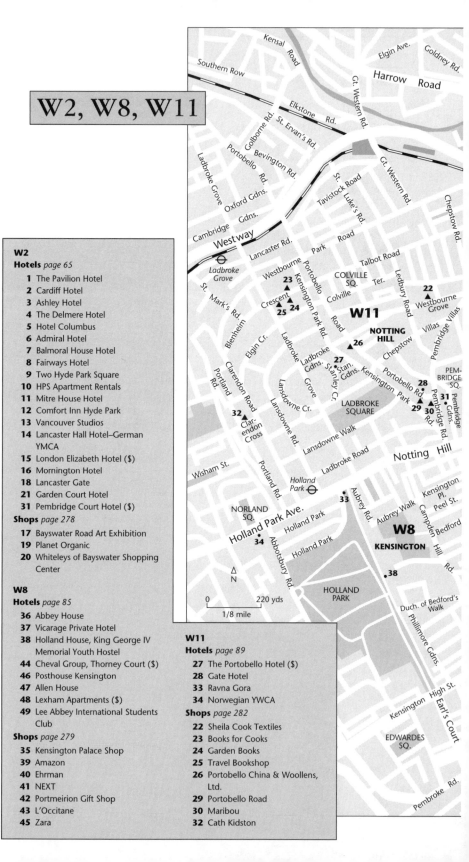

W2, W8, W11

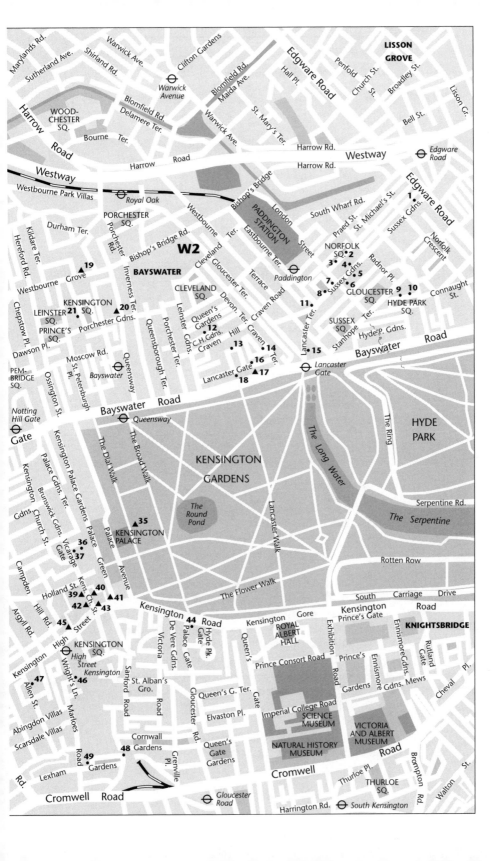

ADMIRAL HOTEL (6)
143 Sussex Gardens, W2
Tube: Lancaster Gate, Paddington

TELEPHONE
020 7723 7309/3975
FAX
020 7723 8731
EMAIL
frank@admiral143.demon.co.uk
INTERNET
www.admiral143.demon.co.uk
CREDIT CARDS
MC, V
RATES
Single £48–50, double £75,
extra person £30
BREAKFAST
English breakfast included

20 rooms, all with shower or bath and toilet

Franco and Gloria Vales continue to run a reliable choice that improves on every visit. This time, new carpets, new bedspreads, and laminated furniture replaced the mixture of colors and styles that were here before. Space is tight in some bathrooms, and the prefab arrangements might turn some off. However, the tidy, completely nonsmoking rooms have drawer and closet space, a chair, and reading lights over the bed. Luggage racks and/or a table would be nice additions in some, but for the price, no one is complaining. Knowing Franco, he will be adding them soon. Breakfast is served on English china in a sweet room that is as clean as the rest of the twenty-room hotel.

FACILITIES AND SERVICES: Ceiling fans in some rooms, central heat, direct-dial phones, double-glazed windows along the front, hair dryer and iron available, electric tea and coffeemakers, one free parking space that must be reserved, office safe, TV, office open 8 A.M.–midnight; no lift, no smoking allowed. The hotel usually closes 4–5 days at Christmas.

NEAREST TOURIST ATTRACTIONS: Hyde Park, Kensington Gardens

ASHLEY HOTEL (3)
15–17 Norfolk Square, W2
Tube: Paddington

TELEPHONE
020 7723 3375
FAX
020 7723 0173
EMAIL
ashhot@btinternet.com
CREDIT CARDS
MC, V
RATES
Single £40–50, double £78,
triple £97, family room £90–
115; add £1 per person if stay is
for one night only.
BREAKFAST
English breakfast included

52 rooms, 43 with shower or bath and toilet

Many hotels around Norfolk Square are leased to managers and show very little pride of ownership, but not so at the Ashley, which has been proudly owned for over a quarter century by Welsh brothers John and David George and is now in the capable hands of David's son Matthew. Matthew is young, enthusiastic, and full of excellent plans, many of which have been well carried out. Twenty rooms have been redone with coordinated fabrics and new furnishings, and ten more are scheduled each year. A genuine interest is taken in each guest, whether it is a first-time stay or repeat visits from couples, families, or businesspeople, many of whom spent their honeymoon here and return now with their children. Near the breakfast room is a bulletin board with helpful hints and tips on what to see and do in London, from street markets and river cruises to day trips in the country, unusual shopping advice, and what to do on a Sunday. In the spring and summer, everyone is invited to enjoy the gardens in front of the hotel.

If you are a family group, you probably will have No. 23, a lower-ground-floor room that sleeps up to five. Despite its location, it is a cheerful room, with pink floral bedspreads and wallpaper. Security rails on the windows ensure safety. Best bets for singles or doubles are on higher floors. Number 9, one of the ten bathless singles, has a view onto Norfolk Square. Two other singles have a shower and toilet on the landing that is private to each room. Number 6 is a quiet double in the back with a neighborhood view. The hotel is closed from December 24 to January 2.

FACILITIES AND SERVICES: Central heat, fans on request, direct-dial phones, hair dryer available, office safe, TV, no lift, office open 8 A.M.–10 P.M.

NEAREST TOURIST ATTRACTIONS: Hyde Park, Kensington Gardens

BALMORAL HOUSE HOTEL (7)
156–157 Sussex Gardens, W2
Tube: Paddington
34 rooms, 31 with shower or bath and toilet

One of the better budget addresses, and one definitely in the top 1 percent for cleanliness along Sussex Gardens, is the Balmoral House, run by the Vieites family. When you reserve, ask to be in the building at 156 Sussex Gardens, unless you like crossing a busy street to have your breakfast, which is served in a plant-filled room at the 156 address. The rooms at both addresses are generally well decorated, with no questionable mixes of color and pattern. Those facing the street will have some noise, but they do have double-glazed windows. Above all, every room in both locations is spotlessly clean, thanks to the daily vigilance of Mrs. Vieites, who lets nothing escape her sharp eyes and told me, "I have a good idea how to care for my guests." She certainly does. When I commented on the cleanliness to one of her daughters, she dutifully replied, "Well, you have met my mother and you know she keeps us marching." The bottom line is a good budget Great Sleep with very few complaints.

TELEPHONE
020 7723 4925

FAX
020 7402 0118

EMAIL
balmoral@freedom2surf.co.uk

INTERNET
www.balmoralhousehotel.co.uk

CREDIT CARDS
MC, V (5% surcharge)

RATES
Single £40–45, double £70–75, extra person £25; off-season rates in winter depending on availability

BREAKFAST
English breakfast included

FACILITIES AND SERVICES: Central heat, hall phone, hair dryer available, electric tea and coffeemakers, free parking for four cars, office safe, TV, desk open 7 A.M.–11 P.M.; no lift

NEAREST TOURIST ATTRACTIONS: Hyde Park, Kensington Gardens

CARDIFF HOTEL (2)
5–9 Norfolk Square, W2
Tube: Paddington
60 rooms, 45 with shower or bath and toilet

TELEPHONE
020 7723 9068/3513

FAX
020 7402 2342

EMAIL
stay@cardiff-hotel.com

INTERNET
www.cardiff-hotel.com

CREDIT CARDS
MC, V

RATES
Single £45–70, double £80, triple £90, quad £100; lower rates in January and February subject to availability

BREAKFAST
English breakfast included

All trains from Wales arrive at Paddington Station, so it is not surprising that many hotels in the neighborhood were once owned by Welsh. These days most of them have been sold, but not the one run by the Davies family, which has been holding strong at the Cardiff for more than forty-five years. Their sixty-room hotel is nothing fancy, but the small, clean rooms are adequately laid out for short-term living. Blond built-ins offer desk and closet space and a place to store luggage. Bathrooms are decidedly small, so I recommend opting for a bathless room. If your sight-seeing includes day trips outside of London to Stratford-upon-Avon, Windsor Castle, Oxford, or Bath, your train leaves from Paddington Station, a few minutes' walk from the hotel's front door. This also means that arrival or departure in London through Heathrow Airport will be a snap, what with the fast-rail link between Paddington Station and the airport, and the check-in desks for most major airlines in Paddington Station.

FACILITIES AND SERVICES: Central heat (morning and evenings only), direct-dial phones, hair dryer in most rooms (otherwise available), electric tea and coffeemakers, office safe, TV, desk open 7 A.M.–11 P.M.; no lift, no smoking in one building

NEAREST TOURIST ATTRACTIONS: Kensington Gardens, Hyde Park

COMFORT INN HYDE PARK (12)
18–19 Craven Hill Gardens, W2
Tube: Paddington, Bayswater
60 rooms, 7 flats, all with shower or bath and toilet

TELEPHONE
020 7262 6644; 800-228-5150 (toll-free from the U.S.)

FAX
020 7262 0673

EMAIL
comfortinn_hydepark@ compuserve.com

The Comfort Inn Hyde Park on Craven Hill Gardens is in a neighborhood of stately Georgian homes with manicured private gardens. The sixty rooms are frankly charm-free (shut your eyes and you could be anywhere), but they do offer the advantage of being nonsmoking if you land on the fourth or fifth floors. These top-floor rooms are also recommended because they have more light and bigger bathrooms than those on the lower floors. Smokers can check into No. 101, a twin in the back with a limited view but with the plus of a sitting area with a desk and chair and a real window in the bathroom. Some of the bathrooms are definitely dated, especially in rooms 10 and 14. If you are staying for a few days or want plenty of space, reserve one of the hotel's flats, which range from roomy one-bedrooms to huge three-bedroom accommodations, all with maid service included. Also included are washing machines and kitchens with microwaves. There is no dishwasher or oven, which shouldn't be a problem unless you were planning on whipping up a turkey dinner with all the trimmings.

FACILITIES AND SERVICES: Bar, central heat, conference room, direct-dial phones, data ports, hair dryer, laundry service, lift, office safe (£1.50 per night), 3–4 parking spaces on first come, first served basis, tea and coffee-makers, TV and radio, 24-hour desk, nonsmoking rooms on 4th and 5th floors. Apartments: all the above plus outfitted kitchen with microwave, washer, and dryer

NEAREST TOURIST ATTRACTIONS: Kensington Gardens, Hyde Park

INTERNET
www.comfortinn.com

CREDIT CARDS
AE, DC, MC, V

RATES
Single £88, double £110, flats £150–2000 per night; lower rates in hotel and flats subject to availability

BREAKFAST
Continental breakfast included

THE DELMERE HOTEL (4)
130 Sussex Gardens, W2
Tube: Paddington

38 rooms, all with shower or bath and toilet

The Delmere Hotel is a townhouse in Sussex Gardens, part of a legacy of early-nineteenth-century design by architect Charles Robert Cockerell, whose star pupil, Benjamin Henry Latrobe, rebuilt the Capitol in Washington, D.C., after its destruction in 1814. This area in London was built to provide luxurious homes for fashionable Victorian families. Lord Baden-Powell, founder of the Boy Scouts (see Baden-Powell House, page 165), was christened in St. James's Church. Sir Arthur Conan Doyle's family lived in Sussex Gardens, and at St. Mary's Hospital, Sir Alexander Fleming discovered penicillin.

As you enter the Delmere, there is a comfortable sitting room and library stocked with daily papers and current magazines, and a black-and-white jazz bar with photos of Louis Armstrong, Geoff Stern, and other legends. Guests can also eat in the hotel restaurant, La Perla, which serves Continental cuisine, but frankly, it needs work. Consult *Great Eats London* for better choices.

TELEPHONE
020 7706 3344

FAX
020 7262 1863

EMAIL
delmerehotel@compuserve.com

INTERNET
www.delemerehotels.com

CREDIT CARDS
AE, DC, MC, V

RATES
Single £90–100, double £110–125, extra bed £20

BREAKFAST
Continental buffet breakfast included

The rooms range from spacious to extremely snug, but almost all are well thought out, with built-ins and compact baths offering good towels and bright lighting. Each color-coordinated room has a soft easy chair, some luggage and desk space, and an electronic key card for extra security. Data ports are standard. Only a few rooms fail to get my stamp of approval, especially Nos. 103 and 204, doubles with twin beds that are simply too small for comfort.

NOTE: The same owners operate the less expensive Hotel Columbus, also in Sussex Gardens. For details, please see page 74.

FACILITIES AND SERVICES: Bar, central heat, data ports, direct-dial phones, hair dryer, electric tea and coffee-makers, laundry service, lift, 2 free parking spaces, restaurant, room safe (£1 per day), satellite TV, radio, nonsmoking rooms, 24-hour desk

NEAREST TOURIST ATTRACTIONS: Kensington Gardens, Hyde Park

FAIRWAYS HOTEL (8)
186 Sussex Gardens, W2
Tube: Lancaster Gate, Paddington
17 rooms, 10 with shower or bath and toilet

TELEPHONE & FAX
020 7723 4871

EMAIL
info@fairways-hotel.co.uk

INTERNET
www.fairways-hotel.co.uk

CREDIT CARDS
MC, V

RATES
Single £52–70, double £75–85; four-poster room £85 for two, triple £100, quad £115; lower rates in January and February

BREAKFAST
English breakfast included

Steve and Jenny Adams run the homey Fairways Hotel, where you will find an abundance of ruffles and flourishes along with large portions of family hospitality. Nothing is modern, but this is part of the charm that keeps their regulars coming back. In an effort to keep up with the times, some rooms have had portable bathroom boxes added to them. Steve had a fit when he saw this comment, but I still maintain that the hall facilities are nice—so why not save a few pounds and avoid the bedrooms with the phone-booth-size bathroom in the corner? That said, I must tell you about their top-selling room, No. 1, which is on the ground floor facing front. It is a pink room (even the ceiling) with lacy curtains, a brass four-poster bed, and a modular (box) bathroom. Number 2, viewless and in blue, has great closets, a double bed, and a full bathroom. Number 9 is a good family room in blue, with bunks for the children and a private bathroom. The photos in the breakfast room tell the story of this friendly family, and the growing collection of worldwide knickknacks and scores of Christmas cards suggest how fond their guests are of them. You, too, will soon feel right at home with all the others who gather here each morning to enjoy a hearty home-cooked breakfast while plotting their day in London. Motorists will appreciate the *free* parking spaces in front of the hotel, and walkers will be able to pace themselves nicely walking through Hyde Park or on to the West End. For the less athletically inclined, bus and tube transportation are within easy reach.

NOTE: If the Fairways Hotel is full, try the James Cartref House, owned by Jenny's brother Derek James and his wife, Sharon (see page 128).

FACILITIES AND SERVICES: Central heat (mornings and evenings), fans, hall phones, hair dryer available, electric tea and coffeemakers, free parking, office safe, room safe in rooms with private facilities, TV, desk open 7 A.M.–10:30 P.M.; there's no lift, and the hotel closes at Christmas (dates vary)

NEAREST TOURIST ATTRACTIONS: Kensington Gardens, Hyde Park

GARDEN COURT HOTEL (21)
30–31 Kensington Gardens Square, W2
Tube: Bayswater, Paddington, Queensway
32 rooms, 16 with shower or bath and toilet

Edward Connolly's grandfather opened the Garden Court Hotel in 1954. Since taking it over a few years ago, Edward has made some needed improvements from top to bottom, but there is still more to do. Plans are in place for a new reception area to be incorporated into a revised sitting area, keeping the fireplace and the present collection of antiques, mirrors, and paintings. Summer guests are invited to enjoy the back garden. Upstairs, the rooms vary from the very narrow No. 25A and compact No. 27 to the larger No. 31, in yellow and white with whitewashed furniture that includes twin beds, a double dresser, a desk, and a folding chair. The bathroom is serviceable, with its stall shower, door hook, tiny basin, and glass-and-tile shelf for your toiletries. I also like No. 7, on the first floor, nicely done in yellow wallpaper with a teapot and china vase pattern in blue and yellow. There is a rattan cushioned chair, two bedside lights, and a view of a tree. A threesome will be given No. 26, which faces out and has mahogany furniture, a double and single bed, luggage and desk space, and a bathtub.

NOTE: If you cancel your reservation within fourteen days of your arrival, you forfeit your deposit, though you can apply the deposit amount toward another stay within a year of your cancellation date.

TELEPHONE
020 7229 2553

FAX
020 7727 2749

CREDIT CARDS
MC, V

RATES
Single £35–55, double £58–88, triple £75–95, quad £85–125

BREAKFAST
Continental breakfast included

FACILITIES AND SERVICES: Central heat, direct-dial phones, hair dryer, office safe, satellite TV, desk open 7 A.M.–midnight; no lift

NEAREST TOURIST ATTRACTIONS: Kensington Gardens

HOTEL COLUMBUS (5)
141 Sussex Gardens, W2
Tube: Paddington

15 rooms, 14 with shower or bath and toilet

TELEPHONE	020 7262 0974
FAX	020 7262 6785
EMAIL	hotelcolumbus@compuserve.com
INTERNET	www.delmerehotels.com
CREDIT CARDS	AE, DC, MC, V
RATES	Single £60, double £80, triple £90, quad £110
BREAKFAST	Continental buffet breakfast

The Columbus is on the south side of this leafy avenue. The building, which is approaching its two hundredth birthday, has been turned into an affordable bed-and-breakfast and is less than a five-minute walk from Paddington Station. As you walk in, note the French-inspired garden breakfast area with modern Miró-like framed prints on your right. There is no getting around the small bathrooms and the noise along the front, despite double glazing (which won't work if you open the windows), but the rooms are color coordinated and offer closet and drawer space, orthopedic beds, and electronic room locks for added safety. I would avoid any of the triples or quads, which are too squeezed for even a chair, but if it's a double you are after, this is a budget Great Sleep worth serious consideration. Ask for No. 603, a tangerine-colored double with a draped bed, dressing area along one wall with full mirror and six drawers, and a glass stall shower. Number 102 is a good double, but too tight a triple, with a terrace. The canopy bed adds a touch of class to the blue-and-green room, but the pod bathroom offers little sink space. For something a bit more upmarket, try its sister hotel across the street, the Delmere (see page 71).

FACILITIES AND SERVICES: Central heat, direct-dial phones, hair dryer available, office safe, satellite TV, desk open 8 A.M.–11 P.M.; no lift

NEAREST TOURIST ATTRACTIONS: Kensington Gardens, Hyde Park

LANCASTER HALL HOTEL–GERMAN YMCA (14)
35 Craven Terrace, W2
Tube: Lancaster Gate, Paddington

In the hotel: 80 rooms, all with shower or bath and toilet

TELEPHONE	020 7723 9276
FAX	020 7706 2870
EMAIL	lhh-info@lhh.ndirect.co.uk
INTERNET	www.lhh.ndirect.co.uk

This is a top Great Sleep in London if there ever was one. The Lancaster Hall Hotel is owned by the German YMCA. The aim is to provide excellent accommodations for any traveler, and I assure you, they succeed in meeting their goal. The setup consists of the hotel itself and the student and group annex. Unless you are around twenty and traveling with a dozen pals, you probably want the hotel section, because the twenty-four-room refurbished annex is geared for groups and those under twenty-six, and none of the rooms have private baths (for complete information on the annex, see the description under YMCAs, page 253). German efficiency and sparseness in detail are reflected from the main hotel lobby, throughout the eighty rooms, and on into the annex. Neither the hotel nor the annex has double beds. An army of uniformed maids pushing heavy-duty vacuum cleaners swoops through each day, making sure everything is shipshape. The basic hotel rooms are coordinated with matching curtains and bedspreads on twin beds, laminated pine furniture, private safes, closets with both hanging and shelf space, and tiled bathrooms that are small but acceptable. For most pleasant results, request a high back room with a sunny view, perhaps Nos. 301 to 304, or 401 to 404. Breakfast is laid out buffet style in a large, sedate dining room. Later on in the day a licensed bar opens in the lounge for guests. The hotel also caters for banquets, conferences, lectures, and seminars in function rooms that may be reserved by the day, or for any three part-day sessions.

FACILITIES AND SERVICES: Bar (6–11 P.M.), central heat, conference rooms, direct-dial phones, hair dryer available, internet terminal for guests, lift, room safe, tea and coffeemakers, satellite TV

NEAREST TOURIST ATTRACTIONS: Kensington Gardens, Hyde Park

CREDIT CARDS
MC, V

RATES
Single £60, double (all with twin beds) £78

BREAKFAST
Continental buffet breakfast included

LONDON ELIZABETH HOTEL ($, 15)
Lancaster Terrace, W2
Tube: Lancaster Gate
49 rooms, all with shower or bath and toilet

There is still only one word to describe the London Elizabeth . . . *wonderful!* It has been in the Newman family since the 1950s and is now run by the dynamic husband and wife duo of Peter and Karen Newman. Karen is an American and met Peter while she was a guest in the hotel. Her attention to detail is evident. She not only decorated all the rooms, she did all the upholstering (with the exception of the sofas) and displays her growing collection of Czech crystal throughout. As soon as you cross the threshold, you enjoy a warm feeling of welcome extended by the Newmans and their helpful

TELEPHONE
020 7402 6641; 800-721-5566 (toll-free from the U.S.)

FAX
020 7224 8900

EMAIL
reservations@ londonelizabethhotel.co.uk

INTERNET
www.londonelizabethhotel.co.uk

CREDIT CARDS
AE, DC, MC, V

RATES
Single £110, double £125–155, deluxe rooms and suites £180–250, child in parents' room: up to age 14 £10, over 14 £25

BREAKFAST
Buffet breakfast included

LONDON BREAKS RATES
THEATRE BREAK
£165–195 per person per night, depending on type of room; includes two nights' accommodation, tickets to a top West End show of your choice, champagne cocktail before three-course dinner in hotel restaurant on evening of your choice, early-morning tea and newspaper, and buffet breakfast; theater tickets cannot be exchanged or canceled if you change your booking.

WELCOME BREAK
£190–335 per person per night, depending on type of room; children under fourteen sharing parents' room £90 per child per night; includes three nights' accommodation, sight-seeing tour of London, champagne cocktail before dinner in the hotel restaurant on evening of your choice, early-morning tea and newspaper, and buffet breakfast.

staff, many of whom are into three decades of service, and whose knowledge of London will go a long way toward making your stay here the best it can be.

The hotel's location, just inches from the Lancaster Gate tube stop and across the road from Kensington Gardens and Hyde Park, allows guests to be almost anywhere in London within twenty to thirty minutes. Another bonus: The bus from Heathrow Airport stops at the hotel's front door. If you prefer the fast-rail link to Paddington, you are only a brief taxi ride from the station.

The reception area and living room display true British ambience, with a mixture of sofas and chairs clustered for good conversation. To one side is the red Theatre Bar and the Rose Garden Restaurant, which has a hand-painted mural along one wall and specializes in an international menu of country classic cuisine. On warm days, guests are invited to sit on the garden terrace, which is encircled with pots of herbs, green shrubs, and blooming flowers.

Many repeat guests have a favorite room and ask for it again and again. However, whatever style or size you have will be a quantum leap ahead of most of the competition, for the rooms display the best in furnishings, fabrics, carpeting, and window treatments. Each has an excellent bathroom stocked with plenty of fluffy towels and nice toiletries. Closet space is adequate. The deluxe rooms and suites are all nonsmoking and air-conditioned and have soft hangers in the closets and a welcome tray of fruit and a bottle of mineral water. If you reserve a suite, you will have fresh flowers, an ornamental fireplace, lighted magnifying mirrors in the bathrooms, televisions with VCRs, a deck of playing cards, and your own library bookshelf.

If you have just won the lottery or are celebrating a very special occasion with an equally special person, treat yourself to the Hyde Park Suite, a real tour de force when it comes to hotel accommodations. Three rooms were combined to make this magnificent suite, and great care was taken to restore it to its original 1850 form. The two marble fireplaces—massive mirrors over them, arched windows and shutters enclosing them—all date from the building's inception. The two-room suite is now graced with beautiful custom-built furnishings that include a set of matching bookshelves. If you are here for work, there is a large desk with the necessary computer hookups to keep you in touch. For entertaining, there is a dining table that seats six, a wet bar, chess and checker sets, two satellite televisions, and your own VCR. On sunny days, you can enjoy a drink on the terrace, which overlooks the Italian fountains in Hyde Park, or step onto the rear balcony. The sumptuous gray marble bathroom has the usual fine points, plus a twelve-inch showerhead, heated towel racks, a half dozen shelves, and a full-length beveled mirror. When you reluctantly have to leave, be sure to sign the guest book, where a Catholic monsignor from Dublin wrote, "A premature taste of paradise for a poor parson. God forgive me for enjoying it so much." I certainly hope he is forgiven, because I am sure he deserved every minute of enjoyment he had staying here, and you will, too.

Another treat for expanded budgets is the Conservatory Room, with its fabulous stained-glass domed ceiling and panoramic, handmade leaded-glass windows designed to flood the room with both sun and moonlight. The bed sits on a raised platform, there is a small rooftop patio, and the view from the desk is of the fountains in the park. The bathroom is divine, the little fireplace warm and comforting, and, of course, the atmosphere speaks of true romance. The double, deluxe Victorian Room, with a crystal chandelier from Czechoslovakia, is bright and airy in soft yellow. The two wing chairs, a fireplace, and large mirrored dressing table make it very livable.

Travelers who judge a room by square footage will be pleased with the lower-ground-floor garden Montagu Suite. The tiled bathroom has a set-in sink, gold fixtures, and plenty of space. The entry, with a closet, leads to a sitting area with a sofa and two high-back chairs covered in soft blue. The coal fireplace, bookshelf, and desk make it even more enjoyable. The Greville Janner Suite, with a private terrace, is named after the Janner family, who lived in this part of the building for many years. The suite was the nursery where Lord Janner of Braunstone, the longest-serving member of Parliament, lived with his sister and their nanny when they were children. He still drops by occasionally for a nostalgic visit. If you are in a standard room, you don't have to feel like Cinderella after the ball. These rooms have sitting areas, writing desks, and enough space to live comfortably. I like No. 116, with a few steps up to a bathroom that has loads of shelf space. Number 110, another

ROMANCE AND CELEBRATION BREAK
£180–260 per person per night, depending on room; includes chilled bottle of champagne, bouquet of flowers, fresh fruit basket, and box of luxury chocolates in room upon arrival; champagne cocktail and gourmet candlelit dinner for two in the hotel restaurant on the evening of your choice and buffet breakfast.

FAMILY FUN HOLIDAY
Fully inclusive family price £250, includes two nights' accommodation in a family bedroom for two adults and up to two children; a family ticket for the London Zoo or for the London Eye, the world's biggest Ferris wheel; cocktails in the bar before a candlelit dinner in the hotel restaurant, or a family dinner on Sunday or Monday at a local Italian restaurant. Early morning tea, a daily newspaper and buffet breakfast are also part of this package, which is available only at selected times of the year.

standard twin room, is rather narrow, but it does have a little balcony facing front and a fan to cool you on hot afternoons.

To entice you further, the hotel offers four special Break Packages: the Theatre Break, the Welcome Break, the Family Fun Holiday, and the Romance and Celebration Break. With your selection of either the Theatre Break, which features a two-night stay and the best available ticket to a top West End show of your choice, or the Welcome Break, which runs for three nights and includes a sight-seeing tour of London on the evening of your choice, you will be served a champagne cocktail in the bar before a three-course dinner in the hotel restaurant. A pot of bracing tea is brought with your morning newspaper before you venture downstairs for the buffet breakfast. The Romance and Celebration Break means you will stay two nights and have a bottle of champagne on ice, a bouquet of flowers, a fresh fruit basket, and a box of chocolates in your room on arrival and will enjoy a gourmet candlelit dinner for two in the hotel restaurant on the night of your choice. These three Breaks are available any night of the week or on the weekend and are priced according to the type of room or suite you choose. The Family Fun Holiday includes two nights in a family bedroom for two adults and up to two children. In addition to cocktails in the bar before a candlelit dinner in the Rose Garden on the evening of your choice, or on Sunday or Monday night a family dinner at a local Italian restaurant, you will receive a day ticket for the London Zoo or "Fly the Eye" on British Airway's London Eye, the world's biggest Ferris Wheel. A buffet breakfast, early-morning tea, and daily newspaper are also included. This holiday is available only during certain periods of the year, but the other three are available anytime.

NOTE: If you have any particular requirements, such as flowers or champagne in your room; tickets to any show, concert, or sporting event; baby-sitting; or anything else, let the staff know and they will provide it if at all possible.

FACILITIES AND SERVICES: Air-conditioning in deluxe rooms and suites; fans in the standard rooms; bar; concierge and porter; direct-dial phones with voice mail; hair dryer; laundry service; lift; data ports in suites; parking (£10 per day); restaurant and 24-hour room service for light snacks; office safe; satellite TV, VCR, and stereo TVs in suites; nonsmoking deluxe rooms, suites, and selected standard rooms; private room for meetings or hosting a private dinner party

NEAREST TOURIST ATTRACTIONS: Kensington Gardens, Hyde Park

MITRE HOUSE HOTEL (11)
178–184 Sussex Gardens, W2
Tube: Lancaster Gate, Paddington

69 rooms, all with shower or bath and toilet

Andrew and Michael Chris grew up in the hotel, which their parents ran for thirty years. Today you can see their father's photo hanging by the lift. The two brothers are now in charge of the hotel, and it is clear they enjoy a friendly rivalry. Andrew is more business-like, Michael more artistic. Michael designed the unusual stained-glass windows in the lounge after a trip to Africa and won a spot for his lion sculpture in the reception area by agreeing to Andrew's demand that he give up his motorcycle parking space in front of the hotel.

The hotel is one of the biggest along Sussex Gardens and includes three junior suites with Jacuzzis. These rooms, which are naturally the largest and most expensive, also have big closets, two television sets, and minibars. Several of the other rooms connect, an advantage for parents with children who still want some privacy. No one would dub any of the rooms stylish, and some of them frankly could benefit from a coat of paint, new fabrics, better carpets, or at least a freshly washed set of sheers on the windows. Those who need sunlight and moonbeams should avoid the viewless ground-floor rooms. If you arrive at Heathrow without a trolley full of luggage, the walk from Paddington Station is less than five minutes by foot. During your stay, the Lancaster Gate tube stop increases your mobility around London. Free parking for a few cars in front is another advantage, as is the outgoing desk staff, who try hard to please.

FACILITIES AND SERVICES: Bar, central heat, fans in suites, direct-dial phones, hair dryer and iron available, laundry service, lift, minibars, trouser press and Jacuzzis in junior suites, free parking, office safe, satellite TV, complimentary tea and coffee, 24-hour desk

NEAREST TOURIST ATTRACTIONS: Kensington Gardens, Hyde Park

TELEPHONE
020 7723 8040

FAX
020 7402 0990

EMAIL
reservations@mitrehousehotel.com

INTERNET
www.mitrehousehotel.com

CREDIT CARDS
AE, DC, MC, V

RATES
Single £70, double £85, junior suite £120, triple £95, quad £105

BREAKFAST
English breakfast included

MORNINGTON HOTEL (16)
12 Lancaster Gate, W2
Tube: Lancaster Gate

71 rooms, all with shower or bath and toilet

TELEPHONE
020 7262 7361; 800-528-1234
(toll-free from the U.S.)

FAX
020 7706 1028

EMAIL
london@mornington.com.uk

INTERNET
www.mornington.se

CREDIT CARDS
AE, DC, MC, V

RATES
Single £120, double £135–145,
split-level rooms £150

BREAKFAST
Scandinavian breakfast included

The Swiss-owned, Swedish-operated Mornington is an exceptional hotel with a delightful staff. The pristine rooms have some of the best, and definitely the cleanest, bathrooms in London. They also have wonderful mirrors, lots of space for your things, a drying rack for your hand washables, and a selection of shampoo, soap, and other items you might have forgotten to pack. The bedrooms display Swedish modern comforts with an easy chair, floor lamp, desk, portable fan in summer, and firm beds with fluffy duvets. I could move right into most of their split-level accommodations, especially No. 84, which has floor-to-ceiling windows and an upstairs bedroom and a downstairs work and sitting room. Numbers 103, 107, and 108 are other split-levels with plenty of light. All rooms on the third floor are nonsmoking, and many rooms throughout the hotel have polished hardwood floors, which are appreciated by allergy sufferers. The only rooms and split-levels to avoid are those facing "The Well," a blank-walled courtyard.

Downstairs by the reception desk is a book-lined library-lounge where you can order a snack from the bar or have afternoon tea. Breakfast is served Scandinavian style, which means a large buffet with fresh orange juice, fruit, hard-boiled eggs, cheese, meat, and herring, plus assorted breads and cereals. It's enough to keep most Great Sleepers going strong until dinner. En route to the dining room, take a few minutes to look at the remarkable bird posters, which are a collection painted by Olof Rudbeck in 1693. Rudbeck, who studied at Oxford, portrayed the birds in their original size, and in great detail. Also by the dining area is an office that allows guests to use a computer to send email or log on to the Internet.

FACILITIES AND SERVICES: Bar, central heat, conference room, direct-dial phones, data ports, fans on request, hair dryers, laundry lines in the bathrooms, laundry service, 2 lifts, office safe, nonsmoking rooms on 3rd and 5th floors, TV with pay movies, guest computer service center, complimentary tea and coffee anytime, airport transfers by prior arrangement

NEAREST TOURIST ATTRACTIONS: Kensington Gardens, Hyde Park

THE PAVILION HOTEL (1)
34–36 Sussex Gardens, W2
Tube: Edgware Road

27 themed rooms, all with shower or bath and toilet

Question: Is this a fantasy land or a hotel?

Answer: It's both . . . and what a place it is!

The Pavilion Hotel exceeds in providing jaw-dropping whimsical glamour for its high-gloss, high-wattage guests, who populate the fashion, media, and music worlds. Brother and sister team Danny and Noshi Karne have combined their talents (she designs the rooms from bits and pieces she constantly collects, he names them and works with her to produce them) to create an amazing boutique hotel that appeals to an artistically minded clientele. If you receive your mail at a Sun City or Leisure World address, need to have a daily Internet fix, or are coolly conservative and buttoned down in thought and deed, please . . . don't check in here. If, on the other hand, you love a kaleidoscope of colors, decor, and people, then check into one of London's hottest crash pads for high-style fashion bees.

All twenty-seven rooms have a different theme to project a funky yet glamorous image. Honky Tonk Afro is an over-the-top tribute to kitsch gone wild. Heart-shaped mirrors hang over twin beds divided by beaded curtains. Pink feather boas ring the lime-green room filled with 1950s-style furnishings, including a cowhide-covered square stool, black chairs with furry pink cushions, fuzzy dice to hold back the sparkling black-and-white curtains, a guitar-shaped mirror, and twirling above it all, a mirrored disco ball. It is one of the hotel's most known and most popular rooms and is routinely used for television backdrops and tapings. One guest aptly summed it up by declaring, "Wow! This looks like Mick Jagger's dressing room!" I have never seen his dressing room, but it couldn't be any more bizarre.

Enter the Dragon is a mystical cocktail of Oriental treasures complete with blue-and-white Chinese-teacup- and -teapot-printed wallpaper, carved wooden window screens, a red and gold chest, and vibrant red and blue satin bedcovers. In Monochrome Marilyn, guests are enveloped by an Andy Warhol–inspired black and silver wall covering of Monroe's face. The black-velvet-draped bed is accented by a satin headboard studded with rhinestones. War and Peace, swathed from top to bottom in red fabric, puts you into a Napoleonic War–style tent,

TELEPHONE
020 7262 0905

FAX
020 7262 1324

EMAIL
pavilionlondon@aol.com

INTERNET
www.msi.com.mt/pavilion/

CREDIT CARDS
AE, DC, MC, V

RATES
Single £65–75, double for single occupancy £85–95, double £100–110, triple £115–125, family £124–130

BREAKFAST
Continental breakfast included and served in the rooms

highlighted with a dozen or more military pictures and a great hat rack hung with Napoleonic hats. There isn't much closet space, but you get atmosphere in spades. History buffs may be interested to know that this building was once occupied by Napoleon's private surgeon.

I don't need to tell you the theme of Highland Fling, lined in MacGregor tartan and showcasing a clan flag. The antlers and other hunting memorabilia will make you want to suit up and ride with the hounds. In the ground-level room Chapter and Verse, a racy love poem wraps itself around the walls, which are hung with Venetian prints. The low-to-the-floor beds are draped in black and gold, and there is a black furry bedside rug in which to wiggle your toes. A marble sideboard doubles as a desk and is lighted by an ornate crystal chandelier. This is the hotel's only nonsmoking room. Better Red than Dead is a voluptuous symphony of vermilion, claret, and crimson, while Casablanca Nights is a deco-inspired Moorish fantasy. Up, Up and Away is a small double with a lighthearted balloon theme and gold damask-clad walls. White Days, Soul Nights, which takes its name from an old song recorded by the Electric Light Orchestra, is a monochromatic room in white and cream tones with an ornate curtain made from an old wedding dress. Indian Summer is in memory of the Indian emperor who built the Taj Mahal in his wife's memory. The bed is from Thailand, the lanterns from Morocco, the 1930 jeweled chandelier from France, the bathroom fringe from the dime store, the screen from Rajasthan, and the rich purple silk and brocade from old Indian costumes. The bubblegum-pink walls have a swirled gold pattern.

Other rooms have equally intriguing names and matching allure: Funky Zebra, Gold Finger, Diamonds Are Forever, Green with Envy, Family Affair, and Three's Company. Downstairs is the Silver Salon, an Ali Baba's cave used for fashion shoots and more television filming. The reception area is based on Josephine's bedroom in Malmaison. In addition to an Italian chandelier from a ballroom and old train racks from the Orient Express, there are two leopard-covered chairs, and check-in is handled on a stack of old luggage. Hanging nearby is a picture of the current "Phone Queen," any model who has stayed at the hotel and managed to ring up telephone charges in excess of £1,000 over a two-week period. In addition to being honored with a framed photo, each

Phone Queen receives a crown, a listing on the hotel Website, and a certificate.

FACILITIES AND SERVICES: Central heat, direct-dial phones, hair dryer available, electric tea and coffee makers, parking (£5 per day), room service for drinks, office safe, 1 nonsmoking room (Chapter and Verse), satellite TV; no lift

NEAREST TOURIST ATTRACTIONS: Hyde Park

PEMBRIDGE COURT HOTEL ($, 31)
34 Pembridge Gardens, W2
Tube: Notting Hill Gate

20 rooms, all with shower or bath and toilet

People always ask me to tell them about my favorite London hotel. I have several, and the Pembridge Court is one of them. I could occupy any of its rooms and be delightfully happy. Nicola, the charming assistant manager, will be at the desk to greet you, ably assisted by Spencer and Churchill, the hotel's famous cat mascots, who have been written up in scores of newspapers and magazines and have even appeared on television. The hotel, and its cats, loves children, and upon arrival each child receives a goodie bag and a box of Lindt chocolate kittens from Spencer and Churchill. Dogs and cats are as welcome as people, but management must be notified in advance and pet owners must be approved by Spencer and Churchill.

It is hard to know just where to begin telling you about the hotel, because everything about it is so well done and beautiful. It has won many certificates of distinction for its excellence in all categories, and after one visit, you will know why. It has, without question, the most colorful flower arrangements and outdoor blooming potted-plant displays I have seen in London. I also love the antique lace collars, Victorian beaded bags, delicate ivory fans, tortoiseshell combs, frilly baby dresses, and other vintage pieces of clothing that have been framed and artistically incorporated throughout the hotel.

Every room is different, and all are fully recommended. If someone told me I would like a stunning orange room facing a wall, I would have thought they were mad, but the ground-floor Chepstow Room is a delight, with a nice bath and a framed flapper dress and pearl belt gracing the bedroom walls. The Churchill Room, named after one of the house cats, looks out

TELEPHONE
020 7229 9977

FAX
020 7727 4982; 800-709-9882 (toll-free from the U.S.)

EMAIL
reservations@pemct.co.uk

INTERNET
www.pemct.co.uk

CREDIT CARDS
AE, DC, MC, V

RATES
Single £130–175, double (small twin) £160, deluxe twin or double £190–200

BREAKFAST
Full English breakfast included

toward Portobello Market. The bed is king size, and the bathroom has a shower and tub with gold fittings and a dressing table. Frames holding Edwardian ladies' gloves, a child's bib, and a sweet camisole decorate the walls. In the Garden Room, on the first floor, you are surrounded by vibrant tulips, which grace the headboard, curtains, and chair coverings. Vintage prints, a framed metal evening bag, and pair of gloves are typical Pembridge touches.

I love the Chelsea Room, which when described sounds wild, but believe me, its drama is not over-whelming. The cream walls are a perfect backdrop for the Black Watch tartan draped over the floral bedspread. The tartan is repeated on the sofa, curtains, desk chair, and pair of matching pillows. The framed dainty doll's dresses, booties, and jeweled collar and buckles make me think of all the treasures one might find in a family attic. For romance, the Belvedere Room, with a four-poster bed and sitting area by a sunny window, is a good choice. The hotel's intimate restaurant is open *only* for guests, and room service is always available for light snacks.

If your travels will take you to Cornwall, please consider their other hotel, the Cross House Hotel, set in the Cornish harbor town of Padstow. It is a charming Georgian house, once owned by John Tredwen, the last of the local sailing-ship builders. The hotel is open from April to October, and all eleven beautifully furnished rooms are nonsmoking. For more information, contact them at Church Street, Padstow, Cornwall PL28 8BG; Tel: 018 4153 2391; Fax: 018 4153 3633.

FACILITIES AND SERVICES: Air-conditioning in all rooms, bar, central heat, direct-dial phones with voice mail, data ports, internet access for guests, hair dryer, laundry service, lift to all floors but the 1st, free parking for 2 cars, restaurant for guests only, room service, office and room safe, trouser press, satellite TV, VCRs in deluxe rooms, CD players, power showers and scales in all bathrooms, 24-hour desk, special arrangements at a nearby health club with gym, swimming pool, steam room and spa, and finally . . . 2 friendly cats for contin-ued spoiling

NEAREST TOURIST ATTRACTIONS: Kensington Gardens, Portobello Road, Notting Hill

W8

Kensington

Kensington, especially in a summer afternoon, has seemed to me as delightful as any place can or ought to be.

—*Nathaniel Hawthorne,* Our Old Home, *1863*

The Royal Borough of Kensington became an important section of London when William III commissioned Sir Christopher Wren to rebuild Kensington Palace. The palace, where Princess Diana lived, stands at one end of Kensington Gardens, which with Hyde Park forms the largest open space in London. Kensington High Street is one of London's premier shopping streets, lined with a wonderful variety of shops and several department store branches. To the north is Kensington Church Street, famous for its magnificent antiques shops filled with museum-quality examples with very high price tags. But it costs nothing to window shop and dream. The area also boasts several excellent restaurants; please see *Great Eats London* for details. Kensington is also not far from London's "Museum District," which includes the Victoria and Albert, Science, and Natural History Museums.

TOURIST ATTRACTIONS
Kensington Palace and Gardens, shopping on Kensington High Street

HOTELS IN W8 (see map on page 66)

Abbey House	**86**
Posthouse Kensington	**86**
Vicarage Private Hotel	**87**

OTHER OPTIONS

Apartment Rental Agencies
Cheval Group, Thorney Court ($)	**189**

Apartment Rentals
Allen House	**202**
Lexham Apartments ($)	**207**

Hostels
Holland House, King George IV Memorial Youth Hostel	**227**

Student-Only Accommodations
Lee Abbey International Students Club	**248**

($) indicates a Big Splurge

ABBEY HOUSE (36)
11 Vicarage Gate, W8
Tube: High Street Kensington

16 rooms, none with shower, bath, or toilet

TELEPHONE
020 7727 2594
FAX
020 7727 1873
INTERNET
www.abbeyhousekensington.com
CREDIT CARDS
None; cash only
RATES
Single £45, double £74, triple £85, quad £100
BREAKFAST
English breakfast included

The Abbey House, on a tranquil Victorian square close to Kensington Gardens, was built around 1860 for a wealthy businessman and has since been the home of a bishop and a member of Parliament. Now it is a small hotel and a classic example of what almost twenty-five years of hard work can do to create a prime budget B&B. The owners, Albert and Carol Nayach, offer clean lodgings to those willing to give up the comfort and convenience of a private bathroom or a lift in the name of saving money. Their hospitality and genuine value is not lost on their regulars, who book rooms far in advance. If you want to stay here in high season, it will never be too early to make a reservation and to secure it with a deposit.

As you enter the front door of the hotel from the wide porch, you will see a beautiful interior staircase that winds up from the entry hall. The rooms are done in a flowery Laura Ashley style and are kept up to snuff with painting and redecorating when needed. Every room has two pillows per person on an orthopedic bed with reading lights, and simple mahogany furniture. Number 12, on the ground floor, is a ruffly double with good drawer and closet space. Number 11 is also on the ground floor and has enough all-around space, and so does No. 39, a family room on the back. The red-carpeted breakfast room has hunting pictures on the walls and white linen napkins and cloths on tables surrounded by red chairs. Free ice, tea, and coffee-making facilities around the clock as well as a pay phone are available for guests.

FACILITIES AND SERVICES: Central heat, hall phones, tea and coffee available, TV, desk open 8:30 A.M.–10 P.M.; no safe, no lift

NEAREST TOURIST ATTRACTIONS: Kensington Palace and Gardens, shopping on High Kensington Street

POSTHOUSE KENSINGTON (46)
Wright's Lane, W8
Tube: High Street Kensington

550 rooms, all with shower or bath and toilet

TELEPHONE
0870 400 9000 (inquiries); 0345 40 40 40 (central booking); 800-225-5843 (toll-free in the U.S.)
FAX
020 7937 8289

The Posthouse Hotels are a division of Forte Hotels and offer their own Posthouse Leisure Breaks scheme (for a further description of these money-saving hotel deals, see page 60). While the Posthouse Kensington is geared principally toward tour groups and business guests, it has a good deal to offer individual guests who want a full-service hotel that includes a restaurant, spa, pool, Jacuzzi, beauty salon, and fully equipped fitness center. Some impressive redecorating has taken place on several floors, during which the hotel employed a sleep therapist to select soothing colors and even design the contour of the headboards behind the beds in the sleekly up-to-date rooms. For the best results, request a superior room on the fourth or seventh floors and positively avoid anything on the first, thanks to poor security on this level, and the fifth, until it has been redone. Guests are given free membership in the hotel health club, which also has a small boutique in case you forgot your bathing suit or workout clothes.

FACILITIES AND SERVICES: Air-conditioning in some superior rooms, central heat; bar; direct-dial phones; hair dryers; free use of hotel health club with pool, Jacuzzi, steam room, spa, beauty salon, and equipped fitness gym; laundry service; lift; data ports in superior rooms; parking (£20 per 24 hours); 2 restaurants; pub; 24-hour room service; room safe; tea and coffee-making facilities; satellite TV; pay movies; concierge; theater bookings; one nonsmoking floor

NEAREST TOURIST ATTRACTIONS: Kensington Palace and Gardens, shopping on Kensington High Street

EMAIL
rm1253@forte-hotels.com

INTERNET
www.posthouse-hotels.com

CREDIT CARDS
AE, DC, MC, V

RATES
Single £100, double £130–150; for special leisure-break packages, see page 61

BREAKFAST
Continental breakfast included

VICARAGE PRIVATE HOTEL (37)
10 Vicarage Gate, W8
Tube: High Street Kensington
18 rooms, 2 with shower and toilet

For the price and the value it represents, the Vicarage Private Hotel is a good buy in this part of London. The hotel is situated in a splendid late-nineteenth-century mansion in a quiet section of the Royal Borough of Kensington. The impressive entry hall has a natural grillwork staircase leading up to the eighteen practical bedrooms, sixteen of which have hot and cold running water but no private bathrooms. The hallways are lined with an impressive collection of oil paintings, prints, and mirrors. The large hall showers and WCs are above average and have attractive touches such as framed prints or playbills on the walls. Number 12 is a spiffy single done in blue and yellow and boasting a view to the flats in the distance. Number 11, on the third floor, has high ceilings, two windows facing out, and bed space for

TELEPHONE
020 7229 4030

FAX
020 7792 5989

EMAIL
reception@
londonvicaragehotel.com

INTERNET
www.londonvicaragehotel.com

CREDIT CARDS
MC, V

RATES
Single £50, double £75–100, triple £100, quad £110

BREAKFAST
English breakfast included (hot porridge available if ordered the night before)

three with room to spare. Number 6 is a front-facing double with 1940s-style furniture, and No. 19 is a top-floor nest for the sturdy solo traveler with a pretty oak armoire and beveled mirror. If you want your own bathroom with shower and toilet but no tub, check into either No. 2 or 3 on the ground floor. I like No. 2, because some of the old furniture has been kept and blends nicely with the soft gold and greens in the room. No. 3 has wrought-iron twin beds, an old chest of drawers, and a small, hand-detailed table and armchair. It also has a television, but no view from the opaque window. A stick-to-your-ribs English breakfast is served downstairs in a room set with assorted antique dining chairs around linen-covered tables and old peasant prints on the walls. For those traveling alone, there is a special "singles" table. Another way to get to know fellow guests is in the television lounge, with its leaded window and framed cameos. If plans to put in more private bathroom facilities and TV sets, and to reupholster the lounge furniture materialize, this already very nice selection will be even better.

FACILITIES AND SERVICES: Central heat, hall phones, hair dryer available, tea and coffeemakers, TV in rooms with private baths, office safe, desk open 7:30 A.M.–10:30 P.M.; no lift

NEAREST TOURIST ATTRACTIONS: Kensington Palace and Gardens, shopping on Kensington High Street

W11

Notting Hill and Portobello Road

Notting Hill is a mixture of media darlings, politicians, hipsters, and Londoners on their way up, as well as those who scrape by on a £100,000 yearly trust, all of whom frequent the area's growing supply of trendy eating places, artistic boutiques, and shops that are either offbeat or trendy, but in either case expensive. Its most interesting feature, from a visitor's point of view, is around Portobello Road, site of the famous outdoor flea and antiques market that is best seen on Saturday morning, when stalls and shops display a bewildering array of goods (see "Indoor and Outdoor Markets," page 312). On the August bank holiday (the last Monday of the month) and the Sunday before, the Notting Hill Carnival, Europe's biggest outdoor festival, is celebrated with nonstop music, dancing, and thousands of revelers.

TOURIST ATTRACTIONS
Portobello Road market

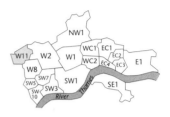

HOTELS IN W11 (see map page 66)

OTHER OPTIONS
YMCAs

($) indicates a Big Splurge

GATE HOTEL (28)
6 Portobello Road, W11
Tube: Notting Hill Gate

6 rooms, 5 with shower or bath and toilet

First of all, I must be frank and say that I am currently on the fence about the Gate Hotel. Longtime manager Debbie Watkins and owner Brian Watkins have semiretired and left the day-to-day running of the hotel to a hired manager. This usually spells disaster, but it is too early to tell what the new setup will entail, because no one seems to be sure about all the details of the transition. There was even some question about the fourteen-year-old resident parrot, Sergeant Bilko, who

TELEPHONE
020 7221 0707

FAX
020 7221 9128

EMAIL
gatehotel@btinternet.com

INTERNET
www.gatehotel.com

CREDIT CARDS
AE, DC, MC (must use to guarantee room; 4% service fee if used to pay final bill)

RATES
Single £60–75, double £85–
100, triple £110

BREAKFAST
Continental breakfast included

served for years as official greeter. Would he stay, or would he also retire?

Fortunately, the bright, compact single and double rooms, most of which offer a measure of comfort and practicality, are still the same. Each has a built-in wardrobe, a full-length mirror, a small refrigerator, some desk space, tea and coffeemakers, and a TV and radio. There are no random styles; everything is coordinated in shades of blue and white. Original paintings depicting the early days of the Portobello Road market and its famous habitués add a touch of local character to each room. Private facilities in five rooms are a bonus, as is the fact that the sixth room's hall facilities are private to that room. A packaged Continental breakfast will be served on white china in your room.

A few additional cautionary words are in order. For those of you who do not like stairs, the ones here are quite steep, and there are many to climb, especially if you have a room above the ground floor. Unless you have youth on your side, some of the extra beds are a backache waiting to happen. The regular beds are orthopedic, but not those that fold out to make a room into a triple. If you are a solo sleeper, opt for something other than No. 3, which is really too small for anyone traveling with more than a meager backpack.

FACILITIES AND SERVICES: Central heat, room fans, direct-dial phones, hair dryer available, tea and coffee-making facilities, TV, radio and clock, minibar, desk open 8:30 A.M.–10:30 P.M.; no lift, no safe

NEAREST TOURIST ATTRACTIONS: Portobello Road, Notting Hill

THE PORTOBELLO HOTEL ($, 27)
22 Stanley Gardens, W11
Tube: Notting Hill Gate

22 rooms, all with shower or bath and toilet

Staying at the Portobello can be the next best thing to sampling life in the "Upstairs-Downstairs" era, but with twentieth-century plumbing. The owners of this sophisticated hotel did not miss a trick in adapting their hotel from several side-by-side Victorian townhouses. Their personal collection of art, rich antiques, and Oriental rugs are only a few of the nice touches that will carry you back to an era when graciousness and lovely surroundings mattered. If all of this plus individually decorated rooms with four-poster beds and soft goose-

TELEPHONE
020 7727 2777

FAX
020 7792 9641

EMAIL
info@portobello-hotel.co.uk

INTERNET
www.portobello-hotel.co.uk

CREDIT CARDS
AE, DC, MC, V

RATES
Single £150–170, double
£195–230, suite £280–380

BREAKFAST
Continental breakfast included

down duvets, with windows overlooking well-tended private gardens, and the company of an arty clientele used to impeccable service is your style, things don't get much better than the Portobello.

The entry and ground-floor sitting room are almost an English stage setting, with lush fabrics on overstuffed furniture and masses of fresh flowers and green plants. It looks like an American idealization of what a London drawing room should be. The twenty-two dramatically decorated rooms are inviting, with both whimsy and flamboyance working together to create unique atmospheres. If your travels have taken you to Morocco, or you hope they will, check into No. 2. It is a large space, with two comfortable armchairs overlooking a wall that has been artfully transformed with a corner table and chairs and an old door, making you feel you are looking across a narrow street into a neighbor's secret garden. The huge bed is enveloped Moroccan style, and the stunning bathroom has a Jacuzzi and free-standing white porcelain sink with gold-leaf mirror above. Room No. 22 has a four-poster bed with cotton drapes. The sitting area overlooks the garden and is furnished with an inlaid antique desk and a fabulous bathroom with a green-and-white enamel shower and working Victorian "bathing machine"—a deep tub on legs surrounded by six shower jets. From a horizontal position in your bubble bath, you can watch television or pop a video in the VCR. A favorite top-floor nest is No. 45, with dormer windows and a sofa and chair. The tub, with gold feet, is painted pink to go with the room, which also has a mirrored bed, an adorable makeup stand, and a small shower.

For a slice of heaven, request No. 13, which is worth the trip to London just to sleep in the bed with angels and clouds painted on the canopy and side curtains. This room has a large bath with mirrors, brass, and all the extra amenities. For something unusual and fabulous, reserve No. 16, with a Chinese motif, a naughty round bed in the middle of the room, and another amazing Victorian bathtub with original copper and brass fittings, also in the main room. Another wonderful room with a Far Eastern theme is No. 1, "The Oriental," which overlooks a small patio with a mosaic shell waterfall. In the room, an antique dresser holds a computer, and a latticed Chinese kitchen cabinet hides tea and coffee-making facilities and the minibar. The stunning bathroom has two freestanding aqua green bowls sitting on a marble sink backed by a large mirror. The deep, white enamel tub is fitted with a Jacuzzi and power shower, set to one side in a small alcove with two chairs and a glass roof. You will feel you are in a Japanese oasis, far from London. Another favorite is No. 6, with a gold-footed bathtub, a "tester" bed—a half four-poster draped in the back and covered with fluffy duvets—and French doors opening onto the garden. Some of the top-floor rooms are referred to as "cabins," and that they are, minuscule havens with bathrooms to match. Despite their size, they have their devotees, who wouldn't stay elsewhere. If this appeals to you, try No. 39, in bright red, which makes you feel enveloped in a big, warm hug.

Besides all the extras you would expect to find in an exceptional hotel, there is room service for light meals; fax, copy, and courier services; Internet access in most rooms; theater bookings; and full-service Nautilus health-club facilities within a four-minute walk (daily charge for hotel guests), and a 10 percent discount and preferential reservations are given at Julie's, a popular upmarket wine bar and restaurant owned by the hotel and not too far away.

NOTE: The hotel is closed from around December 23 to January 3.

FACILITIES AND SERVICES: Air-conditioning in top-floor rooms, fans otherwise; bar; computers in almost every room with charge to log on to the Internet, but not for word processing; direct-dial phones; hair dryer; access to full-service health club; some Jacuzzis; laundry service; lift (to 3rd floor only); office safe; room service for light meals; discount at Julie's Restaurant; satellite TV; VCRs; tea and coffeemakers; minibars; 24-hour desk; business services; theater bookings; limousine and courier service

NEAREST TOURIST ATTRACTIONS: Portobello Road, Notting Hill

RAVNA GORA (33)
29 Holland Park Avenue, W11
Tube: Holland Park

TELEPHONE
020 7727 7725

FAX
020 7221 4282

CREDIT CARDS
MC, V

RATES
Single £35, double £60–70, triple £70–90, quad £90–100

21 rooms, 5 with shower or bath and toilet

The Ravna Gora is a no-frills address that budgeteers have been visiting for years. In its heyday, this palatial mansion, set back from busy and noisy Holland Park Avenue, must have been something. Standing in the rotunda and looking up at the sweeping staircase, I can just imagine the grand parties and balls that were staged here. Since 1956 it has been a B&B, and for the last twenty years or so it has been managed by the hardworking Jovanovic family and Mica, their gray-and-white cat. I have always wished that more than just the morning meal was served to guests, because the smells floating out from Mrs. Jovanovic's kitchen every time I have been to the hotel are tantalizing indeed.

The clean, back-to-basics rooms, geared for the frugal traveler with limited needs, are generally snag- and tear-free and offer dependably clean chenille-covered beds for as many as six in a room. Even though the hotel is off the beaten tourist track, the Holland Park tube stop is down the street, and if you are driving, plenty of free parking is available in a locked lot right by the hotel.

FACILITIES AND SERVICES: Central heat, hair dryer available, public hall phones, free parking, office safe, TV, desk open 7 A.M.–midnight; no lift

NEAREST TOURIST ATTRACTIONS: Holland Park, short walk to Kensington Palace and Gardens

BREAKFAST
English breakfast included

WC1

Bloomsbury

London is incredibly beautiful. . . . I find Bloomsbury so adorably lovely that I could look out of my window all day long.

—Virginia Woolf, letter to Katharine Arnold-Forster, April 12, 1924

Bloomsbury is one of London's most popular areas in which to stay, and for good reason. Transportation is excellent, and it is within walking distance to West End theaters, Soho, shopping on Oxford and Regent Streets, and many good restaurants (see *Great Eats London*). Consisting of elegant and leafy squares and parks surrounded by lovely Georgian townhouses, Bloomsbury is the home of the British Museum, which tops the list of London's most popular tourist attractions, as well as the University of London and many well-known hospitals. In the early 1900s, the area around Gordon Square was the base for the Bloomsbury Group, an intellectual, liberal group whose members included Virginia Woolf, Lytton Strachey, D. H. Lawrence, and John Maynard Keynes. Other places of note in Bloomsbury include some lovely pubs, especially the Lamb, on Lamb's Conduit Street; Coram's Fields, a playground where no adult is admitted unless accompanied by a child; the new British Library, next to St. Pancras Station; and the Gothic wonder formerly known as Midland Grand Hotel but now referred to as St. Pancras Chambers. Next door is King's Cross Station, where you begin your train journey if heading north to Scotland. The area around the station is run-down and should be avoided if alone, and always at night.

HOTELS IN WC1

OTHER OPTIONS

Apartment Rentals

Student Dormitories

Student-Only Accommodations

($) indicates a Big Splurge

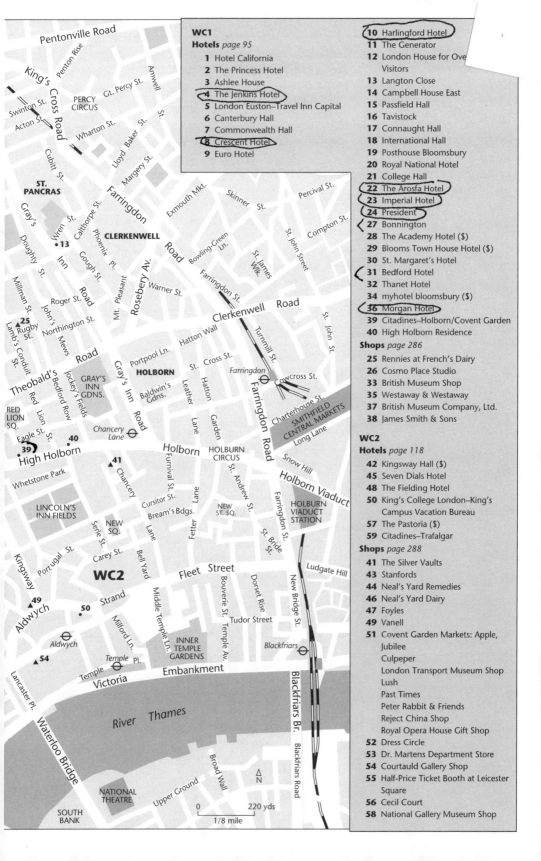

THE ACADEMY HOTEL ($, 28)
17–21 Gower Street, WC1
Tube: Goodge Street

49 rooms, all with shower or bath and toilet

TELEPHONE
020 7631 4115

FAX
020 7636 3442

EMAIL
res_academyh@
etontownhouse.com

INTERNET
www.etontownhouse.com

CREDIT CARDS
AE, DC, MC, V

RATES
Single £135, double £160–190,
suite £210–230, plus 17.5%
VAT

BREAKFAST
Continental or English
breakfast included

In the heart of London's publishing world and very close to the British Museum, the Academy Hotel was once a series of five Georgian houses, which were built in the late 1700s. The original colonnades, the intricate plaster on the facade, and the delicate glass paneling are still in place today, despite several refurbishments, including the most recent one at a cost of £3.5 million. Small groups can reserve one of these houses with eight Georgian rooms and enjoy the exclusive use of the library and garden. The lobby and reception area are enhanced by a series of animal prints and three tufted leather chairs. Dramatic floral arrangements flank a mirrored black marble fireplace. Another sitting area opens onto an enclosed conservatory garden, where drinks are served year-round.

The comfortable rooms are individually decorated with botanical prints, elegant designer fabrics, and luxury bed linens. There are well-lit work areas, excellent closet space, and up-to-date marble bathrooms with shelves, mirrors, dressing gowns, heated towel racks, and plenty of absorbent towels. All guests receive a bowl of fresh fruit and bottle of mineral water on arrival, and turn-down service every evening. There are twelve singles, all with adequate space. I like No. 50, on the back with a garden view and glass shower, and No. 22, with two windows that let in lots of daylight. The junior suites are exceptional, especially Nos. 11 and 27. Both combine bold florals with checks and solids to create very eye-pleasing surroundings, which include marble fireplaces, large sitting areas, ample desk and dressing space, and of course, excellent bathrooms. Breakfast is served in a contemporary azure room with Edward Hopper prints on the walls. When booking, please remember that any room on the front two levels of the hotel has permanently locked windows. Air-conditioning means you won't suffocate, but for some, the lack of fresh air could be unpleasant.

FACILITIES AND SERVICES: Air-conditioning, bar, central heat, conference rooms, direct-dial phones with voice mail, data ports, hair dryer, laundry service, restaurant and 24-hour room service, office and room safe, porter, satellite TV, CD player, tea and coffeemaker, trouser press; no lift

NEAREST TOURIST ATTRACTIONS: British Museum, University College London

THE AROSFA HOTEL (22)
83 Gower Street, WC1
Tube: Euston Square, Goodge Street
16 rooms, 2 with shower or bath and toilet

Hats off once again to Mr. and Mrs. Dorta for sheer determination and elbow grease. Together they have transformed this former crash pad for the homeless into one of the best low-cost Great Sleeps in London. When they bought the hotel a few years ago, it was such a wreck they had to close it completely in order to get rid of all the debris and overcome the neglect by the previous occupants. Murphy's Law was at work, and whatever could go wrong for the hardworking Dortas did, including the boiler breaking. All that is behind them now, and they and their sixteen-room, completely nonsmoking hotel shine with pride.

The rooms don't aim to impress an interior decorator, but at prices this low, they don't have to. They all provide matching laminated furniture, color-coordinated curtains and chenille bedspreads, a television, and some garden views, and a germ doesn't stand a chance in any of them. The hall facilities, which rate among the best in Bloomsbury, are newly tiled and always as clean as the rooms. Windows in the front rooms have double glazing, but for ensured quiet, I like something on the back side facing the hotel garden. Try No. 2, a double; No. 3, which is small but has a wide window view; or No. 4, a triple big enough, as one of my favorite British sayings goes, to "swing a cat." It has its own bathroom and overlooks a garden. The only room I would not recommend is the basement dugout on the back. It has a shower and sink in the room and limited daylight, which I think makes it claustrophobic. Mr. and Mrs. Dorta disagree with me on this every time I visit, promising that this is the quietest room in the hotel and the coolest in the summer. It is up to you to decide. In the morning, an English breakfast will be served in a pretty dining room with abstract print tablecloths and a shelf loaded with touristy memorabilia brought by the growing roster of returning guests who appreciate the Dortas' honest commitment to Great Sleeping in London.

TELEPHONE & FAX
020 7636 2115

CREDIT CARDS
MC, V

RATES
Single £40, double £55–70, triple £72–82, quad £95

BREAKFAST
English breakfast included

FACILITIES AND SERVICES: Central heat, fans, hair dryer available, hall phone, tea and coffee in the lounge, TV, office safe, desk open 7:30 A.M.–10:30 P.M.

NEAREST TOURIST ATTRACTIONS: British Museum, University College London

BLOOMS TOWN HOUSE HOTEL ($, 29)
7 Montague Street, WC1
Tube: Russell Square, Holborn
27 rooms, all with shower or bath and toilet

TELEPHONE
020 7323 1717
FAX
020 7636 6498
EMAIL
blooms@mermaid.co.uk
INTERNET
www.bloomshotel.com
CREDIT CARDS
AE, DC, MC, V
RATES
Single £130–175, double £200–225, extra person £50; welcome drink, fresh fruit and flowers in room, and morning newspaper included
BREAKFAST
Continental breakfast £7.50, English breakfast £10

The hotel building dates from the early 1700s, when it was occupied by Richard Penn, the Whig (liberal) member of Parliament from Liverpool. Today, service and attention to detail are the hallmarks of this very appealing selection, which has an attractive private walled garden backing up to the British Museum. While definitely in the Big Splurge category, it can be a more affordable sleep if you time your stay to take advantage of the weekend rates offered, when available on either the hotel's Web page or by calling the front desk directly.

The richly appointed hotel is decorated with panache in an updated version of classic English style. The drawing room has the comfortable look of a grand house, with antiques positioned around a marble fireplace, and vases of fresh and dried flowers adding color accents. It is a delightful place to order a light snack and sip a cup of afternoon tea or an early evening sherry while catching up on the daily papers or current magazines provided for guests. The color-coordinated rooms have original paintings, a lounge chair, full mirrors, out-of-sight luggage space, and excellent bathrooms. Many of them are attractively themed. Number 4, the Lords, an executive double with a view onto the terrace, is named after the Lords cricket ground, and the autographed cricket bat of former prime minister John Major and a photo of his celebrity team is framed and hanging in the room. If you love going to the theater in London, be sure to request No. 104, the Theatre Royal, which takes its cue from London theaters. In the Dickens Room you will be surrounded with genuine articles on loan to the hotel from the Dickens Museum, including his shaving mirror, a monogrammed dinner plate, and a bust, as well as many photos of the author and a portrait of him hanging over the bed. In the Pickwick Room, a double, guests are treated to a collection of wall-hanging tiles of Mr. Pickwick and Mrs. Bardell, and a framed check written by Dickens to his solicitor for £185—quite a sum in those days. Number 307, facing the street, has no particular theme, but it is especially comfortable, with its four-poster bed, working desk, and bathroom large enough to include a bidet. Numbers 1 and 2 have the advantage of being on the garden. The price of your room includes a cooked-to-order breakfast served in the formally set dining room, or on the garden terrace in summer. In the Malt Library Bar, warmly painted in deep Georgian red, more than thirty-five single malts are served, along with wines by the glass and a selection of snacks. If you don't feel like going out, you can either call 24-hour room service or eat in the hotel dining room, which serves two- and three-course set meals along with à la carte choices.

FACILITIES AND SERVICES: Bar, ceiling fans, central heat, direct-dial phones, hair dryer, laundry service, lift, data ports in all rooms, 24-hour desk and room service, restaurant, office safe, trouser press, satellite TV, radio, terry-cloth robes

NEAREST TOURIST ATTRACTIONS: British Museum, University College London

BONNINGTON (27)
92 Southampton Row, WC1
Tube: Russell Square, Holborn
215 rooms, all with shower or bath and toilet

The Bonnington has an interesting history. When Scotsman John Frame built the hotel in 1911, he used the latest technology. The building was steel and concrete and had central heating, double-glazed windows, and lifts to every floor. He named it the Bonnington, a nostalgic reminder of the spectacular falls on his native River Clyde. With its two hundred bedrooms, large lounges, and noted dining room, it was hailed as something new and exciting in London, because for a modest five shillings, visitors were treated as valued guests and given a taste of luxury. The Bonnington, which is still owned by John Frame's family, is now a 215-room business hotel. But it's useful for Great Sleepers if they are able to take advantage of the Bonnington's Special Weekend Breaks, which include bed, breakfast, and dinner. These rates are good for a stay of up to three nights on a Friday, Saturday, and Sunday. Also available are Easter, summer (mid-July to end of August), and Christmas special rates. The hotel is a good choice anytime for those who want a pivotal location close to

TELEPHONE
020 7242 2828

FAX
020 7831 9170

EMAIL
sales@bonnington-hotels.com

INTERNET
www.bonnington.com

CREDIT CARDS
AE, DC, MC, V

RATES
Single £120, double £155, triple £185, quad £245, Executive Single £150, Anniversary Room with spa and bottle of champagne £220; Special Weekend Break £60 per person, per night; ask for special rates, which are available at Christmas, Easter, and during the summer.

BREAKFAST
Buffet breakfast included

excellent tube and bus connections. In general, the well-kept rooms are efficient and practical, but mundane when it comes to imagination. Many are designated for nonsmokers. Some older bathrooms fall into the dated category, but most have both a tub and shower. Many of the doubles offer a small sitting area, a built-in wardrobe with shelf space, and a full-length mirror. Decorating caution was tossed to the wind in Nos. 259 and 359. Number 259, the Anniversary Room, "is designed for romance," with a draped bed and an ornate, gaudy bath complete with a mirrored double Jacuzzi and swan fittings. Slightly less over the top is No. 359, the Executive Single, done up in red velvet and shiny mahogany, also with a Jacuzzi, but no swans.

The dining room has a pitched glass ceiling, and in the lobby is a baby grand that guests can play.

NOTE: All Special Weekend Breaks include an English breakfast, as well as dinner in the hotel restaurant Friday and Saturday and in the bar on Sunday.

FACILITIES AND SERVICES: Bar, central heat, conference rooms, direct-dial phones, hair dryer, laundry service, lift, office safe, restaurant (3 meals Mon–Fri, breakfast and dinner Sat–Sun), room service, satellite TV, rooms for disabled persons, trouser press, tea and coffeemaker, email terminal in the bar, and an Internet café

NEAREST TOURIST ATTRACTIONS: British Museum

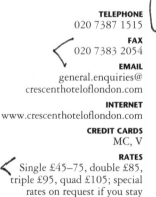

CRESCENT HOTEL (8)
49–50 Cartwright Gardens, WC1
Tube: Euston, King's Cross, Russell Square
27 rooms, 18 with shower or bath and toilet

TELEPHONE
020 7387 1515

FAX
020 7383 2054

EMAIL
general.enquiries@
crescenthoteloflondon.com

INTERNET
www.crescenthoteloflondon.com

CREDIT CARDS
MC, V

RATES
Single £45–75, double £85, triple £95, quad £105; special rates on request if you stay longer than 7 nights in low season

BREAKFAST
English breakfast included

The Crescent Hotel occupies a quiet position directly on Cartwright Gardens, a private square owned by the City Guild of Skinners and looked after by the University of London, whose residence halls are across the street. Keys to the garden and the four tennis courts are available to hotel guests (£1.50 per hour), and if you forgot your tennis racket and balls, they are available on loan from the hotel.

What sets this family-owned hotel apart from dozens like it? Aside from the clean, well-kept rooms, the sitting room with a fireplace, and the impressive perfume-bottle collection in a glass display case in the dining room, which also has a cast-iron range found during a recent renovation project, the key to success here is the warmth and genuine hospitality of Mrs. Cockle and her mother, Mrs. Bessolo. Mrs. Cockle admits she was not formally trained in hotel management, but she did not need to be. She grew up in this hotel and inherited her mother's charm and graciousness. Visitors from among word-of-mouth clientele, including many readers, have been returning for more than forty years and are welcomed each time as family. As Mrs. Cockle said, "The hotel is an extension of our home, and we treat our guests accordingly."

The simple rooms are put together with the odd piece of vintage furniture to give them a hint of character. Colors and fabrics generally blend, and chenille bedspreads cover most of the beds. The largest family room is No. 5, on the ground floor, which has three twin beds and in the bathroom a curtained shower, pedestal sink, and a shelf for toiletries. For a more quiet stay, and in my opinion a more secure one, ask for No. 18, a sunny triple on the back, again with a stall shower. For a peaceful double, request No. 6, also on the back, which looks onto a patio. Three singles have a shower but no toilet. The other singles are completely bathless, but public facilities are above average and boast an enviable collection of plants the family has been nurturing for years. Also well-nurtured is the collection of flea market and jumble sale finds gathered by Mrs. Cockle and her daughter and displayed in a glass cabinet in the main hall. Everything is for sale, and chances are you will find some little treasure you can't resist.

FACILITIES AND SERVICES: Central heat, fans, direct-dial phones, hair dryer and iron available, office safe, TV, tea and coffeemaker, desk open 7:30 A.M.–10 P.M.; no lift

NEAREST TOURIST ATTRACTIONS: Coram's Fields, British Museum, British Library, University College London

EURO HOTEL (9)
53 Cartwright Gardens, WC1
Tube: Russell Square, Euston, Kings Cross

34 rooms, 9 with bath or shower and toilet

Despite its uninspiring name and lack of en suite rooms, the Euro has more in the plus column than in the minus. Its location on the leafy crescent known as Cartwright Gardens means you are close to all public transportation, yet have the peace and quiet of a London neighborhood to return to at the end of the day. Children are as valued as the adults they bring with them. This is evident by the young guests' artwork that is

TELEPHONE
020 7387 4321
FAX
020 7383 5044
EMAIL
reception@eurohotel.co.uk
INTERNET
www.eurohotel.co.uk
CREDIT CARDS
AE, MC, V

importantly displayed behind the front desk. Children sixteen and under are also given a proper bed whenever possible and charged a very nominal rate that includes an English breakfast. Babies sleep in a free cot. There are four steps at the front of the hotel and four ground-floor rooms suitable for those unable to climb any more stairs, but these rooms are not outfitted for the handicapped.

Because the hotel consists of three Georgian townhouses built in 1807 for wealthy merchants, identikit modernity is not part of the ambience—old-fashioned English hospitality is. Pink seems to be the color of choice along the halls and frames the doors to all the rooms, which are furnished mainly in pine. A family of four would be happy in 01, a spacious choice with a double bed and two twins, and a tub in the bathroom. G3 is a roomy, bathless double that faces a wall, which means it will be quiet. Threesomes will like No. 17, with a window on the back and sky views and their own bathtub and shower. Complimentary coffee and tea are served all day; daily newspapers, current magazines, luggage storage, September to March discounts, and an exceptionally nice staff increase the appeal of this thrifty Great Sleep in London.

FACILITIES AND SERVICES: Central heat, direct-dial phone, hair dryer available, tea and coffee-making facilities, TV, radio, office safe, keys for gardens opposite hotel, rackets and balls for tennis court, office open 7 A.M.– 11 P.M.; no lift (4 floors)

NEAREST TOURIST ATTRACTIONS: British Library, British Museum, University College London, Coram's Fields

HARLINGFORD HOTEL (10)
61–63 Cartwright Gardens, WC1
Tube: King's Cross, Russell Square, Euston
43 rooms, all with shower or bath and toilet

The caring management of the Davies family at their B&B in Bloomsbury is reflected in the many repeat customers who value consistency in the hotel and its upkeep. The breakfast room is one of the nicest on the Cartwright Gardens crescent, because it has three big windows overlooking the park in front. In addition to the usual cholesterol-laden English breakfast, they offer a buffet of yogurt, fresh fruit, cheese, croissants, and more than twenty cereal choices (I counted).

All the rooms are generally light and pleasing, with floral prints, tiled baths, and double-glazed windows.

The best ones are on the second and third floors facing front or on the top floor with views over the gardens. These perches on the top require climbing stairs, because there is no lift in the hotel. The basement rooms have been renovated, but you can still hear the tube rumble from Nos. 4 and 8. Keys are available for the tennis courts in front of the hotel, and the nominal fee charged goes to the University of London to maintain them.

NOTE: The Thanet Hotel (please see page 115) is also owned by members of the Davies family.

FACILITIES AND SERVICES: Central heat, direct-dial phones, hair dryer available, Internet access at nominal charge, office safe, TV, desk open 7 A.M.–midnight; no lift

NEAREST TOURIST ATTRACTIONS: British Library, British Museum, Coram's Fields, University College London

HOTEL CALIFORNIA (1)
4–8 Belgrove Street, WC1
Tube: King's Cross, St. Pancras
65 rooms, all with shower or bath and toilet

Welcome to the Hotel California.

Simplicity and convenience prevail in the small but spunky rooms at Tony Megaro's hotel; they are identically dressed with built-ins and complemented by matching duvet covers and curtains. All of them have tiled baths, and some even have tubs and heated towel racks. You can also bank on closet space, a color television, a private safe, but not always a chair or desk. A buffet breakfast is served in a stunning modern room with fruit prints hanging on a backdrop of orange and yellow faux-finished walls.

FACILITIES AND SERVICES: Central heat, hall phones, hair dryer and electric kettle available, Internet terminal, room safe, TV, 24-hour desk; no lift

NEAREST TOURIST ATTRACTIONS: British Library

TELEPHONE
020 7837 7629

FAX
020 7278 5836

EMAIL
enqueries@californiahotel.co.uk

INTERNET
www.californiahotel.co.uk

CREDIT CARDS
None

RATES
Single £50, double £60, triple £80, quad £95

BREAKFAST
Buffet breakfast included

IMPERIAL LONDON HOTELS LTD.

The Imperial London Hotels Ltd. is a group of six centrally located hotels with more than six thousand beds. They are recommendable thanks to their central location, amenities including paid parking, use of a health club, and "Let's Go" Weekend package rates. The hotels deal mainly with budget tour groups, so personalized service is nowhere on the list of benefits for guests.

General Information for all Imperial London Hotels

TELEPHONE
020 7278 7871 (central reservations)

FAX
020 7837 4653 (central fax)

EMAIL
info@imperialhotels.co.uk

INTERNET
www.imperialhotels.co.uk

CREDIT CARDS
MC, V

RATES
For daily rates, please see individual hotel listings. "Let's Go" Weekend rates: £95 per person per night for a 2-night stay; optional supplementary Sunday night (dinner, bed, and breakfast, including parking) when booked together with the 2-night weekend is £50 per person. In addition to the "Let's Go" Weekend base rate, some of the hotels have a per person, per night supplement; please check below for details on each hotel.

BREAKFAST
English breakfast included except at the Royal National, where it is Continental

Expect big, bustling, impersonal, unimaginative hotels that move the herds in and out in processed precision. The hotels are within a five-minute walk of each other near Russell Square in Bloomsbury, and less than a mile from the City of London, main northern railway stations, and tube stops on the Central and Piccadilly lines going directly to Heathrow Airport.

Lower daily rates are available on request for groups. The "Let's Go" Weekends are good from Friday through Sunday and include two nights; daily English breakfast in all but the Royal National, where it is Continental; two three-course meals (lunch or dinner) in any of the hotel restaurants in the group; two days' free parking in the underground garage; a welcome cocktail in the hotel bar on arrival; no single-room supplement; first child under fourteen occupying a cot or minibed in parents' room is free; other children in parents' room are half price. An optional third night that includes dinner, bed, and breakfast is available at all the hotels. It is important to note that no special offers or package rates are available through travel agents.

NOTE: The sixth hotel in the group, the County, is not recommended.

FACILITIES AND SERVICES: In all Imperial London Hotels are a bar, central heat, direct-dial phones, hair dryers available, data ports on request, laundry service, lifts, restaurants, office safe (50p per day, some large enough for a laptop, no additional charge), satellite TV, radio, restaurant, room service, tea and coffeemakers and trouser presses in the room or on request, theater bookings, nonsmoking rooms, conference facilities, underground parking (£20 per day), 24-hour desk. Consult listings below for other specific services offered by each hotel.

NEAREST TOURIST ATTRACTIONS: British Museum, University College London

BEDFORD HOTEL (31)
83–93 Southampton Row, WC1
Tube: Russell Square

TELEPHONE
020 7636 7822

RATES
Single £75, double £98, 3rd person (folding bed) add £20 to double rate, 3rd person (cot) add £8 to double rate; "Let's Go" Weekend supplement £24 per person per night

184 rooms, all with shower or bath and toilet

The Bedford, close to the British Museum, has uniformly boring rooms equipped with built-in furniture, luggage racks, good closet space (especially in the twin-bedded rooms), and pretty back views over the hotel garden and row houses beyond. Those with windows facing the busy street have double glazing to reduce the traffic noise. For an increase in sleep time and a breath of fresh air away from the traffic fumes on the clogged London road in front, book a room facing the back garden. In warm weather, tables are arranged on the patio, which has a reflecting pond and a fountain. The hotel has a coffee shop and a computer with Internet access.

BREAKFAST
English breakfast included

IMPERIAL HOTEL (23)
Russell Square, WC1
Tube: Russell Square
447 rooms, all with shower or bath and toilet

The Imperial has everything from a car park to a casino next door. The rooms have been renovated, and those on the third and eighth floors have minibars. The best rooms for sleeping are on the eighth floor, with Russell Square views that overlook the entry and fountain area. A computer with Internet access is available, as is a currency exchange (with terrible rates), and the hotel shares a shopping arcade with the President (see next listing).

TELEPHONE
020 7837 3655

RATES
Single £75, double £98, 3rd person (folding bed) add £20 to double rate, 3rd person (cot) add £8 to double rate; "Let's Go" Weekend supplement £30 per person per night

BREAKFAST
English breakfast included

PRESIDENT (24)
Russell Square, WC1
Tube: Russell Square
523 rooms, all with shower or bath and toilet

The President has been revamped in budget style and now includes data ports in all the rooms on the first floor. It has all the goodies the others do in this group, but because volume is so high here, the prices are a bit less for standard nightly rates. A shopping arcade joins this hotel with the Imperial.

TELEPHONE
020 7837 8844

RATES
Single £70, double £92, 3rd person (folding bed) add £20 to double rate, 3rd person (cot) add £8 to double rate; "Let's Go" Weekend supplement £24 per person per night

BREAKFAST
English breakfast included

ROYAL NATIONAL HOTEL (20)
Bedford Way, WC1
Tube: Russell Square
1,635 rooms, all with shower or bath and toilet

The Royal National sleeps two thousand persons in more than sixteen hundred rooms, making it the biggest hotel in London. The hideous lifeboat-orange-colored curtains in this monstrous piece of architectural blight are gone, but the fleets of tour buses that disgorge budget revelers in from the sticks for a few days of booze and fun are not. The utilitarian rooms, reached by seemingly never-ending hikes down endless corridors, are clean and reasonably large, with only a few dings here

TELEPHONE
020 7637 2488

RATES
Single £70, double £88, 3rd person (folding bed) add £20 to double rate, 3rd person (cot) add £8 to double rate; "Let's Go" Weekend supplement £22 per person per night

BREAKFAST
Continental breakfast included

and there, but the faded pink color scheme gives them a dull feeling. If you can take the hotel's "bus station at rush hour" atmosphere, you will find everything you need, from an underground car park and a money changer (poor rates unless you are desperate) to a bar, gift shop, fitness center, Internet terminal, theater booking agency, and restaurants that serve predictable English fare.

NOTE: The corridors are very long; be sure you learn the fire escape route from your room.

TAVISTOCK (16)
Tavistock Square, WC1
Tube: Russell Square
343 rooms, all with shower or bath and toilet

TELEPHONE
020 7636 8383

RATES
Single £62, double £85, 3rd person (folding bed) add £20 to double rate, 3rd person (cot) add £8 to double rate; no supplement for "Let's Go" Weekend package deal

BREAKFAST
English breakfast included

The Tavistock is another of this chain's "tour group central" hotels, and with more than three hundred rooms catering mainly to large groups, one could hardly expect much of a personalized approach from the staff. They simply don't have the time or the training. Like at all the others, the rooms are bigger than average, and every possible convenience is offered within the hotel, from a wine bar to laundry services. The best rooms here are those overlooking Tavistock Square.

THE JENKINS HOTEL (4)
45 Cartwright Gardens, WC1
Tube: Euston, King's Cross, Russell Square
13 rooms, 12 with shower or bath and toilet

TELEPHONE
020 7387 2067

FAX
020 7383 3139

EMAIL
reservations@
jenkinshotel.demon.co.uk

INTERNET
www.jenkinshotel.demon.co.uk

CREDIT CARDS
MC, V

RATES
Single £52–72, double £85, triple £95

BREAKFAST
English breakfast included

Great Sleeping readers return to the thirteen-room Jenkins year after year, drawn by the tranquil location and the outgoing manner of owners Felicity Langley-Hunt and Sam Bellingham and their Labradors Georgie, Charlie, and the youngest, Tiggy, who take their duties as official greeters very seriously. Many guests have been known to actually complain if the dogs are not around, but as Sam told me, "They do go on holiday, and they like to go together." Many well-meaning guests have become coconspirators in playing havoc with the dogs' girth. To try to keep the dogs in fit form, Sam has been forced to place a sign in the dining room asking guests, "Please, do not feed the dogs." No one makes any bones about the presence of these appealing canines, so if they pose a problem, look elsewhere. I recommend three other hotels right on Cartwright Gardens, which do not have visible pets of any kind.

The Jenkins Hotel has been listed in every edition of my book, and I am especially glad to include it in this one, because it has been totally redone. Now all rooms but one single have en suite baths, and the outside one for the single is private to it. Each room has been recarpeted and has coordinated fabrics, dark wood furnishings, new beds and refurbished baths with plenty of strong hot water. Many of the interesting bits and pieces of furniture scattered throughout the rooms in the past have been kept, adding just the right note of English character. The poems framed with delicately hand-embroidered silk flowers are still hung throughout the hotel. In the 1920s, these flowers came in cigarette packages along with seeds, instructions on how to grow them, and a poem describing each flower variety. Sam Bellingham found a large collection of these in a box belonging to his grandfather and had them framed for the hotel. They are a special touch that everyone seems to enjoy. The hotel continues to hold firm to its policy of no smoking, a great feature for most Great Sleepers in London.

Guests gather each morning in the cozy breakfast room, with fresh flowers on the tables. Keys to the gardens opposite the hotel are available for anyone who wants to play a set or two of tennis or just relax for an hour or two from sight-seeing and shopping.

FACILITIES AND SERVICES: Central heat, fans, direct-dial phones, hair dryers, minibars, room safe, TV, completely nonsmoking; no lift

NEAREST TOURIST ATTRACTIONS: British Museum, University College London, Coram's Fields

LONDON EUSTON–TRAVEL INN CAPITAL (5)
1 Duke's Road, WC1
Tube: Euston, King's Cross
220 rooms, all with shower or bath and toilet

"We guarantee good quality rooms, friendly service and comfortable surroundings—everything you want for a good night's sleep. If you are not completely satisfied, we don't expect you to pay."

Quite a statement from Travel Inns Capital, and not one many other London hotels are prepared to make, but because the Travel Inns are the McDonald's of the English chain hotel business and deal in volume, they can afford such a guarantee. Their pricing structure is simple: one price for all rooms. Whether you are a single Great Sleeper or a family of four (with two adults and two children under sixteen) willing to share the same room, the price per room per night is £85, breakfast extra. The

TELEPHONE
0870 242 8000 (central reservations); 020 7554 3400 (London Euston)

FAX
0870 241 9000 (central fax); 020 7554 3419 (London Euston)

INTERNET
www.travelinn.co.uk (central Website)

CREDIT CARDS
AE, DC, MC, V

RATES
All rooms £85 per night

BREAKFAST
Continental breakfast £5, English breakfast £7

plain, identical rooms have private bathrooms, hanging space, TV, tea and coffeemaking facilities, and a telephone that requires a phone card (sold at the desk) or a credit card to activate it. Each Travel Inn has a bar and restaurant. In addition to this hotel, there are two other Travel Inns in central London: the London County Hall, with some great views over the River Thames, and the London Tower Bridge, near the Tower of London. Please see page 184 for information on these two. Other than the telephone and fax numbers, the information given in the margin applies to all three locations.

FACILITIES AND SERVICES: Bar, central heat, direct-dial phone, hair dryer available, lift, restaurant, office safe, parking (£10 per night) tea and coffeemakers, TV, one floor for nonsmokers

NEAREST TOURIST ATTRACTIONS: British Library

MORGAN HOTEL (36)
24 Bloomsbury Street, WC1
Tube: Tottenham Court Road

17 rooms, 4 flats, all with shower or bath and toilet

For a stay of a few nights, a week, or a month or more, the Morgan Hotel and apartments is a favorite Bloomsbury address for many Great Sleepers in London. In fact, it is so popular that reservations are important as far in advance as possible, and a year ahead is not *too* soon to begin making your plans.

The Morgan Hotel and the four adjacent apartments are owned by Joy Ward and her brothers, John and David. They are so dedicated to their high level of excellence that they do most of the work in the hotel themselves, from greeting guests at the door to cleaning the rooms and preparing breakfast each morning.

David Ward, a carpenter and craftsperson, did the interior paneling and cabinetry. Everything is well planned, from the blooming flower boxes under the windows to the carefully maintained rooms, most of which are air-conditioned at no extra cost. Bathrooms are equally as nice, with a magnifying mirror and enough shelf and counter space. The dining room is comfortably fitted with booths and accented with fresh and dried flower arrangements. Adding to the warmth here is an impressive collection of English china, a display case of crystal and ceramics, and toby jugs and early London photographs.

TELEPHONE
020 7636 3735

FAX
020 7636 3045

CREDIT CARDS
MC, V with a 3% surcharge unless it is a direct debit charge card

RATES
Hotel: single £60–70, double £85, triple £130. Apartments £120, extra person £50. For apartments, 5-night stays preferred, but shorter stays possible depending on availability. Must cancel reservations more than 48 hours prior to arrival or forfeit deposit.

BREAKFAST
English breakfast included for hotel and apartment guests

The four apartments, which can sleep only up to three, are decorated with attractive furniture and framed English prints. All include a television and VCR, an eat-in kitchen with a view, an en suite bathroom with a separate shower and bathtub, a security system, daily maid service, and breakfast each morning at the hotel.

FACILITIES AND SERVICES: Air-conditioning in all but 3 hotel rooms, but not in the 4 apartments, central heat, direct-dial phones, hair dryer, magnifying mirrors in bathrooms, room safe, satellite TV in hotel and apartments; no lift

NEAREST TOURIST ATTRACTIONS: British Museum

myhotel bloomsbury ($, 34)
11–13 Bayley Street, Bedford Square, WC1
Tube: Tottenham Court Road, Goodge Street
76 rooms, all with shower, bath, and toilet

Owner Andrew Thrasyvoulou's philosophy best sums up his unique hotel: "myhotel will offer you a release from the stresses of this modern age. . . . Relax and let us give call to your needs. We are dedicated to making your stay an experience which will leave you wishing to come back. Enjoy!"

myhotel bloomsbury is a contemporary townhouse hotel where the influence of *feng shui* plays an important part in creating a stylish, welcoming experience designed to assure guests tranquility and relaxation in an atmosphere that combines the culture and technological drive of the West with the graceful and respectful service of the East. Indeed, myhotel is a calm oasis where positive energy flows smoothly and productively in both the communal areas and individual guest rooms. Unobtrusive service and a commitment to care for every guest's needs are vital aspects of the hotel's high standards. myhotel operates on a "personal assistant" system where one contact, met on arrival, is responsible for looking after each guest, personally ensuring their stay will be as smooth as possible from check-in to departure. Tipping is discouraged, and guests are asked to brief the hotel before their arrival on personal likes and dislikes.

From singles to suites, all rooms are uncluttered spaces where careful attention to style and color is reflected in their overall comfort. Every possible modern convenience has been included, from air-conditioning and data ports to safes large enough for a laptop and piles of fluffy towels in the well-lit bathrooms. The mychi

TELEPHONE
020 7667 6000

FAX
020 7667 6001

EMAIL
guest_services@myhotels.co.uk

INTERNET
www.myhotels.co.uk

CREDIT CARDS
AE, DC, MC, V

RATES
Singles from £170; doubles from £195; special weekend rates subject to availability

BREAKFAST
Buffet £15, English £20

restaurant follows the same East-West philosophy, serving light, healthy meals using fresh ingredients. You can further rejuvenate the body in myhotel's fitness room, and use their affiliated health and holistic center to relax the mind and revive the spirit. The myhotel library is a quiet place to enjoy a few minutes reading the daily papers or use the Internet terminal and printer.

FACILITIES AND SERVICES: Air-conditioning, bar, 2 conference rooms, direct-dial phone, hair dryer, Internet terminal and printer for guest use, data ports, laundry service, lift, restaurant, 24-hour room service, room safe large enough for laptop, tea and coffee-making facilities, satellite TV with pay-for-view movies, CD players with a selection of music offered, nonsmoking on 3 floors, fitness room, health club and holistic center affiliation, 24-hour desk with "personal assistant" assigned to each guest

NEAREST TOURIST ATTRACTIONS: British Museum

POSTHOUSE BLOOMSBURY (19)
Coram Street, WC1
Tube: Russell Square
284 rooms, all with shower or bath and toilet

For years this huge hotel was about as exciting as a bowl of stewed prunes. Now, thanks to an £8.5 million ongoing refurbishment, things are looking up, but you can say that only if you land on one of the new floors. The hotel is targeted toward businesspeople who want comfort and convenience in a modern facility with no unpleasant surprises. The new superior rooms do provide that. Strong colors of purple, navy blue, and rust red are mixed and mingled in a style that can be described as Art Deco with Oriental overtones. Air-conditioning, work space with a comfortable chair and halogen lighting, data ports, satellite television reception with pay-for-view movies, and twenty-four-hour room service are standard issue. Meals are served in a dramatically purple and brown dining room that is softened by orchid plants, or in the bar if guests want something light.

FACILITIES AND SERVICES: Air-conditioning in superior rooms, bar, central heat, conference facilities, direct-dial phones, data ports in superior rooms, hair dryer, lift, minibar in superior rooms, restaurant, room service, office safe, satellite TV and pay-for-view movies, tea and coffeemakers, trouser press, 24-hour desk, 3 nonsmoking floors

TELEPHONE
0870 400 9222; 800-225-5843
(toll-free from the U.S.)

FAX
020 7837 5374

INTERNET
www.posthotels.com

CREDIT CARDS
AE, DC, MC, V

RATES
Rates depend on day of week and type of room, either standard or superior. Singles £110–198, doubles £110–210; the hotel participates in the Posthouse Leisure Breaks, described on page 60, and has lower rates on Friday and Saturday nights, as well as special offers subject to availability; always ask

BREAKFAST
Continental or English breakfast £15

NEAREST TOURIST ATTRACTIONS: University College London, British Museum, Coram's Fields

THE PRINCESS HOTEL (2)
35–37 Argyle Square, WC1
Tube: King's Cross, St. Pancras
21 rooms, 3 with shower or bath and toilet

TELEPHONE
020 7278 6895

FAX
020 7833 0984

EMAIL
princesshotel@btinternet.com

INTERNET
www.princesshotel.co.uk

CREDIT CARDS
MC, V

RATES
Hotel: single £32, double £42–55, triple £70; apartments: all prices per night, per room; single £25, double £35–40, triple £45–60

BREAKFAST
English breakfast included

I love surprises, especially when I can pass the good news on to readers. On all of my visits to this hotel, I am reminded by Coco, one of the friendly owners, of my first visit a few years ago, which was on a cold March day. I was in the neighborhood looking for a pub and passed her as she was perched on a ladder washing the windows in what I considered to be arctic conditions. We struck up a conversation, she invited me in, I liked what I saw, and the rest, as they say, is history: the discovery of this clean Great Sleep in London run by Coco, her brothers Jessie and Frank, and their families.

Argyle Square is in the northern tip of Bloomsbury and quickly accessible to the St. Pancras railroad station. It is far (thirty minutes) from the usual tourist trails in London, and to get to them you will have to depend on tube, bus, taxi, and shank's mare. However, if you are a certified bargain-seeking Great Sleeper, the Princess Hotel definitely lives up to its name. It is as well scrubbed inside as it is out, with rooms a big step up from the dark Dickensian decor that is the rule in most of the area's budget lodgings. The rooms are snug and lean, with pine furniture and minimal color coordination. Couples can check into No. 6, a twin on the front, or into Nos. 9 or 11, identical doubles with a glass-enclosed shower in each of the bathrooms. Hall shared facilities are absolutely spotless (none of the singles have private facilities). The public areas are done in easy-care materials that are a cinch to keep washed and don't show wear and tear. The tiled dining room is set with three communal tables where guests can stoke up for the day on bacon, eggs, beans, and all the trimmings.

New this time around is the listed building next door, which the family has purchased and turned into six long-term accommodations. Four of them have private facilities, and two doubles share a bath. Everyone shares a communal equipped kitchen. The rooms themselves are simple, with a television, electric kettle, and table and chair. The bigger ones have an additional lounge chair. The prices are almost philanthropic for the minimum stay, which is two weeks, and even more so if you qualify for a long-stay discount.

FACILITIES AND SERVICES: Central heat, hall phones, hair dryer and iron available, TV, tea and coffeemakers, 24-hour desk; no lift; the same applies to the apartments next door

NEAREST TOURIST ATTRACTIONS: British Library

ST. MARGARET'S HOTEL (30)
26 Bedford Place, WC1
Tube: Holborn, Russell Square
64 rooms, 10 with shower or bath and toilet

TELEPHONE
020 7636 4277/7580 2352

FAX
020 7323 3066

CREDIT CARDS
MC, V

RATES
Single (none with private bath) £50, double £65–95 (No. 53 is £105); £3.50 supplement for 1-night stays; £10.50 cancellation fee

BREAKFAST
English breakfast included

During their many years at St. Margaret's, Rosanna and Betino Marazzi have served a quiet circle of regulars, the sort of people who would not return if they were not fully satisfied. My next-door neighbor and his family have been coming here for more than thirty-five years and have no plans of staying in any other London hotel. The keynote of the hotel is friendly, personal service by a dedicated staff that has worked here for years. As Mrs. Marazzi told me, "My staff changes only when someone retires!"

The eclectically furnished, slightly old-fashioned rooms are fresh and bright and impeccably maintained. The views along the back overlook the Duke of Bedford's gardens and are truly magnificent in the spring and early summer, when the trees and flowers are in full bloom. Top-floor roosts look at the dome of the British Museum. Even the tiniest single has a generosity of space and is clean. Almost all the rooms still have their original fireplaces, which in the early days maids had to stoke several times a day to keep the guests warm. With the addition of central heat, stoking the fires is no longer one of the maids' responsibilities, and the fireplaces serve as decorative reminders of a long-lost era in hotel living. For a family, or anyone, actually, No. 53 is a great room, with a glassed-in conservatory along the gardens, the original marble fireplace dating from 1803, and a nicely tiled bathroom. I can't imagine that anyone could be disappointed by it. There are other rooms that are very nice, and most of them have their own baths and face the gardens, which are available for guests to enjoy. Try for No. 40, a family room for four; No. 28, a double or triple with windows onto the garden and a tiled stall shower in the bathroom; No. 33, with a large closet, chest of drawers, comfortable seating, a new bathroom, and garden view; or No. 23, a favorite because it is so light and has excellent closet and luggage space. You will save money sleeping in Nos. 24 and 41, quiet L-shaped bathless singles with enough room to fully unpack and stay for a week or more, or in No. 44, a spacious, bathless double or triple on the garden.

I think the dining room is one of the nicest in Bloomsbury, because it is bright and airy, with fresh flowers and green plants. I like to sit in the back section, overlooking the gardens below. As you walk from the lounge to the dining room, please be sure to take a minute to look at the series of interesting photographs taken by the Marazzis' son of important events in and around Bedford Place.

FACILITIES AND SERVICES: Central heat, direct-dial phones, satellite TV, hair dryer available and in most rooms with private baths, office safe, tea and coffee served anytime; no lift

NEAREST TOURIST ATTRACTIONS: British Museum, Coram's Fields

THANET HOTEL (32)
8 Bedford Place, WC1
Tube: Holborn, Russell Square
16 rooms, all with shower or bath and toilet

The Thanet Hotel is an exceptionally good value and very nice for the price. Hotels around Russell Square are a dime a dozen and range from luxury stays to utter dumps. The key is to find one that is not only clean and fairly priced but comes without the usual dime-store style of decor that pits clashing colors against patched carpets, shrunken bedspreads, and furnishings that can charitably be called "curbside." If you like Bloomsbury and want to be close to the British Museum, Covent Garden, and the theaters, the Thanet should be a top contender for your stay, because now it is even better than before. The hotel is owned and managed by third-generation hoteliers Richard and Lynwen Orchard. Thanks to their continued efforts, the hotel has improved by leaps and bounds since my last visit. This time, Lynwen happily pointed out, "When we renewed the lease, we called in the decorators." I arrived just as the work was starting, but I could see by the installation of new beds, neutrally matched carpets and curtains, and refreshed bathrooms that the Thanet was in the process

TELEPHONE
020 7636 2869/7580 3377

FAX
020 7323 6676

EMAIL
thanet-lon@aol.com

INTERNET
www.freepages.co.uk/
thanet_hotel

CREDIT CARDS
AE, MC, V

RATES
Single £70, double £90, triple £110, quad £115

BREAKFAST
English breakfast included

of a super facelift. Naturally, the ornamental fireplaces in all but two rooms have been kept, and the garden views from Nos. 5, 9, and 10 are as lovely as before.

The hotel stands out along Bedford Place with a bright-blue awning over the door and the colored-tile entry leading up two steps from the street. As you enter, look up to admire the original glass dome in the ceiling, which sheds light on a winding staircase. A ground-floor dining room with linen-covered tables looks over window boxes to the street.

NOTE: Another Bloomsbury hotel run by family members is the Harlingford Hotel (please see page 104).

FACILITIES AND SERVICES: Central heat, direct-dial phones, fans, hair dryers, office safe, TV and radio, tea and coffeemakers, office open 7 A.M.–midnight; no lift

NEAREST TOURIST ATTRACTIONS: British Museum, Coram's Fields

WC2

Covent Garden, Leicester Square, and the Strand

Why are Trafalgar Square fountains like Government Clerks?
Because they play from 10 till 4.
—Punch, *July 17, 1858*

All distances in London are measured from Charing Cross, the official center of the city, just south of Trafalgar Square.

Covent Garden, London's first planned square, was laid out in 1630 by architect Inigo Jones on behalf of the Duke of Bedford, who owned the land. Before that, it was the Covent Garden for Westminster Abbey, thus the name. In Victorian times, Covent Garden was London's fruit and vegetable market, the place where the legendary Professor Henry Higgins met Eliza Doolittle. In the mid-1960s, the market was converted into a complex of shops, cafés, restaurants, and wine bars that draw crowds every day and night of the week. Because of the density of theaters in the area (including Drury Lane), and the stunning Royal Opera House, many of these restaurants offer well-priced pre- and posttheater menus. There always seems to be something going on around Covent Garden—street entertainers perform in the plaza, and the narrow streets fanning out from the market are lined with interesting boutiques and dozens of coffeehouses that can easily take up an afternoon of browsing and sipping.

Leicester Square, sandwiched between Piccadilly Circus and Charing Cross Road, is perpetually crowded with people milling about, waiting to attend one of the first-run cinemas, or queuing at the Half-Price Ticket Booth (see "Discounts—Theaters and Concerts," page 21). Chinatown is close, and so are the stage theaters along Shaftesbury Avenue.

The Strand is a rich assortment of former noblemen's homes occupying the area between the Strand and the River Thames. For the tourist, it is the principal route between the West End and the City.

TOURIST ATTRACTIONS
Charing Cross, Trafalgar Square, Nelson's Column, Royal Courts of Justice, St.-Martin-in-the-Fields Church, National Portrait Gallery, Royal Opera House, London Transport Museum, National Gallery, Thames River

HOTELS IN WC2 (see map page 96)

OTHER OPTIONS

Apartment Rentals

Student Dormitories

($) indicates a Big Splurge

THE FIELDING HOTEL (48)
4 Broad Court, WC2
Tube: Covent Garden

24 rooms, all with shower and toilet

TELEPHONE
020 7836 8305

FAX
020 7497 0064

EMAIL
reservations@the-fielding-hotel.co.uk

INTERNET
www.the-fielding-hotel.co.uk

CREDIT CARDS
AE, DC, MC, V

RATES
Single £85, double £115–145; must cancel within 72 hours of arrival or forfeit deposit; reservations for a 1-night stay on Saturday are not accepted

BREAKFAST
Not served

For those London visitors who want to be only a heartbeat away from theaters, Soho, Piccadilly Circus, and West End restaurants and shopping, the Fielding is a popular destination. The hotel is named after the novelist Henry Fielding, who lived in Broad Court with his brother; both were magistrates at the Bow Street Magistrates' Court next door. The building seems to have been here since time began. Some of my readers love the hotel, calling it "quaint" and/or "historical." Others find it dreadfully cramped, with depressing views and lacking in flashy amenities. I am somewhere in between, believing that the location, pleasant management, and several of the rooms with new bathrooms save the day.

The hotel is on a paved pedestrian walkway next to the Bow Street Magistrates' Court, site of the world's first police station, and almost opposite the Royal Opera House in Covent Garden. Diamond-paned windows and flower-filled window boxes frame the entrance. Breakfast is not served, but countless cafés and coffeehouses are within a five-minute walk.

Most of the rooms are far from spacious, and thanks to their city-center location, more than a few have gloomy vistas, but in general they do have a cozy cottage air and showers in every bathroom (no tubs). Numbers 10, 20, and 30 are corner locations on Broad Court and are choice picks. Their small sleeping areas are bolstered by well-lit sitting areas and new bathrooms. Hiking enthusiasts who climb to the top floor will live in No. 35, which has a rather interesting view to a block of apartments that once were government council flats (i.e., subsidized). Number 5 is a viewless room to keep in mind, because you certainly do not want to get it until the carpet has been relaid, and new, spot-free bedspreads that fit have been installed. The bathroom has a regulation glass-enclosed shower and heated towel rack, and the room itself features a dressing area and newer pine furnishings. Number 3, a standard twin, has another grim view and has needed redoing from start to finish for several years. Until that has happened, this room is also a definite no-no.

NOTE: The Fielding Hotel is closed between Christmas and New Year's.

FACILITIES AND SERVICES: Bar, central heat, direct-dial phones, hair dryer available, office safe, tea and coffee-making facilities, TV; no lift, no children under 12 allowed

NEAREST TOURIST ATTRACTIONS: Covent Garden, Royal Opera House, Leicester Square

KINGSWAY HALL ($, 42)
Great Queen Street, WC1 (no street #)
Tube: Holborn, Covent Garden
170 rooms, all with bath, shower, and toilet

The monolithic Kingsway Hall was built to serve London's corporate market. Despite its size and postindustrial-chic use of glass and bold colored textures, the hotel feels welcoming, not intimidating. Smart Great Sleepers who time their visit on the weekends will be able to take advantage of impressive rate reductions and still will enjoy the amenities and location this dramatically modern hotel offers. To work off the stress and strains of a long London day, there is a fully equipped gym with a whirlpool and his and her saunas. Dining choices include room service, light snacks in a street-side bar, or something more substantial in the dining room. Rooms vary from standard to superior, but for the leisure traveler, the standard rooms are more than adequate, each with a private telephone number and voice mail, data port, in-room safe for a laptop, and power shower in the bathroom.

Also under the same ownership is the Harrington Hall, in South Kensington, which is perfectly positioned

TELEPHONE
020 7309 0909

FAX
020 7309 9696

EMAIL
kingswayhall@compuserve.com

INTERNET
www.kingswayhall.co.uk

CREDIT CARDS
AE, DC, MC, V

RATES
Single from £220, double from £230, suite £310; discounted weekend rates include English breakfast

BREAKFAST
Continental breakfast £15, English breakfast £20

for the Victoria and Albert, Science, and Natural History Museums and the Royal Albert Hall. Shopping in Knightsbridge or along the King's Road is an easy bus or tube ride away. For further details, please see page 169.

FACILITIES AND SERVICES: Air-conditioning, bar, concierge, 9 conference rooms for up to 150 people, doctor on call, direct-dial phone with voice mail and your own personal number, hair dryer, iron, laundry service, lift, minibar, data port, restaurant, 24-hour desk and room service, room safe for computer, tea and coffee-making facilities, satellite TV, trouser press, fitness center with whirlpool and 2 saunas, several nonsmoking floors

NEAREST TOURIST ATTRACTIONS: Oxford Street shopping, Royal Opera House, Royal Courts of Justice, West End theaters

THE PASTORIA ($, 57)
3 St. Martin's Street, WC2
Tube: Leicester Square
58 rooms, all with shower or bath and toilet

TELEPHONE
020 7930 8641; 800-333-3333 (toll-free from the U.S. through Radisson)

FAX
020 7451 0191

EMAIL
reshamp@radison.com

INTERNET
www.RadissonEdwardian.com

CREDIT CARDS
AE, DC, MC, V

RATES
Single £220, double £240–255; always ask about Corporate, Super Saver, and Weekend rates, which are much less

BREAKFAST
Continental breakfast £11, English breakfast £12

Tucked away in a traffic-free side street off Leicester Square is the Pastoria. For those with flexible budgets and more demanding needs who want a key location in the center of the West End, this lovely hotel has a great deal to offer, especially if you take advantage of the Weekend, Corporate, or other special rates, which in some cases can cut the rack rate almost in half and toss in an English breakfast. Look at it this way: what you save on time, taxi, and tube costs at this location you can apply to upgrading your stay. Piccadilly Circus, Regent Street, Covent Garden, Parliament Square, and Buckingham Palace are all within walking distance, and with Leicester and Trafalgar Squares on the hotel's doorstep, many of London's top theaters and cinemas are only minutes away.

The Pastoria began as a gentlemen's private club and restaurant, and was converted into a hotel in 1931. The rooms have an intimate Edwardian theme, with a hint of the Orient provided by the rich red and green fabrics that enhance the walls and upholstery. The only drawback to the hotel would be the singles facing the back, with creepy views of a fire escape. Some of the nicer rooms, with marble baths, are on the sixth floor, which is also one of the hotel's four nonsmoking floors. Number 608, a double, has a peekaboo look at Big Ben and Nelson's Column. Number 603, which can be made up as either a king or twin, is as well presented as all the other rooms and has even more closet and drawer space, plus a bathroom window, but the view from both the room and the bathroom is nothing. Number 308, also on a nonsmoking floor, is a pretty double done in burgundy and green. I like the big bathroom, with a deep tub and three windows.

The hotel's dining room faces Leicester Square, but the food is only okay if you just want a quick bite. Consult *Great Eats London* for better choices that are all within easy walking distance.

FACILITIES AND SERVICES: Bar, central heat, conference room, fans, direct-dial phones, hair dryer, laundry service, lift, data ports, porter, restaurant, room service, room safe, satellite TV, pay movies, radio, clock, tea and coffeemakers, 24-hour desk, 4 nonsmoking floors

NEAREST TOURIST ATTRACTIONS: Piccadilly Circus, Regent Street, Covent Garden, Leicester Square, Trafalgar Square, National Gallery, Buckingham Palace

SEVEN DIALS HOTEL (45)
7 Monmouth Street, WC2
Tube: Covent Garden, Leicester Square
10 rooms, 7 with shower or bath and toilet

As my Scottish auntie used to say, "You never know what's 'round the corner, dear, until you look." I am glad I kept looking "'round the corner" in this high-priced neck of the London woods, determined to find another acceptably priced Great Sleep. The ten rooms at the Seven Dials Hotel don't offer all the amenities of the big-spender neighbor down the block, which has tabs in the high triple digits, but they do offer clean, cut-rate sleeps for those coming to London to concentrate on the theater. The building is old and narrow with some gloomy views, and there are stairs to climb, but the small rooms are just fine if you are looking for a safe crash pad between curtain calls. In your room, where everything matches, you can brew a cup of tea, call your friends anywhere in the world, or watch the BBC news reports on the telly. Your choice of an English or Continental breakfast is included, and so is the friendly charm of Hanna, the sweet Polish woman who oversees the running of the hotel.

FACILITIES AND SERVICES: Central heat, fans, direct-dial phones, hair dryer and iron available, office safe, tea and coffeemakers, TV; no lift

NEAREST TOURIST ATTRACTIONS: Covent Garden, Soho, Leicester Square

TELEPHONE
020 7681 0791/7240 0823
FAX
020 7681 0792
CREDIT CARDS
AE, EC, MC, V
RATES
Single £60–80, double £75–95, triple £110; 72-hour cancellation policy enforced
BREAKFAST
English or Continental breakfast included

SW1

Belgravia, Knightsbridge, Pimlico, and Victoria

TOURIST ATTRACTIONS
Buckingham Palace,
Westminster Abbey, Houses of
Parliament, Whitehall,
Westminster Cathedral, Big
Ben, Royal Mews, Green Park,
St. James's Park, Tate Britain

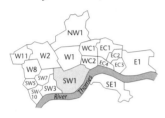

Belgravia is owned by the Duke of Westminster, one of the richest men in England. It is no wonder, then, that Belgravia has the most expensive real estate in London, especially around Eaton Square, where £2 million or £3 million for a fixer-upper is considered a bargain. Ebury Street, one of London's better B&B streets, is on the edge of Eaton Square. Mozart lived at 180 Ebury Street and composed his first symphony here. Noël Coward lived for twenty-five years with his mother at 111 Ebury Street in what is now the Noël Coward Hotel (see page 132). There are several good restaurants and charming small pubs in this area (see *Great Eats London*).

Knightsbridge is another top-drawer address, where residents can shop at Harrods and the even more expensive and exclusive Harvey Nichols, gaze longingly at the designer boutiques on Sloane Street, and browse through the tempting shops along Beauchamp Place.

Other than the Tate Britain, a strip of antiques shops along Pimlico Road, Princess Margaret's son Lord David Linley's design shop, and a cluster of shops around Warwick Way, Pimlico does not have tourist sites drawing crowds of visitors. Belgrave Road features an expanse of terraced town homes, many of which house a variety of bottom-budget B&Bs, most of which are definitely not included in this book.

Victoria hasn't much to recommend it, other than the massive Victoria Station, through which every visitor to London probably passes at least once. If you are leaving London via coach (on the bus), you will leave from the Victoria Coach Station, about a five-minute walk from the Victoria rail and tube station. Restaurants in this area are geared mainly toward the hungry tourist, so you know they are basically terrible.

Westminster and Whitehall are devoted to running the country. In Westminster you will set your watch according to Big Ben; visit the Houses of Parliament and Westminster Abbey, the burial site of many historical figures; and tour the Cabinet War Rooms used by Winston Churchill and his generals during World War II.

Two of the most famous addresses in the world are here: No. 10 Downing Street, home of the British prime minister, and Buckingham Palace. You can't even get close to No. 10 Downing Street, but you can to Buckingham Palace when you witness the famous changing of the guard, or in August, when the queen is away and the doors are opened to the paying public.

HOTELS IN SW1

OTHER OPTIONS
Apartment Rentals

Bed and Breakfast in a Private Home

Student Dormitories

($) indicates a Big Splurge

SW1

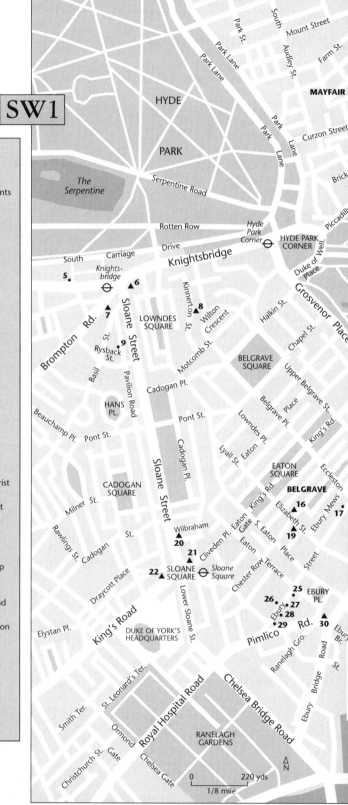

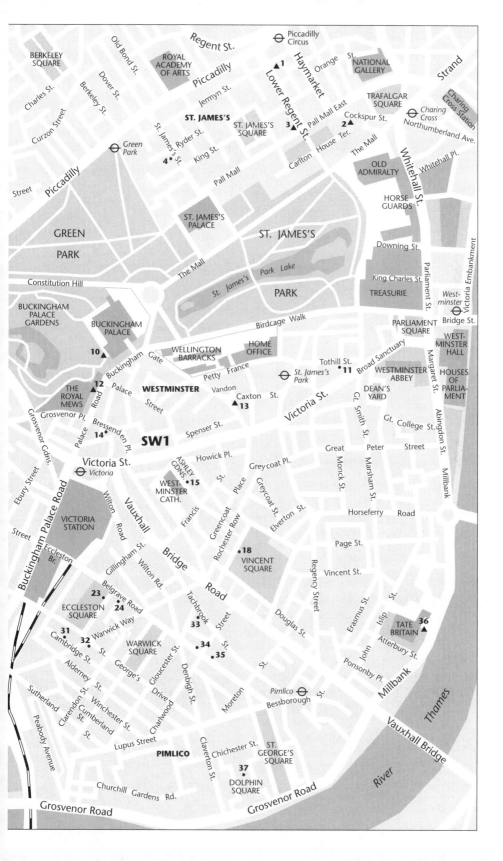

EATON HOUSE HOTEL (25)
125 Ebury Street, SW1
Tube: Victoria, Sloane Square
10 rooms, 5 with shower or bath and toilet

TELEPHONE & FAX
020 7730 8781
CREDIT CARDS
MC, V
RATES
Single £40–60, double £65–75, triple £75–85; lower winter rates
BREAKFAST
English breakfast included

Devoted regulars know that checking into Eaton House means staying with a genuinely friendly family in a small and tidy B&B minutes from Victoria Station. Owner Josephine Belgrano and her daughters Anabel and Maria have been treating their guests like long-lost relatives for thirty years. All of the rooms are painted white and kept clean. Each has its own tea and coffeemaker and color television, in case you want to brew a cup of tea and catch up on your British telly programming. Private facilities have been added to six rooms, but if you are trying to cut costs, you can safely book a room without a private bathroom—the hall toilet and tiled communal bath facilities (on alternate floors) are some of the best of any B&B on the entire street. Breakfast is served piping hot each morning in a room with green and white cushioned chairs and shared tables, where guests swap shopping discoveries and restaurant tips. Both Anabel and Maria are former London tour guides and are happy to help plan your days in London.

FACILITIES AND SERVICES: Central heat, fans in the summer, hall phone, hair dryer, iron available, office safe, tea and coffeemakers, TV, desk open 7:30 A.M.–11 P.M.; no lift

NEAREST TOURIST ATTRACTIONS: Royal Mews, Buckingham Palace

THE GORING HOTEL ($, 14)
Beeston Place, SW1
Tube: Victoria
74 rooms, all with bath, shower, and toilet

TELEPHONE
020 7396 9000; 800-323-5463
(toll-free in the U.S.)
FAX
020 7834 4393
EMAIL
reception@goringhotel.co.uk
INTERNET
www.goringhotel.co.uk
CREDIT CARDS
AE, DC, MC, V

The *London Times* states, "The Goring Hotel is the most distinguished privately owned hotel in London." It would be hard to disagree. Owned and personally managed by three generations of the Goring family, the hotel has a proud history of providing excellent service, outstanding facilities, and a warm, personalized welcome to all its guests. When it opened on March 2, 1910, it was the first hotel in the world with private bathrooms and central heating in every room. In 1937, the Crown Prince of Norway stayed at the Goring because "I don't have a bathroom to myself in Buckingham Palace."

The public areas of the hotel are grand, but hardly pretentious, thanks to the flock of whimsical sheep footstools you see grazing in the lounge and gracing many of the bedrooms. The Garden Bar is an ideal meeting place, and the glassed-in terrace overlooking the private garden a lovely setting in which to relax over a proper afternoon tea with warm scones and clotted cream. Dinner is served in a traditional dining room with quiet piano music, or if you are hosting an event, in one of the private dining rooms designed to serve from four to a hundred guests.

Every room, from the smallest single to the magnificent suites, is luxuriously appointed and decorated and has workspaces and comfortable seating. In addition to the usual facilities, each provides a private safe, data port, two telephone lines, and two ISDN lines. Terrycloth dressing gowns hang in every closet, and lovely toiletries accessorize the beautiful baths. Individual fax lines are in all the suites and deluxe rooms. It would be difficult to pick definitive favorites, but No. 36, with a balcony opening onto the hotel's private garden, is one. So is No. 70, a huge double room done in blue and white, and No. 86, a Junior Suite that has a separate sitting room with its own wooly lamb footstool. The marble bathroom has two sinks and excellent lighting, and the luxurious king-size bedroom has closet and drawer space that is more than ample. Admittedly, the Goring Hotel is a Big Splurge, but occasionally there are very attractive weekend rates, especially in August, and excellent Christmas and New Year's packages that will appeal to many. Final note: Children are welcomed with great pleasure.

FACILITIES AND SERVICES: Air-conditioning, central heat, bar, concierge and porters, 2 direct-dial phone lines, data ports, ISDN lines, private faxes in deluxe rooms and suites, hair dryer, laundry service, lift, parking (£25 per 24 hours), restaurant, room safe, room service, cable TV, nonsmoking rooms, 24-hour desk

NEAREST TOURIST ATTRACTIONS: Buckingham Palace, Royal Mews, St. James's Park, Westminster

RATES
Single £185, double £225–275, Junior Suite £300, Executive Suite £390; occasionally lower weekend rates, Christmas and New Year's packages. Rates include service, but not the 17.5% VAT.

BREAKFAST
Continental breakfast £12.50, English breakfast £16.50, VAT included

THE JAMES CARTREF HOUSE (27)
108/129 Ebury Street, SW1
Tube: Victoria, Sloane Square

James House: 9 rooms, 3 with shower and toilet
Cartref House: 11 rooms, 8 with shower and toilet

TELEPHONE
020 7730 7338 (James House);
020 7730 6176 (Cartref House)

FAX
020 7730 7338

EMAIL
jandchouse@cs.com

INTERNET
www.jamesandcartref.co.uk

CREDIT CARDS
AE, MC, V

RATES
Single £54–65, double £72–88,
triple £95–108, family room
£135; these rates apply to both
houses

BREAKFAST
English breakfast included

It would be hard to imagine a better London B&B than the two-in-one James Cartref House on Ebury Street, run by Derek and Sharon James, energetic hosts who are adept at making everyone feel right at home. Ranking high on my list of top budget bets in London, these two small hotels reflect the couple's dedication to the needs of their guests, who receive the kind of attention seldom seen in this busy, impersonal world. They have now taken a bold step that is appreciated by most of their guests and declared both of their B&Bs to be completely nonsmoking. Hooray!

Both Sharon and Derek take tremendous pride in keeping everything in tip-top condition by repainting, refinishing, and redecorating whenever necessary. The addition of a glass conservatory breakfast room at the James House is a huge success, and so is the newly painted breakfast room at the Cartref House, with pretty fruit-printed curtains and a rogues' gallery of family photos. At the Cartref House, each floor has its own color scheme, with the differently decorated rooms designed to give guests a sense of cozy comfort. In the nine-room James House, each room is individually done in a different color scheme. The sense of coziness in them all is achieved by Sharon's use of simple and sweet fabrics that are coordinated with the carpeting, color of the walls, and the window treatments. Families with children will appreciate the low rates, large rooms (some with bunk beds), and proximity to the Victoria train, bus, and tube station. If you arrive via British Air at Gatwick, the train whisks you from the airport directly to Victoria for a fraction of the taxi fare and in half the time a bus ride takes. After a stay with the James family in either of their two B&Bs, you will undoubtedly join the many Great Sleepers who have come before you, returning each time you are in London.

NOTE: If the James Cartref House is fully booked, try the Fairways Hotel, run by Derek's sister, Jenny, and her husband, Steve Adams (see page 72).

FACILITIES AND SERVICES: Central heat, fans in the summer, hall phone, hair dryer, tea and coffeemakers, TV, desk open 7 A.M.–10 P.M.; no lift or safe, no smoking

NEAREST TOURIST ATTRACTIONS: Buckingham Palace, Royal Mews

KNIGHTSBRIDGE GREEN HOTEL (5)
159 Knightsbridge, SW1
Tube: Knightsbridge

28 rooms, all with shower or bath and toilet

"I can't wait to come back!" wrote one contented guest. Another described the Knightsbridge Green as "intimate, elegant, and warm." I am equally enthusiastic about this special hotel, especially after inspecting it again for the fifth edition of *Great Sleeps London*.

The area known as Knightsbridge epitomizes classic fashionable London, and this wonderful hotel fits the image perfectly. It is situated adjacent to Hyde Park and is within easy bag-carrying distance of Harrods, Harvey Nichols, and the designer boutiques lining Sloane Street and Beauchamp Place. From the outside, it resembles many other London townhouse hotels. However, the minute you walk into the sea green entryway and step up to the marble reception desk, you know that this hotel is several notches above the rest. The Marler family opened it in 1967 and began a tradition of quality and service their friendly staff upholds to this day. The rooms, most of which are spacious suites, are exquisitely planned in decorator colors, have enough storage space for you to stay almost forever, and offer marble baths with power showers and plenty of daylight. Number 10, done in lime green and brick tones, has a modern canopy bed, three workspaces, and a marble bathroom you will love. Number 35, a quiet double facing the back, is decorated in soft green and burgundy, and in No. 44, a standard twin, you will have a room with ample workspace and a bathroom loaded with shelf space. If you want even more room, ask for No. 43, a twin suite with a wall of windows and a peek at Hyde Park, or No. 24, with a bay window and sofa in the sitting room and a large bedroom facing the back that ensures calm and quiet. If you are traveling alone, you will definitely want to book No. 62, a spacious room with a large writing desk, ample shelf space, and a new bathroom with a tub and shower. Number 61 is also a great single, but just a bit smaller.

In the smartly attired Club Room you can read the daily papers while sipping a hot or cold drink. An express, Continental, or full-English breakfast, which you order the night before, is served in the comfort and privacy of your room.

TELEPHONE
020 7584 6274

FAX
020 7225 1635

EMAIL
theKGHotel@aol.com

INTERNET
www.theKGHotel.co.uk

CREDIT CARDS
AE, DC, MC, V

RATES
Single £110, double £145, suite £170, 3rd person in a room, £25; lower off-season rates subject to availability

BREAKFAST
Express £4, Continental £7, English £10.50

FACILITIES AND SERVICES: Air-conditioning, bar service, central heat, 2 direct-dial lines for phone and fax with private incoming numbers, hair dryers, laundry service, lift, data ports, room safe, satellite TV, tea and coffeemakers, trouser press, desk open 7:30 A.M.–10:30 P.M.; no smoking allowed

NEAREST TOURIST ATTRACTIONS: Shopping in Knightsbridge, Museum District, Royal Albert Hall

LUNA SIMONE HOTEL (34)
47–49 Belgrave Road, SW1
Tube: Pimlico, Victoria
36 rooms, 27 with shower or bath and toilet

TELEPHONE
020 7834 5897

FAX
020 7828 2474

EMAIL
lunasimone@talk21.com

INTERNET
www.lunasimonehotel.com

CREDIT CARDS
MC, V

RATES
Single £35–60, double £55–80, triple £80–110

BREAKFAST
English breakfast included

Belgrave Road is a good location if Victoria Station plays heavily in your London plans. However, because the street is loaded with grubby little B&Bs catering to determined budget travelers of all nationalities, it's all too easy to get stuck in a certified dump. To avoid that, head for one of the best selections on the street: the Luna Simone Hotel, owned for over thirty years by twin brothers Peter and Bernard Desira. The modern reception area has a curved desk backed by four clocks showing the time in New York, London, Tokyo, and Sydney. Keeping pace with the modern theme are two downstairs breakfast rooms with wooden bench and slat chair seating, recessed lighting, and a no-smoking policy. Eight bedrooms were refurbished in 2000, and more are scheduled to be done. The noise in rooms on the street will drive insomniacs mad, and those on the back have uninspiring views. Since there is no lift, those who are not prone to stair climbing should avoid No. 16, on the top floor, which requires a hike up eighty-six steps. But—and this is important—this very well maintained family-run hotel provides friendly, great-value accommodations consisting of a clean bed in a plain room with double-locked doors, your own cable TV, room safe, direct-dial telephone, electric kettle and hair dryer, plus a substantial English breakfast.

FACILITIES AND SERVICES: Central heat, direct-dial phones, hair dryers, office and room safe, cable TV, 24-hour desk; no lift

NEAREST TOURIST ATTRACTIONS: Victoria Station, Tate Britain

MELBOURNE HOUSE (35)
79 Belgrave Road, SW1
Tube: Pimlico, Victoria

16 rooms, 14 with shower or bath and toilet

When you look up and down Belgrave Road, all you see are signs for the numerous B&Bs that line both sides. These rooms range from cheap and cheerful to down-and-out dirty and depressing. Melbourne House falls into the cheap and cheerful category, thanks to the enthusiastic owners, John and Manuela Desira, whose cousins operate the Luna Simone down the street (see above). All sixteen exceptionally clean and whitewashed rooms are the same, with hot-pink chenille spreads, burgundy carpets, and brownish curtains. Laminated knotty-pine furniture and tiled baths with stall showers behind glass doors make housekeeping easy, as does the fact that the rooms are small and have limited or nonexistent seating space. The worst example of this is No. 5, nothing more than a small sleeping cubicle with no space for even a table. Numbers 7 and 8 seem a little larger, and are the only two with little balconies. The double-glazed windows in front drown out the incessant traffic noise that starts at 0-dark-hundred and goes until the wee hours, and wardrobes are there for a few hanging clothes. No smoking is allowed in any of the bedrooms. You are invited to watch cable TV or plug in a video in the lounge.

FACILITIES AND SERVICES: Central heat, direct-dial phones, free luggage storage, office safe, TV, tea and coffeemakers, desk open 7:30 A.M.–midnight; no lift, no smoking

NEAREST TOURIST ATTRACTIONS: Victoria Station, Tate Britain

TELEPHONE
020 7828 3516
FAX
020 7828 7120
EMAIL
melbournehousehotel@virgin.net
INTERNET
www.melbournehousehotel.co.uk
CREDIT CARDS
MC, V
RATES
Single £35–60, double £75–80, triple £100, family room £110–120
BREAKFAST
English or Continental breakfast included

MORGAN HOUSE (26)
120 Ebury Street, SW1
Tube: Victoria, Sloane Square

11 rooms, 3 with shower or bath and toilet

Rachel Joplin and Ian Berry are the friendly owners of two B&Bs on Ebury Street: this one and the Woodville, a little farther along the road (see page 141). For a small operation, the entryway at Morgan House is indeed grand, with a crystal chandelier hanging over white wainscoted walls with gold floral wallpaper on top. The miniature breakfast room is brightly outfitted in yellow, green, and blue, with a pine buffet. In the summer, there is a pretty garden in the back. Rooms are more than you

TELEPHONE
020 7730 2384
FAX
020 7730 8442
INTERNET
www.morganhouse.co.uk
CREDIT CARDS
MC, V
RATES
Single £45–65, double £65–85, triple £85–100, quad £95–100
BREAKFAST
English breakfast included

would expect for the price, offering an imaginative blend of mirrors, a black marble fireplace or two, and a smattering of antiques and metal bed frames added for spice. Bits and pieces of contemporary furniture à la Pier One or Cost Plus round out the picture. If you like noise, Nos. 3 and 7 are full of it, but it's better to request other rooms—perhaps No. 2, a basic double with some space; Room B, on the back, with a old, iron fireplace, twin beds, and shared facilities; or No. 9, the family room with a new white-tiled bathroom and a clever curtained wardrobe-closet. I would avoid Room A, a double on the street, with zip in the security department. Singles don't have private facilities, but you can rent a double (with bathroom) as a single for £70.

FACILITIES AND SERVICES: Electric heat, hair dryer available or in some rooms, office safe, TV, tea and coffeemakers, desk open 7:30 A.M.–10 P.M.; no private phones, no lift

NEAREST TOURIST ATTRACTIONS: Buckingham Palace, Royal Mews

NOËL COWARD HOTEL (28)
111 Ebury Street, SW1
Tube: Victoria, Sloane Square
14 rooms, 6 with shower, none with toilet

TELEPHONE
020 7730 2094
FAX
020 7730 8697
EMAIL
sirncoward@aol.com
INTERNET
www.noelcowardhotel.com
CREDIT CARDS
AE, DC, MC, V
RATES
Single £60–65, double £70–80, triple £95
BREAKFAST
Continental or English

From 1917 until 1930, actor and playwright Sir Noël Coward occupied the first two floors of this house, which belonged to his mother, who ran it as a boardinghouse. She lived in the bungalow that is still in back of the hotel with a garden beyond it, the servants lived in what is now the basement dining room, and Noël Coward had his room on the first floor (now No. 3 Piccadilly). After he moved out to much grander quarters, his mother sold the property, and since then a series of proprietors has run it as a B&B of varying quality. Now, thanks to owner Mark dos Santos, a true film buff and unabashed Noël Coward fan, the fourteen rooms, all named after tube stops in central London, are recommendable for anyone who can climb stairs and live in small rooms without private facilities. Fancy and large they are not . . . serviceable they are, each one with a framed film poster. Victoria, facing front, has two double beds, a shower, washbasin, television, and minibar. In Covent Gardens and Piccadilly you will find a marble fireplace and original bookshelf but no chairs. For stair climbers, Wimbledon, almost to the top, has twin beds but no sitting space. Because some of the hall bathrooms are unheated in winter, it would be wise to request a room with its own shower, even if they are what I call "phone booths" in the corner of the room. For theatergoers, the hotel can book tickets and sometimes offers theater promotions that give two tickets for the price of one for popular West End shows that have been selected by the hotel.

FACILITIES AND SERVICES: Individual room heaters and fans, hall phone, hair dryer available, laundry service, minibars, office safe, secretarial service and mobile phones on request, tea and coffeemakers, TV, theater promotions and bookings, advance arrangements can be made for guests to be met at Heathrow Airport, desk open 7:30 A.M.–11 P.M.; no lift

NEAREST TOURIST ATTRACTIONS: Buckingham Palace, Royal Mews

OXFORD HOUSE HOTEL (31)
92–94 Cambridge Street, SW1
Tube: Victoria
15 rooms, none with shower, bath, or toilet

If you want a family sort of place to stay, this could be your spot. All rooms have American-style wallpaper reasonably color coordinated with the curtains. Nothing is remotely contemporary, but the chenille spreads, stretched to almost cover the beds, blend in most of the time, and so do the carpets. The owners, Mr. and Mrs. Kader, live at the hotel with their two grown sons and their young families, along with pet rabbits, whistling birds, and cats. Over the years I have watched the boys grow from little chaps in short pants to one now an engineering graduate from Imperial College and married with children and another studying law. Before going to his office in the morning, Mr. Kader prepares breakfast in the open kitchen just off their downstairs dining room. During the day, Mrs. Kader or someone from the family is on duty. If you like this sort of old-hat, homespun lodging, send your one-night deposit soon. You must guarantee your first night with a credit card when booking, but avoid using your credit card to pay your bill at the hotel, as there will be a 5 percent surcharge.

FACILITIES AND SERVICES: Central heat, hall phones, hair dryer available, iron and ironing board in the kitchen, TV in lounge, desk open 7 A.M.–10 P.M.; no safe, no lift

NEAREST TOURIST ATTRACTIONS: Victoria Station

TELEPHONE
020 7834 6467/9681

FAX
020 7834 0225

CREDIT CARDS
MC, V to guarantee reservation (5% surcharge if bill is paid by credit card)

RATES
Single £40–45, double £50–55, triple £66–75, quad £90–95

BREAKFAST
English breakfast included

RYDER STREET CHAMBERS (4)
3 Ryder Street, SW1
Tube: Green Park, Piccadilly Circus
11 rooms, all with private bath and toilet

TELEPHONE
020 7930 2241

FAX
020 7839 2108

CREDIT CARDS
V

RATES
Single or double £110–130 per night, additional persons £18 per night

BREAKFAST
Not served

The Ryder Street Chambers are a Great Sleep in London run for years by a no-nonsense manager named Valerie May. No one could call them contemporary, but they are comfortable. Each "chamber" has a sitting room with a sofa bed, proper double or twin bedroom, bathroom, and a breakfast bar fitted with a toaster, electric kettle, small refrigerator, and the necessary dishes and utensils to prepare a simple breakfast or light meal. Fortnum and Mason's world-famous food hall is almost next door, in case you want to really indulge in wonderful gourmet goodies. Even though the chambers are not classified as a hotel, you will get Monday to Friday maid service, weekly linen changes, and twice weekly towel changes. Strongly in their favor, aside from their size, is the dynamite location, smack in the middle of St. James's, an enclave of London that is not known for anything in the budget category. From here you can easily walk to most West End theaters, Regent Street, Piccadilly Circus, Covent Garden, the National Gallery, the National Portrait Gallery, and the Royal Academy of Art. If your stay in London is going to be more than a few days, please consider the Valerie May London Apartments, see Other Options, page 213.

FACILITIES AND SERVICES: Central heat, direct-dial phone, lightly fitted kitchenette, lift, TV, office open Mon–Fri 9 A.M.–5 P.M.

NEAREST TOURIST ATTRACTIONS: Superb shopping, Green Park, West End

THE SANCTUARY HOUSE (11)
33 Tothill Street, SW1
Tube: St. James's Park
35 rooms, all with shower or bath and toilet

TELEPHONE
020 7799 4044

FAX
020 7799 3657

EMAIL
sanctuary@fullers.co.uk

INTERNET
www.fullers.co.uk

CREDIT CARDS
AE, DC, MC, V

RATES
Single or double £100, superior single or double £115, extra person £12, baby cots free

When I first heard about a Fuller's Brewery hotel with a pub below, I thought it would be a real dump, a hot sheet shop, or a bad joke. Let me tell you, it is none of these. The Sanctuary House is a very nice hotel with a no-surprise, coordinated decor that doesn't scream budget, and considering the central location, it has unbeatable rates, especially on the weekends. For trips farther afield, the tube stop is on the corner. The well-planned rooms are air-conditioned and have cable television, adequate space, open closets, and modern bathrooms. Two are fitted for handicapped travelers, and two floors are reserved for nonsmokers. If you like pub food and atmosphere, look no further than their pub downstairs, which serves everything from soup to traditional fish and chips, steak and ale pie, or a pastrami sandwich. For visitors who want to be on the other side of the River Thames, near Waterloo and all the exciting development taking place nearby, please see another Fuller's hotel and pub, The Mad Hatter, on page 184.

NOTE: The hotel generally closes between Christmas and New Year's; call to check.

FACILITIES AND SERVICES: Air-conditioning, central heat, bar/pub, direct-dial phone, hair dryer, laundry service, lift, office safe, restaurant, cable TV, tea and coffee-making facilities, trouser press, 2 floors with nonsmoking rooms, 2 rooms for handicapped, 24-hour desk

NEAREST TOURIST ATTRACTIONS: Westminster Abbey, Buckingham Palace, short walk to Trafalgar Square, Covent Garden, and the Strand

BREAKFAST
Continental breakfast £5,
English breakfast £8

SEARCY'S ROOF GARDEN ROOMS (9)
30 Pavilion Road, SW1
Tube: Knightsbridge

11 rooms, 2 flats, all with shower or bath and toilet

As the saying goes, you can't tell a book by its cover. Truer words were never spoken when it comes to this hotel only a heartbeat and credit card toss from Harrods, the designer boutiques along Sloane Street, and all of exclusive Knightsbridge. You arrive on a back street in front of an unassuming white building with a green door. You must press the buzzer by the door to be let in, then ride a red freight elevator to the third floor, where you will step into the comfortable world of Searcy's Roof Garden Rooms, a surprisingly peaceful London oasis owned and operated by Searcy's, one of London's finest catering firms. Each room is individually designed, the service is good, and the prices considerably lower than at most hotels in the area. All rooms are nonsmoking and nicely furnished, with pretty fabrics and a sprinkling of antiques you wish you could sneak home with you. Some rooms have canopy beds; others have sitting alcoves. A few of the rooms with baths are just that—a bathtub is right in the room, not in a separate bathroom. You are just going to have to trust me on this: Everything fits right in, and you *will* like it. A special room is No. 15, with a forest mural wrapping from the bedroom into the bathroom. Number 7 is a comfortable double with lots

TELEPHONE
020 7584 4921
FAX
020 7823 8694
EMAIL
rgr@searcys.co.uk
INTERNET
www.searcys.co.uk
CREDIT CARDS
AE, DC, MC, V
RATES
Single £95–125; double £135; suite £170 for two, £140 for one; apartment £200 per night; extra bed £15 per night
BREAKFAST
Continental breakfast included in hotel rate only

of space, especially in the bathroom, with a stretch tub and mirrored wall. *Lavender, pink,* and *feminine* are the words to describe single room No. 14, with a mural, tiled bath, and stall shower. Room 9, with a purple spring flower motif, is pictured on the brochure, and No. 5, with a sofa bed, comfortable wing chairs in a small lounge, end-to-end twins, and the bathtub in the room, is the only suite. A Continental breakfast is included, and it will be served in the comfort of your own room. Throughout the day, tea or coffee can be brought to your room, and in the summer, there is a sunny roof garden for guests to use.

If your stay is longer or you need more room, *one* of their two flats is worth consideration. The first is on Brompton Road and still is so desperately in need of renovation that it is out of the question until it is totally revamped and soundproofed. However, the second flat, on Beaufort Gardens, is completely recommended, provided you can be happy in a basement (lower ground floor) setting. It offers a sitting room, two bedrooms, a little terrace, a washer and dryer, and a small but fully fitted kitchen. You will never feel cheated by excessive add-on charges when dialing your friends and business colleagues, because the telephone is a pay phone that accepts credit cards and phone cards.

FACILITIES AND SERVICES: Electric heat, fans, direct-dial phones with private number, hair dryer, lift (but not to 4th floor), room service for breakfast, tea and coffee during the day, office safe, TV, some trouser presses, desk open 7:30 A.M.–11 P.M.

NEAREST TOURIST ATTRACTIONS: Hyde Park, Sloane Street, Knightsbridge shopping

TOPHAMS BELGRAVIA ($, 17)
28 Ebury Street, SW1
Tube: Knightsbridge
39 rooms, 37 with shower or bath and toilet

TELEPHONE
020 7730 8147

FAX
020 7823 5966

EMAIL
Tophams_Belgravia@
compuserve.com

INTERNET
www.tophams.co.uk

CREDIT CARDS
AE, DC, MC, V

How do I love Tophams Belgravia? I can't begin to count the ways. Behind the long success of this lovely hotel, wrapped in understated elegance and discreet British good taste, are three generations of the Topham family. Currently run by Marianne Topham and her husband, Nicholas Kingsford, the hotel has earned a worldwide reputation for caring for guests, who return year after year. Marianne Topham's artistic background is impressive. Her great-great-grandfather, noted artist

F. W. Topham, was a contemporary and friend of Charles Dickens and also illustrated some of his work. Marianne studied art at the Byam School of Art and, having worked with many prominent interior designers and architects, including Nina Campbell, David Hicks, and Christopher Smallwood, has developed into one of England's best-known visual artists. In addition to her beautiful decoration of the entire hotel, guests are also treated to displays of her lovely oils and watercolors, which are available for purchase.

The individually created bedrooms in the five adjoining buildings have the friendly feel of a country home, with flowery Colefax and Fowler fabrics, little sitting alcoves where guests can take tea or read a newspaper, and loads of family antiques. The dedicated staff has been with the hotel for decades. While the rates dictate that your stay will be a Big Splurge, there is often a package of some sort on offer during the off-seasons.

The comfort of each guest is always the primary consideration. Bedrooms are furnished in the genteel style of an old-fashioned home, with attention to the details that transform an impersonal hotel room into a pleasing temporary residence: a pretty plate hanging on the wall, a framed lithograph, a Limoges vase filled with spring flowers, hidden televisions, comfortable chairs, writing space, and plenty of closets. With thirty-nine outstanding rooms, it is almost impossible to select a favorite (two of the single rooms have hall bathrooms, but they are completely private to those rooms). However, some stand out, such as No. 9, with a tiny room sink and a canopy bed; it was the favorite of Sir Michael Redgrave when he stayed at the hotel in his early theater days. It is a quiet room, with soft chairs and French floral prints on the bed pillows, canopy, and drapes. Newer and slightly more expensive are the seven mews rooms on the lower ground floor. They are a sterling example of how to use otherwise wasted space and transform it into rooms filled with charm and appeal. Mews 5 is tucked into the old cellars and decorated in pink and white stripes. There is no real view, but no one seems to mind. In Mews 4 you will sleep in a four-poster bed, and in Mews 2, a popular triple, there is a separate room with a twin bed—ideal for a small family with one child or to use as a sitting room. Another popular family room is No. 39, done in white wicker with a separate sleeping loft under a sloping roof that is a favorite with children.

RATES
Single £120, double £130–160, triple £180; cancellations must be made at least 48 hours prior to date of intended arrival or there will be a 1-night room charge; off-season package rates on request

BREAKFAST
English breakfast included

If you are a man traveling alone, request No. 17, which was especially decorated for a particular American guest who visits London frequently. The theme of the room is cricket, carried out by hanging cricket bats, trophies, and a series of black-and-white photos of this man's school days. An interesting room for some might be No. 15, a small double or perfect single, with a direct view of Margaret Thatcher's London townhouse.

Lunch, Monday through Friday, and dinner, Monday through Saturday, are served in No. 26, the street-side restaurant, which is also open to the general public. The menu runs from simple sandwiches, omelettes, and filled jacket potatoes to three-course meals, all well prepared and served with care.

Another *very* special feature of this extraordinary hotel is Jennifer Dorn. Ms. Dorn is a noted travel authority on Great Britain, and she runs her own consulting business in New York called Oh, to Be in England. As a complimentary favor of the hotel to its American guests, the services of Ms. Dorn are included. When your reservation is confirmed, she will contact you and, if you wish, help you to organize your trip to London or anywhere else you might be traveling in the U.K. Even if you don't stay at Tophams Belgravia, please consider using her services. When you think of what you could save in time, energy, and money on costly mistakes, it is worth the investment. You can contact her by writing, calling, faxing, or emailing her at: Oh, to Be in England, 2 Charlton Street, No. 10E, New York, NY 10014; Tel: 212-255-8739; Fax: 646-336-8692; Email: randjdorn@aol.com; Internet: www.tobeinengland.com.

NOTE: The hotel is closed from December 23 until January 2 or 3.

FACILITIES AND SERVICES: Bar, central heat, direct-dial phones, hair dryer, laundry service, lift, restaurant and room service, office safe, satellite TV, tea and coffee-makers, 24-hour desk, complimentary travel planning services with Jennifer Dorn's Oh to Be in England

NEAREST TOURIST ATTRACTIONS: Buckingham Palace, Royal Mews, Westminster

WINCHESTER HOTEL (24)
17 Belgrave Road, SW1
Tube: Victoria

18 rooms, 4 flats, all with shower or bath and toilet

If you are a Great Sleeper looking for a bed for the night with grease-infused bacon, eggs, and beans on your breakfast plate in the morning, you are in the right place on Belgrave Road. Of course, there are exceptions, and the Winchester Hotel is one of them. The hotel also goes on to prove that you don't absolutely have to be high-tech or accept plastic money to be a success in the hotel business. Jimmy McGoldrick's Winchester Hotel is a class act, offering all the benefits of a small hostelry that prides itself on the high standards of comfort and service expected by today's travelers. It is not cute and cozy, nor is it filled with English antiques and picture-postcard floral displays. However, it is well thought out, with acceptable color and fabric coordination and good maintenance. All rooms have an armchair, enough closet space, reading lights, and tiled private bathrooms with high-pressure showers, a real bonus for those tired of holding a limp nozzle with two weak squirts of water erratically spraying. If noise disturbs your sleeping patterns, avoid front-facing rooms. For guests looking for the space and independence of a private apartment, four fully equipped units display the same attention to detail as the hotel rooms. An added treat for both hotel and flat residents is the English breakfast, cooked personally for you by Jimmy in his stainless-steel kitchen.

NOTE: The hotel is closed Christmas day.

FACILITIES AND SERVICES: Central heat, hair dryer available, office safe, TV, all flats have daily maid service and linen change, office open 7 A.M.–midnight; no private phones, no lift, no tea or coffee-making facilities

NEAREST TOURIST ATTRACTIONS: Victoria Station, walk to Tate Britain

TELEPHONE
020 7828 2972

FAX
020 7828 5191

CREDIT CARDS
None; cash only

RATES
No singles, 1–2 people £85, triple £120, family room £140; *flats* (no children under 12): 1 bedroom £120 per night, 2 bedroom for 4 people £240 per night; 7-day cancellation policy

BREAKFAST
English breakfast included for both hotel and flats

WINDERMERE HOTEL (32)
142–144 Warwick Way, SW1
Tube: Victoria

22 rooms, 20 with shower or bath and toilet

Nick and Sylvia Hambi are a hardworking, friendly couple who take very good care of their guests. Just glance through their visitors' book at reception to see the comments from contented travelers from around the world who stay here time and again.

TELEPHONE
020 7834 5163/5480

FAX
020 7630 8831

EMAIL
windermere@compuserve.com

INTERNET
www.windermere-hotel.co.uk

CREDIT CARDS
AE, MC, V

RATES
Single £70–95, double £90–
140, triple £150, quad £140;
cancellations must be received
72 hours in advance

BREAKFAST
English breakfast included

The building has an interesting history dating back to medieval England, when Warwick Way was called "The Abbot's Lane" because it was the road that connected Westminster Abbey with the abbot's residence, known as Abbot's Grange. The hotel stands at the point where the gate to the Abbot's Grange existed. The Victorian building now housing the hotel was constructed in 1857 and was known as the "Pimlico Rooms," the earliest B&B in the area. During the past twelve years that I have been including the Windermere Hotel in *Cheap Sleeps in London* and now in *Great Sleeps London,* I have watched it grow and improve by leaps and bounds. Nick is a go-getter who must lie awake nights devising ways to improve his twenty-two-room hotel, and he succeeds on every level. All the individually arranged and decorated rooms offer travelers up-to-the-minute benefits. In addition to color coordination, recessed lighting, satellite television, and a private safe, he has installed data ports so you can check your email or go on the Internet. I like the Cartmel Room, named after an area near Lake Windermere. Newly decorated in soft yellow and green, it offers a sitting area, two phones, two windows, and is exclusively nonsmoking. No. 11 is a floral-themed, nonsmoking corner room with plenty of natural light and a king-size bed that can be split into twins if requested. In the bathroom, you will have a glass stall shower, heated towel racks, and plenty of towels. Some rooms on the front are noisy. Double glazing on the windows helps, but if you are a light snoozer, get a room in the back. Bathrooms come with heated towel racks in most, hair dryers in all, and very good showerheads. I also like the fact that there is a restaurant, the Pimlico Room, which is open for dinner not only to hotel guests but to the neighborhood regulars. This convenience pays dividends if you are trying to make an early curtain call, cannot face going out again after a hard day traipsing through London, or have tired and hungry children on your hands.

FACILITIES AND SERVICES: Bar and restaurant, central heat, fans, direct-dial phones, hair dryer, ISDN line, data ports, public car park next door with special rates, room service, room safe, satellite TV, 2 floors exclusively nonsmoking, tea and coffeemakers, some trouser presses, 24-hour desk; no lift

NEAREST TOURIST ATTRACTIONS: Victoria Station, brisk walk to Westminster Cathedral and Tate Britain

WOODVILLE HOUSE (29)
107 Ebury Street, SW1
Tube: Victoria, Sloane Square

12 rooms, none with shower, bath, or toilet

Ian Berry and Rachel Joplin own the Woodville House, which reminds me of comfy Olde England thanks to its creatively compacted rooms, many wrapped in typical cabbage-rose wallpaper and highlighted by almost and real antiques. Beyond the narrow Georgian entry are two breakfast rooms, accented by floor-to-ceiling gold-toned silk draperies and a view onto a garden wall. The house cat, Beasty, who has a definite preference for men, reigns supreme here and on the hotel patio.

Room A, designed for families, is on the ground level. If you like warm and fuzzy, this is your room. Bunk beds help create more space, and the collection of teddy bears occupying a corner spot adds a welcoming touch that is appreciated by young guests. Family Room C is also home to related bears and has access to the patio, but I think it needs a quick facelift. If you like English flowered wallpaper, No. 6, a twin with minicoronets over the bed, a detailed ceiling, and wooden window shutters, should satisfy all cravings for some time to come. Aside from the overdose of florals, the focal piece in this room is a Parisian Victorian morning clock. Another handsome clock, a copy of a Louis XIV timepiece, sits in No. 4, a more subdued choice with a white and brass-tipped metal bed draped in a lacey cover. The hotel is under the same ownership as the Morgan House, also on Ebury Street (see page 131).

FACILITIES AND SERVICES: Air-conditioning in three rooms, electric heat, hall phones, hair dryer, iron and ironing board available, TV, guest refrigerator, electric kettle, complimentary cookies to go with your tea or coffee, desk open 7 A.M.–11 P.M.; no lift, no safe

NEAREST TOURIST ATTRACTIONS: Buckingham Palace, Royal Mews

TELEPHONE
020 7730 1048

FAX
020 7730 2574

INTERNET
www.woodvillehouse.co.uk

CREDIT CARDS
MC, V

RATES
Single £45, double £65, family rooms for 3–5 people £85–115

BREAKFAST
English breakfast included

SW3

Chelsea

TOURIST ATTRACTIONS
Chelsea Old Church, Thames
River, Chelsea Royal Hospital,
Sloane Square, King's Road

In the nineteenth century, Chelsea gained fame as London's Bohemia, where writers and artists lived. Stroll along Cheyne Walk (pronounced chainy), which runs along the Thames, and look for the plaques marking the homes where George Eliot, Charles Swinburne, George Meredith, Henry James, James McNeill Whistler, and J. M. W. Turner lived. Thomas Carlyle and Oscar Wilde also lived in the neighborhood. Outside the Chelsea Old Church is a statue of Thomas More, the first famous resident. It is unlikely the area will ever again be an impoverished artists' colony, because now it is one of the most desirable London neighborhoods, and one of the most costly. Chelsea is also where garden and flower enthusiasts from around the globe congregate in May for the dazzling Chelsea Flower Show. The rest of the year, the serene Chelsea Physic Garden, London's first botanical garden, draws visitors. King's Road, starting at Sloane Square and lined with boutiques and restaurants, two supermarkets, and a movie theater, runs the length of Chelsea. When you are walking along, keep your eye out for the distinguished elderly gentlemen wearing smart dark blue and red uniforms and black hats. These are the well-loved Chelsea pensioners, who live at the Royal Hospital Chelsea and serve as the area's goodwill ambassadors. King's Road is one of London's most popular upmarket shopping destinations for everyone from pre-teens to thirty- or forty-somethings. Sloane Square is where you will rub cashmere-clad elbows with the Sloane Rangers, London's equivalent of yuppies and DINKS (Double Income, No Kids couples). You will find them out in full force on Saturdays around Peter Jones department store and browsing through the General Trading Company or in Habitat, picking up a few essentials for their newly redone townhouse. As you wander down King's Road, take a few detours on some of the side streets, where you will see brightly painted mews houses with manicured postage-stamp gardens.

HOTELS IN SW3

OTHER OPTIONS

Apartment Rentals

Bed and Breakfast in a Private Home

Student Dormitories

($) indicates a Big Splurge

SW3

HYDE PARK

Kensington

Kensington Gore

ROYAL ALBERT HALL

KNIGHTSBRIDGE

Ennismore

Prince's

Queen's Gate

Prince Consort Road

Exhibition

Ennismore Gardens

Gardens

Queen's Gate Ter.

Imperial College Road

Gardens

Garden

Elvaston Place

SCIENCE MUSEUM

Road

VICTORIA AND ALBERT MUSEUM

Queen's Gate Pl.

NATURAL HISTORY MUSEUM

Brompton

Cromwell Road

THURLOE SQUARE

Gloucester Road ⊖

Stanhope

Queen's

Thurloe St.

South Ter.

⊖ South Kensington

Gardens

Harrington Road

Pelham Street

Pelham Cr.

Gate

SOUTH KENSINGTON

Gloucester Rd.

Brompton

Road

Sumner

ONSLOW SQUARE

Cranley Pl.

Place

Road

Rosary Gdns.

Old

Onslow Gdns.

Foulis Ter.

Fulham

Pond Place

Sydney

Cranley Gdns.

Neville Ter.

Roland Gardens

South Parade

Street

Drayton

Evelyn

CHELSEA SQ.

Dovehouse Street

19▲

Priory Wk.

Gardens

Gardens

Elm Park

Old Church St.

Manresa Rd.

CARLYLE SQ.

Gilston Road

Fulham Road

Gardens

Glebe Pl.

Redcliffe Rd.

•21 Elm Park Rd.

Mulberry Walk

Seymour Walk

Park

Beaufort St.

King's Road

Old Church St.

Limerston St.

Walk

PAULTONS SQUARE

Up. Cheyne St.

Edith Grove

Gertrude St.

Beaufort St.

Danvers St.

Lamont Rd.

King's Road

Cheyne

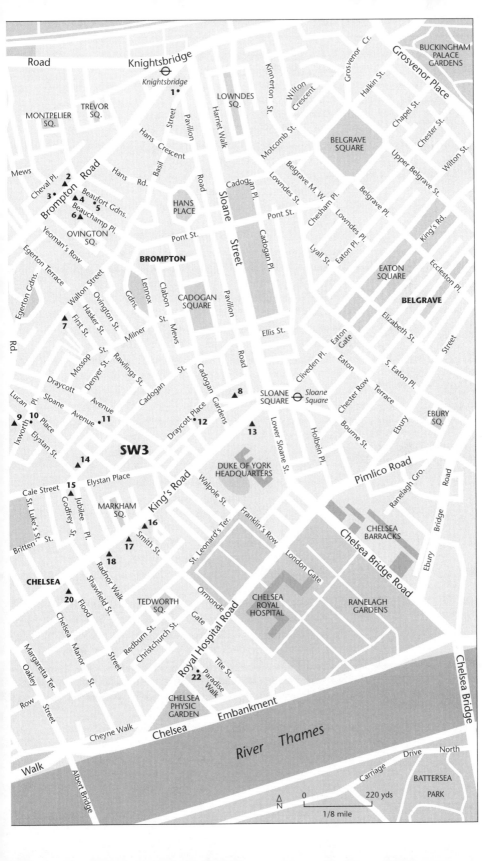

THE BASIL STREET HOTEL ($, 1)
Basil Street, SW3
Tube: Knightsbridge

93 rooms, all with shower or bath and toilet

TELEPHONE
020 7581 3311/7225 9807,
800-448-8355 (toll-free in the
U.S., UTELL International)

FAX
020 7581 3693

EMAIL
reservations@thebasil.com

INTERNET
www.thebasil.com

CREDIT CARDS
AE, DC, MC, V

RATES
Single from £135, double from
£195, family room from £260
(2 bedrooms and 1 bath for 2
adults and up to 3 children),
extra bed £20; Rack rates do
not include 17.5% VAT.
Reduced rates for stays of 5
nights or longer, on weekends
with a minimum stay of 2
nights, during Christmas, the
January sales, throughout
August and on bank holidays.
The Basilite Scheme, with
special rates and privileges, is
available to guests who visit 5
times in 3 consecutive years.

BREAKFAST
Continental breakfast £10,
English breakfast £15

The Basil Street Hotel began when Mr. Charles Winslow-Taylor bought the hotel in 1910. During the 1920s, extensive construction enabled him to realize his dream of creating a home away from home in the heart of Knightsbridge, one of London's most exclusive areas. Today the Basil Street Hotel remains family owned, one among a handful of large London hotels that do not belong to a larger group or consortium. With two grand-daughters now at the helm, the Basil Street celebrates more than ninety years of providing a "hotel for people who don't like hotels." As one guest said, "I knew I would like the hotel when I arrived and discovered that my room, No. 278 I think, was on the third floor, and that No. 305 was on the second. You've got to love a hotel with that kind of disdain for conformity."

Throughout its long history, the hotel has adapted to the ever more demanding standards of its faithful guests, but one essential quality remains unchanged: the style and personal service we remember from a more generous and gracious age. The staff's devotion to duty is remarkable. The hotel has 106 staff members, and a third of them have served the hotel loyally for ten years or more; seven have more than twenty-five years of service, and two more than thirty-five years. The three senior managers have more than a hundred years of service between them. The real service awards, however, go to the two Polish porters who arrived in 1949 and retired at ages eighty and eighty-four in 1993.

The hotel has the hospitable air of a spacious country home where you would like to live forever. Rooms and corridors are fitted with admirable examples of the family's lovely English furniture and collectibles, including pieces of Sheraton and Hepplewhite, and the largest collection of mezzotints in Great Britain. In the entrance hall is a magnificent lantern that once hung in the Duke of Norfolk's home in St. James's Square. If you look, you will see his crown, which is the hotel's logo. Each bedroom differs in size, shape, and decoration, but all meet every standard of quality, taste, and comfort any guest could ever want. In keeping with today's electronic world, there is now a Business Center with fax, photocopier, computer with a color laser printer and scanner, email, and direct access to the Internet.

In 1971, a unique club for women was established in the stunning Art Deco lounge. The Parrot Club took its name from Basil, the resident parrot who greeted guests for many years. During his hotel residency, the waiters taught him disreputable language, and he had to be retired, so he was sent away to luxurious exile, where he enjoyed himself until a ripe old age. Mothers, daughters, and granddaughters continue to gather at this ladies-only retreat, which is not only a welcome refuge from busy London but a base for businesswomen seeking a quiet place to meet clients, send and receive messages, entertain guests for morning coffee, lunch, or afternoon tea, or use the office facilities. Men are allowed, but only in the company of a woman. Women hotel guests are invited to use the Parrot Club freely during their stay, which is appreciated by those who are traveling alone and need office support or must conduct business meetings. That is not all the club offers. You can order morning coffee, a light lunch, or a glass of champagne, call for a taxi, book theater tickets, take a shower, press your ball gown, change your child's nappy, prepare its bottle and arrange for a baby-sitter, or borrow an umbrella. If you are staying long enough, you may be able to attend one of their interesting lectures or perhaps squeeze in a quick day trip to Paris that includes shopping and guided tours of some of the smaller museums.

For many of the guests who call this their London home, the hotel developed the Basilite Scheme, which entitles frequent visitors (those who've had five stays within the past three years) to significant discounts and privileges; call, fax, or email the hotel for details. There are also special rates for minimum two-night weekend stays and for stays of five nights or more, and discounts are offered through August, on bank holidays, Christmas, and during the January sales. That last discount time period alone could tip the scales for some dedicated shoppers, because Harrods is just around the corner.

If that isn't enough, there is a comfortable lounge where afternoon tea is served, a bar, and a beautifully appointed dining room where members of the Royal College of Music play four nights a week, starting at 7 P.M.

Reservations are not held beyond 4 P.M. unless guaranteed. If rooms are canceled after 12 P.M. on the day prior to arrival, one night's accommodation will be charged unless the room is relet. Whenever you cancel, be sure to get a cancellation number, because claims for refunds are considered only when a cancellation number is quoted.

FACILITIES AND SERVICES: Air-conditioning on request at no additional cost, bar, central heat, direct-dial phones with voice mail, additional phone line on request, data ports, hair dryer, electric kettle on request, ironing room, laundry service, lift, 2 parking spaces (must be booked—£22 per 24 hours), Parrot Club, business center, restaurant and room service, office safe, satellite TV, radio, clock, theater bookings, 24-hour desk, concierge porter, meeting rooms, 1 floor exclusively reserved for nonsmoking guests

NEAREST TOURIST ATTRACTIONS: Hyde Park, Sloane Street, Royal Albert Hall, Museum District, Knightsbridge shopping

CHELSEA GREEN HOTEL (10)
35 Ixworth Place, SW3
Tube: South Kensington, Sloane Square
46 rooms, all with shower, bath, and toilet

TELEPHONE
020 7225 7500

FAX
020 7225 7555

EMAIL
ccghotel@dircon.co.uk

INTERNET
www.welcome2London.com

CREDIT CARDS
AE, DC, MC, V

RATES
Single £150, double £180, suites £240–260, Thai suite £300; special rates on request for direct bookings with the hotel, discounts on weekend stays that include a Saturday night

BREAKFAST
Continental breakfast included, English breakfast £6.95

The Chelsea Green Hotel is a renovated townhouse hotel in a quiet part of Chelsea that is synonymous with style and good taste. The King's Road is only a few blocks away, scores of recommended restaurants are in the neighborhood, and two tube stops plus numerous buses make getting around the rest of London very easy. With one notable exception, the forty-six comfortably spacious rooms and suites are luxuriously furnished in the traditional English manner. All are equipped with air-conditioning, luggage and closet space, and a room safe large enough for a laptop computer. Several connect, many are exclusively nonsmoking, and all face outward. The modern marble bathrooms include magnifying mirrors, terry-cloth robes, a telephone, and a scale. The suites have the added benefit of a separate sitting room with a sofa, easy chairs with ottomans, two televisions, and Jacuzzi bathtubs. If you want to celebrate an anniversary or pamper someone very special, consider the magnificent Thai Suite, which is based on those in the Oriental Hotel in Bangkok. The walls are covered in grass cloth, and the floors are polished wood. All the handmade furniture and Thai silks were shipped in from Thailand. The bed, draped in vibrant colors and pillows, looks like a playing field. In one corner of the suite is a lovely screened cabinet and a walk-in closet with a special dressing area and red silk-covered sitting stools. The bathroom is large enough to house both a Jacuzzi and a steam shower. There is even a little kitchen, in case you aren't tempted to go out for meals. Breakfast is served in a beautiful glass conservatory highlighted with green plants and a real tree in the middle. Those in London on business can reserve either of the two conference rooms, and anyone planning a party can book one to be fitted with a dance floor and orchestra.

FACILITIES AND SERVICES: Air-conditioning, central heat, bar, minibar, 2 conference rooms, 2 direct-dial phones with voice mail in all rooms, hair dryer, laundry service, 2 lifts, data ports, parking with a 10% discount at a nearby car park, room safe, nonsmoking rooms, cable/satellite TV, tea and coffee-making facilities, concierge, porter, 24-hour desk

NEAREST TOURIST ATTRACTIONS: King's Road, brisk walk to Museum District

KNIGHTSBRIDGE HOTEL ($, 5)
12 Beaufort Gardens, SW3
Tube: Knightsbridge

40 rooms, 10 flats, all with shower or bath and toilet

Occupying a prime position on tree-lined Beaufort Gardens, only a whisper away from Harrods, the fully equipped Knightsbridge Hotel meets the needs and expectations of travelers in the Big Splurge category. If I listed every service and facility offered, I would not have space to tell you about the lovely accommodations. Even though there is a full-time maintenance person on duty, ten private apartments with enviable kitchens, and a very outgoing staff, what good is it all if your room is unpleasant and you feel as though you are living in a cell? This will never happen here. The professionally orchestrated rooms are large enough for a long stay and complemented by traditional fabrics, marble and tiled bathrooms with Jacuzzis in some, and walk-on balconies in others. Two executive rooms on the back of the hotel (Nos. 311 and 312) have small sitting rooms with pitched ceilings and gray-tiled baths with gold fixtures. Number 202 is a split-level choice with a king-size bed upstairs and a Jacuzzi with steam jets in the downstairs bathroom, which is off a pleasant sitting room. The deluxe apartments not only have washers and dryers, but also dishwashers and microwaves, plus all the other equipment you'll need to prepare everything from a cup of tea to your Christmas goose. Number 421 is a good example, with two televisions, a large bedroom, and a

TELEPHONE
020 7589 9271

FAX
020 7823 9692

EMAIL
reception@
knightsbridgehotel.co.uk

INTERNET
www.knightsbridgehotel.co.uk

CREDIT CARDS
AE, DC, MC, V

RATES
Single £120–140, double £160–210, triple £210, flats £175–300; 10% discount for weekly stays, special rates on request in low season, promotional rates throughout the year

BREAKFAST
English breakfast included

modern kitchen with a microwave and a four-burner stove. To make the hotel more appealing, there are promotional rates, a 10 percent discount for weekly stays, and special rates during the low seasons.

FACILITIES AND SERVICES: Air-conditioning included in ground-floor rooms, otherwise on request (£10 supplement), central heat, conference facilities and secretarial services, direct-dial phones, fax machine and private line in room or suite on request, hair dryer, ironing facility, laundry service, lift to all hotel rooms and most of the flats, minibar with complimentary drinks, room safe, satellite TV with in-house movies, trouser press, Jacuzzis in some rooms, fully fitted kitchens in all flats

NEAREST TOURIST ATTRACTIONS: Museum District, Royal Albert Hall, Knightsbridge shopping

SLOANE HOTEL ($, 12)
29 Draycott Place, SW3
Tube: Sloane Square, South Kensington
12 rooms, all with shower, bath, and toilet

TELEPHONE
020 7581 5757, 800-324-9960
(toll-free in the U.S.)
FAX
020 7584 1348
EMAIL
sloanehotel@btinternet.com
INTERNET
www.premierhotels.com
CREDIT CARDS
AE, DC, MC, V
RATES
Single or double £150–195,
Gallery Suite £240, 17.5%
VAT extra
BREAKFAST
Continental breakfast £9,
English breakfast £12

The chic Sloane Hotel sits in the middle of a row of red brick Victorian townhouses. You will know you have arrived when you see the British Union Jack flying in front and the discreet brass nameplate by the front door. The hotel is known for offering its eclectic guests the standards of service and style they have come to expect and demand from a distinguished London boutique hotel. Vintage Louis Vuitton luggage is used for decoration throughout the hotel, and if you see a piece you like, it's all for sale. So is everything else, for that matter, including the antiques, objets d'art, the four-poster beds—provided you arrange for the shipping. Most guests are not here to shop, but to sleep, and they will do that very well in the individually designed and fitted rooms. Even the simplest room, a small, standard-ground floor double, has charm and appeal. Number 602 is dramatically done with burgundy enameled walls and a mirrored backdrop behind the bed, which is covered with a white cotton bedspread and needlepoint throw pillows. Two beautiful Chinese vases and a wall hung with assorted framed pictures of Victorian ladies add interest. In the bathroom, there is a long narrow bath with a tub and fixed shower over it, and loads of Molton Brown toiletries. A little larger and definitely more sumptuous is No. 302, the Gallery Suite. This is a duplex that features a small sitting mezzanine, an impressive collection of Blue Willow plates, a romantic four-poster bed, two antique Louis Vuitton trunks, a hand-painted drop-leaf desk, and a marble and mirrored bathroom. No. 402, which is a double with a sitting room, is done in dramatic black and white and features a small terrace. Breakfast, which is generally served in the rooms, can be ordered with organic produce and other healthy foods. On warm days, guests can enjoy breakfast or a drink on the rooftop terrace, with views over Chelsea.

FACILITIES AND SERVICES: Air-conditioning, central heat, direct-dial phone, hair dryer, laundry service, lift to all but top floor, data ports, office safe, 24-hour room service for light meals, cable/satellite TV, VCR and free videos, car and driver available, 24-hour desk

NEAREST TOURIST ATTRACTIONS: King's Road, Sloane Square

SW5

Earl's Court

Earl's Court is usually a reliable, if seedy barometer of the changes in social and political pressure in the world beyond. When anything happens on some outcrop of the globe with an unpronounceable name, it will show up a few months later on Earl's Court Road. The street swarms with the world's latest arrivals.

—*Jonathan Raban,* Arabia through the Looking Glass, *1979*

TOURIST ATTRACTIONS
Earl's Court Exhibition Centre

Earl's Court is often called "Kangaroo Court," because it serves as unofficial headquarters for London's sizable Australian student community. It is also known for its two large exhibition centers: Earl's Court and Olympia. The area has a mixed bag of hotels, ranging from charming antiques-filled restored townhouses to chains and some of the worst fleabags London has to offer. Many accommodations are geared toward people with low budgets. To go with these cheap sleeps are a multitude of low-cost restaurants and chain burger joints, with only a handful serving anything approaching quality food. From a tourist's point of view, the area offers very little. The major reason I see to recommend it is if you are involved in an event at one of the exhibition centers and either need a cheap sleep or can spring for something listed in the following section that does not represent the underside of Earl's Court. Transportation is good from the Earl's Court tube: you have a direct link to Heathrow Airport and about a thirty-minute ride to the action in central London.

HOTELS IN SW5

OTHER OPTIONS
Apartment Rentals

Hostels

($) indicates a Big Splurge

SW5, SW7, SW10

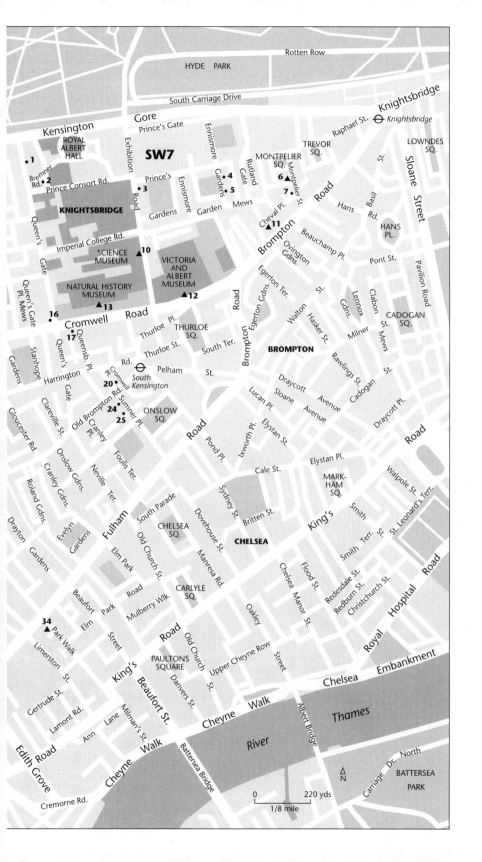

AMSTERDAM HOTEL (29)
7 Trebovir Road, SW5
Tube: Earl's Court

19 rooms, 8 flats, all with shower or bath and toilet

TELEPHONE
020 7370 2814/5084

FAX
020 7244 7608

EMAIL
reservations@
amsterdamhotel.com

INTERNET
www.amsterdamhotel.com

CREDIT CARDS
MC, V

RATES
Single £78–86, double £84–102, triple £112–116, family £122–132; apartments (studio to 2 bedrooms) £105–170

BREAKFAST
Continental breakfast included, English breakfast £3

The appealing plant-lined entry has a corner seating area and a collection of Thomas McKnight prints of world-famous vacation destinations. While the following may not seem like much, in this corner of London they are notable: the Amsterdam has a lift to all floors in the hotel (and to the third floor for the apartments), individually controlled room heat, a twenty-four-hour porter, and guest fax and copying facilities. All the nineteen cheerful and bright rooms have slightly differing colors and functional bathrooms. Number 2 is typical, with the added bonus of being accessible to the garden. In addition to the hotel rooms, there are eight apartments ranging in size from a studio to two bedrooms. On first glance they are very nice, with coordinated fabrics and enough space to move around and live in. On second look I realized the following flat basics were missing in most: a work area, dining table and chairs, and drawer space. The kitchens are fitted with a microwave and small refrigerator. There are no stoves, thanks to the many thoughtless guests who literally trashed the cooking area, thus forcing the owner to redecorate and eliminate them altogether.

FACILITIES AND SERVICES: Central heat, direct-dial phones, hair dryer available, tea and coffeemakers, kitchens with microwave and refrigerator in the apartments, lift to all floors in hotel (and to the 3rd floor for apartments), office safe, nonsmoking rooms, TV, 24-hour desk, guest fax and copy services

NEAREST TOURIST ATTRACTIONS: Earl's Court Exhibition Centre

BEAVER HOTEL (30)
57–59 Philbeach Gardens, SW5
Tube: Earl's Court (take the Warwick Road exit)

38 rooms, 22 with shower or bath and toilet

TELEPHONE
020 7373 4553

FAX
020 7373 4555

CREDIT CARDS
AE, DC, MC, V

RATES
Single £45–60, double £60–85, triple £95; lower rates for weekly stays and readers of this book

In this far corner of London, the well-kept Beaver Hotel delivers more for your battered cheap-sleeping pound than most. Bonus points are earned for their car park, which charges an unbelievably low twenty-four-hour fee of £5; a 5 percent discount for *Great Sleeps London* readers and a 10 percent discount for longer stays; and complimentary tea and coffee available whenever you want. The simple rooms are clean and vary from small without chair space or bath to reasonably spacious with all facilities. They are priced accordingly, starting at £45 for a snug single. Number 27 is new, with a small entryway leading to a simple room with an open closet, three drawers, a built-in desk, two wooden folding chairs, and a nice green and gold fabric used for the curtains and bedspread. The bathroom has an enclosed shower and two windows. It sells as a double, but I think it would make a better single. Other new rooms include Nos. 19, 28, and 44. More are planned. The wood-paneled Austrian-style breakfast room has cushioned chairs and banquettes. For socializing, you can play pool in the next room or join the sports fans who gather around the satellite television in the lounge. The tube stop is only a five-minute walk away, and the management is accommodating—two more reasons this is a good pick if Earl's Court is your stomping ground.

FACILITIES AND SERVICES: Central heat, direct-dial phones, hair dryers in rooms with private bathrooms, laundry service, parking (£5 per day), complimentary tea and coffee, TV in rooms with private bathrooms, office safe, lift, office open 7:30 A.M.–midnight; non-smoking rooms on ground floor

NEAREST TOURIST ATTRACTIONS: Earl's Court Exhibition Centre

BREAKFAST
English breakfast included

BURNS HOTEL (28)
18 Barkston Gardens, SW5
Tube: Earl's Court
105 rooms, all with shower, bath, and toilet

The Burns Hotel offers 105 recently revamped, surprise-free rooms that could be in a mid-range hotel in any large city. The rooms are geared toward the business and convention clientele who stay here when they want to be near the Earl's Court and Olympia exhibition centers and have a direct tube link to Heathrow Airport. Unless you fall into that camp or can get a great corporate rate, I would suggest opting for someplace else at the same price in a more interesting part of London. The lobby and reception area is capped by a chandelier and mirrored ceiling that reflects the tartan carpet and two high-back chairs by the windows. A uniformed, multilingual staff runs the desk. Efficiency is their strong suit; unfortunately, friendliness is replaced by feigned indifference. The rooms have all the usual features, including adequate luggage and wardrobe space and bathrooms

TELEPHONE
020 7373 3151 (direct to hotel), 020 7221 1400 (central reservations)

FAX
020 7370 4090 (direct to hotel), 020 7229 3917 (central reservations)

EMAIL
BurnsHotel@vienna-group.co.uk

INTERNET
www.vienna-group.co.uk

CREDIT CARDS
AE, DC, MC, V

RATES
Single £120, double £145–175, triple £155

BREAKFAST
Continental breakfast £6.75, English breakfast £9.75

with good showers and heated towel bars. There is a dining room overlooking a terrace, but it has a rather forlorn dinner atmosphere, as most of the guests hang out in the comfortable bar in the evening and snack on bar food, probably too full from their business lunches to face much more than a sandwich or fish and chips.

FACILITIES AND SERVICES: Central heat, fans on request, bar, direct-dial phones with data ports planned, hair dryer, laundry service, lift, office safe with £1 access charge, tea and coffeemakers, satellite TV, trouser press, nonsmoking rooms on 3rd and 4th floors, restaurant for breakfast and dinner, 24-hour desk and room service

NEAREST TOURIST ATTRACTIONS: Earl's Court Exhibition Centre, brisk walk to the Museum District

THE CRANLEY ($, 26)
10–12 Bina Gardens, SW5
Tube: Gloucester Road

38 rooms, all with shower or bath and toilet

TELEPHONE
020 7373 0123; 800-553-2582
(toll-free from the U.S.)

FAX
020 7373 9497

EMAIL
info@thecranley.com

INTERNET
www.thecranley.com

CREDIT CARDS
AE, DC, MC, V

RATES
Single £155, double £180, executive double or twin room £190, 4-poster £220, Junior Suite £210, Executive Suite (apartment) £250; special rates in January and February; all rates plus 17½% VAT

BREAKFAST
Continental breakfast £11 extra and served in the rooms

If you appreciate the finer things in life, a stay at the Cranley is guaranteed to be memorable. It is one of the best small hotels in London and serves as a textbook example of how to run a small hotel with great style and elegance. It consists of three beautifully restored townhouses in South Kensington with high ceilings, handsome moldings, floor-to-ceiling windows, and Victorian fireplaces. The stunning interior follows the English country recipe of chintz, traditional antiques, swagged draperies, and beautiful flower arrangements, plus a lovely garden in back. Also incorporated are all the high-tech twenty-first-century touches Americans love to find in a small hotel: ISDN lines, voice mail, and Internet access from the television set. Complimentary fruit baskets, robes and slippers, and a selection of current periodicals are standard in every room. Some of the individually decorated rooms have four-poster beds and include kitchenettes hidden behind paneled doors, complete with a microwave and small refrigerator. Note, however, that these rooms do not include the ISDN line, voice mail, or Internet-access televisions. The new, marble bathrooms are wonderful, with assorted English toiletries, deep bathtubs, ample mirrors and light. All of the rooms, of course, are lovely, but a few stand out. Number 508 has a sitting room and sliding glass doors leading to a private terrace. The fourth-floor one-bedroom suite has a balcony and a view of St. Paul's Cathedral, as does No.

204, a smaller double on the back. I could happily check into No. 101, a front room with a massive four-poster bed, bay windows, and a lilac color scheme. Number 206, also on the front, has twin beds, a soft wing chair, and loads of natural light pouring in from the double windows. For a lot more space, reserve the Executive Suite, a two-bedroom apartment that has a large sitting room, a marble fireplace, two sofas, and an oversize kitchen with a full refrigerator, separate freezer, stove, and microwave. Service is of the old school and taken seriously by the hospitable staff, which does its utmost to provide attentive personal service for each guest. Complimentary tea with scones, jam, and clotted cream is served every afternoon in the lounge between 4 and 5 P.M., and between 7 and 8 P.M., champagne and canapés are offered.

NOTE: The Cranley is one of a number of small hotels represented by Small & Elegant Hotels International, run by American Bonnie DeLoof, who once owned the Cranley. Her company features boutique-style hotels and elegant serviced flats with character and personality in London, Paris, and New York. There are several good reasons to book through her: generally she can get you a better rate; rooms are allotted to her, so if the hotel tells you they are fully booked, she may be able to get you in; and you are dealing with an experienced hotelier who knows what pleases Americans. Another *Great Sleeps London* listing represented by Small & Elegant Hotels International is Harrington Hall hotel (see page 169). For further information on Small & Elegant Hotels, please see page 193.

FACILITIES AND SERVICES: Air-conditioning, central heat, direct-dial phones with voice mail, ISDN lines, Internet access from the television, hair dryer, laundry service, lift to 3rd floor, parking by arrangement, terry robe and slippers, room safe, satellite TV, free use of gym at Harrington Hall (see page 169), kitchenettes with microwaves in some rooms, 1 apartment with a full kitchen, complimentary drink at check-in, fruit basket in the rooms, afternoon tea and evening champagne served in the lounge

NEAREST TOURIST ATTRACTIONS: Moderate walk to the Museum District

HOGARTH HOTEL (22)
Hogarth Road, SW5
Tube: Earl's Court, Gloucester Road
85 rooms, all with shower or bath and toilet

TELEPHONE
020 7370 6831; 800-528-1234
(toll-free from the U.S. and
Canada)

FAX
020 7373 6179

EMAIL
hogarth@marstonhotels.co.uk

INTERNET
www.marstonhotels.co.uk

CREDIT CARDS
MC, V

RATES
Single £105, double £125,
triple £150, executive room
£150; special rates on bank
holidays, Christmas, and New
Year's. Always inquire about
the Leisure Break rates

BREAKFAST
English breakfast buffet £12
extra

If you want a full-service hotel for a reasonable tab near both Earl's Court and Olympia exhibition centers, this is your best bet. The Hogarth has been owned and operated by the Marston family since they built it in 1971. They pride themselves on the level of service offered to all guests and have received many awards for the warm welcome they extend. They are especially proud of the Automobile Association's Courtesy Care Award for outstanding customer care. They are the only hotel in England to have won it twice, which is impressive considering it is awarded to only two London hotels each year. The list of amenities in this modern-style hotel is long and appealing for both tourists and businesspeople. Everyone always appreciates the tasteful and pleasant rooms, especially those on the fifth floor, with balconies. All have a private room safe, data port, and a bathroom drying rack for quick laundries. There is also a convenient car park, 24-hour room service, and a casual dining room with menu choices ranging from a burger and chips to vegetarian and daily specials. There are nonsmoking rooms and a floor with extra security measures geared toward women traveling alone. Business travelers enjoy the eight air-conditioned executive rooms, which have two telephones, a larger television set, minibar, and just enough extra space to make a difference. Leisure Break rates are further enticements at this Best Western–affiliated hotel.

FACILITIES AND SERVICES: Air-conditioning in 8 executive rooms, bar, central heat, direct-dial phones, hair dryer, iron and ironing board available, laundry service, lift, minibars in executive rooms, private car park (£10 per day, £15 for 24 hours), restaurant and 24-hour room service, room safe, nonsmoking rooms on 2nd floor, rooms designed with extra security for women traveling alone, satellite TV, tea and coffeemakers, trouser presses, conference facilities, 24-hour desk

NEAREST TOURIST ATTRACTIONS: Earl's Court Exhibition Centre, moderate walk to the Museum District

SWISS HOUSE HOTEL (33)
171 Old Brompton Road, SW5
Tube: Gloucester Road

15 rooms, all with shower or bath and toilet

When you arrive at the Swiss House, you know immediately that someone is taking care to put the best foot forward. It is a small B&B, only fifteen rooms, but one look at its ivy-covered facade and flower boxes and you will feel as though you have come home. One of the nicest rooms is No. 212, a top-floor triple with a fireplace and a garden view. Other quiet garden rooms to remember are Nos. 2, 5, 8, 12, and 17. Room 201, a street-side triple with a pretty white fireplace outlined in fruit-patterned tiles, is decorated in soft lavender with a light-rose floral-print fabric on the bedspreads and curtains. If you are in one of the street-side rooms, which are the nonsmoking choices, better bring earplugs, because traffic along Old Brompton Road never seems to stop. A quieter room is No. 202, a double or tight triple facing the back with a pretty fireplace and a pine chest and armoire standing on hardwood floors. If it is space you are after, consider lower-ground-floor No. 217, the only room with a tub and a very pink bathroom. It has a walk-in closet and either a king or twin beds. All beds are made up with your choice of blankets or a duvet. A self-service Continental breakfast is offered in the basement breakfast room, with a cheerful blue-and-white color scheme carried out on the china and curtains, complemented by dried floral arrangements and mirrors along one wall. Light snacks, an almost unheard of extra in a modest B&B of this type, include soup, sandwiches, tea, and coffee provided from noon until 9 P.M.

FACILITIES AND SERVICES: Central heat, fans in rooms, direct-dial phones, hair dryer, office safe, light snacks noon–9 P.M., tea and coffeemaking facilities on request, satellite TV, iron and ironing board available office safe, some nonsmoking rooms, office open 8 A.M.–11 P.M.; no lift

NEAREST TOURIST ATTRACTIONS: Short walk to the Museum District

TELEPHONE
020 7373 2769 (reservations);
020 7373 9383 (guests)

FAX
020 7373 4983

EMAIL
recep@swiss-hh.demon.co.uk

INTERNET
www.swiss-hh.demon.co.uk

CREDIT CARDS
MC, V (5% discount for cash payment)

RATES
Single £50–75, double £90–110, triple £125, quad £140

BREAKFAST
Continental breakfast included, full English breakfast £7 extra

YORK HOUSE HOTEL (31)
27–29 Philbeach Gardens, SW5
Tube: Earl's Court (take the Warwick Road exit)

27 rooms, 2 with shower or bath and toilet

TELEPHONE
020 7373 7519/7579

FAX
020 7370 4641

EMAIL
yorkhh@aol.com

CREDIT CARDS
AE, DC, MC, V

RATES
Single £36–50, double £56–75, triple £68–88, quad £80–96; special weekly rates for longer stays in the low season quoted on request

BREAKFAST
English breakfast included

Winnie, the friendly manager, has been welcoming guests to this thrifty Great Sleep since 1981. The hotel is low-tech yet sensible, sturdy, and to the point when it comes to this pocket of London. The rooms are clean and sunny, with high ceilings and no musty odors, nicks, dents, or tears. Rates are indeed bordering on charitable compared to some of the almost obscene prices charged by a few others in the neighborhood. Your final bill will be even less if you stay a week or more and can take advantage of the discount given for long stays in the off-season.

There is the usual television lounge paying homage to overstuffed low seating and a few determined plants. Breakfast is served in two rooms, with red and white tablecloths brightening the morning meal. The good news is that the twenty-seven rooms can house around forty-five people. The bad news is they often do, so make your reservations as early as possible and be *positive* about your dates, because the deposit is nonrefundable, period.

FACILITIES AND SERVICES: Central heat, fans on request, direct-dial phones, hair dryer available, tea and coffee served at reception, TV lounge, office safe, office open 7 A.M.–11 P.M.; no lift

NEAREST TOURIST ATTRACTIONS: Earl's Court Exhibition Centre

SW7

South Kensington

South Kensington (often referred to as "South Ken") is a treasure trove for culture seekers. The Albert Memorial, in honor of the beloved husband of Queen Victoria, and the Royal Albert Hall are here, as well as the vast "Museum District," which includes the Victoria and Albert, Natural History, and Science Museums. Stately Victorian homes, Georgian mansions, and charming mews houses with picture-perfect gardens characterize this very desirable residential area. In springtime, clusters of pink and white blooms on the ornamental cherry trees turn it into a fairyland that draws many photographers. For most of the hotels listed, there is easy tube access from Heathrow Airport.

TOURIST ATTRACTIONS
Albert Memorial, Royal Albert Hall, Kensington Gardens, Hyde Park, Natural History Museum, Science Museum, Victoria and Albert Museum

($) indicates a Big Splurge

ASTER HOUSE (25)
3 Sumner Place, SW7
Tube: South Kensington

14 rooms, all with shower or bath and toilet

TELEPHONE
020 7581 5888
FAX
020 7584 4925
EMAIL
AsterHouse@btinternet.com
INTERNET
www.AsterHouse.com
CREDIT CARDS
MC, V
RATES
Single £100, double £140–180
BREAKFAST
Continental breakfast included

Congratulations are in order for the renovations and friendly staff guests now find at this excellent upmarket B&B in the heart of South Kensington. All rooms are nonsmoking and decorated in a cozy English country style, but there is no lift. Appreciated updates include individually controlled air-conditioning, data ports, and a large room safe. Going from top to bottom, you will find a tiny single with a pod shower and half-wall view that despite its size is still fine for a short stay. If you need more space, request No. 8, with a sleigh bed and a front street view. The Garden Room has its own terrace, queen-size bed, two armchairs, and a marble bathroom with a separate glass-enclosed shower. Number 2, a standard double, faces the charming garden. Desk space is adequate, and so is the bathroom, even though it is on the small side. In the Poster Suite you will sleep in a four-poster bed in a lower-ground-floor room that also has a sofa, two armchairs, and a fireplace. The top highlight of the hotel is the stunning, plant-filled L'Orangerie conservatory breakfast room, which comes into full glory in the spring, when the chestnut tree beside it is a riot of pink blossoms. Over the fireplace is an interesting lighted clock that shows the time worldwide.

The Aster House is so welcoming that some guests have become permanent residents with no apparent plans to leave. You will meet Donald, Jemima, and Martha Duck if you venture into the hotel garden. Donald was born here, and because he has a slight limp, decided to stay; Jemima, born on a South Hampton farm, came to keep him company. Martha arrives every year around February with a male entourage and stays through August, allowing plenty of time for her to have her babies. No one knows where she resides between September and February, because she leaves no forwarding address.

FACILITIES AND SERVICES: Air-conditioning, central heat, direct-dial phones, hair dryer, laundry service, data ports, room safe large enough for a laptop, tea and coffeemakers, satellite TV, 24-hour desk, daily photo ops with the ducks; no lift, no smoking

NEAREST TOURIST ATTRACTIONS: Museum District, Royal Albert Hall, brisk walk to Knightsbridge shopping

BADEN-POWELL HOUSE (16)
Queen's Gate at Cromwell Road, SW7
Tube: Gloucester Road

180 beds, all rooms with shower or bath and toilet

Every time I go back to the Baden-Powell House I cannot believe how much more is offered. For serious budgeteers with a Scout in the family, you can't afford not to take advantage of the outstanding value offered at this Great Sleep in London.

Opened in 1961 by Queen Elizabeth, the Baden-Powell House fulfills the dream of the founder of the Boy Scouts, Lord Baden-Powell, that there be a permanent place where the Boy Scouts and Girl Guides of the world might meet or stay when they come to London. I think it is interesting to note that the Scouts purchased the site in 1956 for the net cost of £39,000 and in 1997 spent £2 million to totally refurbish the facility. Talk about rising costs! The wonderful part is that the facilities of this remarkable hotel are open not only to members of the Scouts and Guides, but to their families as well. Even if your child is a first-year Cub Scout or Brownie, you are eligible to take advantage of this Great Sleeping deal.

The hotel is situated in the heart of London's museum district. Also within easy reach are the Royal Albert Hall, Kensington Gardens, and Kensington Palace. Other famous places such as the Tower of London, Westminster Abbey, and the West End are an easy tube or bus ride away. The simple rooms vary from singles to bunk-bedded dorms and are all nonsmoking. No liquor is served, nor is it allowed onto the premises. In addition to private bathrooms and air-conditioning, you will have duvets on the bed, an electric kettle for making your own tea and coffee, a color television, and daily maid service. If you forgot your hair dryer, you can borrow one from the front desk. Other attractive bonus points include conference rooms, fax machine, and photocopying (fee charged), a coin-operated laundry and dryer, ironing facilities, cafeteria-style restaurant, a few first-come, first-served parking spaces (the only nonbargain offered), a young staff happy to help with your sight-seeing plans, and a notice board to keep everyone up to the minute on theater and concert performances.

Breakfast is included in the nominal rate, and for very little more, two- and three-course lunches and dinners are served daily in the cafeteria. If you are going on a day

TELEPHONE
020 7584 7031

FAX
020 7590 6902

EMAIL
bph.hostel@scoutbase.org.uk

INTERNET
www.scoutbase.org.uk

CREDIT CARDS
AE, MC, V

RATES
All rates are per person, per night. Dorm rooms have bunk beds. Scout Rate: single £50, double (with twin beds) £40, triple £35, extra bed £15; family room £35 for adult, £20 for those under 16; dorm room for those under 16 £20, over 16 £27; Non-Scout Rate: single £70, double (with twin beds) £50, triple £45, extra bed £20; family room £35 for adult, £25 for those under 16; dorm room for those under 16 £25, over 16 £35

BREAKFAST
Continental breakfast included

trip or leaving London via train, consider having the kitchen pack you a box lunch to avoid subjecting yourself to the poor quality of food offered on all the British rail lines.

NOTE: Be sure to request copy of the Booking Policies, details of which are too complicated to outline here. These policies differ between British and non-British guests and groups. The hotel is closed from two days before Christmas until after New Year's.

FACILITIES AND SERVICES: Air-conditioning, central heat, conference facilities, direct-dial phones, garage (£3 per hour, £15 9 A.M.–5 P.M. or 5 P.M.–9 A.M.), hair dryer available, tea and coffeemaking facilities, coin-operated washer and dryer, iron and ironing board, cafeteria-style restaurant open for 3 meals a day to residents and non-residents, office safe, TV, 24-hour desk, luggage room; no smoking or liquor allowed in any part of the building

NEAREST TOURIST ATTRACTIONS: Museum District, Kensington Gardens, Royal Albert Hall, brisk walk to Knightsbridge shopping

FIVE SUMNER PLACE (24)
5 Sumner Place, SW7
Tube: South Kensington

13 rooms, all with shower or bath and toilet

TELEPHONE
020 7584 7586

FAX
020 7823 9962

EMAIL
reservations@sumnerplace.com

INTERNET
www.sumnerplace.com

CREDIT CARDS
AE, MC, V

RATES
Single £105, double £160, triple £185; lower rates November through February

BREAKFAST
Buffet breakfast included

Many small, select London hotels have turned genteel coziness into an art form. Five Sumner Place is no exception. The hotel's guests give it top marks for its lovely tone, pleasing service, and appealing residential location along a beautiful row of white Victorian townhouses built in 1848. When you arrive, you will recognize the understated air of a well-run country home. Comfortable furnishings are in the guest rooms that, because of the nature of the building, vary in size and shape. If you want to face the front, No. 3, in soft gray with mahogany furniture and a white-tiled bath with a shower, is a popular selection. So is No. 6, in deep rose and burgundy. This room has a small balcony and a good shower in a well-lit bathroom. Number 4, a double overlooking the garden on the first floor, with a comfortable wing chair and writing desk, is one of the biggest rooms. If subterraneous living does not bother you, check into No. 2, in the basement. The soft yellow room itself is certainly quiet, and the new bathroom with a tub and shower adds to its appeal. Number 11, a single, needs to have a facelift.

A stunning glass breakfast room with hanging plants overlooks a pretty side garden. What a wonderful place to begin your London day, enjoying a buffet breakfast while glancing through a stack of complimentary daily newspapers. The hotel is ideally placed for visiting the sights of London by bus, tube, or taxi. The South Kensington tube, with a direct link to Heathrow Airport, is less than five minutes away on foot, and major museums and a score of shops and restaurants in all price ranges are within an easy stroll (see *Great Eats London*).

FACILITIES AND SERVICES: Central heat, fans, direct-dial phones, hair dryer, laundry service, lift, office safe, TV, trouser press, 24-hour desk

NEAREST TOURIST ATTRACTIONS: Museum District, Royal Albert Hall, walk to Knightsbridge shopping

THE GORE ($, 1)
189 Queen's Gate, SW7
Tube: Gloucester Road
53 rooms, all with shower or bath and toilet

"Pure joy . . . about as far as you can get from an American corporate hotel," writes the *Wall Street Journal*. *Elle* states, "Six storeys of Old English charm, made cosy with open fires and 5,500 paintings and prints that cover the walls." "The only plastic you will find is the telephone and TV," says the *Financial Times*. Everything said about this charming hotel is absolutely true. It is a very special one-of-a-kind hotel filled with character and personality, where the owners strive to provide for their guests what they themselves want in a hotel: mellow surroundings; an intelligent, friendly staff; good food and wine.

The two impressive townhouses have quite a history. They were first developed into a hotel in the late 1800s when a William Kirby converted them into "discreet hotel suites" and advertised to visitors as "an hotel in all but name." It was listed as "an establishment of superior standard, in the most favourite and fashionable part of the Metropolis," boasting menservants in livery, hot and cold running water, carriages for the use of clients, and a hydraulic lift worked by underground pressure supplied by the London Hydraulic Company. In 1904, Kirby fell on hard times and sublet 189 Queen's Gate to the Turkish Embassy. Four years later, Misses Fanny and Ada Cook took over, and the Gore has been a privately owned hotel ever since, still filled, as the hotel's history

TELEPHONE
020 7584 6601; 800-637-7200 (toll-free from the U.S.)

FAX
020 7589 8127

EMAIL
reservations@gorehotel.co.uk

INTERNET
www.gorehotel.co.uk

CREDIT CARDS
AE, DC, MC, V

RATES
Single £125–165, double £185–275, Tudor Room £295; all rates exclusive of 17.5% VAT

BREAKFAST
Continental breakfast £10, English £12

puts it, with "the kind of Victorian clutter the sisters would have been proud of." It is also well known for its magnificent collection of more than five thousand vintage English prints and paintings hung throughout the hotel and in each room. As you enter, beautiful old paintings of Queen Victoria line the back of the reception area and the walkway leading to an emerald green sitting room filled with large, comfortable sofas and chairs. A roaring winter fire adds a cheerful touch. For a stylish and delicious meal, you can walk into Bistrot 190 (see *Great Eats London*); for a more formal experience, the downstairs dining room serves traditional food in elegant and expensive surroundings.

There are regular single and double rooms with all the nice antique furnishings and appointments one expects to find in a small hotel of this caliber. However, the *real* fun at the Gore begins when you reserve one of their special suites. Probably the best known and most popular is No. 101, the Tudor Room, where a dark-wood-paneled entrance leads to a massive Gothic room with Oriental rugs scattered on its wooden plank floors. Further touches include a huge carved wood-burning fireplace, leaded stained-glass windows, and a carved beamed ceiling with gargoyles. To one side, a ladder, or a secret door, takes you to the "minstrel's gallery," which is a perfect sleeping loft for children. Downstairs, Mom and Dad can share the four-poster canopy bed. The bathroom keeps pace with a Victorian bathtub and throne-seat lavatory. For another unusual experience in hotel living, check into Venus, No. 211, and sleep in a gilded bed that once belonged to Judy Garland and was used in the 1963 musical *I Could Go on Singing,* in which she and Dirk Bogarde costarred. A four-by-six-foot copy of Titian's *Lady of Modena* looms over the room, and in the marbled bathroom, a hand-painted Zeus driving a chariot rides over the bathtub.

The Miss Ada and Miss Fanny rooms (Nos. 208 and 308) are named after the spinster sisters who ran the Gore as a rooming house. In No. 308 you will sleep in Miss Fanny's four-poster bed, which is so high it has a set of steps that actually are from her Georgian commode. In both rooms the bathrooms have improved. They have mahogany paneling with wonderful throne-seat toilets and cast-iron baths with showerheads the size of large dinner plates. Another suite of note is No. 314, the Dame Nellie, named after Dame Nellie Melba, an

Australian opera singer renowned during Queen Victoria's time; Dame Nellie's picture hangs to the right of the fireplace in the hotel lounge (King Edward III is on the left). The bedroom itself, popular with honeymooners, is an opulent mixture of mirrors, nineteenth-century French cupboards, and Victorian chaise longues. The hotel admits that "the bathroom is an experience in itself," with its two bronze statues.

Rates are high at the Gore, but for its many fans, it is well worth the extra money for its unique atmosphere and cordial service. Also under the same ownership and management is Hazlitt's in Soho (see page 58), and the Rookery, near the City in Clerkenwell (see page 178).

FACILITIES AND SERVICES: Air-conditioning in 5th-floor rooms, bar, central heat, direct-dial phones with voice-mail, hair dryer, ISDN lines, laundry service, lift to 4th floor, minibar, room safe, restaurant, room service, robes in deluxe rooms, satellite TV, nonsmoking rooms, conference rooms, 24-hour desk

NEAREST TOURIST ATTRACTIONS: Kensington Gardens, Royal Albert Hall, Museum District

HARRINGTON HALL ($, 21)
5–25 Harrington Gardens, SW7
Tube: Gloucester Road
200 rooms, all with shower or bath and toilet

Harrington Hall sets a benchmark for every possible comfort and convenience and, more important, at lower prices if you go on a weekend or in the off-season. The elegant marbled lobby and reception areas are the curtain-raisers for what awaits beyond. The bar, finished in exotic Burr Vavona, and the beautiful marble fireplace combine warmth and comfort with traditional furniture in complementary colors. The large dining room is overseen by David Shalland, a renowned chef known for his modern English cooking with Mediterranean overtones. The rooms and suites offer stylish accommodations and pour on the extras for their appreciative occupants. In addition to air-conditioning and rooms exclusively reserved for nonsmokers, you will find cable television, in-house movies, a minibar, a private safe big enough to lock up a laptop, and a telephone with data port and an answering machine. Bathrooms are stocked with a variety of toiletries and absorbent towels and offer power showers, good light, and plenty of mirrors. The business center, for the exclusive use of guests, has secretarial

TELEPHONE
020 7396 9696; can also be booked through Small & Elegant Hotels International (see page 193) and 800-44-UTELL (Utell International)

FAX
020 7396 9090; 402-398-5484 (from the U.S.)

EMAIL
harringtonhall@compuserve.com

INTERNET
www.harringtonhall.co.uk

CREDIT CARDS
AE, DC, MC, V

RATES
Single or double £190–200, triple £220, suite that sleeps 4 £250; lower corporate and weekend rates subject to availability

BREAKFAST
Continental breakfast £12 extra, English breakfast £16 extra

services, Internet access, photocopying, and fax services. Conference and banquet facilities for several hundred are beautifully arranged. In addition to all this, guests can work out in the hotel gym, which is fitted with cardiovascular equipment, relax in the sauna, listen to quiet piano music while sipping a drink before dinner, or order something from room service and watch a video. The concierge will secure tickets for any West End production, and uniformed porters will see to it that you never lift anything heavier than your purse.

For guests preferring a location closer to Covent Garden and the West End, the Kingsway Hall on Great Queen Street is under the same ownership. For details, please see page 119.

FACILITIES AND SERVICES: Air-conditioning, bar, central heat, direct-dial phones, data ports, answering machines, hair dryer, minibar, same-day laundry and dry cleaning, lift, room safe, restaurant, 24-hour room service, business and conference facilities, satellite TV, VCR, in-house movies, radio, tea and coffeemakers, trouser press, fitness center with sauna and cardiovascular workout room, 24-hour desk, nonsmoking rooms, porter, and concierge

NEAREST TOURIST ATTRACTIONS: Museum District, Royal Albert Hall

THE PELHAM HOTEL ($, 20)
15 Cromwell Place, SW7
Tube: South Kensington

51 rooms, all with shower, bath, and toilet

"If a man's character can be read in his home, his sense of style is written in the hotels he chooses to stay in. The Pelham Hotel's fine blend of originality and classic English quality will appeal to the lovers of tradition who dare to be a little different." —Elspeth Thompson

The Pelham is a wonderful hotel, catering to discriminating guests who have distinctive taste and a great appreciation of English tradition. All the rooms and suites are furnished with antiques and paintings personally selected by owners Kit and Tim Kemp. Beautiful fresh floral arrangements and blooming orchid plants add soft color to the overall charm and beauty of this very special South Kensington townhouse hotel. Bold patterned and printed fabrics and tapestries are mixed and matched with luxurious abandon, and a fire glows in the eighteenth-century pine-paneled sitting room, which

TELEPHONE
020 7589 8288; 800-553-6674 (toll-free in the U.S.)

FAX
020 7584 8444

EMAIL
pelham@firmdale.com

INTERNET
www.firmdale.com

CREDIT CARDS
AE, MC, V

RATES
Single from £145, double £175–265, suites £300–400, 2-bedroom King Suite £600; all rates are exclusive of 17.5% VAT

BREAKFAST
Continental breakfast £14, English breakfast £16

is filled with soft, overstuffed sofas and lovely chairs. A bit of whimsy is tucked here and there: a Victorian chair is covered in a lively tartan pattern, an old bottle holds one perfect colorful bloom, a framed portrait of a stern, anonymous ancestor peers over a tray of drinks. All rooms are individually designed and executed, from the smallest room under the eaves to the stunning suites with high ceilings, marble fireplaces, and heavily draped floor-to-ceiling windows. Thoughtful extras that do make a difference include lighted closets with shelf space and softly padded hangers, fresh flowers, guest umbrellas, mobile phones for hire, dressing gowns, and of course a data port for your laptop. The only rooms I would prefer not to have are those on the back that overlook a blank wall, but that is their only drawback. For breakfast, lunch, or dinner, or perhaps a drink before the theater, guests can go downstairs to the very popular Kemps bar and restaurant.

Of course this is a Big Splurge of the highest category, but remember, you don't have to check into the King Suite to experience the amenities and services offered. If the Pelham is your kind of hotel, you will also like the Dorset Square Hotel, on page 173, and their latest venture not far away, scheduled to open in early 2003. This new hotel, formerly Number Sixteen, Sumner Place, was purchased by the Kemps and closed for months during the total renovation.

FACILITIES AND SERVICES: Air-conditioning, central heat, honor bar, direct dial phones, mobile phone rental, hair dryer, laundry service, data ports, parking (£24 for 24 hours), office and room safes, satellite TV, videos, restaurant and bar, 24-hour desk and room service, concierge, porter

NEAREST TOURIST ATTRACTIONS: Museum District, Royal Albert Hall, walk to Kensington shopping

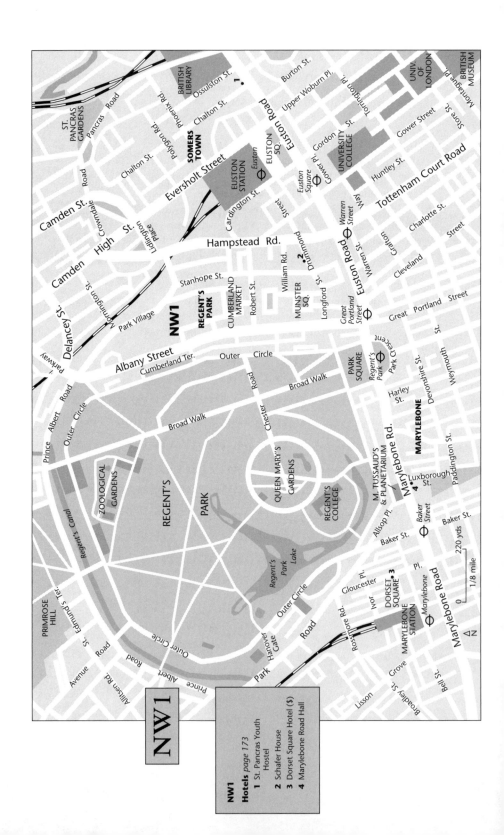

NW1

NW1
Hotels page 173
1 St. Pancras Youth Hostel
2 Schafer House
3 Dorset Square Hotel ($)
4 Marylebone Road Hall

NW1

Regent's Park

Originally the private hunting ground for Henry VIII, this four-hundred-acre park is famous for its zoo, concerts, summer open-air theater, puppet shows, and live bandstand. There is a boat pond, gardens and lawns to stroll along, and the Regent's Canal, where you can take a leisurely boat ride on a lazy Sunday afternoon and contemplate moving to London for good.

TOURIST ATTRACTIONS
London Planetarium, Madame Tussaud's, London Zoo, British Library, Sherlock Holmes Museum

HOTELS IN NW1

Dorset Square Hotel ($)	**173**

OTHER OPTIONS
Hostels

St. Pancras Youth Hostel	**228**

Student Dormitories

Schafer House	**241**
Marylebone Road Hall	**243**

($) indicates a Big Splurge

DORSET SQUARE HOTEL ($, 3)
39–40 Dorset Square, NW1
Tube: Baker Street, Marylebone
38 rooms, all with shower or bath and toilet

For whatever reason you can think of—a birthday, an anniversary, or just to celebrate being in London with someone special—the Dorset Square Hotel, a beautifully restored Regency townhouse, receives high recommendation and praise.

The hotel overlooks two acres of gardens that in 1784 were the site of famous English cricket player Thomas Lord's first cricket ground. Everything about this beautiful hotel is in magnificent taste, from the exclusive, individually designed bedrooms to the Potting Shed, a rustic garden restaurant. Like all rooms in the hotel, the sitting room is furnished with lovely pieces that owners Kit and Tim Kemp would select for their own home. In the lounge, an honor bar laid out with wines, spirits, and champagne sits along one wall. Staffordshire bowls of potpourri, artistic faux finishes, lovely fabrics on overstuffed sofas and chairs, silk draperies, and beautiful

TELEPHONE
020 7723 7874; 800-553-6674 (toll-free from the U.S.)

FAX
020 7724 3328

EMAIL
dorset@firmdale.com

INTERNET
www.firmdale.com

CREDIT CARDS
AE, MC, V

RATES
Single £110, double £150–230, 4-poster double £250; rates do not include 17.5% VAT; ask for seasonal rates

BREAKFAST
Continental breakfast £12 extra, English breakfast £15 extra

floral arrangements and potted plants complete the serene room.

No detail has been overlooked in any of the thirty-eight bedrooms and suites, all of which are a pure joy to occupy. Everything you can imagine has been done in each one to create a luxurious yet livable atmosphere, where antiques, bold color pairings, laces, lush green plants, and flowers are mixed with lavish abandon. The polished bathrooms have scales; baskets of Molton Brown soaps, creams, and shampoos; terry-cloth robes; huge towels; big mirrors; telephones; and even a tissue box covered in a fabric that coordinates with those used in the adjoining bedroom. For that very special person in your life, reserve room No. 202. The sitting room, with its fireplace and view of the square and private gardens, the divine four-poster bed with side curtains, the marble bath, and the double-mirrored armoire are guaranteed to capture anyone's heart. Just below it on the first floor is No. 102, a deluxe double with two comfortable chairs and two big windows on the square. Number 301 is a single in soft greens with a small double bed, writing desk with a view, and two walls of mirrors in the marble bathroom. Even the standard rooms are exceptional, though somewhat smaller, and of course have all the amenities. In addition, a full complement of maids, porters, and valets is always on hand to see to a guest's every need. This is, of course, a Big Splurge, but one you will never regret.

NOTE: The hotel has one side that is not serviced by a lift, and some of the stairs here are steep and narrow. If stair climbing is not part of your daily workout routine, be sure to request accommodations on the side with the lift. If you would enjoy staying in South Kensington, the Pelham (see page 170) and the Kemps' latest endeavor, due to open in 2003 on nearby Sumner Place, are two excellent choices.

FACILITIES AND SERVICES: Air-conditioning, central heat, honor bar, direct-dial phones with voice mail in rooms and bathrooms, hair dryer, laundry and cleaning services, lift to most rooms, minibar, data ports, restaurant, 24-hour room service, satellite TV, radio, clock, office and room safe, access to gym with swimming pool (£15 for a day pass), 24-hour desk, porter, concierge, office and secretarial facilities

NEAREST TOURIST ATTRACTION: Madame Tussaud's, Planetarium, Regent's Park

EC1

Farringdon and Clerkenwell

While not the West End or near any tourist excitement, the area of London known as Farringdon and Clerkenwell is becoming more popular thanks to its growing number of trendy eating places and more affordable real estate prices. It is close to the Barbican Centre, where the Royal Shakespeare Company and the London Symphony Orchestra perform and where the Museum of London and the Barbican Art Gallery are located. St. Giles Church and the City of London School for Girls are in the central courtyard of the center. Early birds can raise a pint or two with the market workers in pubs around the famous Smithfield Market, a meat and poultry wholesale market since the twelfth century. One of the tube stops, Farringdon Station, is the original terminus of the Metropolitan Line, the world's first underground. The walk to the City, Old Bailey, and Fleet Street is not far.

TOURIST ATTRACTIONS
Barbican Centre, Museum of London

HOTELS IN EC1

The Rookery ($)	**178**

OTHER OPTIONS
Serviced Apartments

Citadines–Barbican	**198**

Student Dormitories

Rosebery Avenue Hall	**239**

YMCAs

London City YMCA	**253**

($) indicates a Big Splurge

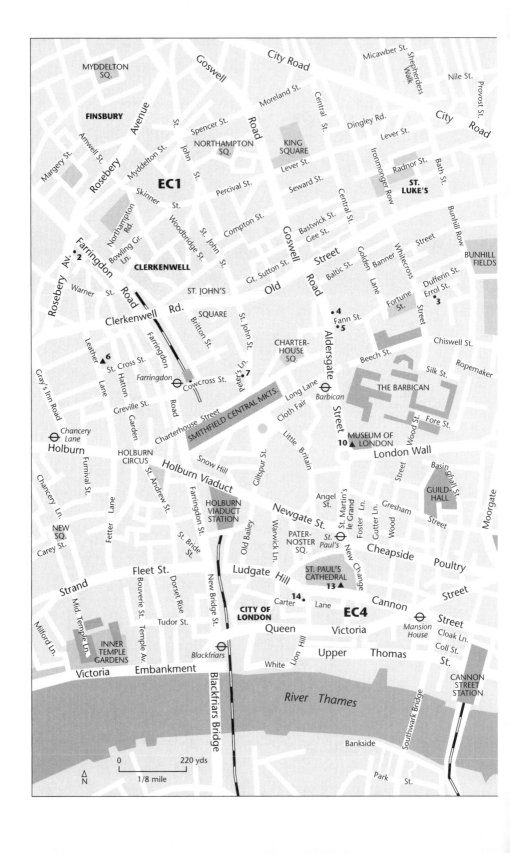

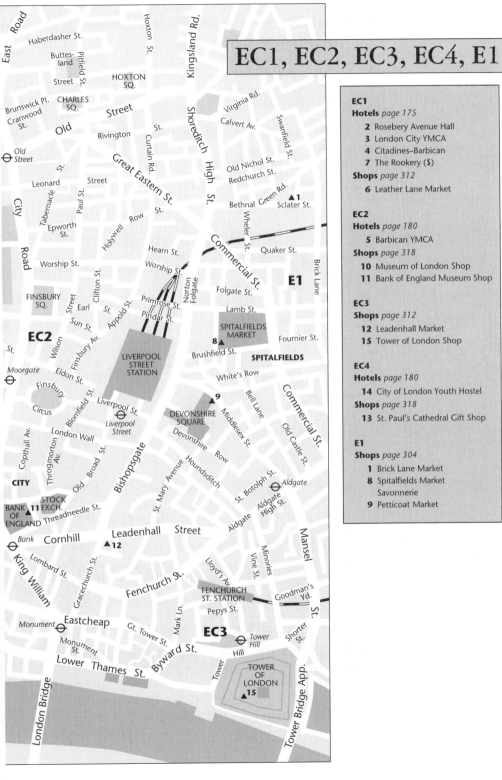

EC1, EC2, EC3, EC4, E1

THE ROOKERY ($, 7)
Peter's Lane, Cowcross Street, EC1 (no street #)
Tube: Farringdon

33 rooms, all with shower or bath and toilet

TELEPHONE
020 7336 0931

FAX
020 7336 0932

EMAIL
reservations@rookery.co.uk

INTERNET
www.rookeryhotel.com

CREDIT CARDS
AE, DC, MC, V

RATES
Single £175–200, double £205, suite £265, the Rook's Nest £475; all rates plus 17.5% VAT

BREAKFAST
Continental breakfast £8.50

The Rookery is the latest hotel venture of Peter McKay and Douglas Blain, who also own Hazlitt's (see page 58) and The Gore (see page 167). If you like these two unique hotels, you will be fascinated by their newest, which as one journalist put it, "appeals to men wearing either pinstripes or pigtails." You will find the hotel on a side street in Clerkenwell. Just look for the lantern outside and a brass plaque lit above the doorway reading, "The Rookery." Clerkenwell is now an up-and-coming area about halfway between St. Paul's Cathedral and the financial center of London, known as the City.

Years ago, the Rookeries were known as run-down slum areas filled with criminals. The name of the hotel comes from the bands of murderers, robbers, and other villains who lived in the Rookeries and who used to haunt these parts. A sign in a bookcase next to the reception desk gives you some idea of the area's past life: "Fourpence a night for a bed, sixpence with supper, no more than five to sleep in one bed, no boots to be worn in bed. Organ grinders to sleep in the wash house, no dogs allowed upstairs, no beer allowed in the kitchen, and no razor grinders or tinkers taken in." In its previous life, the building was the London headquarters and smokehouse for Danish Bacon. When McKay and Blain bought it, there were no floors at all and the outside walls were covered with an inch of black bacon fat. These two farsighted hotel owners certainly take the top prize for vision! Now the hotel consists of thirty-three rooms and a suite to behold, all handsomely furnished with beautifully restored antiques and graced with scores of old paintings. There is not a traditional lobby, but drinks and breakfast can be served in the conservatory lounge overlooking a small terrace. Eventually, the area beyond it will be a walkway to shops and restaurants.

Each room is named after a person who lived in the area and includes a brief history of that person. In the Henry Bennett Smith room, you learn that he was a surgeon who lived at 8 Cowcross Street in 1855. A queen-size bed with a dramatic duvet cover and wooden headboard is the focal point, accented by a fireplace, two leather chairs, and an Oriental rug. The room wouldn't suit someone who needs to plug in a computer, because there is no real workspace and the data port is all but inaccessible. A better choice for a working stay would be the Mary Lane room, on the top floor, with a pitched, beamed roof. The functionally amusing bathroom has a wonderful black iron tub with claw feet and a toilet with copper fittings and a pull chain. Even more fun is the bathroom in the Edward Cave room. Mr. Cave was the editor of *Gentleman's Magazine,* whose office was in St. John's Gate. The glassed-in stall shower in the bathroom has a copper showerhead the size of a massive pizza, and the toilet sits two steps up on a polished wooden three-sided throne. The bedroom itself has a sculpted wooden bed with two lions and an angel incorporated into it. There is a long work area, but the closet is strange: hangers are hung down, in pyramid fashion, one after another, with the bottom hanger only inches from the bottom of the closet. No woman would have designed this! The pièce de résistance of the hotel is the Rook's Nest, which is entered through a door hidden within a trompe l'oeil painting of a maid peeping from behind it. The huge main room has a thirty-five-foot pitched ceiling with a study behind a balustrade, which can be closed off with the switch of a button. A circular stairway leads upstairs to this study, with its executive-size desk and a leather office chair, two cushy sofas, and television set. The rough cedar roof has three round and two pie-shaped windows that let in some light. Downstairs in the main part, the amazing bed is quite something, and it's absolutely no wonder there is only one other like it on the planet. The bedposts are anchored by two attached black male cherubs and two menservants, all with manes of golden hair. The two on each side of the top of the bed, flanking a mirror, are holding feathers with a light on top and have their feet touching a gold ball. The rest of the suite pales by comparison, but it is by no means dull. In one corner of the bedroom is a claw-footed Victorian "bathing machine," where you can either soak in the deep tub or take a shower.

FACILITIES AND SERVICES: Central heat, fans, bar, direct-dial phone with voice mail, hair dryer, laundry service, minibar, data ports, room safe large enough for small laptop, room service for light meals, nonsmoking rooms, satellite TV, conference room; no lift (3 floors)

NEAREST TOURIST ATTRACTION: The City, Old Bailey, Fleet Street

EC2

The Barbican

The Barbican Centre is one of London's arts centers and is home to the London Symphony Orchestra. In addition to attending concerts, you can visit the art gallery, cinema, or theater. Other than this center, the neighborhood is chiefly a business area and offers little of interest to most visitors.

OTHER OPTIONS IN EC2 (see map page 176)
YMCAs

Barbican YMCA   **251**

EC4

The City

The one-and-a-quarter-square-mile area known as the City was, in fact, the original city of London and is loaded with history and beautiful churches, including St. Paul's Cathedral and St. Brides. One of the most famous Fleet Street pubs, Ye Olde Cheshire Cheese, is as popular as it was when Dr. Samuel Johnson was a regular. Today the City is the heart of London's business and financial world and fills each working day with a quarter of a million people, who lend it an air of importance and excitement. On the weekends it is a ghost town; even some of the pubs and most of the restaurants are closed. You definitely want to visit here on a weekday, and I recommend going on one of the walking tours that concentrate on the importance of this interesting part of London (see page 23).

OTHER OPTIONS IN EC4 (see map page 176)
Hostels

City of London Youth Hostel   **226**

SE1

South Bank and Waterloo

Development along the South Bank of the River Thames has brought this once run-down and neglected area of London into prominence. The area takes in Shakespeare's Globe Theatre and museum, Southwark Cathedral, the wharves housing several well-known restaurants in Sir Terence Conran's vast empire, and the new Tate Modern, which is dramatically housed in a former power station. The sprawling area also includes the Royal Festival Hall and South Bank Centre on one side of the Waterloo Bridge, and the Royal National Theatre on the other. A riverside walkway links the Royal Festival Hall to Waterloo Station. The magnificent view of the City from the Waterloo Bridge that has inspired artists for centuries continues to be spectacular, as does the sweeping twenty-five-mile view (on a clear day) of the city from the London Eye, the tallest observation wheel in the world.

HOTELS IN SE1

OTHER OPTIONS

Student Dormitories

Student-Only Accommodations

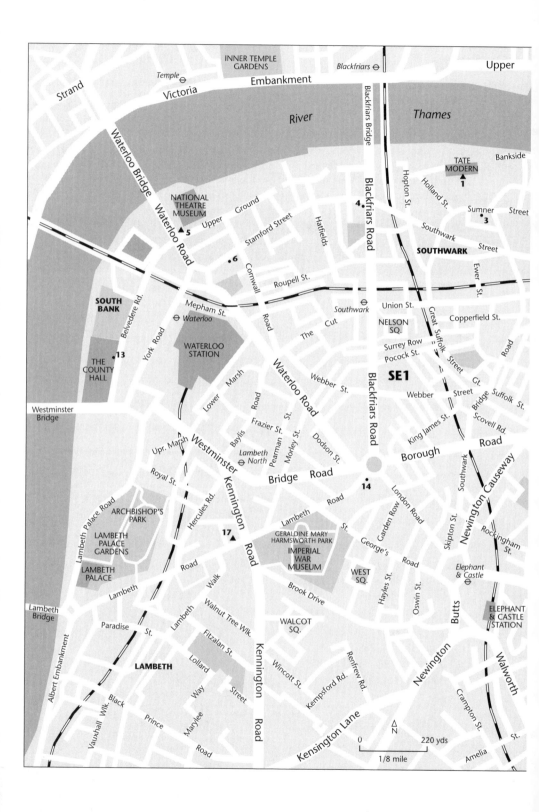

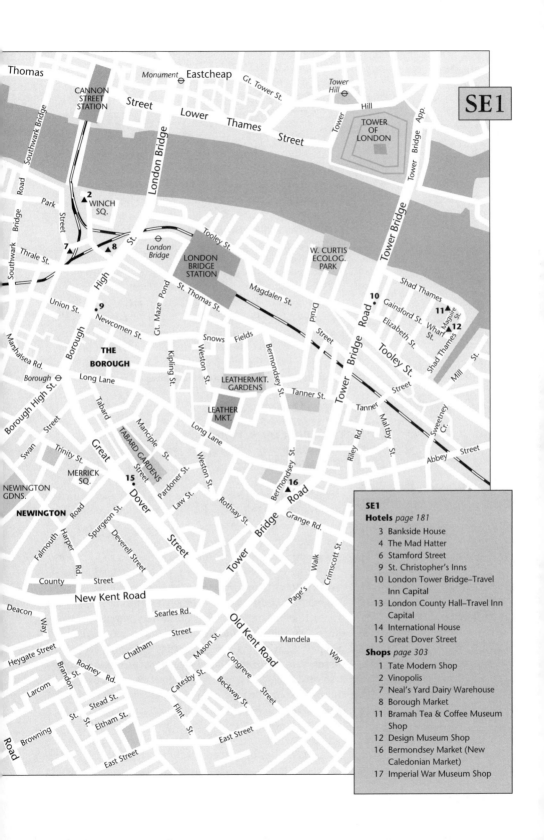

Thomas

Monument ⊖ Eastcheap   Gt. Tower St.

CANNON
STREET
STATION   Street   Lower   Thames   Street

Tower
Hill ⊖

Hill

TOWER
OF
LONDON

Southwark Bridge

Road   Park   Street

Southwark Bridge

Thrale St.

▲2
WINCH
SQ.

7 ▲   ▲8   St.   ⊖
London
Bridge

High

Tooley St.

LONDON
BRIDGE
STATION

W. CURTIS
ECOLOG.
PARK

Tower Bridge

Tower Bridge App.

Shad Thames

Union St.   •9
Newcomen St.

Gt. Maze Pond

St. Thomas St.

Magdalen St.

Druid   Street

Tower Bridge Road

10
• Gainsford St.
Elizabeth St.

Tooley St.

11▲
Maguire St.
▲12
Shad Thames St.

Mill St.

Borough ⊖

THE
BOROUGH

Long Lane

Snows   Fields
Weston St.
Kipling St.

Bermondsey St.

Tanner St.

Tanner   Street
Riley Rd.
Maltby   St.

Sweetney Cr.

Borough High St.

Tabard   Street

Long Lane

LEATHERMKT.
GARDENS

LEATHER
MKT.

Abbey   Street

Marshalsea Rd.

Borough ⊖   Long Lane

Swan   Street
Trinity St.

MERRICK
SQ.

NEWINGTON
GDNS.

NEWINGTON

Great   TABARD GARDENS   Manciple St.
Street   Dover   Street

15
•

Pardoner St.

Law St.

Weston St.

Rothsay St.

Bermondsey

16
▲

Grange Rd.

Road

Tower   Bridge   Road

Falmouth   Harper Rd.
Spurgeon St.
Deverell Street

County   Street

Page's   Walk

Crimscott St.

New Kent Road

Deacon   Way

Searles Rd.

Street

Mandela   Way

Heygate Street
Brandon St.
Rodney   Rd.
Larcom   St.
Browning   St.
Stead St.
Eltham St.

Chatham

Mason St.
Catesby St.
Beckway St.
Flint   St.

Congreve   Street

Old Kent Road

East Street

East Street

Road

East Street

LONDON COUNTY HALL–TRAVEL INN CAPITAL (13)

TELEPHONE
020 7902 1600

FAX
020 7902 1619

Belvedere Road, SE1
Tube: Waterloo

313 rooms, all with shower or bath or toilet

This Travel Inn is on the River Thames next to the London Eye and opposite the Houses of Parliament. For central reservations information, rates, and a description of this hotel chain, see the London Euston, page 109.

NEAREST TOURIST ATTRACTION: Royal National Theatre

LONDON TOWER BRIDGE–TRAVEL INN CAPITAL (10)

TELEPHONE
020 7940 3700

FAX
020 7940 3719

159 Tower Bridge Road, SE1
Tube: London Bridge

195 rooms, all with shower or bath and toilet

The London Tower Bridge hotel is situated south of the Tower Bridge, close to the Tower of London, HMS *Belfast*, and the City of London. For central reservations information, rates, and a description of this hotel chain, see the London Euston, page 109.

NEAREST TOURIST ATTRACTION: Tower of London

THE MAD HATTER (4)

TELEPHONE
020 7401 9222

FAX
020 7401 7111

EMAIL
madhatter@fullers.co.uk

INTERNET
www.fullers.co.uk

CREDIT CARDS
MC, V

RATES
Single or double £99, extra person £15, Fri–Sat single or double £79, extra person £15

BREAKFAST
Continental breakfast £5.50, English breakfast £8.50

3–7 Stamford Street, SE1
Tube: Blackfriars, Waterloo

30 rooms, all with shower or bath and toilet

The Mad Hatter pays homage to its building, which was a hat factory in the nineteenth century. The theme is carried on along the hallways, which display framed pictures of hats. Now the building is a Fuller's English Inn upstairs and an Ale and Pie House downstairs (see the Sanctuary House, page 134, for another Fuller's good-value Great Sleeps in London).

The hotel is well situated for business and leisure visitors, located near Waterloo, a short walk across the Thames on the Blackfriars Bridge. The rooms are all cut from the same cloth, with absolutely no unpleasant quirks. Single occupants are given rooms with a double bed, the open closets have decent hangers, and the bathrooms, some with stretch tubs, are very nice and include a selection of toiletries. Both nonsmoking rooms and those fitted for the handicapped are available. The pub is open daily and serves both lunch and dinner. Prices are kept to a minimum, especially on the weekends, because Fuller's is a monolithic company that has its fingers in all sorts of pies, so it doesn't rely on the success of just one venture to keep its doors open. With the almost obscene hotel prices insulting a majority of London visitors, this is a welcome addition. Bravo Fuller's!

FACILITIES AND SERVICES: Central heat, bar (there's a pub here), direct-dial phones, hair dryer, laundry service, lift, office safe, satellite TV, tea and coffeemakers, trouser press, nonsmoking rooms, handicapped rooms that are alarmed

NEAREST TOURIST ATTRACTION: Tate Modern

Other Options

London hotels are among the most expensive in the world, and the busiest. What does a visitor do when everything is booked and the budget purse strings cannot be stretched one pound further? The answer is: seek other options.

Besides traditional hotel rooms, visitors to London have a wide variety of other options that make Great Sleeping sense; they include everything from staying in an apartment to pitching a tent under the stars. With some of these alternative Great Sleeps, you will be asked to pay in cash and will be required to make a hefty deposit in advance of arrival. Many private B&Bs and flat rentals demand that the balance of your stay be paid on arrival. Refund policies can be merciless and are *never* in your favor. Many keep their policies simple and to the point: no refunds if a cancellation is made after a certain date prior to arrival, and no recourse should you cut your stay short—period. To avoid costly headaches and financial anguish if you have to cancel or cut your trip short, *please* invest in trip-cancellation insurance whenever possible (see "Insurance," page 29). These policies are available through state automobile associations, travel agents, various agencies that specialize in travel insurance, and in some cases, from the flat rental agency you are dealing with in London. I cannot overemphasize the importance of carrying this insurance. I hope you never need it, but if you do, it could save you thousands of dollars in forfeited money.

OTHER OPTIONS

Apartments

There is no place like home, so on your next trip to London, why not consider renting a flat? At first glance, the prices of some may seem high, but on second evaluation, the benefits gained add up to a well-priced Great Sleep. First of all, a stay in a flat gives you more space than a hotel, and for less money. In many instances, you will have more comfortable furnishings in elegant surroundings that would cost dearly in a hotel. Almost as important, it allows you the freedom and independence to get to know a neighborhood of London that you will soon think of as your own. If you are staying longer than a few days, a flat makes sense, because discounts can often be negotiated based on the time of year and length of stay. If you are traveling with children, the kitchen convenience can be a big money-saver, even if you fix only breakfast and a few snacks a day.

When researching the London flat scene, I can promise you I ran across some real bomb sites that were not only ugly, run-down, and depressing but also dirty and operated by unfriendly people who would never darken the door of your flat if you faced any sort of maintenance problem. Others, sadly, have not followed routine maintenance or done any upgrading and thus have been dropped from this edition. Just as with all of the hotels and shops listed in *Great Sleeps London,* I have personally inspected all of the apartments I recommend to you.

In addition, some hotels have a few rooms that are equipped for light cooking or else maintain fully contained apartments (which may or may not be located in the hotel itself). For a list of these hotels, see "Hotels with Apartments and/or Kitchens" in the index, page 339.

Even though I mention it as the number-one tip for apartment rentals, it is so important it bears repeating here: If you plan on renting a flat, be sure you clearly understand the payment, cancellation, and refund policies. It is beyond the scope of this book to detail the various policies you will encounter, but they are usually draconian and will hit hardest when the chips are down and you must change your plans. If you accept only one piece of advice from me on apartment rentals, this is it: *Buy cancellation insurance.* This small investment will pay off handsomely if you have to change plans about dates, cancel altogether, or must suddenly cut your stay short.

Tips on Renting a London Apartment

1. Most important: Know the cancellation policy and buy cancellation insurance.

2. Be very specific when stating your needs: size of flat and number of occupants; whether you prefer a stall shower or a handheld shower nozzle in a tub; required kitchen equipment (must it be fully outfitted for major cooking sprees, or are you just going to peel an orange, drink instant coffee, and heat food in a microwave?). Don't

forget to consider the beds. Do you want a double or twin beds, or will a pullout sofa or Murphy bed do?

3. Ask that color photographs of the flat you are considering be sent to you.

4. Is there a phone, and is it digital? How much are the calls? Is there an answering machine in your flat or a switchboard to take calls when you are out? What about a fax in your apartment or access to one in the office? And don't forget about a data port if you plan on accessing the Internet and sending and receiving email.

5. Who pays for utilities (other than the telephone, which you are always charged for)? Be careful on this one . . . especially if you are going to run the heat or air-conditioning full blast.

6. How far is the flat from *your* center of interest in London? Where is the nearest market, laundry and dry cleaner, tube and bus stops, pub, restaurant? Ask for a map with the location of the flat, nearest tube stop, and grocery shopping pinpointed.

7. Is maid service included, and if not, is it available, and how much does it cost?

8. Who is responsible for laundering the sheets and towels? If you are, you will probably want a washer and dryer in the unit, or at least in the building.

9. Is the apartment suitable for children? Is a park or playground nearby?

10. Is there a lift to your flat? While that fifth-floor penthouse has a million-dollar view, do you really want to lug suitcases up and down, as well as bags of groceries and shopping finds? Think about this one carefully—stairs get old *fast*.

11. If dealing with an apartment rental agency, find out about other services the company may offer, such as airport transfers, sight-seeing in London, help with ongoing travel in the U.K., and air travel arrangements. The list can be long, cost effective, and very helpful.

APARTMENT RENTAL AGENCIES

($) indicates a Big Splurge

CHEVAL GROUP ($)
140 Brompton Road, Knightsbridge, SW3 (main office)
Tube: Knightsbridge (main office only)

Over 200 fully equipped and serviced apartments and houses

The Cheval Group offers great value for the money, especially if you require splendid accommodations at fashionable addresses in central London, such as Knightsbridge, Kensington, or overlooking Hyde Park. If you are planning to stay three months or more, the Gloucester Park apartments in Kensington (see map page 154) offer the latest word in luxury, sophistication, and security. The beautifully appointed, air-conditioned one-, two-, and three-bedroom apartments have balconies, fully equipped Miele kitchens, double sets of high-quality china, crystal, and cutlery, beautiful granite bathrooms with separate power showers for each bedroom, cable television, VCR, two private voice mail telephones, and maid service. In addition, there is a gym, sauna, 24-hour concierge, and private parking.

For stays of at least three weeks in the absolute lap of luxury, reserve a two- or three-bedroom apartment at Thorney Court, overlooking the Kensington Palace Gardens. Each charming apartment is decorated in the classic English style with rich fabrics, bold colors, and tasteful appointments. The upper-floor penthouses have spectacular views of the palace and across the park.

Stays of one week or more are available at the Cheval Apartments in the heart of Knightsbridge (see map page 144). These wonderfully posh accommodations provide elegance and space, beautifully equipped kitchens, and large, comfortably furnished living rooms in apartments, secluded mews houses, and townhouses with two or

TELEPHONE
020 7225 3325

FAX
020 7581 2869

EMAIL
cheval@chevalgroup.com

INTERNET
www.chevalgroup.com

CREDIT CARDS
AE, DC, MC, V (1.75% to 3.5% added if payment is by credit card)

RATES
Cheval Place: £1,225–1,900 per week (minimum stay 7 days); Gloucester Park £945–2,245 per week (minimum stay 90 days); Thorney Court £1,250–3,150 per week (minimum stay 90 days) or £1,900-4,200 per week (minimum stay 22 days). For longer stays, rates vary and are negotiable. All are exclusive of 17.5% VAT for the first 28 days; thereafter then the VAT rate drops to 3.5%.

three bedrooms. All the extras are included—even a free membership to a local health club.

FACILITIES AND SERVICES: Vary somewhat with each location, but the following are always provided: central heat, direct-dial phones with voice mail, fully equipped kitchen with dishwasher and beautiful tableware, lift in most, satellite TV, VCR, washer and dryer, membership in a health club, maid service, video-entry security system. The following also are available in some locations: air-conditioning, fax, stereo and CD player, concierge service, private parking

CHEZ VOUS
1001 Bridgeway, Suite 245, Sausalito, CA 94965

TELEPHONE
415-331-2535

FAX
415-331-5296

EMAIL
bonjour@chezvous.com

INTERNET
www.chezvous.com

CREDIT CARDS
None; cash only

RATES
$1,000–4,000 per week, depending on size and amenities

Chez Vous, as its name implies, began with apartment rentals in Paris (see their listing in *Great Sleeps Paris* as well), and as with all success stories, they grew by leaps and bounds, because they found a niche and provided good services at affordable prices. Now they can provide you with a home away from home in London. By consulting their Website or flipping through their fifty-page catalog of London flats, you are bound to find something of interest. The catalog also clearly explains all the ins and outs of their payment and cancellation policies. The locations are desirably upmarket: Chelsea, Kensington, Mayfair, Knightsbridge, and Belgravia, and range from lower-ground-floor one-bedrooms to a four-bedroom family home with a garden. There is a minimum one-week rental period, which can begin any day of the week. All reservations are made through their office in Northern California, so payment is in U.S. dollars.

FACILITIES AND SERVICES: Vary with each apartment

HOBART SLATER (7)
6–8 Montpelier Street, SW7
Tube: Knightsbridge (office)

TELEPHONE
020 7590 1200

FAX
020 7590 1210

EMAIL
shortlets@hobartslater.co.uk

INTERNET
www.hobartslater.co.uk

CREDIT CARDS
None; all payments by bank transfer or cash in hand

If you are in the market for an exceptional short let in London, Hobart Slater is one of the best I have found, not only for remarkably good value, but also for follow-through once you have moved in. I frankly did not see one apartment in any size or category that I could not have moved into and lived contentedly in for months. For some, the one-month minimum poses no problem, and if you are planning to stay three or more months, the rates get even better. Flats are situated right where we all want to be in Knightsbridge, Chelsea, and Kensington and range in size from smartly modern penthouse studio perches to four-bedroom period homes complete with garden space for your children and dogs. All are exceptional for their furnishings, amenities, and overall appeal and generally include washers and dryers, dishwashers, telephones with answering machines on request, and data ports. Maid service is always available. Every taste and desire can be catered to; just let them know your needs, and their competent office will do all the rest.

FACILITIES AND SERVICES: Vary with each flat, but you can generally count on all the basics plus washer and dryer, dishwashers, data ports, and maid service by arrangement.

RATES
Studios from £400 per week, 1 bedroom from £450 per week, 2 bedroom from £550 per week, 3 bedroom from £1,250 per week, 4 bedroom from £1,300 per week; minimum stay 1 month, payable weekly; negotiated rates for stays over 3 months

THE INDEPENDENT TRAVELLER
Thorverton, Exeter EX5 5NT, England

The Independent Traveller was established in 1980 for those who enjoy traveling on their own. Headed by Mary and Simon Ette, this business lists central and suburban London apartments, country cottages, small inns, hotels, and B&Bs from Cornwall to Inverness. They are used to working with people from around the globe and regularly get inquiries from faraway places such as Papua New Guinea and Kathmandu. The prize for their most isolated request is still shared between missionaries in Nepal, who sent a letter that required a week's donkey journey just to get it to the post office to be sent to London, and another from archaeologists on a remote island in the Pacific with one mail boat per month. How did they book? By sending exact requirements, a deposit, and instructions to "get on with it." So, as you can see, wherever you may be in the world, Mary and Simon are only a letter, telephone call, fax, or email away.

When requesting information about London properties, I recommend looking for something central. While their suburban London addresses are cheaper and give you more living space, weigh carefully what you save in money and gain in space against what you will spend in time commuting back and forth to London, if that is going to be the focal point of your trip. If it isn't, then living on the fringes should be fine.

While the accommodations are inspected regularly and there is an excellent group of owners, many of whom have been with Mary for years, you must remember that you are staying in a private flat. Maybe the sofa needs

TELEPHONE
01392 860807

FAX
01392 860552

EMAIL
Independenttrav@cs.com

INTERNET
www.gowithIT.co.uk

CREDIT CARDS
MC, V

RATES
£450–950, per week, with most properties somewhere in the mid-range. Rates depend on property, what type of maid service is included, and the location; lower rates for longer stays and repeat clients.

reupholstering, the paint redoing, or the bathroom modernization. It is *not* a hotel—please don't expect one. More than half the clientele consists of repeat customers, which is a very strong recommendation. One guest liked his flat so much that he married the owner!

There is a three-night minimum stay, low-season rates are offered from November through March, and cancellation insurance is always available. While you can't always take advantage of the lower seasonal rates, you should definitely take out cancellation insurance.

FACILITIES AND SERVICES: Vary with each property

IN THE ENGLISH MANNER
515 South Figueroa, Suite 1000, Los Angeles, CA 90071-3327

TELEPHONE
213-629-1811; 800-422-0799 (toll-free from the U.S. and Canada)

FAX
213-689-8784

EMAIL
usa@english-manner.com

INTERNET
www.english-manner.com

CREDIT CARDS
AE, MC, V

RATES
Weekly rates are around $1,150 (including VAT) for a studio or 1 bedroom; there is a minimum 1-week stay

"Sketch us your idea of the dream vacation house and location and we will do our best to deliver." This is the motto of In the English Manner, which takes the guesswork and anguish out of spending a week or more in a flat in the heart of London, or in your own home almost anywhere in Great Britain. All properties are privately owned by well-to-do, and in some instances illustrious, British families and reflect the owners' individual living styles and tastes. All are beautifully equipped and maintained to high standards. In London their properties are some of the best I encountered. You have a choice of delightful flats or homes in the best neighborhoods. You can live in a classical house in the heart of Belgravia, a contemporary apartment on the second floor of a building near Harrods, a bright flat overlooking the banks of the River Thames, or a three-story mews house in popular Chelsea. If your London stay will be less than one week, In the English Manner has serviced flats in Mayfair and Kensington available on a nightly basis. Prices depend on time of year and size of the flat. Rates begin at £200 per night. If you're traveling beyond London and staying in one place a week or longer, consider one of their period and historic country cottages.

Traveling "in the English manner" allows you the luxury of arranging for a chauffeured car for airport transfers, food to be purchased for you and placed in your kitchen.

NOTE: They strongly advise cancellation insurance and can provide you with the details.

FACILITIES AND SERVICES: Vary with each property, but almost all needs and desires can be met

PERFECT PLACES APARTMENTS LONDON
53 Margravine Gardens, Barons Court, London W6

Rita Rose knows quality, and well she should. For five years she worked as sales manager at the famed London Ritz. In 1985 she decided to start her own business, and Perfect Places is the result. With great energy and boundless goodwill, she runs her company with a firm and practiced hand. Her apartments are owned by people who use them only occasionally when they are in London, or who live abroad most of the time. Although they are all different, because they are individually owned and decorated, you will find nothing out of whack in decor, cleanliness, or general maintenance. The standards of cleanliness are controlled by Perfect Places, and all flats are thoroughly cleaned before and after each arrival. A maid comes once a week to clean and change the linens if you stay at least two weeks, but additional maid service is always available. The apartments are in pleasant residential areas in central London, close to public transportation, shopping, and places of interest. Clients are met at the apartment and given a briefing about running it, as well about how to best enjoy the location. Someone is available twenty-four hours a day to help with emergencies. There is a one-week minimum stay.

FACILITIES AND SERVICES: Vary with each apartment, but always include a phone, TV, and generally a washing machine. Fax, VCR, and airport transfers can be arranged

TELEPHONE
020 8748 6095

FAX
020 8741 4213

EMAIL
permatch@netcomuk.co.uk

INTERNET
www.perfectplaceslondon.co.uk

CREDIT CARDS
AE, MC, V

RATES
£550–1500 per week

SMALL & ELEGANT HOTELS INTERNATIONAL
9425 Whispering Sands, West Olive, MI 49460

American Bonnie DeLoof knows what she is doing when it comes to hotel and apartment accommodations in London. She is the former owner of the Cranley, which in my opinion represents the quintessence of British taste and style at a cost many can afford. Although I write about the Cranley and her services as a hotel booking agent on page 158, her services concerning apartment rentals bear repeating here, because she is able to book a wide range of apartments in London. If you want to be thirty seconds from the main door of Harrods, call Bonnie. If it's a flat near Kensington Palace you're after, she has it. For a Big Splurge, ask her about the company she represents called Manors & Co. With Bonnie handling the details, you can sit back, relax, and

TELEPHONE
616-844-6000, 800-553-2582

FAX
616-844-6402

EMAIL
res@smallandeleganthotels.com

INTERNET
www.smallandeleganthotels.com

RATES
£90–280 per night for hotels, £123–390 per night for apartments

Branch Office in Tampa, Florida
TELEPHONE
813-251-4777, 866-365-7211 (toll-free)

FAX
813-254-5899

EMAIL
adeloof@tampabay.com

pleasantly anticipate a memorable stay in London. For travels further afield, Bonnie also represents hotels in New York, Edinburgh, Prague, Paris, and Dublin.

FACILITIES AND SERVICES: Vary with each property

VILLAS INTERNATIONAL
4340 Redwood Highway, Suite D-309, San Rafael, CA 94903

TELEPHONE
415-499-9490; 800-221-2260
(toll-free in the U.S.)

FAX
415-499-9491

EMAIL
villas@best.com

INTERNET
www.villasintl.com

CREDIT CARDS
None; cash or check only

RATES
Vary with each location, but start around $750 per week for a small studio

Villas International offers one of the widest selections of overseas rental properties for the independent traveler. With more than twenty-five thousand villas, cottages, châteaus, flats, and castles, surely they will have one that fits your needs and budget. Write, call, fax, or email them and describe your needs, where you want to be in London, and your price range. If you need a rental car, that can also be arranged, but I don't recommend a car in London unless you use it to get out of town. When calling, speak with David Kendall, who maintains office hours Mon–Fri 9 A.M.–6 P.M. (Pacific time).

FACILITIES AND SERVICES: Vary with each property

SERVICED APARTMENTS

($) indicates a Big Splurge

ASHBURN GARDEN APARTMENTS (18)
3–4 Ashburn Gardens, South Kensington, SW7
Tube: Gloucester Road

25 flats, all with shower or bath and toilet

For an economical sleep, an apartment at Ashburn Garden is an improved budget bet that has price and location in its favor. The building consists of twenty-five purpose-built apartments that have been in the same family ownership since 1974. The kitchens in the functional accommodations have been redone and now include a proper stove, oven, and microwave. New furnishings, a fresh coat of paint, and white tiled baths added a much needed spark. The best flats are those on the higher floors because the bedrooms in these are on

TELEPHONE
020 7370 2663

FAX
020 7370 6743

EMAIL
info@ashburngardens.co.uk

INTERNET
www.ashburngardens.co.uk

CREDIT CARDS
MC, V

Minimum of 1 week booking;
1 bedroom for 1–2 persons
from £665 weekly, 2 bedrooms
for 4 from £1,050 weekly; lower
rates November–March;
additional beds/cots £100
weekly

BREAKFAST
Not served

the quiet side of the building and get more light. There
is a launderette close by, and a huge Sainsbury's and a
Waitrose, two of London's best supermarkets, are only a
block away. Public transportation is a snap and less than
five minutes away by foot.

FACILITIES AND SERVICES: Central heat, direct-dial
phones with private number, lift, equipped kitchens,
satellite TV, office safe, iron and ironing board, maid
service Monday through Friday, desk open 7:30 A.M.–
10:30 P.M.

NEAREST TOURIST ATTRACTIONS: Museum District, Royal
Albert Hall

ASTONS APARTMENTS (27)
39 Rosary Gardens, South Kensington, SW7
Tube: Gloucester Road
54 flats, all with shower or bath and toilet

TELEPHONE
020 7590 6000; 800-525-2810
(toll-free from the U.S.)

FAX
020 7590 6060

EMAIL
sales@astons-apartments.com

INTERNET
www.astons-apartments.com

CREDIT CARDS
AE, MC, V

RATES
Standard single £60 per day,
double £85–90 per day, triple
£120 per day, quad £160 per
day; designer studios for 1–2
£120 per day; 5% discount for
weekly stays. All rates exclusive
of 17.5% VAT. Strict 48-hour
cancellation or change of plans
policy absolutely enforced.

BREAKFAST
Not served

The three stately Victorian homes that make up
Astons are tucked away in South Kensington on a quiet
side street off Old Brompton Road. The apartments are
streamlined units with equipped kitchens and private
bathrooms. Despite some severe drawbacks for some
people, they are popular because of their location and
contemporary styling. The coordinated units are divided
into standard and designer studios. The standard studios
are small, basic, and cramped for long stays involving
more than one person with any degree of luggage. The
modular bathrooms feature a shower nozzle on the wall
encircled by a shower curtain that would barely prevent
the rest of this minispace from being drenched. The
studios do have equipped kitchens with microwaves and
hot plates, satellite television, and ISDN lines. The
designer choices are on the back and overlook a garden.
They have a touch more space and include a marble
shower, hair dryer, trouser press, robe, and private room
safe in addition to all of the above amenities. Best bets
are the three basement quads, thanks to their tile bathrooms with an enclosed stall shower and cooking areas
with a proper stove and oven. My complaints with *all* of
their apartments are the woefully inadequate closets,
total lack of drawer space, and dearth of comfortable
seating. This was quite apparent when I witnessed a
guest booking a second studio to use chiefly as closet
and storage space, and to gain an extra chair! On
the brochure, a man is pictured using the bed as a desk

for his laptop and assorted paperwork. No wonder . . . workspace is virtually nonexistent here. When booking, please be aware that management strictly adheres to a forty-eight-hour cancellation policy, which will not be waived for any reason whatsoever. In addition, if you cut your stay short without giving this forty-eight hours' notice, you will pay for the entire stay. They also quote their rates without the 17.5 percent VAT, but you do get a 5 percent discount for stays of a week or more.

FACILITIES AND SERVICES: Central heat, direct-dial phones, hair dryer in designer studios, on request in standard studios, equipped kitchens, ISDN lines, iron, ironing board on request, trouser press in designer studios, office safe (standard studios), room safe (designer studios), satellite TV, daily maid service with linen changes twice a week, desk open 8 A.M.–9 P.M.; no lift

NEAREST TOURIST ATTRACTIONS: Museum District, Royal Albert Hall

CITADINES APART'HOTELS

Leave it to French ingenuity to design a good-value apartment hotel that doesn't remind you that you're on a *budget* at every turn, or make you feel *nouveau pauvre* while staying there. The exteriors are institutionally correct, and so are the studios (for one or two persons) and the large one- or two-bedroom flats (for up to six), which are decorated in cookie-cutter style but have all the basics, plus a few extras that vary according to location. In all, besides pots, pans, nice crockery, and glassware in the kitchen, you will have a microwave and a dishwasher. The bathrooms are worth the price alone, with their sink space *and* shelves, plus a tub and shower. The living space includes a good-size table, bookshelves, satellite television, and a CD player. There are coin-operated laundries, or you can send your laundry and cleaning out in the morning and have it returned that evening; luggage storage can be arranged, and there is always message and mail service. Bed linen changes and maid services are included once a week, and towels are changed twice weekly. The desk is open twenty-four hours a day. Another positive for many are the rooms reserved for nonsmokers.

The studios interconnect, and are all about the same size: twenty-five square meters. That, for the metrically challenged, is about three hundred square feet. The Citadines Apart'hotels include the Barbican, Holborn/

TELEPHONE
020 7766 3800
FAX
020 7766 3866
EMAIL
reslondon@citadines.com
INTERNET
www.citadines.com

Covent Garden, South Kensington, and Trafalgar. Details on each follow.

Central Reservations is open daily 8:30 A.M.–7 P.M.

FACILITIES AND SERVICES: In all Citadines Apart'hotels are central heat; direct-dial phone; double-glazed windows; hair dryer; ironing facilities; equipped kitchen with dishwasher, 2 burners, microwave; lift; coin-operated laundry; laundry services; office services at nominal fees; parking spaces (£18 per day); satellite TV; CD and tape player (BYO music); office or private room safe; rooms for the disabled; baby cots with changing tables on request; nonsmoking rooms; 24-hour desk; maid and linen service once a week; towels changed twice a week; vacuum provided. Consult listings below for other specific services offered by each hotel.

CITADINES–BARBICAN (4)
7–21 Goswell Road, Barbican, EC1
Tube: Barbican

129 studios and flats for 1-4 people, all with shower or bath and toilet

TELEPHONE
020 7566 8000

FAX
020 7566 8130

EMAIL
barbican@citadines.com

CREDIT CARDS
AE, DC, MC, V

RATES
Daily rates start at £110 for a studio and £155 for a flat for up to 4; the longer the stay, the lower the rate

BREAKFAST
Continental breakfast £8, English breakfast £10

This is the lowest-priced Citadines apartment building in London. The area around the Barbican is not tourist central, but there is tube and bus transportation, a modern Safeway grocery store, and use of the Barbican Y Fitness Center or swimming at a nearby pool for lower fees. The rooms are not air-conditioned, but the building does have an air-cooling system. Besides the Barbican Centre, which is home to the London Symphony Orchestra, you are reasonably close to the historical City of London, Saint Paul's Cathedral, and the London Museum. If you want to take a peek at suburban London living, Islington, which has some interesting restaurants and shops, is close by. The Barbican also accepts pets. (Oh . . . how French!)

NEAREST TOURIST ATTRACTIONS: Barbican Centre

CITADINES–HOLBORN/COVENT GARDEN (39)
94–99 High Holborn, Covent Garden, WC1
Tube: Holborn

192 flats, all with shower or bath and toilet

TELEPHONE
020 7395 8800

FAX
020 7395 8799

EMAIL
holborn@citadines.com

CREDIT CARDS
AE, DC, MC, V

For pleasure visitors to London, this is a super address. From here you can walk to the British Museum and Covent Garden, one of the most vibrant and fashionable parts of London, and you are within striking distance of the banks of the Thames, Piccadilly Circus, Oxford Street, and Charles Dickens' house. In all, there are 152 studios for one to two people and 40 one-bedroom flats for one to four people. All have air-conditioning, and conference rooms are available as well.

NEAREST TOURIST ATTRACTIONS: British Museum, Covent Garden, Royal Opera House, Oxford Street

RATES
Studio £118, flat £165, lower rates for longer stays

BREAKFAST
Continental breakfast £8

CITADINES–SOUTH KENSINGTON (8)
35A Gloucester Road, South Kensington, SW7
Tube: Gloucester Road
92 flats, all with shower or bath and toilet

The ninety-two apartments at the Citadines in South Kensington offer the choice of a studio or a two-level apartment, but I think the studios have a better layout than the apartments. There is no dining room, but special rates can be arranged for guests to have breakfast at the restaurant next door. From the doorstep, you are within walking distance of Hyde Park, the museum district, and for more mundane outings, grocery shopping at the mammoth twenty-four-hour Sainsbury's on Cromwell Road. The apartments are air-conditioned and have room safes large enough for a laptop, and there's a fitness studio.

NEAREST TOURIST ATTRACTIONS: Museum District, Royal Albert Hall, Kensington Palace and Gardens

TELEPHONE
020 7543 7878

FAX
020 7584 9166

EMAIL
kensington@citadines.com

CREDIT CARDS
AE, MC, V

RATES
Studio for 1–2 persons £120–130, 1 bedroom for 1–4 persons £170; lower rates for longer stays starting with one week, and during the off-season

BREAKFAST
Continental or English breakfast £8

CITADINES–TRAFALGAR (59)
18–21 Northumberland Avenue, Trafalgar Square, WC2
Tube: Charing Cross, Embankment
187 flats, all with shower or bath and toilet

The Citadines–Trafalgar right next to Trafalgar Square and close to the South Bank. A bonus for guests is the use of the Royal Commonwealth Society's dining room, which has been dramatically redone in a stunning, colorful modern theme. All flats are air-conditioned.

NEAREST TOURIST ATTRACTIONS: National Gallery, Trafalgar Square, South Bank, National Theatre, Royal Festival Hall, Queen Elizabeth Hall

TELEPHONE
020 7766 3700

FAX
020 7766 3766

EMAIL
trafalgar@citadines.com

CREDIT CARDS
AE, DC, MC, V

RATES
Studio for 1–2 people £118, flat for 1–4 people £170, flat for 1–6 people £210; discounts for longer stays

BREAKFAST
Continental breakfast £7, English breakfast £9

DOLPHIN SQUARE (37)
Chichester Street, Dolphin Square, Pimlico, SW1
Tube: Pimlico
151 flats, all with shower or bath and toilet

Dolphin Square, a three-and-a-half-acre riverside block of flats and gardens near the Tate Gallery, has been called home by an illustrious—and notorious—group of residents, including Christine Keeler, the prostitute at

TELEPHONE
020 7834 3800; 800-44-UTELL (toll-free from the U.S.)

FAX
020 7798 8735

EMAIL
reservations@
dolphinsquarehotel.co.uk

INTERNET
www.dolphinsquarehotel.co.uk

CREDIT CARDS
AE, DC, MC, V

RATES
Studio single use £150–185,
double use £175–185; classic
suites: 1 bedroom £185–195,
2 bedrooms £250–300,
3 bedrooms, 3 baths, sleeps 6
£420; corporate and monthly
rates depending on availability
and time of year

BREAKFAST
Continental breakfast £11,
English breakfast £15

the center of the Profumo scandal; Sir Oswald Mosley, the World War II leader of the British Fascists; John Vassal, the Admiralty spy; and, more recently, Princess Anne and her husband, Commander Timothy Laurence, both of whom spent a few months in a flat here.

If you enjoy the services offered by a deluxe hotel, plus the advantages of sports facilities, shops, gourmet dining, and a place to park your car, it would be hard to imagine a better address than Dolphin Square. The flats range from studios to three-bedroom accommodations with fireplaces, above-average kitchens, large baths, and loads of storage and living space. All are highly recommendable. Aside from just staying in nice surroundings, guests are extended free membership in the health club, with a sixty-foot heated indoor swimming pool, a sauna, and a steam room. A staff is on hand to provide massages and beauty treatments at reasonable rates. Energetic visitors can book a tennis court or join a squash game on one of eight courts. Others can attend yoga or aerobics classes. Two restaurants, including Gary Rhodes's award winning restaurant, Rhodes in the Square, and room service take care of those not in the mood to cook. For those who are, shopping in the arcade is a cinch: there's a greengrocer, minimarket, deli, and wine shop, plus a travel and theater booking agent, car hire, chemist, newsstand, and dry cleaner.

All flats have fully equipped kitchens and seven-day-a-week maid service, but the prices do *not* include breakfast.

FACILITIES AND SERVICES: "The works," including but not limited to: bar, baby-sitting, business center with Internet and email access at nominal charge, conference center, central heat and ceiling fans, direct-dial phones, answering machine in all flats, hair dryer, iron and ironing board, fully fitted kitchens, microwaves in smaller flats or on request in larger flats, laundry and dry cleaning shop on premises, lift, office safe, parking (£20 per 24 hours), restaurants (Rhodes in the Square and a brasserie), room service, satellite TV, sports club, swimming pool, squash and tennis courts, full-service beauty salon, fax and data port in all rooms, mobile phone rental, travel agency, shops, full concierge service, theater booking, car hire, porters, 24-hour desk

NEAREST TOURIST ATTRACTIONS: Tate Britain

EIGHT KNARESBOROUGH PLACE (23)
8 Knaresborough Place, Earl's Court, SW5
Tube: Earl's Court, Gloucester Road

12 flats, all with shower or bath and toilet

Eight Knaresborough Place and Five Emperor's Gate (below) are owned and managed by Robert and Polly Arnold, his sister Susan Noah, and their father, Walter Arnold. Robert is in charge of the business end, while the others handle the day-to-day running of these two blocks of serviced flats. I prefer the block of twelve flats at Knaresborough Place because they are better located, have good security, and offer the added convenience of a laundry room. The interiors are furnished in a way that is suitable for families; in other words, nothing is precious. Several have their own private patio gardens or balconies with chairs and tables for sunny days. A word of caution, however, there is no lift in either building, and the climb to the top floors can be treacherous for some, especially if carrying anything heavy. For shopping needs, you will have to go no farther than Cromwell Road to two of the best supermarkets in London, which have everything you could ever need and then some.

There is always someone at the desk from 7 A.M. to 11 P.M. at Knaresborough Place, whereas at Emperor's Gate there is no office or on-site manager at any time.

FACILITIES AND SERVICES: Central heat, fans on request, direct-line private phones with payment for each call by credit card, hair dryer available, fitted kitchens, iron and ironing board, drying rack, coin-operated laundry, TV, linen and maid service 6 days a week, office at Knaresborough Place open 7 A.M.–11 P.M.; no lift, no safe

NEAREST TOURIST ATTRACTIONS: Museum District, Royal Albert Hall

TELEPHONE
020 7244 8409/7373 0323

FAX
020 7373 6455

EMAIL
info@apartment-hotels.com

INTERNET
www.apartment-hotels.com

CREDIT CARDS
AE, DC, MC, V

RATES
£100–160 per night for up to 5 people; minimum stay of 2 days; lower rates on request for stays of more than 3 weeks

BREAKFAST
Not served

FIVE EMPEROR'S GATE (14)
5 Emperor's Gate, South Kensington, SW7
Tube: Gloucester Road

6 flats, all with shower or bath and toilet

The six flats at Five Emperor's Gate—which is run by the same people who run Eight Knaresborough Place (above)—have their devotees, especially those rooms with the newer bathrooms and kitchens hidden behind folding louvered doors. If you are willing to climb some steep stairs, ask for Flat F, with a sofa bed and a bird's-eye view from the arched windows. It's a bit of a tight squeeze in the twin bedroom, but it does have appeal. So does the Flat First Level West, with a large mirrored

TELEPHONE
020 7244 8409/7373 0323

FAX
020 7373 6455

EMAIL & INTERNET
See Eight Knaresborough Place

CREDIT CARDS
AE, DC, MC, V

RATES
£110–175 per night for up to 4 people; minimum stay of 2 days; lower rates on request for stays of more than 3 weeks

closet, small balcony, and a separate sitting area. If stairs are not part of your program, reserve Flat A, a basement location with a separate entrance and a bricked-floor entry. There isn't much sunshine here, but that doesn't seem to bother those who appreciate the cozy electric fireplace, rather modern furniture, and one of the better kitchens in the building.

Emperor's Gate has no office or on-site manager; contact the office at Eight Knaresborough Place for information and reservations.

FACILITIES AND SERVICES: Central heat, direct-line private phones in each flat with payment for calls by credit card, hair dryer available, fitted kitchens, iron and ironing board, drying rack, TV, linen and maid service 6 days a week; no lift, no safe, no on-site manager

NEAREST TOURIST ATTRACTIONS: Museum District, Royal Albert Hall

HPS APARTMENT RENTALS (10)
2 Hyde Park Square, W2
Tube: Lancaster Gate, Marble Arch, Paddington

TELEPHONE
020 7262 8271

FAX
020 7262 7626

EMAIL
reservation@
apartments2book.com

INTERNET
www.apartments2book.com

CREDIT CARDS
AE, DC, MC, V

RATES
See individual apartment rental
write-ups

BREAKFAST
Not served

Where there is a need, there is always a way to fill it. Martyn Lawson recognized the need in London for serviced apartments of a high standard, offering excellent value for money and situated in prime London areas. The result is HPS Apartment Rentals, which offers some of the most spacious, well-decorated apartments for the money that can be found in London. All are central; none is located in a tourist fringe that requires long commutes to get to anything more marginally interesting than the local pub. If you are going to Rome, Paris, Madrid, Barcelona, or New York, HPS Apartment Rentals also has apartments in those cities. The following four apartment buildings represent a good cross-section of what HPS has available in London. For further information and to reserve, contact HPS directly. Apartments include Allen House, Lancaster Gate, Mayfair Pied et Terre, and Two Hyde Park Square, which are described below.

ALLEN HOUSE (47)
Allen Street, Kensington, W8
Tube: High Street Kensington
35 flats, all with shower or bath and toilet

RATES
All rates include VAT: 1–2
bedrooms £150–190 per night;
3 bedroom, 2 bath from £225
per night; lower rates subject to
season, availability, and length
of stay

These flats, in the Royal Borough of Kensington and Chelsea, just a block or so off High Street Kensington, provide you with all the conveniences of shopping, restaurants, and transportation around Kensington, while still maintaining a quiet, neighborhood feel. All of the spacious flats are named after famous London areas or streets. One of my favorites is No. 29, Savile, on the front, with two beautifully arched windows letting in loads of light. I also like the large No. 38, Winchester, and No. 25, Portobello. All have great closets. However, be sure your unit has been recently redone. That is not to say the older units are in shambles, but since the bright coordinated colors, new bathrooms, and modern kitchens in the redone units are the same price as the older units, why not? An extra summer bonus is the large enclosed garden. Allen House flats can be booked through HPS Apartment Rentals (above).

FACILITIES AND SERVICES: Central heat, direct-dial phones with security entry, fax machines on request, lifts, 5-day maid service, porter, office safe, satellite TV, some washers, dryers, and dishwashers

NEAREST TOURIST ATTRACTIONS: Shopping along Kensington High Street, Museum District, Kensington Palace and Gardens

LANCASTER GATE (18)
49 Lancaster Gate, W2
Tube: Lancaster Gate, Queensway
6 flats, all with shower or bath and toilet

The six beautifully furnished two- and three-bedroom flats at Lancaster Gate are only a few minutes from Hyde Park, in a quiet London square between Queensway and Marble Arch. The units are well equipped, meticulously maintained, and totally coordinated. All come with washers, dryers, dishwashers, and two television sets. Kitchens have a proper stove, microwave, and quality cooking utensils, crockery, and silver. It probably has become evident that I am a great fan of closet and drawer space, but one of the oversize bedrooms here exceeds my wildest dreams, with six chests that hold twenty-seven drawers! Ah . . . heaven, and all in one room! The ground-floor bedrooms have no view, so if that is a problem, I would suggest a flat on a higher floor.

FACILITIES AND SERVICES: Central heat, direct-dial phones with security entry, fax on request, lift, maid service, satellite TV, VCR, washer, dryer, dishwasher, 5-day maid service

NEAREST TOURIST ATTRACTIONS: Hyde Park, Kensington Gardens

RATES
All rates are per day and include VAT: 2 bedrooms/2 bathrooms £190; 3 bedrooms/ 2 bathrooms £225; lower rates depending on season, availability, and length of stay

MAYFAIR PIED ET TERRE
Tube: Depends on apartment location
20 flats, all with shower or bath and toilet

RATES
All rates are per day and include VAT: 1 bedroom £130–150; 2 bedrooms/2 bathrooms £155–270, lower rates subject to season, availability, and length of stay

These apartments are so popular that people never want to leave. In fact, they want to buy them. Considering the platinum locations, scattered around the heart of Mayfair and on the edge of Grosvenor Square and Park Lane, I would hate to think what the prices would be if they actually were for sale. As with all HPS Apartments, these are comfortably livable and nicely decorated with all the conveniences to make your stay easy and pleasant. These apartments are in various Mayfair locations.

FACILITIES AND SERVICES: Central heat, direct-dial phones with security entry, fax on request, lift, 5-day maid service, car park (rates on request), satellite TV, VCR available, washer, dryer

NEAREST TOURIST ATTRACTIONS: Depends on location

KENSBRIDGE APARTMENTS
Main office: 38 Emperor's Gate, South Kensington, SW7
Tube: Gloucester Road

TELEPHONE
020 7589 2923 (central reservations)
FAX
020 7373 6183 (central reservations)
CREDIT CARDS
None; British sterling only
RATES
Singles start at £155 per week (shared facilities—no singles have bath, shower, or toilet); doubles start at £320 per week (shared facilities), £380 (private facilities); triple or quad with private facilities £420–450; extra bed £25 per week; a deposit of £100, paid in British sterling, is required to secure the reservation
BREAKFAST
Not served

There is not a chance you will become bored with perfection in one of Walter Harris's unsophisticated bottom-of-the-barrel budget flats. If you need a really cheap place for a long-term London stay and can keep expectations to a rock-bottom level while living in a no-frills, no-charm spot with 1950s veneer, dated colors, and user-friendly furniture and bathrooms, you will no doubt be just fine staying here and certainly will be pleased with the money you will save. If you are willing to share a bathroom with another flat, the sleeping gets even cheaper. Some of the singles are mighty small, closets are minuscule, and the kitchen (of sorts) does not always have a sink—you might have to use the one in the bathroom. Most of the flats have twin beds, but doubles can be requested. The locations are close to bus and tube transport, and household shopping needs can easily be met in nearby supermarkets and neighborhood shops. Despite the time-warp feel of these flats, they are very popular with determined budgeteers, so if you fall in that category, get your reservation in early . . . and read the fine print about refunds, cancellations, and so on. There is a one-week minimum stay.

Apartments in the group include Eccleston House, Elvaston Lodge, and Kensgate House, all briefly described below. For reservations, contact the main office.

FACILITIES AND SERVICES: All flats have heat, hall phones, equipped kitchens, Mon–Fri maid service, linen changed weekly, TV, office hours Mon–Fri 9:30 A.M.–5:30 P.M., Sat 9 A.M.–2 P.M., offices in all closed Sunday and holidays; no safes

ECCLESTON HOUSE (23)
64–66 Eccleston Square, Victoria, SW1
Tube: Victoria

TELEPHONE
020 7839 0985

Despite the historic location on lovely Eccleston Square, only three doors from one of Winston Churchill's former homes, the Eccleston House flats are recommended only for the hardest-core cheap-sleeping enthusiasts. The flats are clean and the location good, but you know you are on a lean budget when you are forced to sleep here.

NEAREST TOURIST ATTRACTIONS: Victoria, Westminster

ELVASTON LODGE (9)
12 Elvaston Place, South Kensington, SW7
Tube: Gloucester Road

TELEPHONE
020 7589 9412 (office); 020 7584 0873 (guests)

This block of flats in South Kensington features studios and two-room apartments and is the best of this group. That is not saying much, however, because just like all the others, it is very, very budget-basic, with no decorating thought given to any of the flats. Forget bringing any electronic equipment more sophisticated than a transistor radio with earphones. Email hookup? Please . . . you can't be serious! The only guest telephone in the building is the one by the entryway in the downstairs hall. Top flat picks are No. 8, with a loft bedroom, and No. 9, a front studio for two with a porch.

NEAREST TOURIST ATTRACTIONS: Museum District, Royal Albert Hall

KENSGATE HOUSE (15)
38 Emperor's Gate, South Kensington, SW7
Tube: Gloucester Road
17 flats, 13 with shower or bath and toilet

TELEPHONE
020 7370 1040 (office); 020 7370 6624 (guests)

The decorating theme here follows the same "any chair will do" mentality as the others in the Kensbridge group. The four single flats do not have private facilities, and in No. 10, the tiniest, the same sink doubles as your bathroom and kitchen washing facility. If you land in No. 1, a small basement double with facilities, you will get a double bed, two chairs, and a fold-down table mounted on one wall. A better choice is No. 9, with a separate kitchen, two chairs, and a proper table. Number 2, on the ground floor facing the street, is the largest and lightest choice. There is a double bed on the main level, but on the mezzanine above, anyone over four feet tall would not be able to stand erect.

NEAREST TOURIST ATTRACTIONS: Museum District, Royal Albert Hall

KNIGHTSBRIDGE SERVICE FLATS (4)
45 Ennismore Gardens, Knightsbridge, SW7
Tube: Knightsbridge
12 flats, all with shower or bath and toilet

Because these simple flats, owned for many years by Martin Raphael, are functional, clean, well located, and reasonably priced, I consider them a Great Sleep in London.

For the ultimate in London shopping, you can take a shortcut and sneak through "the hole-in-the-wall" and be at Harrods' door in minutes. However, if you are expecting to entertain dignitaries or want high-roller surroundings, these flats are not for you, despite the celebrity-studded neighborhood of stately mansions. Ava Gardner lived across the street for twenty years in a flat that rumor has it was paid for by Frank Sinatra, and Charles Gray, who played in early James Bond films, lived next door.

These twelve units are furnished in a mix from the 1940s and 1950s. Some have been redecorated in bland beige, others are still in off-greens and oranges. Most have beds in the sitting room and too many chairs. Workspace is minimal, and the flats are certainly not geared toward those who travel in the electronic, high-tech fast track. On the plus side, the bathrooms are good and have bathtubs with showers above. The kitchens, even though they are old style, have microwaves and everything else you will need for boiling water or preparing a feast. The top-floor flats are the best because they have better views; No. 12 even has a walk-in closet, and remember, there *is* a lift. The basement garden flat, with an eat-in kitchen, opens onto a patio and has a sunroom with a sofa and two chairs.

FACILITIES AND SERVICES: Wall heaters, direct-dial phones with private number, lift, satellite TV, iron and ironing board, maid service Mon–Fri, office open 8 A.M.–8 P.M.; no safe

TELEPHONE
020 7584 4123
FAX
020 7584 9058
EMAIL
info@ksflats.demon.co.uk
INTERNET
www.ksflats.demon.co.uk
CREDIT CARDS
MC, V
RATES
£570–640 per week, depending on size, location, and number of people; lower off-season rates. A week's stay is preferred, but shorter stays can be accommodated if there is room. Reservations are guaranteed on receipt of 1 week's rent in advance, and all rents thereafter are payable weekly in advance. If you leave before your reservation is over, you will be charged for the full period unless the flat can be relet.
BREAKFAST
Not served

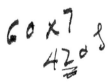

NEAREST TOURIST ATTRACTIONS: Museum District, Royal Albert Hall, Knightsbridge shopping

LEXHAM APARTMENTS ($, 48)
32–38 Lexham Gardens, W8
Tube: Gloucester Road, High Street Kensington

31 studio to 2-bedroom apartments

Sitting on a leafy Kensington square in one of the most fashionable neighborhoods of London are the elegant Lexham Apartments, done in beautiful taste and offering every modern appliance in streamlined kitchens with hardwood floors and eating spaces. Additional amenities are fax, voice mail, data port, private safe, Monday to Friday maid service, 24-hour porter, and complimentary membership at a health club. With the exception of the ground-floor studio, each apartment has plenty of closet, living, and working space. The one-bedroom apartments have a sofa bed in the living room, so they could accommodate up to four people. Most of us could just move right in to No. 12, a two-bedroom choice with the sunny master bedroom overlooking a private back garden. The marble bathroom has space galore, and oh, those double closets! The well-equipped kitchen would inspire me to make frequent trips to the nearby Sainsbury's supermarket. Number 16, with high ceilings and plenty of daylight, faces the street. It has a beautiful bath off the double bedroom and a small guest bath along the hall. You can reserve for one night or a year, but of course the longer you stay, the better the rate.

FACILITIES AND SERVICES: Central heat; fans; 2 telephones with voice mail; fax; data ports; ISDN line; security entrance phone; hair dryer; fully fitted kitchen with freezer dishwasher, washer, and dryer; lift; maid service Mon–Fri; towels and linens changed twice weekly; satellite TV with VCR on request; 24-hour porter; health club membership

NEAREST TOURIST ATTRACTIONS: Museum District, shopping along Kensington High Street

TELEPHONE
020 7559 4444

FAX
020 7559 4400

EMAIL
reservations@lexham.com

INTERNET
www.lexham.com

CREDIT CARDS
MC, V

RATES
1-bedroom £1,175 per week, 2-bedroom £1,475 per week; 17.5% VAT extra, lower rates for longer stays. There is no minimum stay, and rates can be negotiated for longer stays. The Lexham Apartments can also be booked through HPS Apartment Rentals; please see page 202.

BREAKFAST
Not served

NELL GWYNN HOUSE APARTMENTS AND THE ACCOMMODATION OFFICE (11)
Sloane Avenue, Chelsea, SW3
Tube: Sloane Square, South Kensington

NGH: 170 flats, all with shower or bath and toilet
The Accommodation Office: 200 flats, all with shower or bath and toilet

This massive apartment block is so well known in London that it doesn't even need a street number—all you need to know is Nell Gwynn House, Sloane Avenue.

Over the years I have inspected many, many London flats, but when I am in London for any length of time I stay at Nell Gwynn. For its price and location, between Old Brompton Road and King's Road, I cannot imagine wanting more than this location has to offer.

The apartments stand in the heart of Chelsea, one of the most exclusive residential districts in London. The spacious choices range from studios to one- and two-bedroom apartments. Most of the accommodations have abundant closets with plenty of shelves, hanging space, and out-of-sight luggage storage. There is an equipped kitchen, some with microwaves; a color television, some with cable; an iron and ironing board; a bathroom with good light and a tub with shower or a stall shower; central heat; direct-dial phones; and answering machines available for a small weekly charge. Washers, dryers, and dishwashers are available in many of the newer flats. At Nell Gwynn House Apartments, mandatory maid service is from Monday through Friday; towels are changed twice a week and bed linens once a week. Mail is delivered to your flat. An apartment rented through the Accommodations Office includes this maid service.

If you can't find what you want in the neighborhood, chances are you don't really need it. Across the street is a row of shops, including a dry cleaner, convenience grocery, pharmacy, and real estate agent in case you decide to extend your stay to a more permanent status. For long-term housekeeping and cooking needs, King's Road, with two supermarkets, is just a five-minute walk away; Harrods is fifteen. Walton Street, a wonderful street full of tempting boutiques and several restaurants listed in *Great Eats London,* is a block away. Elystan Place and Chelsea Green, an aristocratic square, is another block in the other direction. Here you can indulge in magnificent French pastries and breads, have your hair done, do your laundry, buy an expensive antique or

---

Nell Gwynn House Apartments

TELEPHONE
020 7589 1105

FAX
020 7589 9433

EMAIL
reservations@
nghapartments.co.uk

INTERNET
www.nghapartments.co.uk

CREDIT CARDS
AE, MC, V

RATES
All rates are per week and include VAT. There is a 1-week minimum stay. Studios for 1–2 persons £425–460, studio for 2–4 persons £545–585, 1 bedroom for 2–4 £620–825, 2 bedrooms for 3–5 £970, extra large 2-bedroom for 4 persons £1,215; mandatory maid service is £55–60 per week depending on size of apartment; a refundable deposit of £350–700 is required in advance to reserve against cancellation, for the use of the telephone, and for any potential damages. The balance of the deposit is refunded in about 10 days, after the monthly phone bill has been received and paid. 4 weeks' cancellation notice required. Payment for the 1st week is due upon arrival. Discounts for longer stays. Each April, rates are reviewed and can raise slightly.

BREAKFAST
Not served

---

custom-designed gown or a toy for a special little one, stop by the hardware store, have your clothes cleaned, and get your shoes shined. You can also buy fresh fish, meat, cheese, flowers, and the finest produce in London. If you are not in the mood to cook, there is an excellent deli, plus are a dozen or more excellent *Great Eats London* restaurants, wine bars, and pubs within a two- to ten-minute walk. Taxis on Sloane Avenue take only three or four minutes to flag down, even during rush hour. Otherwise you can easily walk to two tube stops or buses that go directly to the West End and most points beyond. As you can see, when I say this location has it all, I am *not* stretching the truth.

Two rental offices operate from here, one representing individual owners (the Accommodation Office) and the other a corporation managing its own flats (Nell Gwynn House Apartments). At Nell Gwynn House Apartments, the minimum stay is one week and the flats range in size from studios for up to three to large two-bedroom units that can sleep six. While redecoration has improved things somewhat over the past few years, there is no getting away from the older-style building and the dated bathroom colors in many of their flats. That is not to say that they are not serviceable and don't have plenty of space . . . but avocado-green bathroom fixtures are definitely way past their sell-by date.

The flats at the Accommodation Office have a twenty-two-night minimum stay and are either studios or one-bedroom units. Because each flat is individually owned, many of them have been completely modernized and refitted, but some others definitely need to be. The problem here is that you cannot request a particular flat, and if you decide to extend, you might not be able to stay put, because the owner may have blocked the dates following your intended departure. If the flat you do get does not have a toaster, or some other amenity you want or need, you are out of luck: there is no source of extra supplies, so what you see is what you get.

FACILITIES AND SERVICES: Central heat; direct-dial phones with your own private number; answering machines on request; iron and ironing board; washers, dryers, and dishwashers in some units; laundry service; lifts; maid service Mon–Fri; bed linen changed weekly, towels twice weekly; parking, individual safes in office; TV (most with satellite); 24-hour porter; concierge; car hire; ticket bookings; fax and secretarial services during

The Accommodation Office

TELEPHONE
020 7584 8317

FAX
020 7823 7133

CREDIT CARDS
AE, MC, V

RATES
All rates include VAT and maid service. Studio £395–540 per week, 1 bedroom £600–790 per week. Minimum 22-day stay may be extended by the day or week thereafter and is payable accordingly. 22 days' rent is payable in advance, and a minimum of 1 week's rent is required as a refundable deposit against telephone charges and damages.

BREAKFAST
Not served

business hours, which are Mon–Fri 9 A.M.–6 P.M. (and Sat for NGH Apartments)

NEAREST TOURIST ATTRACTIONS: King's Road, Knightsbridge shopping, walk to Museum District

SNOW WHITE PROPERTIES (5)
55 Ennismore Gardens, Knightsbridge, SW7
Tube: Knightsbridge

12 flats, all with shower or bath and toilet

TELEPHONE
020 7584 3307

FAX
020 7581 4686

EMAIL
snow.white@virgin.net

INTERNET
www.freespace.virgin.net/
snow.white

CREDIT CARDS
MC, V

RATES
Studios £720–800 per week, 1 bedroom £840–1020 per week, extra person £15 daily, £80 weekly; lower off-season rates and for long stays; 2-bedroom apartment near Harrods, £1,300 per week, cash only

BREAKFAST
Not served

Maxine White, along with the help of her friendly assistant and Custard the cat, offers twelve nicely appointed flats on Ennismore Gardens. They are well situated for shopping trips to Knightsbridge, performances at the Royal Albert Hall, the museum complex that includes the Victoria and Albert, and leisurely strolls or bracing morning jogs through Hyde Park. I can recommend all of the flats, which are charmingly done in the English school of decorating that leaves no ruffle or frill undone or overlooked. Everything is coordinated, right down to the colors of the shower curtains and the bows on the bowls of scented potpourri. In addition, the closet space is good, the bathrooms are nice, and the kitchens are especially well equipped, some with Maxine's own china. Number 2, a basement twin or double in pink florals, opens onto a small plant-filled terrace. Contrary to most lower-level accommodations in London, this one is cheerful and light. Flat No. 8 is a large studio with a terrace. Number 12 is also a studio, done in green and yellow, with adequate closet space, a place to store luggage, and a nice bathroom. Everyone loves No. 7, with two windows overlooking the gardens and a larger kitchen. It is charmingly decorated in blue, white, and yellow with blue-and-white Chinese porcelain pieces dominating the living room. I also like the top-floor flat, with the living area smartly done in gray and white, with yellow, cerise, and plum accent cushions. The twin bedroom has antique beds covered in gray quilted spreads, and the bathroom has a skylight. The large kitchen should inspire trips to Harrods' fabulous food halls, and the brick terrace, with its table and chairs, is the perfect place for a summer breakfast or late-afternoon drink before going out to the theater. Maxine and her assistant are charming hostesses, and their devoted regulars adore them, so if this is your kind of place, please book as far ahead as possible.

Maxine also has a large two-bedroom flat behind Harrods, near the Basil Street and Capital Hotels. It is done in Maxine's style and has its own phone, fax, washer, dryer, and dishwasher. At the moment there is one bath, with a second planned. The price is £1,300 a week, cash only.

FACILITIES AND SERVICES: Air-conditioning (portable) in some; central heat; direct telephone line for each flat (no answering machines); iron and ironing board; fitted kitchens with stoves and microwaves; lift to 2nd, 3rd, and 4th floors, not to the top flat but the walk up is easy; office safe, satellite TV, washer and dryer in the building, maid service 5 days a week; security phone at entrance with bell to each flat; fax facilities in the office, which is open Mon–Fri 9:30 A.M.–5:30 P.M.

NEAREST TOURIST ATTRACTIONS: Hyde Park, Royal Albert Hall, Museum District, Knightsbridge shopping

23 GREENGARDEN HOUSE ($, 14)
St. Cristopher's Place (no number), W1
Tube: Bond Street

23 1–2 bedroom apartments

St. Christopher's Place is reached by entering a narrow passageway off Oxford Street, opposite the Bond Street tube stop. This charming and secluded enclave is full of cafés, restaurants, and shops most people never stumble upon. The elegant accommodations at 23 Greengarden House, owned by the Athenaeum Hotel, are almost as secret and unknown. These distinctive one- and two-bedroom units provide space, independence, and very high quality service. Each is furnished with the type of style and taste that creates a beautiful setting with a character all its own. Bathrooms are marble tiled, and the kitchens are equipped with all the modern appliances, including a full stove, refrigerator, and microwave, so you can boil water for a cup of tea or prepare a party and set the table with lovely china, cutlery, and glassware. Minimalists will feel at home in No. 41, a two-bedroom masculine setting that mixes offbeat colors with stark, hard-edged furnishings featuring chrome, glass, and metal. Traditionalists will feel warm and cozy in No. 33, a one-bedroom flat with rose wallpaper and two comfortable sofas in the living room, which is accessorized with beautiful lamps and lush fabrics. The queen-size blue-and-yellow bedroom has a second television and plenty of lighted closets.

TELEPHONE
020 7935 9191

FAX
020 7935 8858

EMAIL
info@greengardenhouse.com

INTERNET
www.greengardenhouse.com

CREDIT CARDS
AE, DC, MC, V

RATES
1 bedroom £205–240 per night, £1,435–1,655 per week; 2 bedroom £270–330 per night, £1,875–2,315 per week. Prices vary according to size of the apartment and do not include 17.5% VAT. No minimum or maximum stay, but prices can be negotiated for long stays.

BREAKFAST
Not served

None of the apartments has a view, but they all are so lovely inside that an expansive view doesn't seem to be important. The level of service provided is amazing and includes staff who will do your shopping at no extra charge. In addition guests have the convenience and enjoyment of three phone lines per apartment, a dedicated ISDN line, voice mail, satellite television, video, CD player, and a maid to keep it all clean and do your dishes from Monday to Friday.

FACILITIES AND SERVICES: Air-conditioning (portable units in some), central heat, direct-dial phone with 3 lines, dedicated ISDN line, voice mail, personal fax, security entrance phone, hair dryer, same-day laundry service, washers and dryers, lift, room safe, satellite TV, VCR, CD player, Mon–Fri maid service, free shopping service, baby-sitting, secretarial service, office open Mon–Fri 9 A.M.–6 P.M.

NEAREST TOURIST ATTRACTIONS: Oxford Street, Old and New Bond Streets, Mayfair

TWO HYDE PARK SQUARE (9)
2 Hyde Park Square, Hyde Park, W2
Tube: Lancaster Gate, Marble Arch, Paddington
73 flats, all with shower or bath and toilet

RATES
Studios standard £95–115; 1-bedroom flats £120–140. All rates include VAT; lower rates for stays of more than 1 month

With more than seventy studios and one-bedroom flats, Two Hyde Park Square is not only positioned with perfection, it offers value for money for those who insist on high standards of comfort in a secure and private environment. This part of London boasts some of the most expensive real estate in the city, and these units keep pace except, surprisingly enough, in price. A variety of nearby shops and restaurants make wining and dining a pleasure either in your own flat or out. Business guests will find secretarial and office backup services, and motorists will have a secure car park for a nominal fee. All guests will be well located to strike out for all of London's major attractions.

Almost all of the units have been rejuvenated, with coordination well carried out. In my opinion, the older-style flats are very nice, and besides, they cost less and have more closet space. I think the redone studios are worth the extra cost, especially the ones with windows overlooking Hyde Park Square. The drawback for some is their lack of a washer and dryer. The kitchens are small but well equipped. If you plan on roasting your Christmas goose here, you will want No. 74, a top-floor, corner one-bedroom that has a large, bright kitchen with a four-burner stove, oven, and microwave. The view of the trees in the small park below makes you pinch yourself to remember this is London.

FACILITIES AND SERVICES: Central heat; direct-dial phones; hair dryer available; laundry service; lift; parking (£10 per night); office safe (£3 for entire stay); satellite TV; washers, dryers, and dishwashers in some; maid service Mon–Fri; linen changed twice weekly; fully fitted kitchens; concierge; business services access to private gardens, 24-hour desk

NEAREST TOURIST ATTRACTIONS: Hyde Park, Kensington Gardens

VALERIE MAY LONDON APARTMENTS (4)
3 Ryder Street, Duke Street, SW1
Tube: St. James's or Green Park
11 flats, all with shower or bath and toilet

Close to the Ryder Street Chambers (see page 134) are eleven small, fully furnished apartments to let for a week or more. Considering the platinum location, the price is amazing. All come with an equipped kitchen, separate sitting room, bedroom, and a bathroom. Some have fireplaces or faxes and even washing machines. They all are spacious and personally decorated with an English hand, and the maid comes once a week. None of them have inspiring views, but the neighborhood is one of the most expensive retail parcels in all of London. From here you are minutes to Fortnum and Mason, London's fabled grocer where Buckingham Palace places regular orders. A jog in St. James's Park or Green Park will work off the calories, and pleasant walks to the National Gallery and the National Portrait Gallery, St. Martins in the Field Church, Regent Street shopping, and Piccadilly Circus for bright lights and constant traffic will take care of tourist pursuits.

FACILITIES AND SERVICES: Central heat, direct-dial phone, fitted kitchen, lift, same-day laundry service, weekly maid service, satellite TV, some with fax or washer and dryer; no safe

NEAREST TOURIST ATTRACTIONS: Piccadilly, West End, Royal Academy of Arts

TELEPHONE
020 7930 2241

FAX
020 7839 2108

CREDIT CARDS
V

RATES
From £600 per week; all payment is strictly in advance

BREAKFAST
Not served

VANCOUVER STUDIOS (13)
30 Prince's Square, W2
Tube: Bayswater, Queensway

45 studios, all with shower or bath and toilet

TELEPHONE
020 7243 1270

FAX
020 7221 8678

EMAIL
vancouverstudios@vienna-group.co.uk

INTERNET
www.vienna-group.co.uk

CREDIT CARDS
AE, DC, MC, V

RATES
Rates are per day: single studio £75–80, double £95–110, triple £130; 10% discount for stays over 1 month

BREAKFAST
Continental breakfast pack £6

I have one word for Vancouver Studios: amazing! For a budget Bayswater address, it will be tough to top any of these forty-five one-room, fully equipped studios. When you see the list of amenities, the Great Sleeping price is even more remarkable. Let's start with power showers and maid service that includes fresh towels each day and weekly bed linens. The fitted kitchens have a two-burner stove and microwave, electric kettle, toaster, and an adequate refrigerator. The contemporary studios house from one to three people in twin or queen-size beds with a sofa bed for the third person. When not busy elsewhere in London, homebodies can watch satellite TV, plug in to the data port and check their email, or sit in the private garden and talk with other Great Sleepers in London.

FACILITIES AND SERVICES: Central heat, direct-dial phone, data ports, fitted kitchen with microwave, hair dryer, coin laundry and dryer in building, office safe, satellite TV, daily maid service, security entry system, 24-hour desk with on-site manager at all times; no lift (4 floors)

NEAREST TOURIST ATTRACTIONS: Kensington Palace and Gardens

Bed and Breakfast in a Private Home

It is an unfortunate fact of travel life: London hotel rates are some of the highest in the world, and show no signs of spiraling anywhere but up. In addition to the high rates, too much of London hotel service you will encounter is impersonal, dictated by computers, fax machines, voice mail, and guests referred to by numbers, not names. As a result, many travelers on holiday are becoming nostalgic for the personal touch accompanied by a genuinely friendly smile and warm hospitality. For a quality alternative to staying in a hotel, one of the best ways to save considerable money and add a personal approach to your next trip to London is to consider staying in a private home.

London is full of small establishments advertising themselves as B&Bs. These are usually mum-and-pop hotel operations with homespun decor in fewer than twenty rooms with hall facilities, or with private facilities consisting of tiny, airless modular units. There's often no lift, so there will be daily stair-climbing workouts to your room and down to the basement dining room for breakfast. These have their place, and many are listed in *Great Sleeps London.* However, if you want to gain a greater insight into life in London, go for the real thing: a bed-and-breakfast stay in a private London home.

Facilities and prices vary widely, depending on each residence and what it has to offer. Think about it carefully before you reserve, because you are, in effect, a guest in someone's home and thus do not have hotel services as part of the package. Nor do you have kitchen privileges or the right to stretch out on the living-room sofa with a drink and read the Sunday papers. You also will have to carry your own luggage, and that may mean up and down several flights of stairs. To avoid disappointment, *be sure* to lay out all your needs and expectations in advance. Specify such things as whether a nonsmoking household is a must and whether you are allergic to dogs, cats, children, or noise; if you can't negotiate stairs, say so. And if you need a private bathroom or have specific dietary requirements for breakfast, make all this clear up front. You may also want to know whether liquor is allowed in your room, if entertaining in the host's living room is permitted, and if you have access to a telephone and fax.

NOTE: Each bed-and-breakfast agency has cancellation, no-show, and refund policies. Read and understand the fine print before reserving, please.

BED AND BREAKFAST IN A PRIVATE HOME

AT HOME IN LONDON
70 Black Lion Lane, W6

TELEPHONE
020 8748 1943

FAX
020 8748 2701

EMAIL
info@athomeinlondon.co.uk

INTERNET
www.athomeinlondon.co.uk

CREDIT CARDS
MC, V

RATES
Rates are per night for the room and include breakfast. Location One: single £42–65 double £66–90; Location Two: single £30–40, double £55–65. In all homes, there is a minimum stay of 2 consecutive nights.

BREAKFAST
Generally included

With more than seventy homes in greater London, Maggie Dobson's At Home in London will surely have just the B&B to suit you. Those that are the least expensive on her roster are *not* in central London, and require some lengthy commutes on the tube or bus to get to the center of things. These "Location Two" areas include Chiswick, Hammersmith, Kew, Putney, and so on. "Location One" B&Bs are more centrally located in areas such as Knightsbridge, Kensington, Mayfair, and Chelsea. Wherever you stay, your hosts, who include lawyers, teachers, architects, designers, and writers, will provide you with a comfortable bedroom and bathroom, plus breakfast in the morning. You will have your own key so you can come and go as you like. Remember, these B&Bs are in someone's private home, so expect some homey touches: dogs, cats, children, comfy but well-loved furniture, personal collections, and probably some stairs. On the other hand, be sure to state your bottom-line requirements when reserving. If you want nonsmoking or no pets and/or children in the household, say so, and Maggie will do her best to please you and match you with a compatible host family. She also has a few apartments in Location One and Two. If you are willing to travel one stop beyond Earl's Court to West Kensington, and do some walking to get to it, ask her about the flat on Matheson Road. For something better located, she has an attractive one-bedroom flat in the basement level of a townhouse on a well-known street in Notting Hill, London's currently "in" neighborhood.

If you plan to travel elsewhere in the U.K., At Home in London can provide similar accommodations for you.

FACILITIES AND SERVICES: Vary with each home

THE BULLDOG CLUB
14 Dewhurst Road, W14

There is no question about it: the Bulldog Club is fabulous and offers the finest imaginable alternative to an expensive hotel stay—indeed, at a fraction of the cost. Before I tell you just a few of the wonderful things about this bed-and-breakfast service, there is some interesting background information.

With her last child off to boarding school and nothing to do while she and her husband rattled around in their large London home, founder Amanda St. George began to take in paying guests who were friends of friends. This was such an unqualified success that she convinced pals in Kensington, Chelsea, and other parts of central London to do the same. Thus was born the Bulldog Club, named for her bulldog, Emily. A few years ago Amanda moved to South Africa, and the Club is now owned and beautifully run by the charming and energetic Maggie Jackson. It is in its fourteenth year and flourishing more than ever with stunning properties in London and the countryside.

By paying a £25 five-year membership fee per adult, you become a member of the Club and can stay in some of London's most beautifully appointed homes, filled with museum-quality antiques, paintings, books, tapestries, and objets d'art at rates considerably lower than those of a more moderately decorated hotel. The prices quoted are the same for any of Bulldog Club homes; are per room, per night; and include breakfast and all taxes. All of the five-star-quality properties are magnificent, down to the last detail, offering guests personal and exclusive attention from the moment of arrival until departure. Many lone women travelers and businesspeople now think of their favorite Bulldog home as their own and would never consider the impersonal Hilton or Sheraton hotels again.

Each lovely room in a Bulldog Club home is equipped with a color television, tea and coffee-making facilities, telephone, and in some cases a fax. Fresh flowers and fruit are always in each room, and a bottle of mineral water is by the bedside. The luxurious private bathrooms are complete with hair dryer, a basket of the best English bath soaps and oils, a terry robe, and beautiful towels. Each day guests are given a menu from which to decide what to have for breakfast the next morning. They might choose from juices and fruit, yogurt, cereals,

TELEPHONE
020 7371 3202; 800-727-3004 (toll-free from the U.S.)

FAX
020 7371 2015

EMAIL
jackson@bulldogclub.u-net.com

INTERNET
www.bulldogclub.com

CREDIT CARDS
AE, MC, V

RATES
London locations (all rates are per room, per night): single £85 (when available), double £110. Country locations: single £60, double £80; 3-course dinner, £25–30 per person. 10% single-night supplement; all rates are paid to the Club, not your host. Properties are open only to members of the Bulldog Club; 5-year membership is £25 per adult and includes a yearly newsletter.

BREAKFAST
English breakfast included

eggs any style with bacon, sausages, mushrooms, and tomatoes, followed by toast and rolls, jams, and coffee or a pot of tea. If you're staying more than a few days, the host makes sure the menu changes. Breakfast is served in the guest's private dining area, and a complimentary newspaper is beside the tea or coffee cup. For relaxing during the day, the guest has the use of a sitting room. All homes maintain a nonsmoking policy.

There's more! Bulldog also offers country stays at more than twenty privately owned estates throughout the English, Welsh, and Scottish countrysides, as well as in Edinburgh, Oxford, and Salisbury. These historic private castles, mansions, and manor homes are set in exquisite gardens and parklands and cost even less than the Bulldog homes in London. Dinner, with three courses, can be booked at least forty-eight hours in advance at £25–30 per person. All of these beautiful locations are selected and monitored by Maggie, and they must meet the same exacting standards required of the London properties.

It is important to note two further points: Every London Bulldog home, and most in the country, are exclusive to the Club, and because they are such special private residences, no general list is offered. Guests are told what is available when they give specific dates.

It is all very British, terribly upper crust, and "really a must for every civilized person visiting London or the countryside," as one delighted guest put it. I think he is 100 percent correct. The Bulldog Club stands alone at the top of its class and, as always, receives my highest recommendation and endorsement.

FACILITIES AND SERVICES: All locations include central heat, telephone (sometimes private), and fax in some, private sitting and dining rooms, TV, mineral water, hair dryer, terry robe, map and description of the location of the home. Homes are in South Kensington, Holland Park, Parsons Green, Limehouse (the Docklands), Marble Arch, Notting Hill Gate, and Knightsbridge. *Country locations:* Many have tennis courts, swimming pools, and can provide dinner if booked in advance. There are country locations in or near Bath, Oxford, Suffolk, Salisbury, York, the Cotswolds, Leicestershire, Cornwall, and the Scottish Highlands. Of course, they do change, so if you have a particular area in mind, please be sure to ask. All Bulldog homes are nonsmoking.

HOST AND GUEST SERVICES
103 Dawes Road, SW6

Host and Guest Services is run by Craig Wood and includes accommodations in family homes in and around London and throughout the British Isles. On the drawing board are plans to expand to other cities in Europe, so if your travels are taking you to Rome or Paris, they may be able to meet your needs. Prices range from definitely budget to top-of-the-line luxury, depending on location and whether or not you are sharing a bathroom with a family or have one of your own. Many of the hosts have had varied, interesting careers and include well-known actors and government officials. As with all B&Bs, be sure to state your needs and requirements, remembering that few homes are equipped with lifts, but there is no shortage of stairs.

FACILITIES AND SERVICES: Vary with the home

TELEPHONE
020 7385 9922/3434

FAX
020 7386 7575

EMAIL
Acc@host-guest.co.uk

INTERNET
www.host-guest.co.uk

CREDIT CARDS
AE, MC, V

RATES
All rates are per person, per night unless otherwise noted. Luxury: central areas with private facilities from £35; Superior: somewhat central with varied facilities from £20; Standard: nowhere near central, all shared facilities from £18; Budget: long-term student accommodations, far out, minimum stay 2 weeks, £85 per person, per week. Half-board (includes dinner, bed, and breakfast *not* available in central London), from £110 per person, per week.

AGENCY FEES
Up to 5 days £10 per person, £15 per couple; 5–13 days £20 per person, £25 per couple; 2 weeks–2 months £40 per person, £50 per couple; over 2 months £60 per person, £75 per couple

BREAKFAST
Continental breakfast included in London, English breakfast included in countryside

THE LONDON BED & BREAKFAST AGENCY
71 Fellows Road, NW3

Dynamic Julia Stebbing runs her B&B agency with boundless energy coupled with a dose of British good sense. She provides rooms in private homes in and around London in four categories. Prices are quoted per person, include breakfast, and depend on the category location and whether or not you will share a bathroom. No one-night reservations are accepted—a two-night minimum is required—and a £5 booking fee is added for all reservations.

For most Great Sleepers, homes in Category A will be the most appealing, even though they are the most

TELEPHONE
020 7586 2768

FAX
020 7586 6567

EMAIL
stay@londonbb.com

INTERNET
www.londonbb.com

CREDIT CARDS
MC, V

RATES
Rates are per person per night and include breakfast plus a £5 booking fee. There is a 2-consecutive-night minimum stay, and the these can be reserved only 7 days in advance. Stays of 3 nights or longer should be booked as far in advance as possible. Category A (Greater London): from £45 per person per night; Category B+ to B (edges of London and beyond): from £35 per person per night; Category C (far out): singles from £25 and doubles from £22 per person per night.

BREAKFAST
Included

expensive. This category includes central London and the immediate suburbs. If you stay in a Category B or C home, the quality will be at least the same, and the price lower, but the distance to Piccadilly Circus is another matter. Even some in the A category are what I would consider on the tourist fringes, so be careful. Check them out on a map first and find out the tube and/or bus connections, remembering that the cost of the accommodations in this category will be the same, so why waste valuable vacation time commuting back and forth to whatever action and bright lights you want to see in London?

All accommodations offer guest rooms in nice homes with friendly hosts who have what Julia describes as "a generosity of spirit." None have what she termed "heaving bosoms," which she translated as "having problems that would affect a guest in any way." That is reassuring. Each home and host is, of course, different, but whether you stay in a large home toward outer London, in Knightsbridge minutes from Harrods, or in a lovely row house with a prize-winning garden overlooking the River Thames, you will be warmly received by your host family. Many but not all of the homes are nonsmoking, so be sure to state if that is a priority for you.

FACILITIES AND SERVICES: Vary with each home, but expect stairs

NUMBER NINETY-SIX (33)
96 Tachbrook Street, Pimlico, SW1
Tube: Pimlico (take the Rampayne Street exit)

TELEPHONE
020 7932 0969

FAX
020 7821 5454

EMAIL
helen@numberninety-six.co.uk

INTERNET
www.numberninety-six.co.uk

CREDIT CARDS
None; cash only

RATES
Single £95, double £105

BREAKFAST
Continental breakfast included, English breakfast £8 extra

2 rooms, each with shower or bath and toilet

Unless you had insider knowledge about Helen Douglas's bed-and-breakfast home in Pimlico, you would never know about this marvelous place, which, quite frankly, rates as one of my favorite entries for this edition of *Great Sleeps London*. In my opinion, Number Ninety-Six is the perfect choice for discriminating guests who value personal service in a quiet, elegant home surrounded by lovely heirloom antiques and chintzes. There is only one problem: once settled in, you will never want to leave!

Several years ago, Helen Douglas opened her large, beautifully furnished home to London visitors. Along with the help of her housekeeper, Jennie, who began as her children's nanny three decades ago and is now adored by all the guests, everything is done to make you feel welcome and comfortably at home. There are only two graciously appointed bedrooms, each with a sitting area. There is one downstairs, with a large sitting room and breakfast area, and another upstairs, with a four-poster bed and a fabulous gold mirror. If you are staying in this room, your breakfast will be served in the main living room on the ground floor. The Continental breakfast includes freshly squeezed orange juice, yogurt, home-made jam and marmalade to spread on your croissants, brioche, and toast, and hot tea and coffee. A full English breakfast is available for a supplemental charge. During the day, sandwiches and tea and coffee may be ordered. They also provide fax services and will do your laundry and ironing (guests cannot do their own laundry; there is a nominal charge for this service).

At Number Ninety-Six you will be within easy reach of most of London's must-see tourist sites, and, several longtime popular Great Eats are close by. You are also within five or ten minutes of Victoria Train and Coach Stations, which have easy links to Heathrow and Gatwick Airports.

NOTE: The B&B is closed for a few days around Christmas.

FACILITIES AND SERVICES: Central heat, direct-dial phones, laundry service, TV and radio, sandwiches, tea and coffee to order, daily newspaper, fax; no lift

NEAREST TOURIST ATTRACTIONS: Short walk to Bucking-ham Palace, Houses of Parliament, Westminster Abbey, Westminster Cathedral, Thames River, shopping in Knightsbridge, Tate Gallery

UPTOWN RESERVATIONS (22)
41 Paradise Walk, SW3

Uptown Reservations offers exclusive B&B accom-modations *only* in the posh districts of London: Knightsbridge, Sloane Square, Chelsea, Mayfair, St. James's, and Kensington. They are now affiliated with Wolsey Lodges, which is the U.K.'s most prestigious group offering in-home hospitality in the British coun-tryside. By working together, these two companies are able to offer the best in B&Bs to visitors in London or touring the U.K. The Wolsey Lodges range from Geor-gian mansions to quaint country cottages where guests are entertained as family and have the option of dining with their hosts. The difference between the two organi-zations is that Uptown hosts do not provide dinner, but

TELEPHONE
020 7351 3445

FAX
020 7351 9383

EMAIL
inquiries@uptownres.co.uk

INTERNET
www.uptownres.co.uk

CREDIT CARDS
AE, MC, V

RATES

Single £70, double £90, family room £120–125, £5 supplement for a single-night stay; deposit of 28% of the total booking is nonrefundable but may be applied to a later booking if canceled at least 7 days ahead. Deposits can be made by credit card, but the balance must be paid in cash to the host upon arrival.

For information and prices for Wolsey Lodges
Contact Procter Naylor at Wolsey Lodges Ltd., 9 Market Place, Hadleigh, Ipswich, Suffolk IP7 5Dl

TELEPHONE
1473 822058

FAX
1473 827 444

EMAIL
wolsey@wolseylo.demon.co.uk

INTERNET
www.wolsey-lodges.co.uk

they are happy to make suggestions for all types of local restaurants. The homes Uptown Reservations represents are carefully selected by Monica Barrington and Keith Stables, who personally monitor each to ensure that it is keeping pace with their standards, paying as much attention to the attitude of the hosts as to the quality of accommodations. All will have private baths, and the price includes breakfast. From minimalist modern to mews houses filled with enviable antiques and heirlooms, Uptown has it all. Many of the homes look as though Martha Stewart or Laura Ashley lived in them, or that *House Beautiful* should be called in to do a feature story. Efforts are made to match guests with hosts, who come from a variety of interesting backgrounds and professions. Be sure to state your needs when booking, and remember, you are a guest in a private home, so even though you will be staying in lovely surroundings, you must not expect hotel services.

FACILITIES AND SERVICES: Depends on home. Nonsmoking homes are available. They offer car hire for general uses as well as airport transfer, and individually guided sight-seeing or shopping tours; details of all these services are given on request

Camping Out

You are not going to get a cheaper sleep in London than sleeping under the stars in your own tent or camper in a campground on the edges of the city. You may not be a happy camper, however, when you realize these sites are far removed from the center of the city, thus forcing you to make commutes of one or two hours each way, using a combination of foot, train, bus, and tube to get to your final London destination. If you have your own transportation, consider the heavy traffic, confusing one-way London streets, and steep parking fees before you drive yourself.

CAMPING OUT

ABBEY WOOD CO-OP CAMPING & CARAVANING SITE
Federation Road, Abbey Wood, near Greenwich, SE2
Train stop: Abbey Wood Station, then a 10-minute walk

This campground is open all year, but advance reservations are necessary for Easter, spring holidays, July, and August. If you are in a motor home or have a car trailer, you can always reserve ahead. Send a £5 deposit and self-addressed envelope (with International Postal Coupon) for confirmation. No advance reservations made for tents, bicycles, or hikers. If you belong to a trailer or caravan club, bring your card for a discount, otherwise there is a £6 fee for nonmembers.

FACILITIES AND SERVICES: Electrical hookups, public phones for outgoing calls only, no incoming calls, laundry room with iron, children's play area, free showers, toilets

TELEPHONE
020 8311 7708
FAX
020 8311 1465
CREDIT CARDS
MC, V
RATES
Pitch fee for motor homes or caravans £9.50, plus £6 per person per night for adults over 17, £1.50 per person per night for children under 17; pitch fee for tents with cars £5 per night; with motorcycles, bicycles, or hikers £4 per night; electrical hookup £2 per night

CRYSTAL PALACE, CARAVAN CLUB SITE
Crystal Palace Parade, Crystal Palace, SE19
Train and bus stop: See note below

TELEPHONE
020 8778 7155
FAX
020 8676 0980
EMAIL
cc73@gofornet.co.uk
CREDIT CARDS
MC, V
RATES
Caravan pitch fee £10 plus £6 per person per day; children under 5 free, children 5–16 £1.50 per day; electrical hookup £2.25; tent pitch fee £2–5 depending on mode of transport (foot, motorbike, or car); maximum stay 21 nights; lower rates in off-season

Advance booking for motor vans and trailers: send £5 to secure a spot (this will be deducted from total charge when you arrive). Tent space given out on first-come, first-served basis. Open all year.

NOTE: To get there, get off at the Brixton tube stop, and then there's a twenty-minute walk to the campground, uphill all the way. Buses are a five- to ten-minute walk to and from the campground. Going to London you can get off at Oxford Circus; coming back, get the No. 3 bus from Piccadilly or Trafalgar Square.

FACILITIES AND SERVICES: Coin-operated laundry, free showers and toilets, small convenience store selling milk, juice, and eggs

LEE VALLEY PARK
Picketts Lock Centre, Picketts Lock Lane, Picketts Lock, N9
Train stop: See note below

TELEPHONE
020 8803 6900
FAX
020 8884 4975
EMAIL
leisurecentre@ leevalleypark.org.uk
INTERNET
www.leevalleypark.org.uk
CREDIT CARDS
MC, V
RATES
No pitch fee; adults 16 years and up £6 per person per day, children under 16 £3 per child per day, electrical hookups £3 per night

This campground is six miles from center of London, and the trip takes forty-five minutes each way. But the site is loaded with extras. When was the last time you played eighteen holes of golf at your campsite? Open year-round, office open daily 8 A.M.–10 P.M.

NOTE: To get there, from Liverpool Station in London, take British Rail to Edmonton Green, then bus W8 to Picketts Lock; bus stops in front of the cinema, and it is another hundred yards to the campsite.

FACILITIES AND SERVICES: Free showers and toilet, coin-operated laundry, swimming pool (£1.50 per person per swim), 18-hole golf course (greens fee £12), golf pro and golf shop, two gyms, sauna, convenience store, public phone for outgoing calls only, no incoming calls, 12-screen cinema next door, restaurant; no tents provided

Hostels

The London hostels listed here are associated with the nonprofit International Youth Hostel Association and are some of the best values going. Other crash pads may call themselves hostels, but with the exception of those listed in these pages in addition to the YHA hostels, those independently owned hostels are some of the worst excuses for accommodations I have ever seen—anywhere.

Despite their name, youth hostels are open to all ages, but those under fourteen years of age should be accompanied by an adult. Most hostels offer a variety of accommodation options—you can find single, double, family, and dormitory rooms in most major locations. To stay at a hostel, you must be a member of your national Youth Hostel Association (YHA), or pay a nominal extra fee for up to six nights, after which you become a member. Members can stay at any of the five thousand hostels in more than seventy countries, from the United States to New Zealand, from South Africa to Ireland. In London there are seven hostels, five of which are central and two of which are in the boonies. In addition, members are eligible for a "suitcase of travel bargains" ranging from discounts on transportation, museums, theaters, restaurants, and shops to special travel packages to language courses. Hostels also provide a variety of programs and activities, such as walking tours, pub crawls, and movies, which all add up to much more than just a cheap sleep.

The YHA value is significant for anyone looking for a Great Eat and/or a Great Sleep in London. Sleeping accommodations range from modern bunk-bedded rooms for singles to fifteen-bed dorms with bathrooms on every floor. The hostels provide TV lounges, kitchens (except at the City of London Youth Hostel), cafeteria-style lunches and/or dinners in some, a coin-operated laundry, and convenient extras that include money changing at bank rates, personal storage lockers (bring your own locks), onward bookings, discount tickets to major attractions, and theater reservations. Bed linen is provided, but towels and soap are not, so BYO or pay a nominal charge to buy them. Few have lifts; all have a nonsmoking policy in the bedrooms.

If the hostel way of traveling appeals to you, plan as far ahead as possible because hostel locations in popular destinations (especially London) fill up quickly, and you don't want to be left out in the cold. Reservations can be

U.S. Booking Information
Hosteling International/American Youth Hostels (HI-AYH), 733 15th Street, Suite 840, NW, Washington, D.C. 20005
EMAIL
hiayhserv@hiayh.org.com
INTERNET
www.hiayh.org; www.iyhf.org

London Booking Information
TELEPHONE
020 7373 3400
FAX
020 7373 3455
EMAIL
lonres@yha.org.uk
INTERNET
www.yha.org.uk

England and Wales Booking Information
YHA Ltd., Trevelyan House 8 St. Stephen's Hill St. Albans, Hertfordshire AL12DY England
TELEPHONE
1727 845047
FAX
1727 844126
EMAIL
customerservices@yha.org.uk

made six months in advance using the on-line computer-ized booking network (IBN), with payment by either MasterCard or Visa. The IBN Reservations Line in the United States is 202-783-6161. The cost is $5 per hostel booking. Allow at least five days to receive your written confirmation, which must be presented at the hostel upon your arrival. You can also reserve your space by contacting an American Youth Hostel in most major American cities, through the central hostel office in London, or with the individual hostels. Most hostels can also reserve ongoing reservations for you.

CENTRAL LONDON YOUTH HOSTELS

CITY OF LONDON YOUTH HOSTEL (14)
36 Carter Lane, the City, EC4
Tube: St. Paul's, Blackfriars

197 beds, no private facilities

TELEPHONE
020 7236 4965

FAX
020 7236 7681

EMAIL
city@yha.org.uk

INTERNET
www.yha.org.uk

CREDIT CARDS
MC, V

RATES
All rates are per person. Single: over 18 years £26.50, under 18 years £23; slightly lower rates in family rooms with bunk beds

BREAKFAST
Continental or English breakfast included; picnic lunch £4–5; dinner from £6

This Victorian building is opposite St. Paul's Cathedral and was, until 1968, the school for St. Paul's choirboys. It is the only London YHA hostel that has single rooms; most rooms hold four to six beds. There are no kitchen privileges, but there is a restaurant for dinners, and packed lunches can be ordered.

FACILITIES AND SERVICES: Central heat, public phones, TV in lounge, restaurant, Internet access, money changing (bad rates), coin-operated laundry, luggage storage, no smoking in bedrooms

NEAREST TOURIST ATTRACTIONS: St. Paul's, City of London

EARL'S COURT YOUTH HOSTEL (32)
38 Bolton Gardens, Earl's Court, SW5
Tube: Earl's Court, Gloucester Road
154 beds, no private facilities

An old townhouse offering 154 beds with rooms packed full of up to a dozen snoozers. The area is popular with cheap sleepers, and within a fifteen-minute journey to museums. There is no curfew, no lift or safe, and no smoking allowed in the bedrooms.

FACILITIES AND SERVICES: Central heat, public phones, Internet access, coin-operated laundry, lockers, kitchen privileges, money changing, satellite TV lounge; no lift

NEAREST TOURIST ATTRACTIONS: Earl's Court Exhibition Centre

TELEPHONE
020 7373 7083

FAX
020 7835 2034

EMAIL
earlscourt@yha.org.uk

INTERNET
www.yha.org.uk

CREDIT CARDS
MC, V

RATES
All rates are per person. Single over 18 years £22, under 18 years £20, £1 discount per day for students of any age; slightly lower rates as the number of beds per room increases

BREAKFAST
Not served

HOLLAND HOUSE, KING GEORGE IV MEMORIAL YOUTH HOSTEL (38)
Holland Walk, Holland Park, W8
Tube: Holland Park
201 beds, no private facilities

This refurbished hostel is an old Jacobean mansion built in 1607 and situated in Holland Park. There are a few rooms with only six to eight beds, but most rooms hold twelve to twenty beds.

FACILITIES AND SERVICES: Central heat, public phones, restaurant, kitchen, TV lounge, money changing, coin-operated laundry

NEAREST TOURIST ATTRACTIONS: Holland Park, Notting Hill

TELEPHONE
020 7937 0748

FAX
020 7376 0667

EMAIL
hollandhouse@yha.org.uk

INTERNET
www.yha.org.uk

CREDIT CARDS
MC, V

RATES
Prices are per person no matter how many beds are in the room. Single for those over 18 £22, under 18 £20

BREAKFAST
Continental or English breakfast included

OXFORD STREET YOUTH HOSTEL (26)
14 Noel Street, Soho, W1
Tube: Oxford Circus, Tottenham Court Road
75 beds, no private facilities

The location, right in the heart of Soho, makes this the best choice for a short-term London stay. Rooms are shared between only two to four travelers.

FACILITIES AND SERVICES: Central heat, public phones, lift, TV in lounge, kitchen facilities, coin laundry, lockers

TELEPHONE
020 7734 1618

FAX
020 7734 1657

EMAIL
oxfordst@yha.org.uk

INTERNET
www.yha.org.uk

(BYO lock), money changing (bad rates), theater booking, pay-computer terminal

NEAREST TOURIST ATTRACTIONS: Soho, Oxford Street, Theatre District, West End

ST. PANCRAS YOUTH HOSTEL (1)
79–81 Euston Road, Euston, NW1
Tube: Euston, King's Cross, St. Pancras
150 beds, no private facilities

This is the newest YHA London hostel, with easy access to most attractions and transport links to the north.

FACILITIES AND SERVICES: Central heat, public phones, kitchen, TV lounge, coin-operated laundry, money exchange

NEAREST TOURIST ATTRACTIONS: British Library, walk to British Museum

Student Dormitories

Some of the most impressive Great Sleeping bargains in London are in university and college dormitories after the students have left. The good news is that these are available to anyone, no matter what age. The bad news is that they are available only during holiday periods and in summer, when classes are not in session. Most of these utilitarian sites are well located, and many offer inexpensive cafeteria-style meals or have microwaves and refrigerators on each floor, but few have private bathrooms or any style. Some have dorm rooms that can sleep four to six persons who may or may not be traveling together. Lockers are provided, but theft is common. To protect your belongings, put valuables in the office safe and lock up your baggage using the best lock you can afford. Since most of the bathing facilities are communal, it is a good idea to bring along shower shoes and soap. Linens and towels are usually provided. Each operation has its own payment and cancellation policy. A dim view is taken of cancellations, and penalties are usually at least 10 percent of the entire stay, and in some cases as high as 50 percent. No-shows rarely get one pence refunded. Cancellation insurance is strongly recommended.

ALLEN HALL UNIVERSITY DORMITORY (21)
28 Beaufort Street, Chelsea, SW3
Tube: Sloane Square, then bus No. 19, 22, or 319, or No. 211 or 11 from Victoria

TELEPHONE
020 7351 1296; 020 7349 5615
FAX
020 7349 5601
CREDIT CARDS
None; all payment in advance in British sterling
RATES
Single £30, double £50; nonrefundable £10 deposit is required when booking but is deducted from the final bill
BREAKFAST
English breakfast included

About 40 rooms, none with shower, bath, or toilet

Allen Hall is a seminary where men train for the priesthood ten months of the year. During mid-July and all of August it is open to groups, families, or individuals looking for a budget sleep in London. The building was built on the site of the home of Sir Thomas More and his family, which makes it historically interesting. The location in Chelsea is close to King's Road and all the boutiques and restaurants it has to offer. The majority of rooms are singles, but there are a few twin-bedded rooms and some that are suitable for families. All are reminiscent of military comfort and decorating. Guests are required to make their own beds and empty their trash. The communal bathrooms are recent. There is a television lounge with tea and coffee provided. Breakfast is the only meal provided, but those really watching their money can prepare light snacks in the kitchenettes on each floor. The staff includes some of the students of the college, which creates a friendly, easy atmosphere. There is a nonrefundable deposit of £10, and payment must be made in full upon arrival in *British sterling only*.

FACILITIES AND SERVICES: Central heat, public phone downstairs, kitchen privileges, tea and coffee always available; no lift

NEAREST TOURIST ATTRACTIONS: King's Road, Chelsea Embankment, Thames River

LINSTEAD HALL–IMPERIAL COLLEGE OF SCIENCE, TECHNOLOGY, AND MEDICINE VACATION ACCOMMODATIONS (3)
47 Prince's Gardens, Exhibition Road, South Kensington, SW7
Tube: South Kensington (take the Thurloe Street exit)

TELEPHONE
020 7594 9507/8
FAX
020 7594 9505
EMAIL
reservations@ic.ac.uk
INTERNET
www.imperialcollege-conferencelink.com
CREDIT CARDS
MC, V

724 rooms; during holiday periods, none with shower, bath, or toilet

Linstead Hall is open at Easter and from July through the end of September. Trying to find the reception office in a maze of institutional brick buildings can be discouraging. If you are coming on the tube, you want the South Kensington stop, Thurloe Street exit. The entrance to the building is off Watts Way, not, as the address suggests, Prince's Gardens. To keep your frustration

230 Other Options

level to a minimum when you arrive, be sure to ask that a map of the facility be sent to you when you make your reservations. The rooms are not suitable for the handicapped, none are en suite, and the bathrooms are shared with a maximum of three other people. They are of the usual student variety, are cleaned regularly, and linens and towels are provided. In addition to a dining room and a small grocery store, there is a bookstore, sports center, and bank. The hall is situated in a nice residential area on the boundary of Kensington and Chelsea, not far from museums and the Royal Albert Hall.

FACILITIES AND SERVICES: Central heat, public phones, lifts to some floors, laundry facilities, pizzeria on campus, grocery store, bookshop, bank, sports center, TV in lounge, office safe, some kitchen facilities, 24-hour reception

NEAREST TOURIST ATTRACTIONS: Museum District, Royal Albert Hall

RATES
Single £40 without private facilities, £80 with; double (twin beds only) £65 without private facilities, £110 with

BREAKFAST
English breakfast included

LONDON HOUSE FOR OVERSEAS VISITORS AND GOODENOUGH CLUB (12)
Mecklenburgh Square, Bloomsbury, WC1
Tube: Russell Square
London House: 350 rooms, 6 with shower or bath and toilet
Goodenough Club: 65 rooms, all with shower and toilet

The London House residence is open year-round *only* to postgraduate students doing research and visiting academics here for at least one academic term. The spartan rooms have no private bathrooms. For short term stays in accommodations with private bathrooms, anyone can check into the Goodenough Club.

FACILITIES AND SERVICES: Direct-dial phones, tea and coffeemakers and TV in suites

NEAREST TOURIST ATTRACTIONS: British Museum, British Library

TELEPHONE
020 7837 8888

FAX
020 7837 9321

EMAIL
London House: registry@lgt.org.uk; Goodenough Club: club@lgt.org.uk

INTERNET
London House: www.lgt.org.uk; Goodenough Club: www.club.lgt.org.uk

CREDIT CARDS
MC, V

RATES
London House: single £35–45, double £85–155; prices for long stays available upon request
Goodenough Club: Single £60–95, double £95–135, suite £125–155; discounts available for stays over 4 weeks

BREAKFAST
London House: not included; Goodenough Club: Continental or English included

MORE HOUSE (17)
53 Cromwell Road, South Kensington, SW7
Tube: South Kensington, Gloucester Road
60 rooms, none with shower, bath, or toilet

TELEPHONE
020 7584 2040
FAX
020 7581 5748
EMAIL
more-house@surf3.net
CREDIT CARDS
None; British sterling only
RATES
Single £29 per night, double £44 per night, triple £56 per night, quad £68 per night; 10% discount for each night after the 7th night, and lower rates for stays over 4 weeks; groups of 10 or more pay a 10% advance deposit and are given a 10% discount if total is paid by leader or 5% if paid by individual bills; nonrefundable £20 deposit required on individual bookings, but it's deductible from the bill; deposits may be paid by international money order or banker's draft
BREAKFAST
English breakfast included

If you are interested in a popular Great Sleep open only in summer, where gentle nuns treat their guests with the utmost kindness, get your reservation in at More House ASAP, because the word is out on this one.

More House is named for Sir Thomas More, a famous saint of the English Reformation who was lord chancellor under King Henry VIII and lived in Chelsea. The house is run by the Sisters of St. Augustine, and during the school term it is used as a dorm for students attending London University Colleges. In July and August, More House offers bed-and-breakfast accommodations at prices reminiscent of bygone days. Those planning to stay a week or more will have a 10 percent discount. Groups receive favorable rates, and children under six stay free if they share their parents' room. Each sparse room has hot and cold running water and dormitory decor. Baths, showers, and toilets are on each floor, and so are tea and coffeemakers, a microwave, refrigerator, and telephone to receive incoming calls. A full English breakfast, with juice, bacon, sausage, eggs, beans or tomatoes, cereal, rolls, toast, tea, and coffee is served in the cafeteria. The South Kensington location is prime: right across from the Natural History Museum.

NOTE: To inquire about rooms here, contact the Warden, More House, 53 Cromwell Road, London, SW7 2EH. To reserve, a nonrefundable £20 deposit is required, which is deductible from the total bill. All payment must be in British sterling.

FACILITIES AND SERVICES: Central heat, public phones, microwave, refrigerator, tea and coffeemakers on each floor, TV in lounge, lift, coin-operated laundry, office safe

NEAREST TOURIST ATTRACTIONS: Museum District, Royal Albert Hall, Kensington Gardens

QUEEN ALEXANDRA'S HOUSE (2)
Bremner Road, Kensington Gore, South Kensington, SW7
Tube: Gloucester Road, South Kensington
110 rooms, none with shower, bath, or toilet

TELEPHONE
020 7589 3635
FAX
020 7589 3177
CREDIT CARDS
None; cash only

From July to mid-August (and other times if rooms are available), women of all ages can check into Queen Alexandra's House. It is definitely not sumptuous, but it is a safe, well-located selection next to the Royal Albert

Hall. One advantage is that all of the rooms are singles, so you won't have to bunk with strangers. It is popular, and advance reservations are strongly recommended, because drop-ins can rarely be housed. Microwaves are on each floor, and the coin-operated laundries and ironing facilities are further money-savers for many.

FACILITIES AND SERVICES: Central heat, public phone, iron, coin-operated laundry, microwave on each floor, office safe, TV lounge, lift

NEAREST TOURIST ATTRACTIONS: Museum District, Royal Albert Hall, Kensington Palace and Gardens

RATES
£150 per week if stay is longer than 2 weeks, otherwise £30 per day

BREAKFAST
Continental breakfast included

Intercollegiate Halls

Intercollegiate Halls, which are connected to the University of London but independently operated, are dotted throughout London and open to Great Sleepers during the summer months. Each hall handles its own bookings. Head office contact and basic information about some of the more desirable locations follows. The office is open Mon–Fri 9:30 A.M.–5 P.M. Each location has its own email address, but there is only one general Internet site.

TELEPHONE
020 7862 8880

FAX
020 7862 8084

EMAIL
accom@lon.ac.uk

INTERNET
www.lon.ac.uk/accom

Canterbury Hall and Hughes Parry Hall, WC1	**233**
College Hall, WC1	**234**
Commonwealth Hall, WC1	**234**
Connaught Hall, WC1	**234**
International Hall, WC1	**235**
Nutford House, W1	**235**

CANTERBURY HALL AND HUGHES PARRY HALL (6)
12–18 Cartwright Gardens, Bloomsbury, WC1
Tube: Russell Square
250 rooms, none with shower, bath, or toilet

Most bathrooms are shared by only two or three rooms, which are available from mid-June through August.

FACILITIES AND SERVICES: Central heat, direct-dial phones (need a phone card to activate), TV lounge, squash and tennis courts, coin-operated laundry; lift

NEAREST TOURIST ATTRACTIONS: British Library, Coram's Fields

TELEPHONE
020 685 4000

FAX
020 7383 4328

EMAIL
hughesparry@hotmail.com

CREDIT CARDS
None; cash only

RATES
For groups or individuals £26 for bed and breakfast, £30 with dinner included

BREAKFAST
Included

COLLEGE HALL (21)
Malet Street, Bloomsbury, WC1
Tube: Goodge Street, Russell Square

250 beds, no private facilities

College Hall is open June, July, and September, but is closed in August.

FACILITIES AND SERVICES: Kitchen on each floor, coin-operated laundry, lift, restaurant, TV lounge

NEAREST TOURIST ATTRACTIONS: British Museum, Coram's Fields

TELEPHONE
020 7685 2000

FAX
020 7636 6591

EMAIL
enquires.college@
collegehall.lon.ac.uk

CREDIT CARDS
None; cash only

RATES
£22 per person for bed and breakfast, £27 with dinner included

BREAKFAST
Included

COMMONWEALTH HALL (7)
1–11 Cartwright Gardens, Bloomsbury, WC1
Tube: Russell Square

400 rooms, none with shower, bath, or toilet

Commonwealth Hall is open mid-June through mid-August.

FACILITIES AND SERVICES: Two microwaves per floor, coin-operated laundry, library, lift, squash and tennis courts, TV lounge

NEAREST TOURIST ATTRACTIONS: British Museum, Coram's Fields

TELEPHONE
020 7685 3500

FAX
020 7383 4375

EMAIL
bursar.commonwealth@
commonwealthhall.lon.ac.uk

CREDIT CARDS
None; cash only

RATES
Groups or individuals £30 per person for bed, breakfast, and dinner; reservations must be made in advance

BREAKFAST
Included

CONNAUGHT HALL (17)
41 Tavistock Square, Bloomsbury, WC1
Tube: Euston, Russell Square

200 rooms, none with shower, bath, or toilet

Connaught Hall is open at Easter and in June and August.

FACILITIES AND SERVICES: Coin-operated laundry, direct-dial phone, garden, lift, TV lounge

NEAREST TOURIST ATTRACTIONS: British Museum, British Library

TELEPHONE
020 7685 2800

FAX
020 7383 4109

EMAIL
info.connaught@
connaughthall.lon.ac.uk

CREDIT CARDS
None; cash only

RATES
£24 for single bed and breakfast, £29 dinner included; £22 per person for double bed and breakfast, £27 per person dinner included

INTERNATIONAL HALL (18)
Brunswick Square, Bloomsbury, WC1
Tube: Russell Square
410 rooms, all with shower or bath and toilet

International Hall is open for Christmas and Easter and from late June to early September for academics or students over eighteen years old. All rooms are singles with private bathrooms.

FACILITIES AND SERVICES: Direct-dial phones, microwaves on each floor, coin-operated laundry, lift, squash courts, TV lounge

NEAREST TOURIST ATTRACTIONS: British Museum, British Library

TELEPHONE
020 7685 4500

FAX
020 7278 9720

EMAIL
info.internatl@
internationalhall.lon.ac.uk

CREDIT CARDS
MC, V

RATES
£24 per person for bed and breakfast, £28 per person dinner included

NUTFORD HOUSE (10)
Brown Street at Nutford Place, Marylebone, W1
Tube: Marble Arch
200 rooms, none with shower, bath, or toilet

Nutford House is open for Easter and from mid-June to mid-September in rooms with only twin beds.

FACILITIES AND SERVICES: Kitchen on each floor, coin-operated laundry, leisure center with pool and gym (supplemental charge), TV lounge; no lift, no smoking

NEAREST TOURIST ATTRACTIONS: Oxford Street

TELEPHONE
020 7685 5000

FAX
020 7258 1781

EMAIL
info.nutford@
nutfordhouse.lon.ac.uk

CREDIT CARDS
None; cash only

RATES
£24 single bed and breakfast, £29 dinner included; £36 twin-bedded room for 2 and breakfast, £42 dinner included

BREAKFAST
Included

KING'S COLLEGE LONDON–KING'S CAMPUS VACATION BUREAU (50)
Strand Bridge House, Third Floor, 138–142 Strand, WC2
Tube: Charing Cross

King's Campus Vacation Bureau has various college halls of residence offering single or double dormitory rooms in and around London, providing an impressive number of beds and range of facilities for groups and individuals. Some of the residences offer breakfast. Conference facilities are available in some locations. Only those within central London that take both individuals and groups are described below. For a complete listing of all their London area residence halls, and those specifically for large groups, please contact the main office. The residences are open from early June to mid-September, and Wellington Hall is usually open during the Easter vacation as well. All bookings must be made through the

TELEPHONE
020 7848 1700

FAX
020 7848 1717

EMAIL
vac.bureau@kcl.ac.uk

INTERNET
www.kcl.ac.uk

CREDIT CARDS
MC, V

RATES
Vary with each location; please consult individual listings

BREAKFAST
Continental or English breakfast included, depending on location

King's Campus Vacation Bureau office. When booking, bear in mind that discounts are available to individuals for stays over seven nights, groups, and university students holding current student status. Half- or full-board rates are available for groups of thirty or more.

GREAT DOVER STREET (15)
165 Great Dover Street, London Bridge, SE1
Tube: Borough

TELEPHONE
020 7407 0068/9

FAX
020 7378 7973

RATES
Single £32, twin £49, student rate £25

BREAKFAST
None served

769 rooms, all with shower or bath and toilet

The single and twin-bedded-only rooms are close to the South Bank of the River Thames within a modern residence built around a landscaped quadrangle, and they are within walking distance of Shakespeare's Globe Theatre and the new Tate Gallery of Modern Art. Each has a private bathroom and shares with four others a communal area with a refrigerator and TV. There is access to a small, unequipped cooking area.

FACILITIES AND SERVICES: Central heat, each room shares a communal area with TV and refrigerator, unequipped cooking area, hall phones, some rooms for disabled, coin-operated laundry, lift, 24-hour desk

NEAREST TOURIST ATTRACTIONS: Shakespeare's Globe Theatre, London Dungeon, London Bridge, Southwark Cathedral

STAMFORD STREET (6)
127 Stamford Street, Waterloo, SE1
Tube: Waterloo

TELEPHONE
020 7873 2969 (office hours);
020 7873 2962 (all other times)

FAX
020 773 2964

RATES
All rooms are singles, £35

BREAKFAST
Not served

560 single rooms, all with shower or bath and toilet

The rooms are located on the South Bank of the River Thames, not far from the Tate Modern. Covent Garden is just across the Waterloo Bridge, and the Eurostar Terminal and Waterloo Station, with trains direct to Paris and Brussels, is five minutes away. The building was the first warehouse owned by W. H. Smith, the famous stationers and bookstore, and their crest can still be seen at roof level on the facade—the only part of the original building that's still there. The residence has 560 single bedrooms arranged in self-contained units of four to nine rooms, each with its own bathroom, TV, and small refrigerator.

FACILITIES AND SERVICES: Each unit has a communal area with TV and refrigerator; by arrangement, rooms may have a direct-dial phone; some rooms are equipped for disabled guests and there is limited parking for them, but otherwise there is no parking; unequipped kitchen; lift; 24-hour desk

NEAREST TOURIST ATTRACTIONS: Royal National Theatre, National Film Theatre, Royal Festival and Queen Elizabeth Halls, Hayward Gallery, Tate Modern

WELLINGTON HALL (18)
71 Vincent Square, Victoria, SW1
Tube: Victoria, St. James's Park

125 beds, no private facilities, no double beds

Wellington Hall is in the quiet, green Vincent Square, only a few minutes from Parliament Square. The building was designed by A. C. Martin, an Edwardian architect, and was used by the King's College theology faculty until 1983, when it became a student residence hall. This is the most central of the King's College residences, very close to Victoria Station. There are 125 beds in single and twin-bedded rooms, all with hot and cold water and the other facilities down the hall. There are two lounges with views of the gardens and the square. Lunch and dinner can be arranged for groups only, but an English breakfast is served. This is the only residence that is also open during the Easter break.

FACILITIES AND SERVICES: Central heat, conference room, laundry and ironing facilities, public phone, TV lounge, 24-hour desk; no lift

NEAREST TOURIST ATTRACTIONS: Short walk to Big Ben, Westminster Abbey, Houses of Parliament

TELEPHONE
020 7834 4740

FAX
020 8233 7709

RATES
Singles £29, twins £44 per room

BREAKFAST
Included

LONDON SCHOOL OF ECONOMICS HALLS AND RESIDENCES

The LSE halls and residences offer thousands of comfortable, frugal Great Sleeps during Easter and summer vacation periods. All are within easy access of public transportation and are in the areas most tourists have on their lists. Reservations can be made directly with the residences, and all accept credit cards. Their Internet site gives daily updates on all the LSE halls and residences.

EMAIL
vacations@lse.ac.uk

INTERNET
www.lse.ac.uk/vacations

Bankside House, SE1	**238**
Carr Saunders, W1	**238**
High Holborn Residence, WC1	**238**
Passfield Hall, WC1	**239**
Rosebery Avenue Hall, EC1	**239**

BANKSIDE HOUSE (3)
24 Sumner Street, South Bank, SE1
Tube: London Bridge, Blackfriars, Waterloo

800 beds; some singles have shower and toilet; all twins, triples, and quads do

TELEPHONE
0207633 9877

FAX
020 774 6730

EMAIL
Bankside-
Reservation@lse.ac.uk

CREDIT CARDS
MC, V

RATES
Single £32–45, double £60,
triple £85, quad £98

BREAKFAST
Breakfast included

LSE's largest residence is on the South Bank of the Thames, about a fifteen-minute walk to Tower Bridge and the West End. The residence is open from the end of June to the end of September.

FACILITIES AND SERVICES: Bar, pool table, coin-operated laundry, lift, TV lounge

NEAREST TOURIST ATTRACTIONS: Globe Theatre, Tate Modern, fifteen-minute walk to West End, Tower of London, Tower Bridge, and St. Paul's Cathedral

CARR SAUNDERS (2)
18–24 Fitzroy Street, W1
Tube: Warren Street

156 beds, none with shower or toilet

TELEPHONE
020 7580 6338

FAX
020 7580 4718

EMAIL
Carr-Saunders@lse.ac.uk

CREDIT CARDS
MC, V

RATES
Single £29, twin £47–52

BREAKFAST
Included

Well positioned off the top end of Tottenham Court Road, Carr Saunders is open at Easter and from the end of June until the end of September.

FACILITIES AND SERVICES: Central heat, coin laundry, lift, TV lounge

NEAREST TOURIST ATTRACTIONS: Regent's Park, British Museum

HIGH HOLBORN RESIDENCE (40)
178 High Holborn, Covent Garden, WC1
Tube: Holborn, Chancery Lane

494 beds; 20 clusters have shower and toilet

TELEPHONE
020 7379 5589

FAX
020 7379 5640

EMAIL
High.Holborn@lse.ac.uk

CREDIT CARDS
MC, V

RATES
Single £37, double £59–69,
triple £79

BREAKFAST
Continental or English
breakfast included

You can't get more central than this residence, occupying prime territory in the West End opposite the Shaftesbury Theatre at the top of Drury Lane. Four or five people can stay in single or small twin rooms in clusters that have a shared sitting area and bathroom.

FACILITIES AND SERVICES: Bar, coin-operated laundry, lift, TV lounge

NEAREST TOURIST ATTRACTIONS: Ten-minute walk to Covent Garden, Leicester Square, Oxford Street, Trafalgar Square, the National Gallery, and Bloomsbury

PASSFIELD HALL (15)
1 Endsleigh Place, Bloomsbury, WC1
Tube: Euston

144 rooms, none with shower or toilet

The Georgian building is divided into three blocks around a garden. Passfield Hall is open for Easter and from July to September.

FACILITIES AND SERVICES: Rooms have phones for incoming calls; coin-operated laundry, pool table, TV lounge; no lift

NEAREST TOURIST ATTRACTIONS: British Museum, British Library

TELEPHONE
020 7387 3584

FAX
020 7387 0419

EMAIL
Passfield@lse.ac.uk

CREDIT CARDS
MC, V

RATES
Single £28, twin £50, triple £64

BREAKFAST
English breakfast included

ROSEBERY AVENUE HALL (2)
90 Rosebery Avenue, Clerkenwell, EC1
Tube: Farringdon, Angel

193 rooms, 18 twin rooms with shower or bath and toilet

From some of the rooms at Rosebery Avenue Hall you have a view of the famed Sadler's Wells Theatre, from others a peek at St. Paul's Cathedral. As in all dormitory rooms, you can expect only the basics: hot and cold water, a bed, desk, chair, and closet. Toilets and showers are shared on each floor. The tube stop here is Angel, which may seem like the edge of nowhere, but actually it isn't. The area is called Clerkenwell, and it was here that Oliver Twist was taught to pick pockets by the Artful Dodger. From an entertainment side, you are in exploring distance of the Camden Passage Antiques Market, fringe theater, and a traditional London street market in Chapel Street. Open Easter and mid-June to late September.

FACILITIES AND SERVICES: Bar, central heat, limited disabled access, TV lounge, coin-operated laundry, cafeteria, kitchen on each floor, lift

NEAREST TOURIST ATTRACTIONS: Must use public transportation

TELEPHONE
020 7278 3251

FAX
020 7278 2068

EMAIL
Rosebery@lse.ac.uk

CREDIT CARDS
MC, V

RATES
Single £28–34, twin £38–60, triple £57

BREAKFAST
Continental breakfast included

UNIVERSITY COLLEGE LONDON

University College London has residence halls open to the public during term vacation periods and in the summer. Because of their locations in greater Bloomsbury, these dorms make excellent choices for independent budget seekers and groups of twenty or more who do not want to live in seedy hotels in order to keep sleeping cheaply. The rooms have weekly maid service, and linens and towels are provided. Bathrooms, showers, and toilets are communal. For availability, bookings, and specific information, contact the site manager of the individual colleges directly. Each has the same email address, but as of press time, they did not have an Internet site. Daily office hours are 8 A.M.–6 P.M. in the summer and until 4 P.M. in the winter.

ASTOR COLLEGE (7)

TELEPHONE
020 7580 7262

FAX
020 7636 6385

EMAIL
accommodation@ucl.ac.uk

CREDIT CARDS
None; cash only

RATES
Single less than 7 nights £22, more than 7 nights £20; twin less than 7 nights £38, more than 7 nights £35; flats with kitchen £27 per person

BREAKFAST
Not served

99 Charlotte Street, Bloomsbury, W1
Tube: Goodge Street, Warren Street, Tottenham Court Road
250 rooms, none with shower or toilet, 7 flats for two with shower and toilet

Astor College is a brick pile of rooms about a five-minute walk from Oxford Street that is open from the first part of June until mid-September for groups and individuals.

FACILITIES AND SERVICES: Bar, central heat, private-line telephones in all rooms (require phone cards to call out), gym, squash court, coin-operated laundry, kitchens on each floor, TV lounge

NEAREST TOURIST ATTRACTIONS: Soho, British Museum

CAMPBELL HOUSE EAST (14)

TELEPHONE
020 7679 1479

FAX
020 7388 0060

EMAIL
accommodation@ucl.ac.uk

CREDIT CARDS
None; cash only

RATES
Single less than 7 nights £20, more than 7 nights £19; twin less than 7 nights £37, more than 7 nights £35

BREAKFAST
Not served

5–10 Taviton Street, Bloomsbury, WC1
Tube: Euston Square
200 beds, no private facilities

Converted from eleven early Victorian townhouses, the residence houses more than two hundred people in single or twin rooms that share kitchens and bathrooms. Bed linens are provided, towels are not. The hall is open from mid-June to the last part of September.

FACILITIES AND SERVICES: Central heat, public phone, communal kitchens, TV and music room, coin-operated laundry, garden

NEAREST TOURIST ATTRACTIONS: British Museum, British Library

LANGTON CLOSE (13)
Wren Street at Gray's Inn Road, Clerkenwell, WC1
Tube: Russell Square, King's Cross
272 singles, none with shower, bath, or toilet

Groups only are welcome from June to September at Langton Close, where 272 weary souls sleep in single rooms around clusters that share shower, toilet, and kitchen. Bed linens are provided, BYO towels. Access to central London and the City of London is convenient by foot or public transportation.

FACILITIES AND SERVICES: Central heat, computer room, direct-dial phone that requires a phone card, kitchen, coin-operated laundry, parking can be arranged, TV lounge

NEAREST TOURIST ATTRACTIONS: British Library

TELEPHONE
020 7833 8175

FAX
020 7833 8206

EMAIL
accommodation@ucl.ac.uk

CREDIT CARDS
None; cash only

RATES
£22 per person; groups only, minimum stay 7 nights

BREAKFAST
Not served

RAMSAY HALL (5)
20 Maple Street, W1
Tube: Great Portland Street, Warren Street, Goodge Street
480 rooms, none with shower, bath, or toilet

Ramsay Hall provides mainly single rooms to individuals or groups of students or professors during the Easter holidays and from June to September. The basic rooms have hot and cold running water, and the rates include a cooked breakfast and all linens. Dinner is served, with two meat dishes and one vegetarian selection, but it costs extra. From here the walk to Regent's Park and the British Museum is easy, and the public transportation is good.

FACILITIES AND SERVICES: Bar, central heat, private phone lines that require phone cards to activate, coin-operated laundry, lift, car park, free bicycle storage, satellite TV and VCR in lounge, dining room for breakfast and dinner

NEAREST TOURIST ATTRACTIONS: Regent's Park, British Museum

TELEPHONE
020 7387 4537

FAX
020 7383 0843

EMAIL
accommodation@ucl.ac.uk

CREDIT CARDS
None; cash only

RATES
Under 7 nights: £30 for dinner, bed, and breakfast, £25 for bed and breakfast only; over 7 nights: £28 for dinner, bed, and breakfast, £23 for bed and breakfast only

BREAKFAST
Included

SCHAFER HOUSE (2)
168–182 Drummond Street, Euston, NW1
Tube: Warren Street, Euston Square
363 single rooms, none with shower, bath, or toilet

It is all more of the same: 363 single rooms with sinks, arranged in clusters of up to five rooms around a kitchen/dining room and shower available to groups only. The toilet is in the hall. All rooms have double-glazed windows, and only the bed linens are provided.

TELEPHONE
020 7387 1286

FAX
020 7383 3920

EMAIL
accommodation@ucl.ac.uk

CREDIT CARDS
None; cash only

You can cook here or eat out, which will probably seem like a very good idea after a few nights in these barracklike quarters.

FACILITIES AND SERVICES: Central heat, computer room, communal kitchens, hall phones, coin-operated laundry, TV lounge

NEAREST TOURIST ATTRACTIONS: Regent's Park, British Library

UNIVERSITY OF WESTMINSTER
Central Reservation Information, Head Office
35 Marylebone Road, NW1

TELEPHONE
020 7911 5796/5807/5799

FAX
020 7911 5141

EMAIL
comserv@westminster.ac.uk

INTERNET
www.wmin.ac.uk

CREDIT CARDS
MC, V

RATES
Prices are per person in single or twin-bedded rooms and depend on age and length of stay. Under 26 years: less than 7 nights £25, weekly £155; over 26 years: less than 7 nights £35, no weekly rate; group rates are quoted on request

BREAKFAST
Continental breakfast included at Wigram House only; not served elsewhere

Careful-shopping Great Sleeping budgeteers, sit up straight and pay attention! There is absolutely no need to reduce your stay to a grubby flophouse-style hotel when you can check into a room in one of these residence halls and get a clean, safe bed with weekly linen change, not to mention fringe benefits and a convenient location. The catch is that you have to time your visit for mid-June to mid-September. Groups have first dibs, but with so many rooms scattered over London, individuals do stand a good chance, especially if they can book ahead. All reservations for both groups and individuals should be made through the central booking office, not through the individual halls.

Alexander Fleming Halls, N1	**242**
International House, SE1	**243**
Marylebone Road Hall, NW1	**243**
Wigram House, SW1	**243**

ALEXANDER FLEMING HALLS
3 Hoxton Market, N1
Tube: Old Street, Liverpool Street

TELEPHONE
020 7729 9680

FAX
020 7729 7918

186 single rooms, none with private bath, shower, or toilet

Situated on the edge of the historic City of London, Hoxton Market is close to the traditional East End markets and Brick Lane, famous for its Eastern cuisine. The accommodations consist of single bedrooms arranged in self-contained units of four to eight, each with private bathrooms, kitchen with fridge-freezer, full size oven, microwave, electric kettle, toaster, dining area, and television. There is a coin-operated laundry, and the phones are in the hall.

NEAREST TOURIST ATTRACTIONS: Must use public transportation

INTERNATIONAL HOUSE (14)
1–5 Lambeth Road, South Bank, SE1
Tube: Lambeth North, Waterloo
100 beds

TELEPHONE & FAX
020 7582 9688

International House is a short walk from the Houses of Parliament, the River Thames, the Old Vic Theatre, Waterloo Station, and the Eurostar Terminal. It is a modern nine-story building with singles and doubles for a hundred people. The rooms on high floors have great views of London. Each floor has a communal kitchen and bathrooms. There is a TV lounge and a coin-operated laundry.

NEAREST TOURIST ATTRACTIONS: Imperial War Museum, fifteen-minute walk to South Bank, London Aquarium, and Waterloo

MARYLEBONE ROAD HALL (4)
35 Marylebone Road, Marylebone, NW1
Tube: Baker Street
229 rooms, all singles, none with private bath, shower, or toilet

TELEPHONE
020 7911 5000, ext. 5071
FAX
020 7911 5019

You have to be a card-carrying student to stay at Marylebone Road Hall. Of the twenty-one floors, rooms on the top three are the best, because they have washbasins, large wardrobes with good shelf space, and sweeping views of greater London. The floors are coed, but not the rooms or the bathrooms. On every floor there is a bathroom for every six rooms, an equipped kitchen for every twelve, and telephones. There is also a common room with a satellite TV, a bookstore, and a coin-operated laundry. If you don't want to fix something in the hall kitchen, you can dine out at any number of Great Eating spots in the vicinity, or stop by the student canteen and snack bar. The locale is great, across from Madame Tussaud's and the Planetarium.

NEAREST TOURIST ATTRACTIONS: Madame Tussaud's, Planetarium, Regent's Park

WIGRAM HOUSE (15)
84/99 Ashley Gardens, Thirleby Road,
Westminster, SW1
Tube: Victoria
200 beds, none with private bath, shower, or toilet

TELEPHONE
020 7828 5019
FAX
020 7828 3497

On a residential street off the paved piazza of the Westminster Catholic Cathedral, Wigram House is at the heart of London tourist sights. The residence is a seven-story Victorian mansion block that can accommodate up to two hundred guests, most in modernly furnished singles. There are kitchens, bathrooms, and telephones on each floor. On the ground floor is a common room with a TV, and laundry facilities. A Continental breakfast is included.

NEAREST TOURIST ATTRACTIONS: Ten-minute walk to Buckingham Palace, Westminster Abbey, Palace of Westminster, Big Ben, and Thames River

Student-Only Accommodations

There are many places in London to stay that are mainly for students. From what I can see, they can be the pits—run-down hotel dumps with absolutely no regard for cleanliness or safety, let alone eye appeal. Some are so deplorable I wouldn't even let my dog walk in, not to mention a young person, no matter how cash strapped. There are some very good exceptions, and those listed here are recommended and safe.

STUDENT-ONLY ACCOMMODATIONS

ASHLEE HOUSE (3)
261–265 Grays Inn Road, WC1
Tube: King's Cross

186 beds, none with bath, shower, or toilet

For a clean central London bed near the British Library and not far from the funk at Camden Market, book a bunk at Ashlee House, where there is no curfew and no lockout. Sleeping choices range from a single cell to a coed sixteen-bed room. The price includes bedding and a Continental breakfast in the morning, but not towels or soap. There is a coin-operated washer and dryer to refresh clothes stuffed too long in a backpack, two Internet terminals to keep you in touch back home, and kitchen privileges for warming up a take-away meal. Showers are gratis, and so is luggage storage and the wisecracks from the happy desk staff.

FACILITIES AND SERVICES: Central heat, 2 Internet terminals, kitchen privileges, coin laundry, lift, luggage storage, office safe, TV lounge, 24-desk

NEAREST TOURIST ATTRACTIONS: British Library

TELEPHONE
020 7833 9400

FAX
020 7833 9677

EMAIL
info@ashleehouse.co.uk

INTERNET
www.ashleehouse.co.uk

CREDIT CARDS
None, cash only

RATES
Single £41, twin £28 per person, room with 4–6 beds £23 per person, room with 8–10 beds £21 per person; 16-bed dorm £18 per person; towels £1; soap 50p; lower rates November–March

BREAKFAST
Continental breakfast included

THE GENERATOR (11)
MacNaghten House, Compton Place (off 37 Tavistock Place), WC1
Tube: Russell Square, King's Cross

810 beds in 217 rooms, no private facilities

Earth to Mars, come in please.

The Generator is something else. If you know and like the architecture of the Georges Pompidou Centre in Paris, with its exposed piping, swirling neon tube lights, and open-grid ceilings, you will love the Generator. Designed along futuristic lines, with hard-edged graphics and decoration, it is a popular pit stop for Great Sleepers young enough in body, mind, and spirit to appreciate this far-out London sleeping factory designed to provide clean beds and a chance to meet other like-minded voyagers. You will bunk in dorm rooms designed to sleep up to eight, and shower down the hall in cubicles divided by corrugated tin. Food and drink are consumed in the Fuel Stop (cafeteria), the Turbine (dining room), and in the Generator Bar. Talking Heads is an additional facility where groups can meet. Breakfast is an all-you-can-eat affair and included in the room rate. Lunch and dinner are available only to groups with advance notice, but anyone can drink at the bar. Management states that the Generator is really beyond description and that you have to experience it to get the true flavor. Go and try it for yourself, but be sure to book early, because there is going to be a long queue ahead of you.

FACILITIES AND SERVICES: Bar, central heat, hall phones, Internet terminal, lift, luggage storage, restaurant for groups, office safe (50p per opening), all rooms non-smoking, sheets and towels provided, free showers, TV lounge, 24-hour desk

NEAREST TOURIST ATTRACTIONS: British Library, British Museum

TELEPHONE
020 7388 7666

FAX
020 7388 7644

EMAIL
info@the-generator.co.uk

INTERNET
www.the-generator.co.uk

CREDIT CARDS
MC, V

RATES
Single £40, twin £28 per person, room with 3–6 beds £24 per person, room with 7–8 beds £22.50 per person; 1-night Saturday bookings in winter subject to a £2 supplement on all rate categories; lower rates in the off-season

BREAKFAST
Continental breakfast included

INTERNATIONAL STUDENTS HOUSE (1)
229 Great Portland Street, Marylebone/Regent's Park, W1
Tube: Great Portland Street
661 beds in 200 rooms, 4 with shower or bath and toilet

For my money, the International Students House is one of the best of its kind in London. Most important for bargain seekers, it is open throughout the year to anyone who is staying temporarily (less than three weeks) and to students on a long-term basis. All rooms are nonsmoking, and the singles and twins have a minibar. For sheer number of services offered in London, it is unequaled. Even if you are not staying here, but are a full-time student, you can pay a monthly or yearly membership fee and participate in their wide range of planned activities. Better still, if you hold an International Student ID Card, you will get a discount for your room, but not on any of the activities (see "Discounts," page 19, for more about this super money-saver). If you are an au pair or student nurse, you will pay half price. Members are eligible to buy discounted theater and concert tickets; take aerobics, ballroom dancing, yoga, kung fu, or karate lessons; and work out in the fitness center or play snooker, tennis, bridge, or chess. Anyone staying here is automatically a member, and in addition to the above, can eat the bargain meals served in the cafeteria; watch full-length films; surf the Web in the cyber café; check the bulletin board for jobs, rides, or lonely hearts; change money; or join the Travel Club and participate in London walking and sight-seeing tours, day trips into the country, and weekend excursions. If you think you might become a member, bring three passport-size photos and proof of full-time-student status.

FACILITIES AND SERVICES: Bar, cafeteria, central heat, cyber café, direct-dial phone in all rooms, iron available, laundry room, lift in one building, unstocked minibars in singles and twins, office safe, parking (£10 per day), TV lounge, vast array of services and activities, fitness center, conference facilities. Reception desk open daily 7:45 A.M.–10:30 P.M.

NEAREST TOURIST ATTRACTIONS: Regent's Park, long walk to Oxford Street

RATES: There is a complicated array of rates depending on length of stay and level of amenities. There are seasonal and group discounts, as well as breaks for longer stays, but only up to three weeks for nonstudents. If you

TELEPHONE
020 7631 8300

FAX
020 7631 8310

EMAIL
accom@ish.org.uk

INTERNET
www.ish.org.uk

CREDIT CARDS
MC, V

RATES
See below

BREAKFAST
Included in some room rates

hold an ISIC, there will be a 5% discount, except on the weekly rates.

Short stays:

Includes room with hot and cold running water, private telephone, and £2 breakfast voucher:

Single	£35
Twin	£25 per person, sharing
3–4 beds	£23–20 per person, sharing
Multibeds	£12 (bed only, no breakfast)

Includes room with private bathroom, private telephone, and £2 breakfast voucher:

Single	£38
Twin	£30 per person, sharing

Special weekly rates (from September to May):

Includes sink only for a seven-night stay

Single	£195 per person, per week
Twin	£145 per person, per week

Long stays (three-month minimum):

	first 4 weeks	thereafter
Single	£110	£95
Twin	£85	£75
Triple	£68	£58
Dorm	£53	£45

The long-term rates are per person per week and do not include breakfast. There is a nonrefundable booking fee, an annual membership fee, and a security deposit. Long-term residents are issued meal cards, which give discounts in the cafeteria. If there is no prior arrangement, and the duration of your stay is less than three months, weekly rates apply. Permanent/long-stay residents should apply well in advance to the reservations office.

LEE ABBEY INTERNATIONAL STUDENTS CLUB (49)
57–67 Lexham Gardens, Kensington, W8
Tube: Earl's Court, Gloucester Road

100 rooms, 20 with shower or bath and toilet

TELEPHONE
020 7373 7242

FAX
020 7244 8702

EMAIL
studentsclub@leeabbeylondon.freeserve.co.uk

INTERNET
www.leeabbeylondon.freeserve.co.uk

If you want to stay in a place a cut above the usual student digs, check into this Christian-run students' club, founded in 1964 by the Lee Abbey Council, headed by the Right Reverend Lord Coogan, former archbishop of Canterbury. Here you will find clean and pleasing single or shared rooms offered to people of all faiths and nationalities. It is staffed by a group of young men and women who live and work together on site as a Christian community. Breakfast, lunch, and dinner are served Saturday, Sunday, and holidays, breakfast and dinner are served during the week, and vegetarians catered for. A wealth of special programs and visits in and around London are arranged during the academic year, and there is a chapel, large garden, study area, Internet terminal, photocopying service, and coin-operated laundry. Short-term stays are open to anyone over eighteen, but for three months or more, you must be a valid, card-carrying student. No smoking is allowed, except in the garden and the smoking room.

FACILITIES AND SERVICES: Central heat; phones in all rooms; coin-operated laundry; separate smoking, study, and music rooms; dining room; Internet terminal; lift; TV and VCR in lounge; smoking room; pool and Ping-Pong tables

NEAREST TOURIST ATTRACTIONS: Long walk to Museum District and Royal Albert Hall

CREDIT CARDS
MC, V

RATES
Daily: single £36–45, twin with bathroom £66, bed in shared room £27; one-night deposit required for short-term stays; weekly: 10% discount for 5 weeks or more, and even lower rates for longer stays on request

BREAKFAST
Includes breakfast daily, lunch Sat–Sun only; dinner (£6) is served daily

ST. CHRISTOPHER'S INNS (9)
57, 121, 161–165, Borough High Street, SE1
Tube: London Bridge

Over 200 beds in rooms with 2 to 20 beds, none with private facilities

The three St. Christopher's Inns on Borough High Street in South Bank are a super group of budget crash pads designed to accommodate both genuine backpackers as well as budget-conscious travelers. Dubbed "the hostels with attitude," they are only a few minutes' walk from the London Bridge tube and offer a lively atmosphere in which to eat, drink, party, and sleep it all off. Showers and toilets are on every floor; there is satellite TV and a bank of computers for Internet access; a pub on site offers both liquid and solid refreshment; cheap towels, free bed linens, and full coin-operated laundry facilities help make shoestring traveling easier; and a no-curfew policy keeps the places packed and hopping around the clock.

St. Christopher's Orient Expresso, at 57 Borough High Street, has thirty-six beds in rooms for two to eight. It is a good choice for groups, because it is the quietest of the trio; there is no bar or pub attached, but there is a coffee shop and a no-smoking chill-out room for TV viewing.

TELEPHONE
020 7407 1856

FAX
020 7403 7715

EMAIL
bookings@st-christophers.co.uk

INTERNET
www.st-christophers.co.uk

CREDIT CARDS
MC, V

RATES
From £25 in 2-bedded room to £15 in 12-bedded room. All rates are per person, per night

BREAKFAST
Continental breakfast included

The original St. Christopher's Inn is at 121 Borough High Street. Its attached pub has a great reputation as a party destination on the weekends. The forty-eight rooms sleep from two to eight, and there is a chill-out room here as well.

The Village, at 161–165 Borough High Street, is the newest and has 164 beds on three floors with rooms sleeping up to twelve. In addition to a chill-out room there is a roof terrace with a hot tub and sauna, Internet terminals, and bar and dance floor for residents and guests.

A Continental breakfast is included in all three inns. Packed lunches and hot meals are available by prior arrangement for groups. There are also St. Christopher Inns in Camden and Greenwich, and two more are planned in Shepherd's Bush and in Edinburgh. Check the Website for details.

FACILITIES AND SERVICES: Central heat, bar and club with dancing, Internet access, coin laundry, lift, safes (20p per opening), bed linens included, towels £1 per day, satellite TV lounge, handicapped-accessible rooms, no smoking in rooms

NEAREST TOURIST ATTRACTIONS: Tate Modern, Southwark Cathedral

YMCAs

For reliable, clean, safe accommodations at great prices, any penny-pinching Great Sleeper in London must consider staying at one of the YMCAs described below. For the price you will always get bed and breakfast, and in one case lunch and dinner as well. At the Barbican Y and the London City Y, you get the added benefit of gym privileges. For a list of all the greater London YMCAs and more information, contact them.

TELEPHONE
020 8520 5599
FAX
020 8509 3190
INTERNET
www.ymca.org.uk

YMCAS

Barbican YMCA, EC2	**251**
Indian Student YMCA, W1	**252**
Lancaster Hall Hotel–German YMCA, W2	**253**
London City YMCA, EC1	**253**
Norwegian YWCA, W11	**254**

BARBICAN YMCA (5)
2 Fann Street, Barbican, EC2
Tube: Barbican

196 rooms, none with shower, bath, or toilet

Attention fitness fanatics!

If you can handle very, very basic accommodations on the edge of things in London and want to keep fit by pounding the flesh even on holiday, read on.

Some 196 single and double rooms on sixteen floors make this one of the biggest Ys in London. Metal beds, cafeteria food (which includes dishes for vegetarians), shared bathrooms, and low-wattage lights (sometimes bare) in scruffy rooms . . . is this high-class incarceration? No! This is a cheap Great Sleep with a big bonus: free membership in the Y Fitness Center and reduced fees to attend its various classes. The rooms may be a bit over-the-hill, but the Fitness Center is state-of-the-art, with enough equipment and loud, upbeat music to keep you pumping, stepping, and cycling until you drop. If you take advantage of all the features and classes, you won't have much time to see or do much else in London, but you will come home with a bronzed, buffed and and toned bod. Those who want to change their body shape in a hurry should join Body Pump, which is resistance training with rhythm. Move on to Aerobic Fat Burner, guaranteed to get you in a sweat and raise your heart rate, or the Step and Abs/Step and Sculpt class, a great

TELEPHONE
020 7628 0697
FAX
020 7638 2420
EMAIL
barbicanYMCA@aol.com
CREDIT CARDS
MC, V
RATES
Daily rates are per person and include only bed and breakfast. Weekly rates are per person and include bed, breakfast, and dinner. Daily £26, weekly £160, over 3 months £100 per person per week.
BREAKFAST
English breakfast included

workout for your heart, lungs, and motor skills. For low-impact conditioning, the Legs, Bums, and Tums class emphasizes muscular strength and tone. If you're over fifty, join a class of gentle aerobic exercises, or try yoga or khai-bo, no-contact martial arts movements choreographed to music. Worn out? Wrap up your workout with a session on a tanning bed and a steam bath.

FACILITIES AND SERVICES: Central heat, public hall phones, hair dryer available, lift, office safe, cafeteria, TV lounge, 24-hour desk, free use of fitness center and reduced rates for classes, bed linens and maid service provided; BYO towels and soap

NEAREST TOURIST ATTRACTIONS: Barbican Centre, St. Paul's

INDIAN STUDENT YMCA (3)
41 Fitzroy Square, Soho/Fitzrovia, W1
Tube: Warren Street, Great Portland Street
110 rooms, 15 with shower or bath and toilet

TELEPHONE
020 7387 0411
FAX
020 7383 7651
EMAIL
indianymca@aol.com
INTERNET
www.indianymca.org
CREDIT CARDS
None; cash only
RATES
Single £35; double £50–55; family suite £75; extra bed £12; children under 5 are free, children 6–12 have special rates on request; non-YMCA members must pay a membership fee of £1, and everyone must pay a 50p reservation fee
BREAKFAST
Included (dinner too)

The motto of the Indian Student YMCA is, "We serve members, friends, and well wishers and thank you for your patronage." On every visit I have made here, they have lived up to their words.

When I first asked to see these accommodations, I was ready to be unimpressed. However, when I saw how clean the simple rooms are compared to many other cheap sleeping digs in London, I knew I had to include this as a very special Great Sleep. While still operating as a hostel for seventy-five full-time Indian students, it is also open to anyone of any age from any place on a short-term basis. The sunny rooms have light-colored wooden built-in furniture, three-drawer desks with shelves above, a chair, a sink, and acceptable beds. There is daily maid service for all short-stay visitors. If you are alone, be sure to get your room on the side with either the ladies' or men's toilets; otherwise, you must cross an enclosed walkway to get to them. The budget price includes breakfast and "Indian style" dinner, and there is no reduction if you don't eat here. If you like Indian food, this is a deal you will never beat. Even if you skip dinner altogether, it is a deal you will have to go a long way to equal. (See *Great Eats London* for more information about the cafeteria-style restaurant.) If you are a music lover, you are in luck: twice a week, the Westminster Philharmonic Orchestra practices in the basement, and Y guests can listen to the music from the balcony absolutely free.

FACILITIES AND SERVICES: Central heat; direct-dial phones; iron available; lift; cafeteria for breakfast, lunch, and dinner; TV in lounge and in all rooms; minibars in a few rooms; study room; library, coin-operated laundry; badminton courts; billiards; Ping-Pong; 24-hour desk

NEAREST TOURIST ATTRACTIONS: Soho, British Museum, Regent's Park

LANCASTER HALL HOTEL–GERMAN YMCA (14)
35 Craven Terrace, Paddington, W2
Tube: Lancaster Gate, Paddington
In the annex: 25 rooms, none with shower, bath, or toilet

The Lancaster Hall Hotel is owned by the German YMCA and consists of two parts: the hotel proper and the annex, which is geared toward groups and students under twenty-six years old in rooms without private bathrooms. Because it will serve Great Sleepers in London more as a hotel than as a Y, I have also listed it under the hotel section for W2 on page 74.

I think it is interesting that the same architect who designed the hotel and annex in 1973 was asked, at age ninety, to plan the changes that took place in 2000, at a cost of a million pounds. The results are wonderful, especially the beautiful new communal bathrooms and the single rooms, which are huge. The German zeal for cleanliness continues to be apparent throughout. There is a maximum stay of three weeks in the annex.

FACILITIES AND SERVICES: Central heat, bar (6–11 P.M.), conference rooms, hall phone, hair dryer available, lift, office safe, 24-hour desk

NEAREST TOURIST ATTRACTIONS: Kensington Palace and Gardens, Hyde Park

TELEPHONE
020 7723 9276
FAX
020 7706 2870
EMAIL
lhh-info@lhh.ndirect.co.uk
INTERNET
www.lhh.ndirect.co.uk
CREDIT CARDS
MC, V
RATES
Single £25, double £40 (there are only twin beds), triple £51, quad £68; group rates available on request for parties of 20 or more
BREAKFAST
Continental breakfast included

LONDON CITY YMCA (3)
8 Errol Street, Barbican, EC1
Tube: Barbican, Moorgate
111 rooms, 4 with shower or bath and toilet

Only single or double rooms are available at this Y, which is about a block from the Barbican Y and a mile ahead of it in terms of room standards. During the year it is full of students, so getting space can be a problem. In the summer you stand a better chance. Only four rooms have en suite bathrooms, but there is a bathroom for every two rooms, so it really isn't too bad to share. Each room has its own TV and a locked closet. Bed linens are provided, but towels are not. Guests can use the Barbican Y Fitness Center (see page 251 for details).

TELEPHONE
020 7628 8832
FAX
020 7628 4080
CREDIT CARDS
MC, V

RATES
Nightly: single £30, double
£48 for bed and breakfast;
weekly (must include 4
consecutive Saturday nights;
includes bed, breakfast, lunch
Sat–Sun, dinner Mon–Sat):
single £203 for first 4 weeks,
£185 for 5th week; weekly rates
for doubles and long-term rates
(3 months or more) on request

NOTE: A £10 key deposit is taken upon arrival and returned on day of departure. Bookings are accepted by telephone, fax, or email. A nonrefundable full payment or seven-night payment will be required, and no bookings will be accepted without it.

FACILITIES AND SERVICES: Central heat, hall phones, coin-operated laundry, lift, restaurant for breakfast and dinner, TV in room, office safe, ironing facilities, access to Fitness Center at the Barbican Y

NEAREST TOURIST ATTRACTIONS: Barbican Centre, St. Paul's

NORWEGIAN YWCA (34)
52 Holland Park, Holland Park, W11
Tube: Holland Park
20 rooms, 18 with shower only, 2 with shower and toilet

TELEPHONE
020 7727 9346/9897
FAX
020 7727 9897
EMAIL
kfuk.hjemmet@kfuk-ksum.no
INTERNET
www.kfuk.dial.pipex.co
CREDIT CARDS
MC, V
RATES
Single (some tiny) £32, double
£30 per person, triple £26 per
person
BREAKFAST
Breakfast, packed lunch, dinner
included September–June;
breakfast only included July–
August

Oh, how I wish I was younger or Norwegian! Then I could stay at this wonderful YWCA, which is open only to women who are under thirty or carry a Norwegian passport. Men must be Norwegian citizens under thirty, or married and in the company of a woman who is. If you can get past the entrance requirements, let me assure you this is a fabulous Great Sleep in London.

Living in a Y can be an institutional and spartan experience. Not here, though—not by a long shot. I will start with the food. When I arrived I could smell bread baking, and I was told that they do all their own baking, especially the bread, because "English bread is full of air and not nutritional." Already I was hooked. Even more so when I found that the rates from September until the end of June include breakfast, a packed lunch, and dinner, tea, and coffee every evening, and on Wednesday and Sunday nights, homemade cakes are served. In July and August, when the students are gone, only breakfast is available, but there is a microwave, refrigerator, and electric kettle that anyone can use. The rooms are exceptional: simple in their Norwegian pale knotty-pine furniture with duvets on the beds, nightlights, and a wardrobe. All have a shower; two also have a toilet. You will be happy in No. 23, a huge room with a view over the Holland Park mews and the street beyond, where Richard Branson (Virgin Airlines owner and balloon enthusiast) has a home. If there are two of you, No. 17 is a good choice, because it has its own shower and toilet. Whenever you arrive you will receive a welcome note on your bed with a biblical saying, or a poem and a piece of wrapped candy. Of course, inviting anyone to your room, smoking, boozing, and using drugs are absolutely prohibited. The lounge is a dignified yet homey room pleasantly outfitted with comfortable furnishings and a rogues' gallery of the Norwegian founders and benefactors of this YWCA, which was originally a club for Norwegian nannies and maids. The dining room is equally pretty, set with pine furnishings and colorful tablecloths. In back there is a large garden with a barbecue. A few years ago a group of music students raised enough money to build a soundproof music room, where guests can listen to music, study, or use the computer.

NOTE: You must be a member of YWCA, or carry a Norwegian passport, to stay here. Membership is £2 for 1 night–1 week; £6 for 1 week–6 months; £12 for 6 months–1 year.

FACILITIES AND SERVICES: Central heat; phones for incoming calls only; dining room for breakfast, dinner, packed lunches, evening tea and coffee September–June; breakfast only, and use of microwave, refrigerator, and electric kettle July–August; office safe; satellite TV in lounge; soundproof music room; office open daily 8 A.M.–3 P.M.; no lift, no laundry allowed (launderette close by), no smoking (except in the garden), no liquor

NEAREST TOURIST ATTRACTIONS: Holland Park, Notting Hill

Shopping: Great Chic

People who tell you money can't buy happiness don't know where to shop.

—Anonymous

London . . . a kind of Emporium for the whole Earth.

—Joseph Addison, Spectator, *no. 69, May 19, 1711*

According to the British Tourist Authority, shopping is the most popular tourist activity in London, outstripping visits to the Tower of London, Madame Tussaud's, the theater, the Changing of the Guard, and the Elgin Marbles. Whatever you need or want in this world-class shopping city, you can buy it, order it, or have it specially made for you. There are shops catering to everyone from the queen and the English gentry to East End cockneys and those on the wild side of today's fashion. And don't forget the famous London food halls, specifically those at Harrods, where the feast for your senses will entice you to shop for a picnic or a full-blown meal or to purchase gourmet items from around the world to bring home as gifts.

With inflation running in the double digits, you probably won't come home with the bargain of a lifetime, but that's not the point. The great sport of London shopping lies in exploring different places, finding unusual things, and enjoying them once you are home. Despite everything you hear to the contrary, there are finds at the outdoor markets, as well as in china, woolens, and stylish clothing created by the young designers of tomorrow.

Sales are held in January and late June into July, and these events attract buyers from around the globe. People wait all year for these few weeks, when prices are slashed by 30 to 70 percent on most goods. The January sale at Harrods is both theater and legendary shopping. Before the first sale day, some shopping lunatics camp out overnight to be at the head of the line when the doors open. More than 350,000 shoppers surge through the store on day one, and two thousand temporary clerks are added to take care of them. At the height of the sale, £1 million are rung up per hour! The less devoted will still snag some bargains if they can withstand the throngs of shoppers, who seem to lose their usual sense of British decorum during the hunt. Crowd control is handled by London bobbies, who are out en masse. The bargains are good, but be careful of the bin merchandise, which has been brought in specifically for the sale and is of lesser quality than Harrods' regular goods.

Discount shopping as we know and love it in the States is becoming a stronger shopping alternative in London, but many of the best locations are definitely not central. Good sources of discount shopping are found in the *Evening Standard* newspaper and the weekly *Time Out* magazine, which run ads throughout the year for top designers who are having a one- or two-day sale in an empty storefront. Great Chic shoppers should pay close attention to the secondhand couture shops, which are called dress agencies. These are not smelly used-clothing shops hidden on dreary backstreets with fashion castoffs you wouldn't be caught dead wearing. Instead, they are some of the smartest shopping addresses in town. Here customers bring their gently worn designer clothing to sell on consignment. This means you can buy a Chanel suit for a fraction of retail and look like a million dollars.

Besides the myriad shops and department stores, London is famous for street markets. But don't go to one of these huge outdoor circuses expecting to find hidden and valuable treasures for only a few pounds. Go instead for the overall experience, the great vibes, and the fun of just being there. These open-air bazaars are good places to find little gifts and mementos as well as kicky fashions that last a moment or two. Be careful, however, and don't get taken in by a glib dealer who will try to sell you the moon. If it smells like vinyl, it is not a rare leather product out of the Amazonian forest, no matter what the dealer claims. If you remember that a bargain is a bargain only if you like it and can afford it, and more important, that there are no *real* bargains left, just lucky purchases, you will do fine.

It is beyond the scope of *Great Sleeps London* to detail the vast London shopping scene. To get you started, however, I have outlined the main shopping areas and listed major department stores, indoor and outdoor markets, and a sampling of interesting shops that sell everything from buttons to umbrellas. The information about the shops and markets was correct at press time, but details do change. Some places will have closed, changed hands, or altered their hours. If you are making a special trip, I urge you to call ahead and check the facts, so you will not waste time on a false hope.

Tips for Great Shopping

1. Know your prices at home, so you will be able to spot a good buy when you see it in London.

2. If you like it, want it, can get it home, and can afford it, buy it when you see it. If you wait until later and tell yourself you will come back, you probably won't do it, and if you do, it won't be there, and you will kick yourself when you end up paying more for it someplace else.

3. Bring color swatches of anything you are trying to match, try on as much as possible, and if you are buying clothing for other people, bring their measurements and a tape measure (in both inches and centimeters) to make sure the item will fit. Returns are a difficult procedure, and sometimes not accepted at all.

4. Pack an empty, soft folding suitcase in your luggage so you can transport your treasures home with you without the extra hassle and expense of mailing and insuring your package. An extra suitcase over the airline limit of two plus a carry-on will cost you around $100, which is payable at check-in time. This is cheap when you consider the mailing and insurance costs and the worry that the box may not arrive or that it will be damaged en route.

5. Take time to fill out the paperwork for a VAT (value-added tax) refund, and remember to turn it in at the customs office at the airport *after* you go through passport control. (For further details on the ins and outs of VAT, see page 260.)

6. If you are a committed shopaholic, consider a trip to London during the January or June–July sales. Check with the airlines and some of the higher-priced hotel chains in London. Many offer four- and five-day package deals around the sale time, especially in January, when there are fewer tourists (see the Basil Street Hotel, page 146).

7. Unless you are a big-time antiques dealer, buy for the pleasure an object will give you, not for long-term investment qualities the dealer may extol. After all, if you like it, you won't want to part with it.

8. When buying from a street merchant or antiques dealer, cash, not plastic, is king. For more strategies on indoor/outdoor London market shopping, see pages 312.

9. *Never* change money in a shop or at a money-changing booth at an outdoor flea market. The one exception to this rule is Marks & Spencer, which gives good rates and does not charge a commission. In the small shops, the rate will *never* be in your favor.

10. When returning to the United States, remember: when going through U.S. customs, you and every member of your family traveling with you, regardless of age, can bring back $400 worth of purchases duty-free. See "Customs" on page 261 for further pointers.

Shopping Hours

Bette Midler said it all: "When it is three o'clock in New York, it is still 1938 in London." The good news is that all stores are legally able (not required) to stay open for six hours on Sunday. Finally, London merchants have gotten the message that consumers shop on their days off and spend money. Surprise, surprise! The icing on the cake is that more and more shops and large department stores are staying open on Sundays and bank holidays as well, usually from 11 A.M. or noon until 5 or 6 P.M. During the week, large department stores open between 9:30 and 10 A.M. and close between 6 and 7 P.M. The British idea of "late" shopping is that one night a week when stores stay open one hour longer. Many of the shops around Covent Garden stay open nightly until 8 P.M., some even later on the weekends and in summer.

Size Conversion Charts

British sizing can be very confusing if you don't have a head start on how to deal with it. Most manufacturers have their own cuts, and some even put smaller size numbers on larger items to flatter those with a fuller figure. The key to success, of course, is to try everything on. Because this isn't always possible, be sure to bring measurements for those not with you and carry a tape measure in both inches and centimeters. Watch out on men's shirts. The sleeve length is not mentioned, so you will have to measure them. Table and bed sizes are also different from ours, so be careful.

Women's Clothing

American	8	10	12	14	16	18
British	10	12	14	16	18	20
Continental	38	40	42	44	46	48

Women's Shoes

American	5	6	7	8	9	10
British	4	5	6	7	8	9
Continental	36	37	38	39	40	41

Men's Suits

American	34	36	38	40	42	44
British	34	36	38	40	42	44
Continental	44	46	48	50	52	54

Men's Shirts

American	$14\frac{1}{2}$	15	$15\frac{1}{2}$	16	$16\frac{1}{2}$	17	$17\frac{1}{2}$	18
British	$14\frac{1}{2}$	15	$15\frac{1}{2}$	16	$16\frac{1}{2}$	17	$17\frac{1}{2}$	18
Continental	37	38	39	41	42	43	44	45

Men's Shoes

American	7	8	9	10	11	12	13
British	6	7	8	9	10	11	12
Continental	$39\frac{1}{2}$	41	42	43	$44\frac{1}{2}$	46	47

Children's Clothing

American	3	4	5	6	6X
British	18	20	22	24	26
Continental	98	104	110	116	122

Children's Shoes

American	8	9	10	11	12	13	1	2	3
British	7	8	9	10	11	12	13	1	2
Continental	24	25	27	28	29	30	32	33	34

VAT Refund

You *must* ask for the VAT refund; no one will volunteer it. The VAT refund is 17.5 percent in theory, but not in fact.

What Is It?

Value-added taxes (VAT) are taxes included in the price of goods and services, including hotel rooms, cars, books, jewelry, restaurant meals, and clothing. As a tourist, you cannot get a rebate for the hotel or restaurant VAT (some corporate businesses can, but it is complicated and not applicable here), but you can get a rebate for your shopping purchases, unless you are buying from a flea market vendor. It is important to be aware that you will not get the full 17.5 percent back. Your refund is proportionate to the amount you spend and subject to an administration fee, which varies between retailers. Hang in there, though; it can be worth it.

How Does It Work?

If you can answer yes to the following questions, you qualify for the VAT refund.

1. Are you a non–European Union (E.U.) resident?

2. Do you plan to take the goods out of the U.K. within three months of the last day of the month in which they were purchased?

3. Have you spent the required store minimum purchase limit to qualify?

When you are in a store, ask what their minimum expenditure is for you to claim the VAT refund. The amount varies, but all stores have a minimum purchase requirement, usually between £50 and £100, and some (such as Marks & Spencer) insist it be made in one branch, not in a combination of several. You do not have to buy everything all at once, but you must save your receipts and total them when you know you have finished shopping at that store. Most major department stores have VAT departments where they will help you with the paperwork. In smaller stores there are several ways to go: (1) the store gives you the paperwork and you fill it all out, (2) the store clerk fills it out for you, or (3) they offer you a discount to forget all about the VAT. My advice? Take the discount in a New York minute!

Important: You must show your passport at the store granting you the VAT. Without it you won't get to first base. The store will always ask you how you want to take the VAT: refunded to your credit card, or mailed to you in a pounds sterling check. The best way, by far, is to have the amount refunded to your credit card. This way not only provides you with a record of the transaction, but the credit will be in U.S. dollars, not foreign currency that will cost you time and money to convert at your bank, if they will convert it at all.

Turning in the Paperwork to Get Your VAT Refund

Before you leave England (and I assume that will be at either Heathrow or Gatwick airports), you *must* have all the forms completely filled out. Please do this before you leave your hotel for the airport, not standing in the queue waiting your turn. When you arrive at the airport, make this your top priority, and allow extra time for it. During peak travel seasons, lines are lethal. *After* you go through U.K. passport control, go directly to the customs official who deals with VAT. This is done *before* you clear U.K. customs. By law, you are required to have your purchases with you. No one has ever asked to see mine, but these officers have the right to inspect every item you are claiming for your VAT refund. The officer will stamp your papers, and there will be a mailbox by the desk where you deposit the envelopes that the store should have given you along with the paperwork. Unless the stores have already affixed postage to the envelopes, you should stamp them before leaving for the airport, because the VAT customs people don't stock postage stamps.

That is all there is to it. Now you have time to hit the duty-free shops in the airport before boarding your flight. The refund will take up to six weeks to arrive by check or show up on your credit card, so be patient. Naturally, when you made your purchase, you got the name, address, telephone, fax, and email (if they have one) of the store.

Claims are valid for a limited time, usually up to a year from the date of purchase. If you don't get your money in three months, contact the store before the time runs out.

Customs

Each person returning from abroad is allowed to bring back $400 worth of duty-free items. This allowance is per person, and age doesn't matter. Everyone in your family with you on the trip, including a baby, is entitled to $400 worth of duty-free goods, meaning your purchases can be pooled. You pay a flat 10 percent duty on the next $1,000 worth of merchandise. Thereafter, duty is on a product basis and can get expensive. Have your receipts ready, and make sure they coincide with what you filled out on the landing card. Don't cheat, don't lie, don't smuggle, and for heaven's sake, don't do drugs—they will catch you and examine your luggage (and maybe your person) down to the last breath mint.

Any purchase worth *less* than $50 can be shipped back to the States as an unsolicited gift and is duty-free. It does *not* count in your $400 limit. If the value is more than $50, you will pay customs when the package arrives.

Important: Send one unsolicited gift per person for each mailing, and don't mail anything to yourself.

Antiques must be one hundred years old to be duty-free.

A work of art is duty-free, and it doesn't matter when it was painted or who the artist was.

If you have expensive camera gear, lots of imported luggage, or watches, carry the receipts for them, or you could end up paying duty on them.

Finally, people who look like hippies get stopped and have their bags searched. So do bejeweled and bedecked women wrapped in full-length minks and carrying expensive luggage. For more information, send for the free brochure "Know Before You Go," available from the U.S. Customs Service, Box 7407, Washington, D.C. 20044; Tel: 202-927-6724.

Do China in a Day

When the brochure says "Do China in a Day," it is talking about Stoke-on-Trent, the china and pottery bargain capital of England, between Birmingham and Manchester. Here is where you can stock up on seconds, overruns, and pieces you never can find at home, if your pattern happens to be English. You can take the train from Euston Station (156 miles, two hours) for around £65, or the National Express Bus from London Victoria Coach Station, which costs only £20, but takes three to four hours. For more on the bus, contact the Tourist Information Centre in Stoke-on-Trent or telephone First Bus PMT, 01782 207999 for bus routes and times.

Better yet, if there are at least two of you, or you plan to buy in bulk, rent a car and drive from London. The M6 motorway provides easy access; the potteries are off the M6 junction 15 from the south and junction 16 from the north. It is a long day trip, but the car makes life much easier once you arrive in Stoke.

The trip is not worth the effort if you just want to browse and pick up a vase or two. But for brides and serious china shoppers, it is. For noncommitted Great Chic shoppers, there are factory tours on Monday through Friday and interesting exhibits and programs to fill time while the shopper is unearthing one bargain after another. Bridgewater and Royal Stafford have pottery cafés where children and adults can decorate their own pottery masterpieces.

No matter how you get there, your first order of business is to go directly to the Tourist Information Centre. Here you can load up on information about whatever brand you are interested in, and from there, you can drive or take a taxi or the bus that links many of the outlets. Stoke-on-Trent is made up of six towns all blended together. From north to south they are: Tunstall, Burslem, Hanley (the city center), Stoke, Fenton, and Longton. Forget about walking. The thirty-plus factory shops and ceramics museums are located throughout Stoke-on-Trent, which covers thirty-six miles. Obviously, walking is not an option.

What's here? Coalport, Johnson Brothers, Minton, Portmeirion, Royal Doulton, Royal Stafford, Spode, Staffordshire enamels and ceramics, Wedgwood, and much more. Shipping is possible, although some outlets do not mail seconds—but *you* can.

For more information, contact the Tourist Information Centre: Quadrant Road, Hanley, Stoke-on-Trent, ST1 1RZ, Tel: 01782 236000; Fax: 01782 236005; Email: stoke.tic@virgin.net; Internet: www.stoke.gov.uk/tourism. The center is open throughout the year except Christmas week and New Year's Day, 9:15 A.M.–5:15 P.M. Note that most of the factories follow the same schedule, but tours and programs do not. It is advised that you check before you travel.

Special Shopping Services

Shirley Eaton—Shopping Services

Shirley Eaton is an energetic and delightful lady who knows her way around London. For many years she was a noted interior decorator, and one visit to her lovely home underscores her talents in this area. She also owned a restaurant in the countryside; has written a charming book, *A Granny's Guide to London,* which she dedicated to her five grandchildren, who were the catalysts behind her writing it; and is a special inspector for Wolsey Lodges, the premier B&B agency in the U.K. (see Uptown Reservations, page 221). A day spent in Shirley Eaton's capable hands will not only expand your shopping horizons and appreciation for the vast storehouse of wonderful purchases awaiting you on your next trip to London, but also will save you considerable time and money. Naturally, you are not going to engage Shirley to guide you through Harrods or up and down Bond Street, but if you have special needs you want to shop for, especially related to interior design, discuss them with Shirley, and she will guide you to the best antiques, fabrics, and furnishings London has to offer. As she said, "I can do anything . . . within reason." She was too modest to add, "and do it well." The price is £75 per day, from 10 A.M. to 5 P.M. Monday to Friday, and does not include wherever you have lunch.

There is more to Shirley than wonderful shopping. She owns a beautifully appointed three-bedroom, three-bath Chelsea townhouse only minutes from Harrods that she is willing to let. Rates for this are available on request.

TELEPHONE: 020 7581 8429
FAX: 020 7854 0782
CREDIT CARDS: None; cash only

Shopping Areas

Most shopping is concentrated along certain streets and in specific areas, making London an easy city in which to plan a shopping expedition. Each area is different, with its own character and atmosphere. Traditional men's clothing is found on Savile Row; both Old and New Bond Streets are known for their fashionable boutiques, art galleries, and auction houses; Regent Street is noted for high-quality shops such as Liberty, Burberry's, and Aquascutum; Oxford Street, with three hundred stores, is the busiest shopping street in Britain, and many shops on Jermyn Street are more than a hundred years old . . . the famed Floris opened here in 1730. The King's Road, Carnaby Street, and Kensington High Street are the places for the latest word in new-wave fashions; designer shops line Sloane Street; and on Tottenham Court Road, computer buffs will be in high-tech heaven. Book lovers will head for Foyles, at 113–119 Charing Cross Road, and one-stop power shoppers will find everything they need, and generally will overpay for it, at Harrods, the famous Knightsbridge department store with three hundred departments, where you can buy everything from a tube of toothpaste to a ball gown or arrange to sell your house and its contents and move to the tropics. How many lights does it take to illuminate the exterior of Harrods? 11,500.

THE WEST END (W1)

The West End is the heart of London and one of the most important shopping areas of the city. The big shopping streets are here: Oxford and Regent Streets, Savile Row, Jermyn Street, Old and New Bond Streets, and Piccadilly Circus, with the world's largest Tower Records store. Also here is the beautiful and expensive Burlington Arcade, Aquascutum, Hamley's toy store, Liberty, Selfridges, and much more. If you only have time to window-shop for an hour or so, you will not forget your time spent on New and Old Bond Streets. The shops are magnificent; so are the prices.

KNIGHTSBRIDGE (SW1, SW3)

After the West End, Knightsbridge has the largest concentration of shops. The most important streets to remember are Brompton Road (Harrods is here), Sloane Street (Harvey Nichols and designer boutiques), Walton Street (glorious gift and clothing boutiques), and Beauchamp Place (pronounced BEECH-um). This is a block-long strip of exclusive shops where the late Princess Diana's favorite designer, Bruce Oldfield, has a shop. Another of her favorites along here was Janet Reger, a specialist in luxurious lingerie. Her most popular designs are in pure silk, trimmed in handmade lace and in loads of colors. Prices run from £20 for a garter to £350 and up for a silk dressing gown.

KENSINGTON (W8)

When you get off at the High Street Kensington tube station, you will be right in the middle of a shopping area along Kensington High Street and Kensington Church Street. Kensington High Street is one of London's busiest shopping areas, probably because everything is concentrated in a relatively small area. All the chains are here, and good old, stodgy Marks & Spencer is in the center of it all. Barkers of Kensington has everything you want in a department store: a lip and nail bar on one; facials and massages on the mezzanine, housewares on two; women and children on three and four, and menswear and a cappuccino bar in the basement. Antiques lovers will enjoy strolling along Kensington Church Street, where both sides of the street are lined with jewel-like shops featuring museum-quality antiques and collectibles.

CHELSEA (SW3, SW10)

Saturday is the best day to experience Chelsea. Take the tube to Sloane Square and start with a quick look through the General Trading Company, then hit the housewares and linens at Peter Jones Department Store, forgoing their fashions, which are strictly from hunger. Continue to work your way down both sides of King's Road. The shops along here come and go, but they all display every new trend the fashionites under forty-something are wearing. Once the home of punks wearing skintight leather and spiked purple hair, the area has calmed down a bit, because most of these fashion victims have moved on to Notting Hill Gate or are hanging out at Covent Garden. You will probably see more Sloane Rangers (British yuppies) in their Ralph Lauren and Laura Ashley clothes, either behind the wheel of their Range Rover or pushing a magnificent pram holding a picture-perfect baby, than you will freaky dressers toward the Sloane Square end. The farther you go along King's Road toward Fulham, the more bizarre things get. Antiques buffs will want to save time for a look through the Antiquarius Gallery and keep an eye on the notice board outside the Chelsea Town Hall for announcements of weekend antique shows.

While you are in Chelsea, please make a detour to one of my favorite neighborhood shopping areas, Chelsea Green. Allow time to window-shop and peek into these very upmarket and oh so English shops, which are dotted around the charming Chelsea Green. All the basic necessities of life are here. You can buy your daily newspapers, pick up some fresh fish for dinner, have your clothes cleaned, do your laundry, and have your hair done. If you are considering a permanent move to London, there are estate agencies to handle all the details of finding just the right flat for you, and interior decorators to redo it. In addition, you will find antiques and dress shops, a perfume boutique, a framer, the best greengrocer in London, a sweet and savory pie shop, a smart bar, an even smarter restaurant, and a crowded matchbox-size toy store that children of all ages love (see Traditional Toys, page 301). Down Elystan Street leading to Fulham Road is a French pastry shop; La Scala dress agency (see page 298); Elistano, a great Italian restaurant (see *Great Eats London*); a wine shop; a shoe repair shop; a meat market; and a corner pub where you can hoist a few while watching all the important sports events on their wide-screen televisions.

Here's how to find Chelsea Green: Coming from Sloane Square, walk along King's Road until you see the Safeway, turn right on Anderson (which becomes Sloane Avenue), and continue on to Whitehead's Grove. Turn left and after a block you will be at Chelsea Green. If you are coming from the other direction on King's Road, turn left on Markham or Jubilee Place, which are lined with mews houses, and you will walk straight into Chelsea Green. If you are coming from the South Kensington tube, exit on Pelham Street and cross over Brompton Road (you will see Sir Terence Conran's Bibendum Restaurant and Habitat store on your right) to Sloane Avenue. Walk about two blocks and turn right on Whitehead's Grove, just after you pass the Nell Gwynn block of flats on your left and a Europa convenience store on your right. The tube stops are Sloane Square or South Kensington.

COVENT GARDEN (WC2)

The name comes from a "covent garden" where monks grew fruit and vegetables in the Middle Ages. It remained London's fruit, flower, and vegetable market until the 1970s, when the old market was turned into a complex of snazzy shops, market stalls, and boutiques that seem to come and go faster than you can say "Rex Harrison and Julie Andrews in *My Fair Lady*." It is an upbeat, vibrant part of London, jammed with clothing shops, arts and crafts markets, restaurants, pubs, and cafés where you can sit and watch the wild things go by. Outside Covent Garden itself, a carnival atmosphere prevails, with a show put on by sidewalk mimes, jugglers, magicians, and musicians. The whole area is a tourist attraction that is fun and boisterous night and day. You should not leave London without at least walking through it.

WESTBOURN GROVE AND LEDBURY ROAD (W2, W11)

The latest hot hangouts for the trust-fund crowd are the smart boutiques, restaurants, and cafés that cluster around Westbourn Grove as it Crosses Ledbury Road, an elite neighborhood near the famed Notting Hill Gate that is small in everything but price.

Store Listings by Postal Code

ACCESSORIZE (23)
386 Oxford Street, W1
Tube: Oxford Circus

Accessorize sells whatever is "hot" in color-coordinated accessories at very reasonable prices. They have hats, scarves, jewelry, hair ornaments, umbrellas, purses, belts . . . everything you need to pull together an outfit that is very "now." This is the largest and the only shop in the U.K. where both Accessorize and Monsoon Home lines are available. They have dozens of branch stores all over London.

TELEPHONE: 020 7629 0038

INTERNET: www.monsoon.co.uk

CREDIT CARDS: AE, MC, V

OPEN: Mon–Sat 10 A.M.–7 P.M., Sun noon–5 P.M.

THE BODY SHOP (21)
374 Oxford Street, W1
Tube: Bond Street

The Body Shop is Britain's largest skin- and hair-care retailer, specializing in natural products that are as pure as possible and *never* tested on animals. Some of their ingredients are cucumber, carrot, seaweed, strawberry, and grape, in addition to the usual aloe and vitamin-enriched creams and lotions. All shops are self-serve, and each product has an explanation of what it can do for you. Several sizes are available for most products, making it easy and inexpensive to experiment before making investments. The small sizes are great to tuck into a travel bag or to take home as little gifts. Prices are very reasonable, especially for the smallest sizes, many of which cost around a pound or two.

The Body Shop has branches throughout London (and in the United States as well). There are too many to list, but here are a few of the more central locations: 54 King's Road, SW3, Tube: Sloane Square; 203 Kensington High Street, W8, Tube: High Street Kensington; the Market, Covent Garden, WC2, Tube: Covent Garden; 15 Brompton Road, Knightsbridge, SW3, Tube: Knightsbridge; the London Pavilion, Piccadilly Circus, W1, Tube: Piccadilly Circus.

TELEPHONE: 020 7409 7868

INTERNET: www.the-body-shop.com

CREDIT CARDS: AE, DC, MC, V

OPEN: Mon–Sat 9 A.M.–9 P.M., Sun 10 A.M.–7 P.M. (these hours are basic; most of the shops are open late 1 night a week and are open on Sundays and bank holidays)

BOOTS (42)
44–46 Regent Street, W1
Tube: Piccadilly Circus

I never have met a shopper who didn't love Boots, which is one of the U.K.'s best-known chemists (drugstores), with more than ninety locations in London and forty in the West End alone. Actually, most branches are more like mini–department stores, with sections devoted to children's needs, stationery, film and developing, food, household items, cosmetics, and health-care products. They also dispense drugs. The prices are competitive and the supply and selection excellent. They stock my favorite French makeup brand, Bourjois (the prototype for Chanel). I also like their own brand No. 7, a takeoff on Chanel No. 5, their cucumber face scrub, and their fragrance- and additive-free brand of soaps and lotions called Simple. The Boots on Regent Street at Piccadilly Circus is listed here because it is one of the biggest branches, but you will never be too far away from a Boots, because every neighborhood has at least one.

Boots Health and Beauty Experience is a new and very popular service of heath and beauty treatments that includes everything from a simple manicure to aromatherapy, a vast selection of beauty treatments and massage therapy, and advice on general health including nutrition, homeopathy, reflexology, chiropody, and much more. A full-service salon has opened at the High Street Kensington branch, and a nail bar is in full swing at the Piccadilly Boots. Appointments are necessary for all services, but trying to schedule something over the phone is frustrating. I found it better to make my appointment in person.

TELEPHONE: 020 7734 6126
INTERNET: www.boots.co.uk
CREDIT CARDS: AE, MC, V
OPEN: Mon–Sat 8:30 A.M.–8 P.M., Sun noon–6 P.M. Hours at other locations vary but are generally Mon–Sat 10 A.M.–6 P.M., with the larger ones open on Sunday; most of the larger Boots are open bank holidays as well

BROWN'S—LABELS FOR LESS (29)
50 South Molton Street, W1
Tube: Bond Street

All along boutique-lined South Molton Street are several Brown's, which are famous for discovering, encouraging, and featuring U.K. and international fashion talent. All but this one at 50 South Molton Street are beyond the pocketbooks of prudent Great Chic shoppers. At this address, however, you will find men's and women's designer clothing and accessories that did not sell in any of the other Brown's shops. The labels vary, but if you are lucky, they should include Chloe, DKNY, Montana, Moschino, Byblos, Comme des Garçons, and a host of others representing every major fashion trend currently in vogue. Service ranges from cool to downright frosty, but ignore these fashion snobs and do your thing.

TELEPHONE: 020 7514 0052
FAX: 020 7408 1281
EMAIL: brownssms@aol.com
INTERNET: www.brownsfashion.com
CREDIT CARDS: AE, MC, V
OPEN: Mon–Sat 10:30 A.M.–6:30 P.M.

THE BURLINGTON ARCADE (52)
Piccadilly and Old Bond Street, W1
Tube: Green Park, Piccadilly Circus

The Burlington Arcade was built in 1819 by Lord George, and today it is protected by Her Majesty's government as a historical and architectural masterpiece of the Prince Regent in London. Visitors to the arcade are expected to obey its Regency laws, still imposed by top-hatted beadles, who forbid you to whistle, sing, or hurry. The shops are beautiful and very expensive, but it doesn't cost a ha'penny to dream as you look in the windows displaying precious antiques, magnificent cashmeres, Irish linens, perfumes, jewelry (both real and fabulously fake), leather goods, and pure chocolates.

OPEN: Mon–Sat 9:30 A.M.–6 P.M., Sun 10 A.M.–5 P.M.

THE BUTTON QUEEN (20)
19 Marylebone Lane, W1
Tube: Bond Street

Button, button, who has the button? For the definitive word in buttons, this is the place. Owners Martyn and Isabel Frith have an enormous supply of buttons in pearl, wood, glass, silver, and porcelain, as well as buttons for collectors, dress designers, military buffs, or anyone else wanting to have something different in the way of buttons. If you go around lunchtime, stop by Paul Rothe and Son at 35 Marylebone Lane for a great sandwich (see *Great Eats London*).

TELEPHONE & FAX: 020 7935 1505
EMAIL: information@thebuttonqueen.co.uk
INTERNET: www.thebuttonqueen.co.uk
CREDIT CARDS: MC, V
OPEN: Mon–Wed 10 A.M.–5 P.M., Thur–Fri 10 A.M.–6 P.M., Sat 10 A.M.– 4 P.M.

CULPEPER (47)
21 Bruton Street, Berkeley Square, W1
Tube: Bond Street, Green Park

Culpeper products take their name from Nicholas Culpeper (1616–1654), who believed in the healing powers of herbs, pure food, and moderate exercise. The emphasis at Culpeper today has expanded from products made from only natural ingredients (free from chemicals or sprays of any kind, and never tested on animals) to include aromatherapy products and herbal preparations for health and beauty. The two shops stock soaps, lotions, remedies, a wide range of aromatherapy oils, herbs, spices, honeys, and herbal jellies. You can also buy more than seventy-five varieties of herb and wildflower seeds, herb mustards, herb fragrances, and books about herbs. The company has a reputation for quality, simple yet attractive packaging, and excellent value. If you are into this sort of way of life, you will love shopping here. If you can't get to London, you can shop by mail order.

NOTE: There is a branch at 8 The Piazza, Covent Garden, WC2, Tel: 020 7379 6698.

TELEPHONE & FAX: 020 7629 4559
MAIL ORDER & GENERAL ENQUIRIES: 01223 894 054
MAIL ORDER FAX: 01223 893 104
EMAIL: orders@culpeper.co.uk
INTERNET: www.culpeper.co.uk
CREDIT CARDS: AE, MC, V
OPEN: Mon–Fri 9:30 A.M.–6 P.M., Sat 10 A.M.–5 P.M.

DAUNT BOOKS (6)
83 Marylebone High Street, W1
Tube: Baker Street

The *Daily Telegraph* called Daunt Books "the most beautiful bookshop in London—designed for travellers who like reading." It is true! What a fabulous selection of more than twenty-five thousand titles, new and secondhand, arranged by country. Within the sections you will find not only guides, maps, and travelogues, but also novels, histories, biographies, cookbooks . . . anything that will inform, stimulate, or amuse. They can also send you any title in stock on the day of order or find any book currently in print. The staff is well informed and very helpful. Of course, they do carry all the books in the *Great Eats* and *Great Sleeps* series.

TELEPHONE: 020 7224 2295
FAX: 020 7224 6893
EMAIL: orders@dauntbooks.com
CREDIT CARDS: MC, V
OPEN: Mon–Sat 9 A.M.–7:30 P.M., Sun 11 A.M.–6 P.M.

DENNY'S (41)
55A Dean Street, W1
Tube: Leicester Square, Piccadilly Circus

This is a great place to shop if you are looking for serious and proper chef's attire to wear while whipping up gourmet meals. They have an excellent catalog, will personalize any garment, and accept mail orders from the United States.

TELEPHONE & FAX: 020 7287 1239
MAIL ORDER: 01372 377904
EMAIL: sales@dennys.co.uk
INTERNET: www.dennys.co.uk
CREDIT CARDS: AE, MC, V
OPEN: Mon–Fri 9:30 A.M.–6 P.M., Sat 10 A.M.–4 P.M.

HALCYON DAYS (30)
14 Brooke Street, W1
Tube: Bond Street

The delicately hand-painted boxes sold here are famous collector's items and keepsakes.

TELEPHONE: 020 7629 8811
FAX: 020 7409 7901
EMAIL: info@halcyondays.co.uk
INTERNET: www.halcyondays.co.uk
CREDIT CARDS: AE, MC, V
OPEN: Mon–Sat 9:30 A.M.–6 P.M.

HAMLEY'S (38)
188–196 Regent Street, W1
Tube: Oxford Circus

This is the ultimate toy store, with seven floors of pure fun and fantasy for everyone, no matter what age. Even if you have no children, or don't even *like* them, this famous store will captivate you on some level. Prices? Not cheap, but for some of the smaller items, certainly affordable.

TELEPHONE: 020 7494 2000
INTERNET: www.hamleys.com
OPEN: Mon–Fri, 10 A.M.–8 P.M., Sat 9:30 A.M.–8 P.M., Sun noon–6 P.M.

JIGSAW (36)
126–127 New Bond Street, W1
Tube: Bond Street

Lots of coordinated looks in classic clothes that nevertheless have an edge and keep pace with the styles and colors of the moment are available at branches of this better-than-average chain store. There are at least a dozen addresses in central London and throughout the U.K., so if this one doesn't work for you, there is bound to be one near you that does.

TELEPHONE: 020 7491 4484
INTERNET: www.jigsaw-online.com
CREDIT CARDS: AE, MC, V
OPEN: Mon–Wed, Fri–Sat 10 A.M.–6:30 P.M., Thur 10 A.M.–7:30 P.M.

JOHN BELL & CROYDEN (11)
50–54 Wigmore Street, W1
Tube: Bond Street

The motto of John Bell & Croyden is, "Where excellence is an everyday word." This chemist certainly lives up to those words by operating the most amazing "drugstore" you will see in London, perhaps anywhere. Not only will they fill prescriptions for just us folks, they are the chemist for the queen, Prince Philip, and the queen mother. In addition to the pharmacy section, the shop stocks almost every health and beauty aid known to civilization, and many products to aid the disabled, including canes and surgical appliances such as stockings and corsets.

You will also find vitamins, health foods, aromatherapy products, perfume, soaps and shampoos, dental needs, and even a one-hour film-developing service. If you are worn out after doing London, make an appointment at their osteopathic and naturopathic clinic, which is open Monday 9 A.M.–2:30 P.M. and Thursday 2–6 P.M. Even if you don't buy as much as a toothbrush, go just to see it.

TELEPHONE: 020 7935 5555
FAX: 020 7935 9605
CREDIT CARDS: MC, V
OPEN: Mon–Fri 9 A.M.–6:30 P.M., Sat 9 A.M.–5 P.M.

LE CORDON BLEU (12)
114 Marylebone Lane, W1
Tube: Bond Street

If you love good food or just love to cook, spend a half day attending one of this world-famous cooking school's demonstrations. Reservations are required at least one day in advance. If you go to the demonstration, plan on watching, asking questions, tasting at the end, and getting the recipes. Also available are the Guest Chef Demonstrations, from 7:30 to 9:30 P.M., which include tasting. For these, you must telephone ahead and ask to speak to the recipe department, which is responsible for the Guest Chef Demonstration schedule. If you want to get your hands into things, you will have to enroll in a course. There is also the Cordon Bleu boutique, featuring their own gourmet goodies and related culinary items. What fun to go home with an apron or something else from here to give to your favorite chef! The cost of a demonstration is £15, and courses start at £145. Please call ahead to see what the demonstration schedule will be.

TELEPHONE: 020 7935 3503, 800-457-CHEF (toll-free from the U.S.)
FAX: 020 7935 7621
EMAIL: london@cordonbleu.net
INTERNET: www.cordonbleu.net
CREDIT CARDS: MC, V
OPEN: Office hours Mon–Fri 9 A.M.–5 P.M., cooking demonstrations Mon–Fri 9:30 A.M. and 1:30 P.M.

L'OCCITANE (31)
237 Regent Street, W1
Tube: Oxford Street, Piccadilly Circus

Purity and simplicity are the guiding principles behind the L'Occitane line, which is inspired by the natural products from Provence and the sacred shea trees in Africa. Based on essential oils, flower infusions, milk, and honey, their lovely products are a joy to use. Try any of their shea-butter-based soaps or creams, a bottle of their cinnamon-orange aromatic bath gel, a box of their fragrant lavender candles, or any of their excellent cosmetics, and you too will love L'Occitane. Their commitment to customers is evident by the use of Braille on their packaging.

NOTE: If you are going to Paris, *all* L'Occitane products are naturally less expensive there. Other stores in London are on Kensington High Street, W8; the King's Road, SW3; and in Whiteleys Shopping Centre, W2. Please see pages 281 and 299.

TELEPHONE: 020 7290 1420
FAX: 020 7290 1429
MAIL ORDER: 020 7290 1421
EMAIL: mailorder@loccitane.co.uk
INTERNET: www.loccitane.net
CREDIT CARDS: AE, MC, V
OPEN: Mon–Wed 10 A.M.–7 P.M., Fri–Sat 10 A.M.–8 P.M., Sun noon–6 P.M.

LOON FUNG AND LOON MOON CHINESE MARKETS (44)
42–44 Gerrard Street, Chinatown, W1
Tube: Leicester Square, Piccadilly Circus

Billed as supermarkets, these two grocers are on opposite sides of Gerrard Street in Chinatown. You probably are not interested in buying ten-kilogram bags of rice or a gallon jug of soy sauce, but for a glimpse of what veggies you will be served in the area's restaurants, or just to look at the incredible variety of Asian foods the locals crowd in to buy at amazingly low prices; it's an experience. Expect long queues to check out and not much help from the staff, who don't admit to speaking or understanding much English.

TELEPHONE: 020 7437 7332
FAX: 020 7439 1585
CREDIT CARDS: MC, V
OPEN: Daily 9 A.M.–7 P.M.

LUSH (39)
40 Carnaby Street, W1
Tube: Oxford Circus

Lush must be short for *luscious* . . . and that is exactly what these kicky products are. The company believes in "making our own fresh products by hand, printing our own labels, and making our own fragrances. We believe in long candlelit baths, massage, filling the house with perfume, and in the right to make mistakes, lose everything, and start again. We also believe that our products should be good value, that we should make a profit, and that the customer is always right."

The stores are set up to look like a deli, and all their soaps, creams, elixirs, and lotions, which are handcrafted from natural plant-based ingredients, will take care of not only your hair, face, and body, but also your mind. Preservatives are used as little as possible, and all the products are marked with a sell-by date to ensure their freshness and potency. The imaginatively named products are displayed in bulk and cut and sold to order. Huge rounds of soaps can be sliced by the ounce; refrigerated face creams are dispensed from bowls. I can hardly pass one of their stores in London without darting in for a bar of their Red Rooster, Banana Moon, or Honey Waffle soap, a tub of Wow Wow face mask, the Angels on Bare Skin gentle facial scrub, or Truly Madly Veggie, which cleans and conditions the skin. For the ultimate massage, they recommend their "Massage à Trois" bars—Choco Lala, made with dark chocolate scented with violet; Mont Blanc, with orange flowers and white chocolate; and Cherrie Ripe, a fruity bar with the smell of cherries and cassia buds. To jump-start your day and keep you going, Demon in the Dark keeps your brain awake with peppermint and clove fragrances. If you like really crazy, indulgent bath products, treat yourself to one of their Great Balls of Bicarb, which will liven up your bath with fizzing, frothy bathtime ballistics. Drop in a ball of Bom Perignon and watch it hurl and whirl itself around in the water, soothing, moisturizing, or stimulating as it goes. To be wide awake, buy the Slammer or Summer Blues; to stay awake, Waving not Drowning; for aching muscles, it's Fizzy O'Therapy; and to soften everything, you will want a Butterball.

There are Lush branches in Australia, Brazil, Canada, Croatia, Italy, Japan, Singapore, Sweden, and other cities in the U.K., but so far none in the States. To order by mail, consult the Website. There are three other Lush outlets in London: two in Covent Garden and another on the King's Road.

TELEPHONE: 020 7287 5874
EMAIL: sales@lush.co.uk
INTERNET: www.lush.co.uk
CREDIT CARDS: AE, MC, V
OPEN: Mon–Sat 10 A.M.–7 P.M., Sun noon–6 P.M.

PAST TIMES (46)
155 Regent Street, W1
Tube: Piccadilly Circus, Oxford Street

Past Times is an exercise in nostalgia, showcasing replicas of crafts, toys, stationery, jewelry, and many other items, covering Britain's history as far back as the Celts. The selection is excellent, and the items make interesting gifts. At Christmastime the selection is particularly good. They do a color mail-order catalog that is nice for armchair travelers. To order by phone, call 01993 770440 (twenty-four hours a day, seven days a week) or fax 01993 770477.

Other London locations: Covent Garden, Central Arcade, The Piazza, WC2, Tube: Covent Garden, Tel: 020 7240 9265; Knightsbridge, 146 Brompton Road, SW3, Tube: Knightsbridge, Tel: 020 7581 7616.

TELEPHONE: 020 7734 3728
MAIL ORDER: 01993 770440
FAX: 01993 770477
EMAIL: service@past-times.com
INTERNET: www.past-times.com
CREDIT CARDS: AE, DC, MC, V
OPEN: Mon–Sat 9:30 A.M.–6 P.M., Sun 11 A.M.–5 P.M. (hours may vary slightly in the other London locations)

PAUL SMITH SALE SHOP (37)
23 Avery Row, W1
Tube: Bond Street

Paul Smith is a popular London designer for men, women, and children. Items here go for about half price and include knits, jeans, and sportswear.

TELEPHONE: 020 7493 1287

CREDIT CARDS: AE, MC, V

OPEN: Mon–Sat 10 A.M.–7 P.M.

REJECT CHINA SHOP (45)
71 Regent Street, W1
Tube: Piccadilly Circus

Maybe the name fit at one time, but no longer. The stock offered is the same quality, and often the same price, as you will find at Harrods. There are sales in January and June when you might hit a bargain; otherwise, it isn't likely unless you buy in bulk (that is, six place settings of first quality will be 10 percent less), or find a second. You can get the 17.5 percent VAT refunds after you spend £100. It will be automatically deducted from your total if you have them ship your purchase (you still pay the postage); if you hand carry your items, you will pay the VAT and apply for a refund. In either case, the store will pack the china for you.

Other locations: 183 Brompton Road, corner Beauchamp Place, SW3, Tube: Knightsbridge, Tel: 020 7581 0739; the Piazza, Covent Garden, WC2, Tube: Covent Garden, Tel: 020 7379 8374.

TELEPHONE: 020 7734 4915

EMAIL: netsales@chcraft.com

INTERNET: www.chinacraft.co.uk

CREDIT CARDS: AE, DC, MC, V

OPEN: Mon–Sat 9 A.M.–6 P.M., Thur until 8 P.M., Sun 11 A.M.–5 P.M., bank holidays 10 A.M.–5:30 P.M.

SHELLY'S (16)
266–270 Regent Street, W1
Tube: Oxford Circus

If you have a young-at-heart mind-set and sturdy feet to match, shop at Shelly's for the hottest shoe fads at prices that won't leave you teetering as much as their heels and platforms will.

Other locations are all over London, but some of the more central ones are: 159 Oxford Street, W1, Tube: Oxford Circus; 44–45 Carnaby Street, W1, Tube: Oxford Circus; 14 Neal Street, WC2, Tube: Covent Garden; 40 Kensington High Street, W8, Tube: Kensington High Street; 124 King's Road, SW3, Tube: Sloane Square.

TELEPHONE: 020 7287 0939

INTERNET: www.shellys.co.uk

CREDIT CARDS: AE, MC, V

OPEN: Mon–Sat 10 A.M.–7 P.M., Thur until 8 P.M., Sun noon–6 P.M.

STANFORDS AT BRITISH AIRWAYS (43)
156 Regent Street, W1
Tube: Piccadilly Circus, Oxford Circus

At this location and the one at 1 Regent Street, SW1, page 296, there is a selection of travel books and maps dealing with England and Ireland. For books on Scotland, see their shop at the Scottish Tourist Board, SW1, on page 296. For details on their flagship store and on-line ordering, please see page 292.

TELEPHONE: 020 7434 4744
FAX: 020 7434 4636
CREDIT CARDS: MC, V
OPEN: Mon–Sat 9:30 A.M.–6 P.M., Sat 10 A.M.–4 P.M.

VIDAL SASSOON SCHOOL OF HAIRDRESSING (34)
56 Davies Mews, W1
Tube: Bond Street

Have your hair cut and styled by one of the students trained in the ways of Vidal Sassoon. If you really want a do, book at the Advanced Academy, whose students have had a minimum of seven years experience. Appointments are required. Prices start around £10, and are even less if you are a student, a nurse, out of work, or an OAP (old aged person, the British equivalent of a senior citizen—a name I thought I didn't like until I heard OAP).

TELEPHONE: 020 7318 205
INTERNET: www.vidalsassoon.co.uk
CREDIT CARDS: MC, V
OPEN: Mon–Fri 10 A.M.–3 P.M.

YESTERDAY'S BREAD (28)
29 Floubert's Place, off Carnaby Street, W1
Tube: Oxford Circus

From the miniskirt and kinky boots to love beads, it's all here in this shrine to the 1960s and 1970s, when "Peace" and "Love" and "Flower Power" were the slogans of the day and everyone celebrated the Age of Aquarius.

TELEPHONE: 020 7287 1929
FAX: 020 7287 3380
EMAIL: yesterdays.bread@virgin.net
INTERNET: yesterdaysbread.co.uk
CREDIT CARDS: MC, V
OPEN: Mon–Fri 11:30 A.M.–6:30 P.M., Sat 11 A.M.–6 P.M.

YVES ROCHER (22)
7 Gees Court, W1
Tube: Bond Street

There are six hundred Yves Rocher shops in France and only one in London. Be glad you know about this one, because it is a great find. If you are not already familiar with the Yves Rocher line of skin-care products, it is a good one, based on plants and other natural ingredients. Prices are very good, quality is high, and the staff is knowledgeable. In addition, they do reasonably priced facials, body wraps, waxing, and the cheapest and best manicures and pedicures I found in this part of London. Appointments are necessary. When you go, look for the different "specials" that are being featured for both skin-care products and beauty services.

TELEPHONE: 020 7409 2975
CREDIT CARDS: MC, V
OPEN: Mon–Fri 10 A.M.–6:30 P.M., Sat 10 A.M.–6 P.M.

W2—PADDINGTON and BAYSWATER (see map page 66)
Shops

BAYSWATER ROAD ART EXHIBITION (17)
Clarendon Place until Queensway, W2
Tube: Queensway, Lancaster Gate

Smart shoppers arrive early, at least by 10 A.M., when the selection is best. The exhibition runs along the north side of Hyde Park and Kensington Gardens on Bayswater Road. More than 280 artists display their works, which are in all price and quality categories. You can select from modern to romantic, watercolor or oil, pen and ink, or handmade crafts. Most of the artists are present, so you can meet them and discuss the price. Many take credit cards and can arrange shipping. If you don't want to ship and insure your new piece of art, which could cost more than the piece itself, go over to Whiteleys of Bayswater Shopping Center (see below) and buy another suitcase for carting home your extra purchase(s). Even if you have to pay an excess baggage fee to the airline (usually around $100), it will probably be less than shipping and insuring it would cost, and *much* less trouble—believe me.

CREDIT CARDS: Depends on artist, but most will take MC or V
OPEN: Sat–Sun 8 A.M.–5 P.M.

PLANET ORGANIC (19)
42 Westbourne Grove, W2
Tube: Bayswater

When you are through shopping at Whiteleys, walk another few minutes to the top of Queensway, turn left, and enter the American-inspired world of Planet Organic, a natural foods supermarket with one of the largest supplies of organic products in England. Spread out over five thousand square feet is certainly the best selection of health foods and natural products I found in London. In addition to the organic fruits and vegetables that could inspire a sudden conversion to healthiness, there is a complete range of organic meats and poultry, fresh fish, baked goods, frozen foods, vitamins, cosmetics, a full-service deli where you can buy healthy sandwiches and take-away food, a cheese counter, juice and coffee bar, organic wines, fresh flowers, and food for your dog. If you are confused and don't know what to buy, there is a qualified nutritionist to help you. Wherever possible, products are without artificial additives, preservatives, refined sugar, or hydrogenated fat. There is a second location in WC1, opposite the Googe Street tube.

TELEPHONE: 020 7221 7171
FAX: 020 7221 1923
CREDIT CARDS: MC, V
OPEN: Mon–Sat 9:30 A.M.–8 P.M., Sun noon–6 P.M.

WHITELEYS OF BAYSWATER SHOPPING CENTER (20)
Queensway at Porchester Gardens, W2
Tube: Bayswater

An indoor shopping complex with four floors of restaurants, cinemas, and shops, including Marks & Spencer, NEXT, L'Occitane, an Internet café, book and toy stores, and much more. It is a good place to go with family, because there is something for everyone. If you are worn out, your feet hurt, and your back aches, please go directly to Reflexions, on the ground floor next to the Café Rapallo. In this small salon, trained therapists will do foot reflexology or massage your aching back in increments of fifteen minutes to an hour. Trust me, the foot reflexology session is worth its weight in gold, and you will feel like a million dollars afterward, especially if you get Fran to do it. Reflexions is open noon–8 P.M. daily.

TELEPHONE: 020 7229 8844
CREDIT CARDS: Depends on shop
OPEN: *Stores:* Mon–Sat 10 A.M.–8 P.M., Sun noon–6 P.M.; *restaurants:* 10 A.M.–10 P.M. daily; *cinemas:* daily

W8—KENSINGTON (see map page 66)

AMAZON (39)
1–22 Kensington Church Street, W8
Tube: High Street Kensington

Amazon, with its four shops all along one block, is geared toward Great Chic shoppers who want to catch the present fashion vibes and not pay an arm and a leg to do so. The total space adds up to seven floors of discounted merchandise. Each shop has a slightly different emphasis, but the bottom line is always the same: to sell clothes, shoes, and accessories for men, women, and children at lower prices. Amazon buyers are always on the lookout for anything new and fresh that is a good deal. They buy in bulk and pass the discounts along to you. The quality varies, which means you have to look over the garments carefully. You won't recognize all of the names, but a handful of all-stars you can expect to see are the French Connection, Ralph Lauren, and Calvin Klein. The stock changes almost daily, the sales never stop, and the turnover is huge . . . never mind the bargain-hunting shoppers, who are advised to shop with care: there are absolutely, positively no refunds.

CREDIT CARDS: AE, DC, MC, V
OPEN: Mon–Fri 10:30 A.M.–6:30 P.M., Sun noon–5 P.M.

EHRMAN (40)
Lancer Square, off Kensington Church Street, W8
Tube: High Street Kensington

If you are a needlepoint enthusiast, know one, or just appreciate the art, visit this magnificent shop. I promise you will be very impressed, and probably inspired to buy a kit and take up this art form. The shop itself is a blaze of color. Here you will find all the beautiful designs featured in their catalogs plus many more, all done up so you can truly appreciate the vibrant colors, intricate patterns, and general scope of each piece. The only time these display items are available for purchase is during their January sale. The staff can sometimes be quite pleasant and helpful. If you cannot go to the store, at least send for a catalog, which you can do from the toll-free U.S. number given below.

Lancer Square is a development at the bottom of Kensington Church Street. The best landmark to watch for is Café Rouge as you come up from Kensington High Street.

Ordering Information:

Within the U.K.: 020 7937 4568 (general inquiries); 020 8573 4891 (ordering). To order a catalog, send £2 to the following address: Ehrman, Freepost, London, W8 4BR, United Kingdom

From the U.S.: Ehrman Tapestry, 112 Cross Street, Chestertown, MD 21620, Tel: 888-826-8600 (toll-free order line), 410-810-3032 (customer service); Fax: 410-810-3032; Email: usehrman@dmv.com

TELEPHONE: 020 7937 8123
FAX: 020 7937 8552
INTERNET: ehrmankits@btinternet.com

CREDIT CARDS: MC, V

OPEN: Mon–Fri 9:30 A.M.–5:30 P.M., Sat 10:30 A.M.–4:30 P.M.

L'OCCITANE (43)
70 Kensington High Street, W8
Tube: High Street Kensington

There are several L'Occitane locations in London, including: 237 Regent Street, W1; 67 King's Road, SW3; and in Whiteleys Shopping Centre, W2. Please see page 273.

TELEPHONE: 020 7938 4135

FAX: 020 7937 2311

CREDIT CARDS: AE, MC, V

OPEN: Mon–Sat 10 A.M.–7 P.M., Sun noon–6 P.M.

NEXT (41)
54–60 Kensington High Street, W8
Tube: High Street Kensington

NEXT shops are all over London, or as someone aptly put it, "Next to almost everything." These shops sell traditional clothing and accessories popular with those starting out on the corporate ladder. I like their coordinated outfits, which have pants, skirts, blazers, and blouses you can mix and match to create several different looks. The Kensington High Street branch is one of the biggest, with departments for men, women, and children, plus shoes, accessories, lingerie, and interiors.

NOTE: If the prices at the London NEXT shops are too high, consider trying your luck at NEXT to Nothing, their discount shop in Ealing, which is just on the edge of London. Stock consists of men's and women's clothing that has not sold in their London retail shops within the last six months and from their catalog. Prices are guaranteed to be at least 30 percent, and in most cases up to 50 percent, less than full price. If you have a morning to spare and are a NEXT shopper, this could be a worthwhile shopping safari. NEXT to Nothing, Unit 11, Arcadia Centre, Ealing, W5; Tel: 020-8567-2747; Tube: Ealing Broadway; open: Mon–Sat 9:30 A.M.–6 P.M., Sun 11 A.M.–5 P.M.

TELEPHONE: 020 7938 4211

INTERNET: www.next.co.uk

CREDIT CARDS: AE, DC, MC, V

OPEN: Mon–Sat 10 A.M.–7 P.M., Thur until 8 P.M., Sun noon–6 P.M.

PORTMEIRION GIFT SHOP (42)
13 Kensington Church Street, W8
Tube: High Street Kensington

Of course, everything is cheaper at their shop in Stoke-on-Trent (see "Do China in a Day," page 262), but for Portmeirion collectors limited to London, this shop offers the best selection of all their patterns. In January, June, and July there are sales. You can order any piece they make and have your purchases shipped anyplace worldwide. VAT kicks in after you spend £50.

Since Susan and Euan Cooper-Willis founded Portmeirion Potteries more than thirty years ago, the company has developed into an internationally known business. People have always collected the pottery, but recently the market for collecting has grown, and many of their early designs are being bought and sold at prices far above their original cost. In view of this, a Portmeirion Collectors' Club has been formed to help existing collectors and encourage new ones. If you are a tried-and-true Portmeirion lover, you may want to look into joining. Please contact the club secretary at 017 8274 3416, or by Email: dshufflebotham@portmeirion.co.uk.

TELEPHONE: 020 7938 1891
FAX: 020 7376 1770
INTERNET: www.portmeirion.com
CREDIT CARDS: AE, MC, V
OPEN: Mon–Sat 10 A.M.–6 P.M.

ZARA (45)
48–52 Kensington High Street, W8
Tube: High Street Kensington

The quality is not particularly high, and neither are the prices at this international chain of youthful, trendy, wearable clothes. All items are tagged with prices given in thirty-one currencies, including U.S. dollars. This branch is big and open, with good displays and a glass lift to transport you to each floor.

TELEPHONE: 020 7368 4680
FAX: 929 7368 4681
CREDIT CARDS: AE, DC, MC, V
OPEN: Mon–Wed, Fri, Sat 10 A.M.–7 P.M., Thur until 8 P.M., Sun noon–6 P.M.

W11—NOTTING HILL and PORTOBELLO ROAD
(see map page 66)

BOOKS FOR COOKS (23)
4 Blenheim Crescent, W11
Tube: Ladbroke Grove

Books for Cooks stocks the most comprehensive inventory of cookbooks in London. You name it, they have it or can order it or find it for you and have it sent to your home address. Most of the staff doubles as cooks in the test kitchen. Don't miss having lunch in the little restaurant, which features weekly changing menu of gourmet fare and luscious pastries (see *Great Eats London*).

TELEPHONE: 020 7221 1992
FAX: 020 7221 1517
EMAIL: info@booksforcooks.com
INTERNET: www.booksforcooks.com
OPEN: *Store:* Mon–Sat 9:30 A.M.–6 P.M.; *Restaurant:* Mon–Sat lunch 1–3:30 P.M.

CATH KIDSTON (32)
8 Clarendon Cross, W11
Tube: Holland Park

Two floors of English rose and floral prints on fabrics, wallpaper, and clothing keep you enchanted for hours. Everything you see is made exclusively for the shop. All grandmothers are hereby forewarned about the store's captivating children's clothing—I defy you to leave without something! Also featured are small gifts in their own fabrics, perhaps padded hangers, ironing board covers, mother-child matching aprons, cushions, cosmetic bags, or a fabric-covered box tied with a satin ribbon. If you cannot get to the store, they have a mail-order catalog and are on-line. They have a second store in Chelsea Green, SW3; please see page 297.

TELEPHONE: 020 7221 4000
MAIL ORDER: 020 7229 8000
FAX: 020 7221 4388 (mail order only)
EMAIL: mailorder@cathkidston.co.uk
INTERNET: www.cathkidston.co.uk
CREDIT CARDS: AE, MC, V
OPEN: Mon–Fri 10 A.M.–6 P.M., Sat 11 A.M.–6 P.M.

GARDEN BOOKS (24)
11 Blenheim Crescent, W11
Tube: Ladbroke Grove

"If it grows, we have something on it, or can get it for you." That is the promise of this shop, which stocks a vast selection of books devoted to all aspects of the art and pleasure of gardening. In addition, they stock an impressive number of books about design and architecture, flower arranging, botanical art, and interior decorating. If you are a gardener, would-be or otherwise, or know someone who is, this shop is a must. They also have a catalog and will do mail order.

TELEPHONE: 020 7792 0777
FAX: 020 7792 1991
EMAIL: sales@garden-books.co.uk
CREDIT CARDS: AE, MC, V
OPEN: Mon–Sat 9 A.M.–6 P.M.

MARIBOU (30)
55 Pembridge Road (beginning of Portobello Road), W11
Tube: Notting Hill Gate

Ginny De-Bell makes everything in her shop: the hats, bags, coats, jackets, skirts, and blouses. Her specialty is velvet- and tapestry-trimmed jackets. I bought one in red with black velvet appliqué, and it is a sensation with either a cocktail skirt or a pair of jeans. I also have one of her luxurious reversible velvet scarves, which are just the thing to keep the winter chill at bay on a London night out. For warmer climates, consider one of her vintage chiffon skirts. Each item is unique and uses old pieces of tapestry, velvet, and chiffon for decoration. Prices are very reasonable.

TELEPHONE: 020 7727 1166
CREDIT CARDS: AE, MC, V
OPEN: Mon–Sat 10 A.M.–6 P.M., closed three to four days at Christmas

PORTOBELLO CHINA & WOOLLENS, LTD. (26)
89 Portobello Road, W11
Tube: Notting Hill Gate

If you think you are going to scoop up cashmere sweaters anywhere in the British Isles for a song, think again. You will do better to watch the sales at home. However, there are good buys in colors and styles you may not see elsewhere. For the best prices in London, this is the place. Delia Hall sells sweaters, scarves, robes, shawls, hats, and gloves in cashmere, lamb's wool, and blends, which are stacked in bins, boxes, and on shelves in this cluttered shop. Some are seconds; some have imperfections you can barely detect; and some are big names such as Jaeger, Peter Scott, and Robertson. A few have the labels removed.

The shop also stocks first- and second-quality British china: Christmas Tree Spode, Johnston Brothers, Wedgwood, Royal Creamware, and more are always discounted. This place is an absolute zoo on Saturday mornings, when the Portobello Road market is in full swing. For best choice and ease of purchase, go during the week, when you can have the store and the clerk to yourself. Whatever you buy, you can ship and automatically save the VAT.

NOTE: Delia also runs a B&B near Putney, which is outside the parameters covered by *Great Sleeps London*. However, for some, the suburban locale, about ten minutes from the East Putney tube stop, may be of interest. If so, contact her at the fax or email given below. There are two double rooms and one single, neither en suite. Prices are £30 for the single and £50 for the double including English breakfast.

TELEPHONE: 020 7727 3857
FAX: 020 8874 4510
EMAIL: deliahold@portobelloltd.com
INTERNET: www.portobelloltd.com
CREDIT CARDS: AE, MC, V
OPEN: Mon–Fri 10 A.M.–5 P.M., Sat 9 A.M.–5 P.M., Sun 11 A.M.–3 P.M.

SHEILA COOK TEXTILES (22)
184 Westbourne Grove, W11
Tube: Notting Hill Gate

If you are interested in textiles, costumes, and accessories dating from the late eighteenth century through Mary Quant and the 1970s, a visit to Sheila Cook should be on your London shopping list. All of her stock, which is selected for quality, condition, and design, is beautifully displayed and sold to fashion and interior designers, as well as to the public. Doll collectors buy her fabrics and trim to create authentic doll clothing; costume designers keep her name handy for hats, accessories, and shawls. If you saw *Titanic,* the parasols and fans were from Sheila's treasure trove. She also supplied some of the jewelry for the film *Evita.* When you arrive, just ring the bell, and someone will let you in.

TELEPHONE: 020 7792 8001
FAX: 020 7229 3855
EMAIL: sheila.cook@dial.pipex.com
INTERNET: www.sheilacook.co.uk
CREDIT CARDS: AE, MC, V
OPEN: Mon–Wed by appointment, Thur–Sat 10 A.M.–6 P.M.

TRAVEL BOOKSHOP (25)
13–15 Blenheim Crescent, W11
Tube: Ladbroke Grove

Here is a great selection of old and new globe-trotting travel books to interest every voyager, even if your trip is in your dreams from your armchair.

TELEPHONE: 020 7229 5260
FAX: 020 7243 1552
EMAIL: post@thetravelbookshop.co.uk
INTERNET: www.thetravelbookshop.co.uk
CREDIT CARDS: AE, MC, V
OPEN: Mon–Sat 10 A.M.–6 P.M.

WC1—BLOOMSBURY (see map page 96)

BRITISH MUSEUM COMPANY, LTD. (37)
22 Bloomsbury Street, WC1
Tube: Holborn, Tottenham Court Road

Don't look for key chains, postcards, or snow globes in this bright, open, corner location. The upmarket stock centers on jewelry, housewares, and gifts based on the British Museum collection, as well as other museum replicas.

TELEPHONE: 020 7637 9449
CREDIT CARDS: AE, DC, MC, V
OPEN: Mon–Sat 9:30 A.M.–6 P.M., Sun and bank holidays noon–6 P.M.

COSMO PLACE STUDIO (26)
11 Cosmo Place, WC1
Tube: Russell Square

The shop sells Staffordshire china hand-painted by ceramic artists. The designs are bright, bold, and very appealing. You can order a complete dinner set for twelve, or a simple egg cup or mug, all of which can be personalized and shipped to any address you wish.

TELEPHONE: 020 7278 3374
FAX: 020 7278 4153
EMAIL: Cosmochina@connectfree.uk
CREDIT CARDS: MC, V
OPEN: Mon–Sat 10 A.M.–6 P.M.

JAMES SMITH & SONS (38)
Hazelwood House, 53 New Oxford Street, WC1
Tube: Tottenham Court Road

An umbrella or walking stick purchased from James Smith & Sons will not be cheap, but it will last your lifetime, and probably that of your heirs. Just be sure that what you are buying is made by them. They do sell some other brands, but you are not here for those, *only* for the ones displaying the official James Smith & Sons insignia. If you are not in the market for a fine umbrella, please take a few minutes just to look at this fascinating shop, which is the oldest and biggest umbrella shop in Europe. James Smith opened the original shop in 1830 and moved to the present location, which also served as the family home, in 1850s. Almost unaltered in 150 years of doing business in the same spot, the storefront is a perfect example of Victorian shop-front design. Before Smith & Sons occupied it, the building housed a dairy. When you go inside, if you look closely, you can still see some of the original blue and white dairy floor tiles that date from 1857. If you think custom umbrellas have a limited appeal, think again: seven hundred are sold, and two thousand repaired here, every month. Unless you bought your umbrella here, however, they are unable to repair it.

TELEPHONE: 020 7836 4731
FAX: 020 7836 4730
INTERNET: www.james-smith.co.uk
CREDIT CARDS: AE, MC, V
OPEN: Mon–Fri 9:30 A.M.–5:25 P.M., Sat 10 A.M.–5:25 P.M.

RENNIES AT FRENCH'S DAIRY (25)
13 Rugby Street, WC1
Tube: Russell Square

I first noticed this great little shop as I was hurrying along Lamb's Conduit Street to check on the Lamb's Pub (see *Great Eats London*). The colorful tiled front caught my eye, and I made a special trip back to see it. I have always been so glad I did.

The building has quite a history, but the most pertinent concerns the two dairy shops that preceded Rennies. The first dairyman tenant, Mr. French, moved in around the middle of the nineteenth century. His successor, John Davies, was responsible for the tiled facade you see today. Members of his family ran the dairy shop until 1994, when Paul and Karen Rennie restored the shop and opened Rennies at French's Dairy. No, they don't sell milk. They specialize in twentieth-century British art and design of the twenties, thirties, and forties, and the forms modernism took in Britain after World War II. While the furniture will be too big for your suitcase, or to mail, poke around and you are sure to find a must-have or two you can take home. I found a lovely early piece of Scottish Buchan pottery, which I collect, several vintage scarves, and some adorable toys.

Before you leave the area, please take a moment or two and walk down Lamb's Conduit Street to Coram's Fields, a seven-acre playground open to all children, and adults if accompanied by a child. The park has had a recent face-lift, making it even more appealing to all who love it.

TELEPHONE: 020 7405 0220
EMAIL: info@rennart.co.uk
INTERNET: www.rennart.co.uk
CREDIT CARDS: MC, V
OPEN: Tues–Fri, noon–6:30 P.M., Sat noon–6 P.M.

WESTAWAY & WESTAWAY (35)
64 Great Russell Street, WC1
Tube: Holborn, Tottenham Court Road

It is an old-fashioned shop, barely hanging on in today's world, but if you want to look like a real Scottish lad or lassie, Westaway is your London source. Across the street from the British Museum, it offers a vast selection of Scottish Highland dress and knitwear. They can make a kilt from any of more than four hundred tartans, sell you a cashmere or lamb's wool sweater in a variety of colors and shades, outfit your children, and mail goods to your home address. While prices are not in the bargain-basement category, they are some of the best you will find in London. Be sure to check the special offers for tag ends that haven't sold, and remember their sales in late December and June.

TELEPHONE: 020 7405 4479
FAX: 020 7405 1070
EMAIL: westway@compuserve.com
INTERNET: www.westaway.co.uk
CREDIT CARDS: AE, DC, MC, V
OPEN: Mon–Sat 9 A.M.–6 P.M., Sun 10:30 A.M.–5:30 P.M.

WC2—COVENT GARDEN, LEICESTER SQUARE, and THE STRAND (see map page 96)

CECIL COURT (56)
Cecil Court, WC2
Tube: Leicester Square

A sign in a shop window along this picturesque street off Charing Cross Road sums up what you can expect to find: "eclectic items and unusual objects." The selection includes antiquarian prints and engravings, first editions, and a coin and stamp dealer.

CREDIT CARDS: Depends on shop
OPEN: Depends on shop, generally Mon–Sat 10 A.M.–6 P.M.

CULPEPER (51)
8 The Piazza, Covent Garden, WC2
Tube: Covent Garden

For more details about this natural-products shop, please see page 270.
TELEPHONE: 020 7379 6698
OPEN: Mon–Sat 10 A.M.–8 P.M., Sun 10 A.M.–6 P.M., bank holiday hours vary

DR. MARTENS DEPARTMENT STORE (53)
1–4 King Street, Covent Garden, WC2
Tube: Covent Garden

If you don't have a teen in your life, you probably don't know or care about Dr. Martens shoes. (The name is correctly written as Dr. Martens, but pronounced "Doc Martens.") The shoes originated unpretentiously more than fifty years ago in Germany, when Dr. Klaus Marten designed air-cushion shoes to wear after suffering a skiing accident. Soon, the sturdy shoes were being worn by elderly ladies with foot problems. Over time, they found their way to Britain, where the young people transformed the clodhoppers into cult wear and fashion icons that have been spotted on everyone from Madonna to the Pope.

Did someone mention shoes in this galvanized-steel, exposed-brick, multistory mecca for Dr. Martens fans? Besides footwear, which is somewhat cheaper here than in the United States, you can buy, or try to avoid buying, all the essential accessories, including bags, watches, and stationery your teen considers merchandise "to die for."

TELEPHONE: 020 7497 1460
INTERNET: www.drmartens.com
CREDIT CARDS: AE, MC, V
OPEN: Mon–Sat 10 A.M.–7 P.M., Thur until 8 P.M., Sun noon–6 P.M.

DRESS CIRCLE (52)
57–59 Monmouth Street, WC2
Tube: Leicester Square

Called the longest-running showbiz shop in the world, Dress Circle specializes in a huge selection of records, tapes, and CD soundtracks of stage and film musical productions. They produce an impressive catalog and ship worldwide.

TELEPHONE: 020 7240 2227
FAX: 020 7379 8540
EMAIL: info@dresscircle.co.uk
INTERNET: www.dresscircle.com
CREDIT CARDS: AE, DC, MC, V
OPEN: Mon–Sat 10 A.M.–7 P.M.

FOYLES (47)
113–119 Charing Cross Road, WC2
Tube: Tottenham Court Road

Charing Cross Road is synonymous with books in London. Both sides of the street are lined with every type of bookseller imaginable, from antiquarian to new wave. Foyles stands alone in its class and is far and away the most famous. With five floors devoted to the sale of books, Foyles has more titles in stock than any other in the world. Established in 1904, it is considered by many to be one of the world's greatest bookshops, where you can buy the latest best-seller, all the books in the Great Eats and Great Sleeps series, or browse the rows of rare and out-of-print titles.

TELEPHONE: 020 7437 5660
FAX: 020 7434 1574
EMAIL: sales@foyles.co.uk
INTERNET: www.foyles.co.uk
CREDIT CARDS: AE, DC, MC, V
OPEN: Mon–Sat 9:30 A.M.–7:30 P.M., Sun noon–6 P.M.

HALF-PRICE TICKET BOOTH AT LEICESTER SQUARE (55)
Clocktower Building on the South corner of Leicester Square, WC2
Tube: Leicester Square

For details, see "Discounts—Theater and Concerts," page 21.

TELEPHONE: 020 7831 0971
CREDIT CARDS: None, cash only
OPEN: Tues–Sat noon–6:30 P.M.; matinee tickets sold from noon to 30 minutes before curtain; nightly performance tickets sold 2–6:30 P.M.; Sun tickets sold for matinees only noon–3 P.M.

LUSH (51)
Units 7 & 11, The Piazza, Covent Garden, WC2
Tube: Covent Garden

Please see page 274 for information about these handmade cosmetics.

TELEPHONE: 020 7240 4570
OPEN: Mon–Sat 10 A.M.–7 P.M., until 8 P.M. in summer, Sun noon–6 P.M.

NEAL'S YARD DAIRY (46)
17 Short's Gardens, WC2
Tube: Covent Garden

You can smell it as you round the corner. Neal's Yard Dairy, a tiny shop with cheese stacked floor to ceiling, offers the widest range of British and Irish cheese in the country. For cheese lovers, this is heaven. The cheeses are labeled, so not only will you know where the cheese was made, but who made it. All the cheeses are from farms in Britain and Ireland, many of them matured in the dairy's cellars or on its farm in Kent, which also supplies the shop with yogurt and crème fraîche. The selection is seasonal. The staff is great, and sampling is encouraged. Also available are organic bread, vinegar, and olive oil. They also do mail order, but they encourage you to first call them so they can tell you what's particularly good even if you can't come in for a taste.

Their warehouse is at Borough Market, 6 Park Street, London SE1 (see page 303 for details).

TELEPHONE: 020 7240 5700
FAX: 020 7240 2442 (for mail order)
EMAIL: mailorder@nealsyarddairy.co.uk
CREDIT CARDS: MC, V
OPEN: Mon–Sat 9 A.M.–7 P.M., Sun 10 A.M.–5 P.M.

NEAL'S YARD REMEDIES (44)
15 Neal's Yard, WC2
Tube: Covent Garden

Homeopathic remedies, supplements, teas, cosmetics, toiletries, bath and hair products, essential oils . . . if it is natural and geared toward keeping you at your healthy best, it's here, but management needs to train the staff on the benefits of the merchandise they unenthusiastically sell.

TELEPHONE: 020 7379 7222
INTERNET: www.nealsyardremedies.com
CREDIT CARDS: MC, V
OPEN: Mon 10 A.M.–6 P.M., Tues–Fri 10 A.M.–7 P.M., Sat 10 A.M.–5:30 P.M., Sun 11 A.M.–5 P.M.

PAST TIMES (51)
Central Arcade, The Piazza, Covent Garden, WC2
Tube: Covent Garden

This shop is hopelessly crowded with merchandise and customers. For a better shopping experience, try one of the other branches, on Regent Street or on Brompton Road. For details, please see page 275.

TELEPHONE: 020 7240 9265
CREDIT CARDS: AE, MC, V
OPEN: Mon–Sat 10 A.M.–8 P.M., Sun 10 A.M.–6 P.M.

PETER RABBIT & FRIENDS (51)
Unit 42, The Piazza, Covent Garden, WC2
Tube: Covent Garden

The world of Peter Rabbit, Paddington Bear, and Winnie-the-Pooh awaits you on two floors in Covent Garden.

TELEPHONE: 020 7497 1777
EMAIL: info@lakefield.edi.co.uk
INTERNET: www.charactergifts.com
CREDIT CARDS: AE, MC, V
OPEN: Mon–Sat 10 A.M.–8 P.M., Sun 10 A.M.–6 P.M.

REJECT CHINA SHOP (51)
The Piazza, Covent Garden, WC2
Tube: Covent Garden

For details, please see page 276.

TELEPHONE: 020 7379 8374
CREDIT CARDS: AE, MC, V
OPEN: Mon–Sat 10 A.M.–6:45 P.M., Sun 11 A.M.–4:45 P.M.

THE SILVER VAULTS (41)
53–64 Chancery Lane (entrance is just past the address), WC2
Tube: Chancery Lane

No serious lover or collector of silver should miss the Silver Vaults. In the late 1800s, the rich stored their valuables in private underground vaults in central London. These same vaults have been turned into more than forty shops for dealers of modern and antique silver. If it is silver, it is here, and in all price ranges.

TELEPHONE: 020 7242 3844 (general information)
CREDIT CARDS: Depends on dealer
OPEN: Mon–Fri 9 A.M.–5:30 P.M. (no entry after 5:20 P.M.), Sat 9 A.M.–1 P.M. (no entry after 12:50 P.M.)

STANFORDS (43)
12–14 Long Acre, WC2
Tube: Covent Garden

If it is a map of your neighborhood, the world, or the moon, or a travel guide on any destination on the planet, Stanfords has it. There is an amazing selection of books, maps, charts, and globes, and a helpful staff in four locations: Stanfords at British Airways, W1 (see page 277), at the British Tourist Authority, SW1 (see page 296), and at the Scottish Tourist Board, SW1 (see page 296).

TELEPHONE: 020 7836 1321
FAX: 020 7836 0189
EMAIL: sales@stanfords.co.uk
INTERNET: www.stanfords.co.uk
MAIL ORDER: Tel: 020 7836 1321; Fax: 020 7836 0189; Email: customer.services@stanfords.co.uk; Open Mon–Fri 9 A.M.–6 P.M., Sat 10 A.M.–5 P.M.

CREDIT CARDS: MC, V
OPEN: Mon–Fri 9:30 A.M.–7:30 P.M., Sat 10 A.M.–7 P.M., Sun noon–6 P.M.

VANELL (49)
Aldwych (no street number), next door to the Waldorf Hotel, WC2
Tube: Covent Garden

It's fake, fun, gaudy, and priced to sell. If you need a necklace, pair of earrings, or other bauble to complete an outfit or love wearing the current glitzy fad, Vanell no doubt carries just what you are looking for.

TELEPHONE: 020 7497 0557
CREDIT CARDS: AE, DC, MC, V
OPEN: Mon–Tues, Fri–Sat 9 A.M.–6 P.M., Wed–Thur 9 A.M.–7:30 P.M., Sun 10 A.M.–4 P.M.

SW1—BELGRAVIA, KNIGHTSBRIDGE, PIMLICO, and VICTORIA (see map page 124)

Shops

BLEWCOAT SCHOOL GIFT SHOP AND INFORMATION CENTER— NATIONAL TRUST GIFT SHOP AND INFORMATION CENTER (13)
23 Caxton Street, SW1
Tube: St. James's Park

The National Trust is a conservation charity founded to protect Britain's fine homes and beautiful countryside. This gift shop, located in the historic Blewcoat School, has china, glassware, pottery, kitchenware, books, stationery, spices, preserves, crafts, and knitwear, most of which are exclusive to the National Trust. By shopping here you are helping the National Trust's work of conserving and protecting more than 560,000 acres of countryside, 200 houses and castles, 114 gardens, 59 villages, and country parks, churches, and ancient monuments. As a charity, the National Trust is not run or funded by the government, and it depends on the support and generosity of the public to continue its work.

The Blewcoat School was founded in 1688 for the education of poor children and named for the color of the tunic worn by its pupils. The present building was built in 1709. There is a figure of a "Blewcoat Boy" in the niche above the entrance door.

TELEPHONE & FAX: 020 7222 2877
CREDIT CARDS: AE, MC, V
OPEN: Mon–Fri 10 A.M.–5:30 P.M., Thur until 7 P.M.

egg (8)
36/37 Kinnerton Street, SW1
Tube: Knightsbridge

For simple, free-flowing, unstructured clothing made out of silk and cotton, egg offers timeless fashion for the individual who does not follow fads. The men's store is on one side of this hidden Knightsbridge mews street, women's on the other. Prices are not low, but these are one-of-a-kind items of clothing that you will wear and enjoy long after you've forgotten what you paid for them.

TELEPHONE: 020 7235 9315
FAX: 020 7838 9705
EMAIL: info@eggtrading.com
CREDIT CARDS: AE, MC, V
OPEN: Tues–Sat 10 A.M.–6 P.M.

ELIZABETH STREET (19)
Belgravia, SW1
Tube: Sloane Square, Victoria

The butcher, the baker, and the chocolate maker are all positioned along the section of Elizabeth Street anchored by the Ebury Street Wine Bar and Chester Street. The butcher is the prestigious Chatsworth Farm Shop, featuring a delicious deli and the finest Derbyshire meats from the farms owned by the Duke and Duchess of Devonshire. The baker is the renowned Paris bread maker Poilâne, which has opened its first shop outside of Paris here. Valrhona French chocolates have long been recognized as some of the finest in the world, but you no longer have to travel to France to taste their Grand Cru Guanaja bitter chocolate squares, milk-chocolate-coated almonds and hazelnuts, or thick hot chocolate. Oliviers & Co. specializes in the finest imported olive oils and allows you to taste before you buy. At Jeroboams wine shop, you will have a huge selection and a knowledgeable staff to help you. There is more to Elizabeth Street than famous food and wines. Look for both frivolous and wearable hats at Philip Treacy; cards, books, and gifts at Henry Stokes; assorted clothing and jewelry boutiques; a florist; a Havana cigar den; and a beguiling toy store.

THE EXCHANGE BELGRAVIA (16)
30 Elizabeth Street, SW1
Tube: Victoria

Fifty percent of the profits from this dress agency (clothes on consignment) goes to the National Kidney Research Fund. The *bon-ton* location in Belgravia means the gently worn clothes must be as upmarket as the customers, who often cruise by on a regular basis just to see what was brought in the day before. While not worth a taxi ride across town, it is worth a look if you are nearby . . . say, en route to Buckingham Palace for tea.

TELEPHONE: 020 7730 3334
CREDIT CARDS: AE, MC, V
OPEN: Mon–Sat 10 A.M.–4 P.M., Thur until 6 P.M.

JO MALONE (20)
150 SLOANE STREET, SW1
Tube: Sloane Square

Jo Malone is the *oh, so* chic London address for fragrances and skin-care products guaranteed to pamper and spoil you. Once you have tried one, I promise you will be a devotee. The beautiful Sloane Street store displays all her products and invites you to sample as many as you wish. You can also envelop yourself in a fragrance in special booths that allow you experience it in an unadulterated way. The bath oils and soaps, body creams and lotions, shampoos and conditioners, cologne, and scented candles come in five fragrance groups, each with three or four related fragrances. For instance, the Citrus group includes Grapefruit, Lime Basil and Mandarin, and Verbenas of Provence; Spicy offers Nutmeg and Ginger, Amber and Lavender, and Veltver; Green Floral features Honeysuckle and Jasmine, Wild Muguet, and Red Roses; and Woody has Fleurs de la Forêt. If you cannot shop in her London store, mail ordering is simple via Send a Scent.

TELEPHONE: 020 7730 2100
FAX: 020 7730 2125
MAIL ORDER: Send a Scent Tel: 020 7720 0202; Fax: 020 7720 0277
INTERNET: www.jomalone.co.uk

CREDIT CARDS: AE, DC, MC, V

OPEN: Mon–Sat 10 A.M.–6 P.M., Wed–Thur until 7 P.M.

LEVY AND FRIEND (30)
9 Ebury Bridge Road, as it crosses Pimlico Road, SW1
Tube: Sloane Square, Victoria

If retail clothing prices keep rising, consignment dress agencies are going to be the wave of the future. For me, they offer the smart buys of today. More and more stylish Londoners are buying secondhand and not afraid to admit it. Wouldn't you love to find a two-ply cashmere sweater for next to nothing, or an Armani jacket in perfect condition for the equivalent of a mere $50? I have found these items and many more at Levy and Friend. The value is here, the stock is interesting and changes regularly, and the prices are definitely right.

TELEPHONE: 020 7730 5695

CREDIT CARDS: AE, DC, MC, V

OPEN: Tues–Sat 11 A.M.–5 P.M.

STANFORDS AT THE BRITISH TOURIST AUTHORITY (3)
1 Regent Street, SW1
Tube: Piccadilly Circus

This branch specializes in travel books and maps on England and Ireland. For further details on Stanfords travel books and maps, including on-line ordering, please see page 292.

TELEPHONE & FAX: 020 7808 3891

CREDIT CARDS: MC, V

OPEN: Mon–Fri 9 A.M.–6 P.M., Sat–Sun 10 A.M.–6 P.M.

STANFORDS AT THE SCOTTISH TOURIST BOARD (2)
19 Cockspur Street, SW1
Tube: Charing Cross, Piccadilly Circus

For details on Stanfords travel books and maps, including on-line mail ordering, please see page 292.

TELEPHONE: 020 7321 5752

CREDIT CARDS: MC, V

OPEN: Mon–Sat 10 A.M.–6 P.M.

V V ROULEAUX, LTD. (21)
54 Sloane Square, SW1
Tube: Sloane Square

This is heaven if you love trims, tassels, braid, fabulous ribbons, feathers, and fringe. It has been collected from around the world by owner Annabel Lewis, who also redoes old furniture and has a line of accessories using bits and pieces from her tantalizing collections.

TELEPHONE: 020 7730 3125

INTERNET: www.vvrouleaux.com

CREDIT CARDS: AE, MC, V

OPEN: Mon–Tues, Thur–Sat 9:30 A.M.–6 P.M., Wed 10:30 A.M.–6 P.M.

SW3—CHELSEA (see map page 144)

BERTIE GOLIGHTLY (6)
48 Beauchamp Place, SW3
Tube: Knightsbridge

Just look at the address and you can tell this one could be a gold mine. Everyone is here—Chanel, Armani, Yves St. Laurent, Hermes, Gucci—but maybe not all at the same time. Prices may seem high, but have you been to their retail boutiques? Ball gowns and evening wear are featured, and so are samples that go for 50 percent less than their original price.

TELEPHONE: 020 7584 7279
CREDIT CARDS: AE, DC, MC, V
OPEN: Mon–Sat 10 A.M.–6 P.M.

CATH KIDSTON (14)
8 ELYSTAN STREET, CHELSEA, SW3
TUBE: SLOANE SQUARE, SOUTH KENSINGTON

The corner shop on Chelsea Green is the second for this popular designer whose pastel floral fabrics and weathered country chic have captivated the hearts of many. For a complete description and mail-order information, please see page 283.

TELEPHONE: 020 7584 3232
OPEN: Mon–Sat 10 A.M.–6 P.M.

THE CHELSEA GARDENER (19)
125 Sydney Street, SW3
Tube: Sloane Square, then bus No. 11, 22, or 19

The Chelsea Gardener is both a source and an inspiration for those seeking imaginative new ideas for their gardens. They offer help and advice on everything related to gardening and plants, whether yours are planted on a tiny balcony or a vast country estate. They also display a great selection of everything to help out your green thumb, from plants and pots to garden ornaments and furniture. It's worth a visit if you love to dabble in dirt.

TELEPHONE: 020 7352 5656
FAX: 020 7352 3301
CREDIT CARDS: AE, MC, V
OPEN: Mon–Sat 10 A.M.–6 P.M., Sun noon–6 P.M.

GENERAL TRADING COMPANY (8)
2 Symons Street, SW3
Tube: Sloane Square

After being on Sloane Street for almost forty years, the General Trading Company has relocated around the corner in a restored building opposite the back doors of Peter Jones. The GTC continues to offer unusual, stylish living accessories, all artistically displayed. As you walk through the beautifully stocked store, you will be inspired by all you see: books, garden items, children's gifts, stationery, china, glassware, luggage, and a sensational tabletop department.

TELEPHONE: 020 7730 0411
FAX: 020 7823 4624
EMAIL: catalog@general-trading.co.uk
INTERNET: www.general-trading.co.uk
CREDIT CARDS: AE, DC, MC, V
OPEN: Mon–Sat 10 A.M.–6 P.M., Wed until 7 P.M.

LA SCALA (9)
39 Elystan Street, SW3
Tube: South Kensington

Who can afford Chanel off the rack, or even last season's leftovers? You can if you haunt the London dress agencies or resale shops. After one or two runs through designer boutiques, you will recover from your acute case of "sticker shock" by becoming a resale addict, just as the most fashionable London women are. I won't mention any names, but you would be surprised to find out who shops here! Of all the dress agencies in London, including the strip across the street and around the corner from Harrods, this one is head and shoulders above the rest. The stock is up-to-the-minute, in perfect condition, and beautifully displayed according to type and size, and the staff, headed by owner Alexandra Reid, is very helpful. They carry U.S. sizes 6 to 16, with loads in size 8. Also available are shoes, bags, hats, jewelry, and other accessories.

If you go to only one dress agency, let it be La Scala.

TELEPHONE: 020 7589 2784
CREDIT CARDS: MC, V
OPEN: Mon–Sat 10 A.M.–5:30 P.M., closed first week of Aug

L'OCCITANE (17)
67 King's Road, SW3
Tube: Sloane Square, then walk or take bus No. 11, 19, or 22

Please see page 273 for details on this bath and body products and cosmetics store. There are other locations in London, including one on Regent Street (W1) and Kensington High Street (W8).

TELEPHONE: 020 7823 4555

CREDIT CARDS: AE, MC, V

OPEN: Mon–Sat 10 A.M.–7 P.M., Sun noon–6 P.M.

LUSH (18)
123 King's Road, SW3
Tube: Sloane Square, then walk or take bus No. 11, 19, or 22

For more on Lush, please see page 274. Next door to this branch is Starbucks, a perfect refueling stop for anyone in your group who wouldn't get a kick out of a shopping spree at Lush.

TELEPHONE & FAX: 020 7376 8348

CREDIT CARDS: AE, MC, V

OPEN: Mon–Sat 10 A.M.–7 P.M., Sun noon–6 P.M.

MONSOON (13)
33-C King's Road, SW3
Tube: Sloane Square

Monsoon is an English chain with brightly colored clothing designed in England and made in India, Thailand, and Hong Kong. These styles are lean and flirty, with colors and prints coordinated for mixing and matching. Prices are affordable, especially when Monsoon has a sale, but keep in mind they also reflect the quality of the sewing—check them over carefully before buying, as quality varies from piece to piece. Branches of Monsoon are all over London, and many have a Monsoon Home department, devoted to accessories gathered from the Near and Far East.

TELEPHONE: 020 7730 7552

INTERNET: www.monsoon.co.uk

CREDIT CARDS: AE, DC, MC, V

OPEN: Mon–Sat 10 A.M.–6 P.M., Wed until 7:30 P.M., Sun noon–6 P.M.

NURSERY WINDOW (7)
83 Walton Street, SW3
Tube: South Kensington

For the most adorable clothing, accessories, fabrics, and equipment for the well-dressed and -housed babies, children, and teens in your life, this shop is pure paradise. The owners have researched the market and have chosen the best and most practical items with the aim of providing their customers with a package for your child's room that includes fabric and wallpaper to match. Their simple pine cot and nappy changing table will last through several generations of children in your family. The cottons are all 100 percent washable; the spotted voile and lace come from Switzerland and are also washable. All of their accessories are handmade in England. They stress that cheaper products may be out there, but by your third child, theirs will look great and will still be going strong. What is their biggest seller? The hand-washable cashmere pram blanket for £90.The have a mail-order catalog with all of their products attractively pictured and described. If you are contemplating ordering any of their furnishings, you will be pleased to know that they come flat-packed and, according to the catalog, "are easily assembled by normal mortals without a degree in carpentry."

TELEPHONE: 020 7581 3358; 020 7581 3358 (for catalogs)
FAX: 020 7823 8839
EMAIL: nurserywindow@btconnect.co.uk
INTERNET: www.nurserywindow.co.uk
CREDIT CARDS: AE, MC, V
OPEN: Mon–Sat 10 A.M.–6 P.M., closed Dec 24–Jan 2

ONE NIGHT STAND (20)
8 Chelsea Manor Studios, Flood Street, SW3
Tube: Sloane Square, then bus No. 11, 19, or 22

For the uninitiated, the location of One Night Stand will be difficult to find because it is not a shop but a display room in a block of flats and business offices. To help you find it, Flood Street is across the King's Road from Waitrose supermarket and the Chelsea Cinema.

If you have been invited to a black-tie event, to the cocktail party of the season, or to meet the queen, and you didn't pack a thing to wear, don't despair—call One Night Stand. This agency will come to your rescue with a fabulous selection of party dresses for hire (Britspeak for "rent"). You can hire your outfit and all the accessories, including a fur wrap, for up to three days. The clothes, all cleaned after wearing, are from top American and British fashion designers. Dress rental prices range from £70 to £90 for short dresses, £100 to £200 for long ones. Your credit card number is taken as a security deposit. Optional damage insurance is available and recommended. Sizes: U.S. 4–16.

TELEPHONE: 020 7352 4848
FAX: 020 7376 8866
EMAIL: joanna@onenightstand.co.uk
CREDIT CARDS: AE, MC, V
OPEN: By appointment *only* Mon–Fri 10 A.M.–6:30 P.M.; Sat 10 A.M.–4 P.M.

PAST TIMES (2)
146 Brompton Road, SW3
Tube: Knightsbridge

For details, see page 275.
TELEPHONE: 020 7581 7616
FAX: 020 7581 9016
CREDIT CARDS: AE, DC, MC, V
OPEN: Mon–Sat 9:30 A.M.–6 P.M., Sun 11 A.M.–5 P.M.

REJECT CHINA SHOP (4)
183 Brompton Road, SW3
Tube: Knightsbridge

For details, please see page 276.

TELEPHONE: 020 7581 0739/7225 1696

FAX: 020 7225 2283

CREDIT CARDS: AE, DC, MC, V

OPEN: Mon–Sat 9 A.M.–6 P.M., Wed until 7 P.M., Sun noon–6 P.M.

TRADITIONAL TOYS (15)
56 Godfrey Street, Chelsea Green, SW3
Tube: Sloane Square, South Kensington

My London flat was just around the corner from Sarah Campos's enchanting toy store on Chelsea Green. Each day as I passed by I would see some new and adorable treasure in her windows—maybe a cuddly bear with a tartan bow, a funny little pink pig wearing ballerina shoes and a smile, a dolly's pram complete with a lace-trimmed blanket, or a doll that would fit perfectly into a little one's hand. I will admit it: I did most of my Christmas shopping here, and I mean for my own friends as well as the under-ten set. No matter what your price range, what age or gender you are shopping for, Sarah will have something to make you and the recipient very happy.

NOTE: If you are not in the market for toys, you should make time for a delightful shopping detour to Chelsea Green—an oasis in the middle of London (see page 265).

TELEPHONE: 020 7352 1718

FAX: 020 7349 9603

CREDIT CARDS: AE, MC, V

OPEN: Mon–Fri 10 A.M.–5:30 P.M., Sat until 6 P.M.

SW7—SOUTH KENSINGTON (see map page 154)
Shops

DRESS AGENCIES ON CHEVAL PLACE (CONSIGNMENT STORES) (11)
Cheval Place, SW7
Tube: Knightsbridge

For years, fashion-savvy women have brought their designer clothing to these shops to sell. The deal is this: The clothes are brought in (by appointment *only*), the shop accepts them (they must be clean), and puts a price tag on the items. The owner gets a percentage, as does the store. Shoppers get a good price and the chance to wear designer clothing when all we really can afford are Wal-Mart fashions on special. U.S. sizes available are 6–16. If you don't see what you want in one store, just keep working the street. You can also accessorize your wardrobe with belts, bags, hats, jewelry, shoes, and scarves. Quality and choice vary greatly. It isn't easy shopping, but it's fun if you love couturier clothing, but not the prices. Prices may *seem* high, but they are at *least* 50 to 60 percent below retail.

The Dress Box, 8 Cheval Place

Pandora, 16–22 Cheval Place (the biggest; a lot by Chanel and Hermes)

Renate, 4 Cheval Place

Salou, 6 Cheval Place

Strelios, 10 Cheval Place

CREDIT CARDS: MC, V in all, AE, DC in some

OPEN: Generally Mon–Sat 10 A.M.–6 P.M.

THE LINEN MERCHANT (6)
11 Montpelier Street, SW7
Tube: Knightsbridge

In today's world of polyester and drip-dry, many have forgotten all about the beauties and pleasures of magnificent linens. A walk by this lovely store will refresh your memory, and you will be inspired to buy something, even if it is only one of their unusual hankies. Grandmothers, don't say I didn't warn you . . . their baby clothes are captivating. Prices will reflect the quality. The personal attention given to each customer harks back to an earlier era.

TELEPHONE: 020 7584 3654

FAX: 020 7584 3671

INTERNET: www.thelinenmerchant.com

CREDIT CARDS: AE, MC, V

OPEN: Mon–Sat 9:30 A.M.–6 P.M.

SW10—FULHAM (see map page 154)
Shops

Ganesha   **302**

GANESHA (34)
6 Park Walk, SW10
Tube: South Kensington, plus a long walk

It is not worth a special trip from the West End, but if you are around Fulham Road or the far end of King's Road, take a quick detour on Park Walk and browse through this jam-packed Asian-style dime store, which stocks something for every pocketbook. The tiny ground-level room is stuffed with trinkets and treasures from all over Asia and India. It is a good place to buy clever and inexpensive gifts. The downstairs room is devoted to large items—tables, chests, and so on—at reasonable prices.

TELEPHONE: 020 7352 8972
CREDIT CARDS: MC, V
OPEN: Mon–Sat noon–6 P.M., Sun 1–6 P.M.

SE1—SOUTH BANK and WATERLOO (see map page 182)

NEAL'S YARD DAIRY WAREHOUSE (7)
6 Park Street, Borough Market, SE1
Tube: London Bridge

If you like their shop near Covent Garden, you will be mad about this warehouse, where the cheeses are stacked and the aromas are tantalizing. At both shops, sampling is encouraged and the staff very knowledgeable and friendly.

TELEPHONE: 020 7645 3550
FAX: 020 7645 3564
EMAIL: mailorder@nealsyarddairy.co.uk
CREDIT CARDS: MC, V
OPEN: Mon–Fri 9 A.M.–6 P.M., Sat until 4 P.M.

VINOPOLIS (2)
1 Bank End, SE1
Tube: London Bridge

This two-and-a-half-acre theme park devoted entirely to wine sits under the arches of the Southwark Bridge. An audio guide in six languages takes visitors through the history of wine and includes a simulated ride on a Vespa through the countryside of the Italian wine regions. A simulated glass of bubbling champagne in the form of an elevator transports people to a mezzanine, and touch-screen computers advise on what wines to serve with what food. Included in the price of admission is a tasting of five premium wines. Of course there is a gift shop with every possible gizmo and gadget for the wine connoisseur, plus a dazzling selection of wines. Also here are a restaurant and wine bar. Children are welcomed with a glass of fruit juice and a Kid's Fun Book. If you later think of something you wish you had bought while you were here, don't despair. There's a mail-order catalog and on-line ordering.

TELEPHONE: 0870 4444 777 (24 hours), 0870 241 4040 (wine tasting inquiries)

FAX: 020 7940 8302

EMAIL: retail@vinopolis.co.uk

INTERNET: www.vinopolis.co.uk

CREDIT CARDS: AE, DC, MC, V

OPEN: Mon–Sat 10 A.M.–8 P.M., Sun until 6 P.M.

E1—EAST END (see map page 176)

SAVONNERIE (8)
Inside the Spitalfields Market, 57–59 Brushfield Street, E1
Tube: Liverpool Street

Savonnerie boutiques are dotted around the city, including one in the exclusive Burlington Arcade and two at Selfridges, but at this, their main shop, found inside Spitalfields Market, the same products sell for 30 percent less. All their soaps and bath products are handmade from natural ingredients, using essential oils. The soaps are made in huge blocks and sold by weight, which is a perfect way to sample several before deciding which one you cannot be without. Try Cedar soap, the color of burnt clay, which is a "romantic, warm scent with the skin balancing and healing benefits of cedar"; Honey Cake, "a yummy, scrubby soap loaded with Scotch Oats designed to be a mild exfoliating body soap"; or Marmalade, with small pieces of orange within. These natural soaps don't keep well, so buy only what you can use in one or two months.

TELEPHONE: 020 7375 1844

FAX: 020 7375 1886

CREDIT CARDS: AE, MC, V

OPEN: Mon–Sat 11 A.M.–6 P.M., Sun 10 A.M.–5 P.M.

Department Stores

Whatever you need or want, or never imagined you should have, can be found in one of London's many department stores. These large emporiums make good shopping sense if you have only a few hours to shop. All of them are known for their January and July sales. Only people who have earned a black belt in shopping should attempt opening day at a Harrods sale. If you do brave this onslaught, you will need superhuman stamina and patience to withstand the merciless crowds clamoring and clawing for bargains that come only once or twice a year. Shopping hours have improved, at least from a British point of view. Most stores are open five or six hours on Sundays and bank holidays, and one so-called late night during the week. Late means they close one hour later at 7 or 8 P.M. on that night. Each area of London has a different late night, and most of the stores in it comply.

Debenhams, W1	**305**
Dickens & Jones, W1	**305**
Fenwick, W1	**306**
Fortnum & Mason, W1	**306**
Harrods, SW1	**306**
Harvey Nichols, SW1	**307**
John Lewis, W1	**308**
Liberty, W1	**308**
Lillywhite's, SW1	**309**
Marks & Spencer, W1	**309**
Peter Jones, SW1	**309**
Selfridges, W1	**310**

DEBENHAMS (19)
334–338 Oxford Street, W1 (see map page 54)
Tube: Bond Street, Oxford Circus

The store has a decent lingerie and housewares department but otherwise is run-of-the-mill, featuring items that will never find their way into the closets of fashion wildcats.

TELEPHONE: 020 7580 3000
INTERNET: www.debenhams.com
CREDIT CARDS: AE, DC, MC, V
OPEN: Basically Mon–Sat 9 A.M.–7 P.M., Sun noon–6 P.M.

DICKENS & JONES (17)
224–244 Regent Street, W1 (see map page 54)
Tube: Oxford Circus

Part of the House of Fraser, aimed toward the fashion-conscious men and women who care about how they look, but who cannot afford bespoke clothing, this store features some mid-level designers, as well as Kenzo and Burberry for men.

TELEPHONE: 020 7734 7070

INTERNET: www.houseoffraser.co.uk
CREDIT CARDS: AE, DC, MC, V
OPEN: Mon–Tues 10 A.M.–6 P.M., Wed, Fri, Sat until 7 P.M., Thur until 8 P.M., Sun noon–6 P.M.

FENWICK (35)
63 New Bond Street, W1 (see map page 54)
Tube: Bond Street

Say "Fennick," not Fenwick. Affordable clothes are nicely displayed over three floors. Serious price slashing happens during their Designer Sales, held before Christmas and at the end of June. Carlulccio's famous Italian deli and café has a branch on the lower ground floor.

TELEPHONE: 020 7629 9161
FAX: 020 7409 1890
CREDIT CARDS: AE, DC, MC, V
OPEN: Mon–Sat 9:30 A.M.–6 P.M.

FORTNUM & MASON (51)
181 Piccadilly, W1 (see map page 54)
Tube: Green Park, Piccadilly Circus

Fortnum & Mason is famous for its grocery department, with knowledgeable clerks ready to serve you. Where else would you be told which tea is best suited to the water in any particular city? It was opened in 1701, and a major part of its success came from providing expatriate Brits living throughout the Empire with products they otherwise would not have had. It still sells a huge variety of gourmet items, as well as its famous picnic hampers for the races at Ascot, and is a Royal Warrants' holder and supplier to Buckingham Palace and the queen. There is a tableware department in the basement, a stationery and gift department on three, and a women's department on the first floor that stocks designer labels, including Issey Miyake and Missoni. One of the nicest department-store ladies' rooms is next to the lingerie department. Please be sure to look at the clock outside the front entrance on Piccadilly. It is as famous as the store itself.

TELEPHONE: 020 7734 8040
FAX: 020 7437 3828
EMAIL: info@fortnumandmason.co.uk
INTERNET: www.fortnumandmason.co.uk
CREDIT CARDS: AE, DC, MC, V
OPEN: Mon–Sat 9:30 A.M.–6 P.M.

HARRODS (7)
87–135 Brompton Road, SW1 (see map page 124)
Tube: Knightsbridge

The first stop on the yellow brick road of London shopping is Harrods. It is simply not to be missed. You will stand in awe of the sheer size and magnitude of this world-class department store, which covers four and a half acres of land and amounts to fifteen acres of prime shopping territory in Knightsbridge. If you are seriously shopping, get in training: Of the more than three hundred departments spread out over seven floors, there are more than sixty fashion departments alone. The mother of all English food halls covers thirty-five thousand square feet, with eighteen departments filling seven elaborately decorated rooms and the necessary service personnel to wait on you properly. That is just the fresh food! A level below is the grocery department.

Elegance and abundance has its price, but in January the sales are on and special police forces are stationed outside for mob control. Harrods boasts that it can take care of all of your needs from the cradle to the grave (they have a funeral department). Because it is a full-service department store, there just isn't much they don't have or can't arrange, including excellent half-day tours of London in their own air-conditioned buses, with soft drinks served after the tour. You can get either a morning or afternoon tour, both of which leave from right in front of the main entrance. Also available is the Windsor Castle Tour, which includes Runnymede, where you see the memorials to the Magna Carta and John F. Kennedy.

Warning: There are rules and more rules:

1. There is a dress code for crossing the threshold, and armed guards to enforce it. You are not allowed in wearing shorts, vest tops with nothing underneath, backpacks, or torn jeans (no matter how much they cost).

2. You are not allowed to bring, let alone use, your camera; carry or leash your dog; smoke a cigarette; or eat outside the restaurants. You can bring in your mobile telephone, but heaven forbid you use it.

3. You can forget about using the toilet, unless you pay £1 or produce a paid receipt from one of their restaurants (no other department, even the food hall, qualifies) for a meal in excess of £8! This is outrageous. Harrods certainly doesn't need the extra money, and with armed guards at the entrances, certainly the riffraff will be kept out. No other store in London practices this sort of robbery. Harrods should know better.

TELEPHONE: 020 7730 1234
INTERNET: www.harrods.com
CREDIT CARDS: AE, DC, MC, V
OPEN: Mon–Sat 10 A.M.–7 P.M.

HARVEY NICHOLS (6)
109–125 Knightsbridge, SW1 (see map page 124)
Tube: Knightsbridge

"Harvey Nicks" is how you refer to this Knightsbridge shrine to the latest fashions and without question the most luxurious department store in London (sorry, Harrods). If I could afford it, I would never shop anyplace else. All major designers are represented, including many from America. If you are in London during the January sales, your attendance is absolutely required. Designer labels and displays of every major style trend cover three floors; cosmetics and perfumes yet another. If you love housewares, don't miss the fourth floor, a treasure trove of home fashion ideas ranging from the traditional and useful to the completely wacky. On the fifth floor is a very modern food hall selling every exotic piece of produce you ever heard of, and some you have not. Here also are cafés that have long lunch queues and a restaurant with understaffed and over-worked waiters. By the way, the ladies' room on the fifth floor is great, and not only provides an assortment of colognes and creams, and an attendant who keeps it all clean, but it's *free*. (Compare Harrods, page 306.)

TELEPHONE: 020 7235 5000
CREDIT CARDS: AE, DC, MC, V
OPEN: Mon–Sat 10 A.M.–7 P.M., Wed–Fri until 8 P.M., Sun noon–6 P.M.; restaurants open later (call to get hours)

JOHN LEWIS (18)
278–306 Oxford Street, W1 (see map page 54)
Tube: Oxford Circus

Along with Peter Jones, Liberty, Selfridges, and Harrods, this is one of the stores in central London that carries the range of goods you would expect to find in a full-service department store, and if you lived in London, it would be a reliable standby. Clothes are a bit boring, but the electronics section is excellent, and prices are good in all departments, thanks to the store motto that they are "never knowingly undersold."

TELEPHONE: 020 7629 7711
INTERNET: www.johnlewis.co.uk
CREDIT CARDS: MC, V
OPEN: Mon–Wed, Fri 9:30 A.M.–6 P.M., Thur 10 A.M.–8 P.M., Sat 9 A.M.–6 P.M.

LIBERTY (32)
210–220 Regent Street, W1 (see map page 54)
Tube: Oxford Circus

Arthur Lasenby Liberty opened a shop at this address in 1875. The present faux-Tudor building was constructed in 1924 with the timber from two Royal Navy warships. It is easy to get lost in the maze of departments and boutiques that meander over two large buildings, but what a wonderful place to wander. To save yourself wasted shopping time, get a store map and study it before you strike out. Liberty is known worldwide for their fine Liberty print fabrics. A Liberty tie, scarf, covered bracelet, or even a hankie makes a perfect gift that even the most demanding person on your list will recognize and enjoy. There are no bargains here, but if you look carefully, you will find something. If you are in London during the January sales, come on the last day and you can save up to 70 percent on selected goods.

TELEPHONE: 020 7734 1234
INTERNET: www.liberty-of-london.com
CREDIT CARDS: AE, MC, V
OPEN: Mon–Wed 10 A.M.–6 P.M., Thur until 8 P.M., Fri–Sat until 7 P.M.

LILLYWHITE'S (1)
24–36 Lower Regent Street, SW1 (see map page 124)
Tube: Piccadilly Circus

This is the largest sporting goods store in England, with few breathtaking savings unless you hit a sale, and even then it is still questionable. If you are a sportsperson, though, this is mecca—even if you don't buy a single golf ball. All brand names are represented, including American ones. There is no ladies' room.

TELEPHONE: 020 7930 3181

CREDIT CARDS: AE, DC, MC, V

OPEN: Mon–Sat 10 A.M.–8 P.M., Sun noon–6 P.M., open some bank holidays

MARKS & SPENCER (25)
458 Oxford Street, W1 (see map page 54)
Tube: Bond Street, Marble Arch

Marks & Spencer has terrific lingerie, especially the little numbers in silk. There are hundreds of branches of this British shopping standard in the U.K., where it is referred to as "Marks & Sparks." In addition to the silk underwear, best buys include sweaters and the food in the basement. Otherwise, the fashions have an unexciting, middle-age twinge. To get your VAT refund, check with the Marks & Spencer you are in to be sure they participate. All of your purchases at one branch must add up to that store's required total before you get the refund. You cannot shop at several different branches and pool the receipts. There are numerous branches in London, including ones on Kensington High Street, W8, tube: High Street Kensington, and on King's Road, SW3, tube: Sloane Square. Hours may vary slightly.

NOTE: Some of the best rates in London for changing money are at the M&S exchange offices, and they do not charge a commission. Such a deal.

TELEPHONE: 020 7935 7954

INTERNET: www.marksandspencer.co.uk

CREDIT CARDS: AE, MC, V. The clerk at the information booth told me, "Our cash machines take every card under the sun, including American ones I've never heard of." Good luck!

OPEN: Mon–Fri 9 A.M.–8 P.M., Sat until 7 P.M., Sun noon–6 P.M., open bank holidays

PETER JONES (22)
Sloane Square, SW1 (see map page 124)
Tube: Sloane Square

I like Peter Jones for its fine linens, fabrics, china, and housewares departments. The clothing department is boring. Sloane Rangers (British yuppies) shop here in full force on Saturday mornings.

TELEPHONE: 020 7730 3434

EMAIL: peter-jones@johnlewis.co.uk

INTERNET: www.peterjones.co.uk

CREDIT CARDS: MC, V
OPEN: Mon–Sat 9:30 A.M.–6 P.M., Wed until 7 P.M.

SELFRIDGES (24)
400 Oxford Street, W1 (see map page 54)
Tube: Bond Street

American businessman Henry Gordon Selfridge opened the doors of his store in 1901. It had London's first television sales department (1926) and always has fabulous window displays created by specially commissioned artists and designers. Selfridges recently had a £100 million redo, and the results are as impressive as their cost. Now you will find a huge cosmetics and perfume department, a theater booking agent, wonderful food halls, good-looking fashions, a big household section, and a pleasing staff. Miss Selfridge on Duke Street (same telephone, tube: Bond Street) stocks trendy yet affordable fashions for anyone wanting to feel under thirty-five, even if that birthday is in the distant past.

TELEPHONE: 020 7629 1234
INTERNET: www.selfridges.co.uk
CREDIT CARDS: AE, DC, MC, V
OPEN: Mon–Wed, Sat 10 A.M.–7 P.M., Thur and Fri until 8 P.M., Sun and bank holidays noon–6 P.M.

Antique Markets

If you are a collector, try to save some time to wander through the mazes of stalls in these indoor London antique markets. Whatever your fancy, from Art Deco jewelry to old buttons, teddy bears, dolls, boxes, handmade lace, or furniture, you are bound to find it here, and in spades.

Bargaining is expected, but be realistic—the dealer has to make a living. Usually the higher the price, the more room to deal, but *please* don't try to bargain down something priced at £10. As in any market transaction, cash, not plastic, is king. A good phrase to use when dealing is, "What is the trade on that?" which implies that you are in the antiques business. Always buy the best you can afford and don't settle for something cracked, chipped, or otherwise damaged, even if the dealer insists it won't matter. Of course it will, so move on to the next dealer—the competition is stiff.

ALFIES ANTIQUE MARKET
13–25 Church Street, NW8
Tube: Edgware Road, Marylebone

I never miss a swing through Alfies, a sprawling collection of antiques dealers selling at prices that (after you have bargained) are affordable. The location is not central, and it is not one of the mainstream tourist markets, so you are more inclined to find something of quality and value. It bills itself as the biggest permanent covered antiques market in Britain, with forty thousand square feet of space and 350 sellers tucked throughout the joined buildings, plus a greasy-spoon café on the top floor.

NOTE: One of my favorite stalls is Stand G144, run by Stevie Pearce, who has the most amazing collection of costume jewelry on her side of the Atlantic Ocean. She also stocks bags and other accessories, but you are here to zero in on her jewels. When you see her corner, you will wonder how she keeps track of anything, but believe me, she does. If you don't see what you are looking for, just ask, and she is likely to pull it out of one of the boxes stacked on the floor and under her feet. Her prices have been the same for eight years: she sells nothing over £15, and 90 percent of her stock is priced to sell at under £10.

Stevie has quite an international following and does a lot of work with films and television. In the films *Evita* and *Notting Hill,* some of the jewels were by Stevie.

TELEPHONE: 020 7723 6066
FAX: 020 7724 0929
EMAIL: post@eAlfies.com
INTERNET: www.eAlfies.com
CREDIT CARDS: Depends on seller
OPEN: Tues–Sat 10 A.M.–6 P.M.

ANTIQUARIUS (16)
135 King's Road, SW3 (see map page 144)
Tube: Sloane Square, then take bus No. 11, 19, or 22 (if you don't want a long walk)

There are more than a hundred stalls at the Antiquarius market selling everything from clocks and lace to porcelain and watches. It's known for buttons, textiles, Art Deco, and collectibles including corkscrews, pipes, dolls, and teddy bears. It is across King's Road from the Waitrose supermarket and the Chelsea Cinema.

TELEPHONE: 020 7351 5363
CREDIT CARDS: Depends on dealer
OPEN: Mon–Sat 10 A.M.–6 P.M.

GRAY'S ANTIQUES MARKET and GRAY'S IN THE MEWS (33)
58 Davies Street and 1–7 Davies Mews, W1 (see map page 54)
Tube: Bond Street

Called the biggest antiques market in the world, it is a good place to browse to get an idea of what's available. Prices are not in the bargain category, but you are not expected to pay sticker prices. The front section is devoted to antique jewelry, and tin toys highlight in the Mews.

TELEPHONE: 020 7629 7034

INTERNET: www.graysantiques.com

CREDIT CARDS: Depends on stall

TYPE: Two antiques markets with a multitude of individual sellers

OPEN: Mon–Fri 10 A.M.–6 P.M.

Indoor and Outdoor Markets

London markets are entertaining and fun for everyone, even the die-hard couch potato whose idea of shopping is to thumb through a mail-order catalog and dial a toll-free 800 number or order on-line and have the goods delivered. For serious antiques or collectible shopping enthusiasts, a predawn visit to one of London's big outdoor flea markets is something you will never forget. While you probably will not unearth a rare Minton vase for a few pence, you will find something you want and have fun in the bargain. However, never let some aggressive salesperson sell you something you really don't want. If you didn't like the item before someone tried to "sell" it to you, you don't like it, period. Move on.

At all the flea markets, bargaining is expected and part of the game. There are always two prices for everything, the "punter's" and the dealer's. You know who you are. There are two phrases to keep in mind when discussing price: "What is the best you can do?" and, when talking antiques, "What is the trade on that?" which means, what is the dealer price?

For most of these outdoor markets, Saturday and Sunday are the times to shop, and you *must* get there when the market opens. I am talking 5 A.M. for Bermondsey and 6 A.M. for Portobello Road. These are the times for hard-core bargaining and buying. I do not recommend the wee hours at Petticoat Lane; the neighborhood is just too dicey.

No matter which market you go to, it is better to travel in pairs for these early-morning safaris. Dress simply. Dealers will charge what the market will bear, and if you are clad in designer togs and high-visibility jewelry, the prices will not go down. With the exception of Covent Garden and some of the dealers on Portobello Road, don't count on your credit cards because not all, and sometimes not many, sellers take them. Not only that, but credit cards just don't command the same discount attention as folding money does.

Don't kid yourself: Pickpockets work the outdoor markets and are fleet-footed pros who will snatch your wallet or purse before you know what hit you. *Wear a money belt* under your clothing, not strapped around your waist for all to see and dip into.

BERMONDSEY MARKET (ALSO CALLED NEW CALEDONIAN MARKET) (16)
Bermondsey Square, south of Tower Bridge, SE1 (see map page 182)
Tube: Borough or London Bridge and walk south

Bermondsey Market—also called New Caledonian Market—is the most serious and professional antiques market. The sellers set up by 5:30 A.M., and by 9 A.M. the dealers have picked through. Across the street is a covered market called the Bermondsey Antiques Market and Warehouse. The real fun is outside, early in the morning, so get up early, take your flashlight, and keep your money in a money belt. For a real London outing, combine your trip to the market with a meal of pie and mash at Manze's (see *Great Eats London*).

OPEN: Fri 5:30 A.M.–1 P.M. (starts closing at noon)

BERWICK STREET MARKET (40)
Berwick and Rupert Streets, W1 (see map page 54)
Tube: Leicester Square, Piccadilly Circus

The West End's cheapest fruits and vegetables are hawked all day on Berwick Street from Monday to Saturday. If it hasn't sold by 4 P.M. Saturday afternoon, the prices fall to the giveaway level. When you hit Rupert Street, quality goes downhill, and the seedy stalls and shops are devoted to the wholesale and retail rag trade and cheap jewelry.

OPEN: Mon–Sat 8 A.M.–6 P.M.

BOROUGH MARKET (8)
Between Borough High Street, Bedale Street, Winchester Walk, and Stoney Street, SE1 (see map page 182)
Tube: London Bridge

Borough Market, crammed with more than forty quality food stalls every Friday and Saturday, has become the "in-place" for London's foodies. A vast range of foods from all over England is on sale and often available to sample. Try the Garlic Farm's smoked garlic honey, taste the Ginger Pigs' range of hams and sausages, sample cheeses from Neal's Yard Dairy, buy a loaf of bread from De Gustibus, get some fresh fish or vegetable sushi from Feng Sushi, or taste fine French or organic wines. In addition, there are fresh fruit and vegetable stalls, meat and fish vendors, and much, much more. The best day to go is on the third Saturday of the month, when there are more stalls.

INTERNET: londonslarder.org.uk
OPEN: Fri noon–6 P.M., Sat 9 A.M.–4 P.M.

BRICK LANE MARKET (1)
Brick Lane, Cygnet Street, Sclater Street, E1 (see map page 176); Bacon Street, Cheshire Street, Chilton Street, E2
Tube: Aldgate East, Shoreditch, Liverpool Street

These streets are full of locals out for a bargain. Brick Lane itself is the place to go in the East End for leather, junk jewelry, produce, and jellied eels.

OPEN: Sun 8 A.M.–1 P.M.

CAMDEN MARKETS
Camden Lock Place, off Chalk Farm Road, NW1
Stables Yard: Off Chalk Farm Road, opposite Hartland Road
Tube: Camden Town

Even if you don't buy a thing, Camden Markets are worth a visit just to see the animals populating this people's zoo. You won't be alone here: tourists have turned the Camden Markets into London's fourth-biggest tourist attraction, and it can be a virtual madhouse on Sundays. This tells you not to expect the bargain of a shopping lifetime on a rare antique, but you *can* expect to have a good day's outing poking through all there is to see. Camden Lock, a cobbled courtyard leading to the canal, is where the crowds congregate to rifle through the stalls selling crafts and castoffs whose worth and artistic merit vary. There is a street-party atmosphere, with lots of funky young Londoners just hanging out. The Stables Yard is probably the best-value part if you are shopping for furniture—from antique through the 1960s—or lighting fixtures. Techno-groupies will have a field day in Cyberdog. The other three markets under the Camden Market umbrella are Camden Canal Market, Camden Market, and Electric Market, none of which are worth a special trip unless you are into henna tattoos, retro clothes and shoes, or international hippy junk. When you have had enough of the markets, walk along the peaceful Regent's Canal or hop on one of the boats that ply the canal.

CREDIT CARDS: Depends on seller

OPEN: *Camden Lock Place:* Indoor stalls Tues–Sun 10 A.M.–6 P.M., outdoor stalls Sat–Sun 10 A.M.–6 P.M.; *Stables Yard:* Sat–Sun 8 A.M.–6 P.M.

CAMDEN PASSAGE
Upper High Street, N1
Tube: Angel

Camden Passage is *not* to be confused with the Camden Markets. They aren't even in the same postal code. On Wednesday and Saturday, the area is jammed with hundreds of stalls. The rest of the week, shops sell antiques along an alleyway. The focus is on small tchotchkes, and there are few bargains.

TELEPHONE: 020 7359 9969

CREDIT CARDS: Depends on seller

OPEN: Tues, Thur–Fri 10 A.M.–5 P.M., Wed 8 A.M.–2 P.M., Sat 10 A.M.–4 P.M.

COVENT GARDEN MARKETS: APPLE, JUBILEE (51)
Covent Garden, WC2 (see map page 96)
Tube: Covent Garden

The original Covent Garden of Eliza Doolittle's time was a fruit and vegetable market, but now it is a mall of shops and restaurants. The little side streets that go off in every direction are filled with boutiques, coffeehouses, restaurants, and other shops. The whole area is great fun and should not be missed. In addition to the permanent shops in Covent Garden itself, there are three separate markets, which are hard to tell apart. Remember: Monday is antiques *only* at all three; otherwise, Apple sells crafts, and Jubilee sells junk.

Apple Market is inside the Piazza, under the rooftops of Covent Garden in a courtyard between the permanent shops. Monday it sells antiques; Tuesday to Sunday it sells a mixture of the good, the bad, and the ugly in British crafts.

Jubilee is in Jubilee Hall, off Southampton Street. Monday it sells antiques, other days, clothing, jewelry, and crass tourist trash.

OPEN: Daily 10:30 A.M.–6:30 P.M., may vary on bank holidays and in the summer

GREENWICH MARKET
Crafts Market: College Approach; Central Market, Food Market, Village Market: Stockwell Street across from the Hotel Ibis; Antiques Market: Greenwich High Road, SE10
Transportation: Greenwich Rail, or take the boat that leaves every half hour from Westminster Pier

A Saturday or Sunday spent wandering through the Greenwich market stalls used to be a must-do for every serious flea-market fan. The stands and merchandise on display have become a bit tackier and tattier lately, but a Sunday spent taking the boat to historic Greenwich is still great fun. To keep a focus on your shopping, remember that stalls in the

Crafts Market and the Antiques Market have somewhat better quality; books, prints, and records are found in the Village Market; and along King William Passage are some up-and-coming new designers and linens aimed at those who want to spend considerable time washing, starching, and ironing.

Greenwich is not all shopping. You can straddle the meridian line (thus standing simultaneously in the eastern and western hemispheres), wander through the park, or explore the three-masted *Cutty Sark* or *Gypsy Moth* sailing vessels.

OPEN: Generally Sat–Sun 9 A.M.–5 P.M. (some stalls are open Fri)

LEADENHALL MARKET (12)
Whittington Avenue off Gracechurch Street, EC3 (see map page 176)
Tube: Monument

In the fourteenth century, Leadenhall was a meat, poultry, and fish market occupying a series of courts on Leadenhall Street. Parts of the market were destroyed in the Great Fire of 1666. During the early nineteenth century, one of the most famous characters of the market was a gander from Ostend named Old Tom, who had followed a goose from his flock to London. There are no details about his lady-friend, but Tom lived for twenty-eight years and was buried here. Today you will still see some meat and fish stalls, but they are slowly being replaced by the High Street chains, pubs, and restaurants catering to high rollers in the City.

OPEN: Mon–Fri 7 A.M.–4 P.M.

LEATHER LANE MARKET (6)
Leather Lane, EC1 (see map page 176)
Tube: Chancery Lane

From the name, you would think you were entering leather-land. Not so. Yes, there are leather shoes, bags, coats, skirts, and accessories, but there's also luggage, cheap fashion thrills, and junk jewelry that appeals to office workers on their lunch hour. More interesting is the concentration of real jewelry shops that line the street between Holborn Circus and Greville Street.

OPEN: Mon–Fri 10:30 A.M.–2 P.M.

PETTICOAT LANE (9)
Middlesex Street, Goulston Street, New Goulston Street, Toynbee Street, Wentworth Street, Bell Lane, Cobb Street, Old Castle Street, Cutler Street, E1 (see map page 176)
Tube: Liverpool, Aldgate

A morning spent at this famous East End market is an experience: it's a wild kaleidoscope of color, noises, and smells—including that of jellied eels sold from carts. Actually, there is no Petticoat Lane. Look for Middlesex Street and the others, where the thousand-plus stalls attract hordes of buyers and lookers. The best leather goods are found on New Goulston Street; the antiques section is called the New Cutler Street

Market and is known for its scrap gold and silver, coins, medals, and stamps. Take cash, bargain like mad, and have fun. Watch your wallet!

OPEN: Sun 9 A.M.–2 P.M.

PICCADILLY MARKET AT ST. JAMES'S CHURCH (49)
Piccadilly, W1 (see map page 54)
Tube: Green Park, Piccadilly Circus

The market is held in the churchyard of St. James's Church, the only one Sir Christopher Wren designed and built on a new site. The carvings and organ by Grinling Gibbons are magnificent. The market itself has improved and includes a bit of everything, not all of it quality, but definitely worth a browse if you like this sort of shopping. If you time your visit around noon, check to see if a lunchtime concert is being held.

CREDIT CARDS: Depends on the stall and seller

OPEN: Wed–Sat 10 A.M.–6 P.M.

PORTOBELLO ROAD (29)
Portobello Road off Pembridge Road, W11 (see map page 66)
Tube: Notting Hill Gate

On Saturday, Portobello Road is one of Britain's most famous antiques and bric-a-brac markets. The rest of the week it is a quiet street lined with dealers selling antiques from their shops. The Saturday market has three sections. The first and most posh is a five-block strip from Chepstow Villas north, where the street is lined with stalls selling jewelry, lace, objets d'art, paintings, books, and antiques, or would-be antiques. Sellers along here can spot a tourist a mile away and are not above taking them for as much as possible. Be careful. The next section, near Lonsdale Road, is primarily fruit and vegetable hawkers, and from Tavistock Road to Goldborne Road it's chiefly pure, unadulterated junk. *Beware of pickpockets at all times.*

NOTE: The people you see on Saturday with the stands and stalls are *not* extensions of the shops behind them.

OPEN: Sat market 5 A.M.–4 P.M., but best until about 1 P.M. Shops Mon–Sat 10 A.M.–5 P.M.

SPITALFIELDS MARKET (8)
Commercial Street between Lamb Street and Bushfield Street, E1 (see map page 176)
Tube: Liverpool Street

When I went to look at Spitalfields Market a few years ago, there were about three stalls selling tired veggies and a dog show for mutts going on in the center of the open-air building. Hardly the stuff of a write-up. Now, the Sunday market is a major destination for throngs of Londoners, who browse and buy from stalls with vendors just in from Tibet selling unbleached cotton clothing, interesting crafts, leather goods, wooden toys, and enough candles and scented soaps to keep you and your surroundings smelling sweet for a year. Whatever you do, don't miss

Savonnerie, which sells a beautiful selection of pure, handmade soaps and toiletries (see page 304).

Around the edge of the market are various food stalls selling everything from coffee and doughnuts to chili pickles and Oriental noodles. Two of my favorites for a forbidden grease-out are Fat Boy's Diner and the Arkansas Café. At Fat Boy's you can sit on a red leatherette stool at the counter and indulge in a hot dog and a malt, or order a burger and fries washed down by a cherry Coke (see *Great Eats London*), and at the Arkansas Café, you will chow down on finger-licking barbecued pork ribs. During the week the place is utter dullsville. The center section is devoted to practice sessions for men's and women's soccer teams, whose shouts and whoops drown out everything else. The organic produce is gone, and so are most of the market stalls, with the notable exception of Savonnerie and most of the same greasy spoons you will find on Sundays.

CREDIT CARDS: Depends on stall, but usually MC, V
OPEN: Sun 10 A.M.–5 P.M.

Museum Shops

London has such an enormous variety of museums that entire books are devoted to their collections. In the present climate of reduced government grants, museums have had to reinvent themselves and in the process have become more aggressively commercial. For shoppers, this is a bonus because greater emphasis has been placed on luring the museum-goers into the museum shop. Most of London's major museums now have interesting shops, which are definitely worth a look. They all sell reproductions from their own collections, and books about them, which you will not find anyplace else. Quality is high and the items are often unusual and represent good value for the money. In most of the museum stores, you can shop without having to pay admission to get into the museum itself. All the shops listed here take at least two major credit cards. *Tip:* If you have time for just one museum shop, make it the Victoria and Albert.

BANK OF ENGLAND MUSEUM SHOP (11)
Threadneedle Street, entrance on Bartholomew Lane, EC2 (see map page 176)
Tube: Bank

The bank covers three acres, and its vaults hold the country's gold reserves. The only part open to the public is the Bank Museum and its shop, which sells postcards and the usual posters. Hardly a shopping thrill.

TELEPHONE: 020 7601 5545
INTERNET: www.bankofengland.co.uk
CREDIT CARDS: MC, V
OPEN: Mon–Fri 10 A.M.–5 P.M.

BRAMAH TEA & COFFEE MUSEUM SHOP (11)
Maguire Street, Butler's Wharf (near the Design Center), SE1 (see map page 182)
Tube: Tower Hill, and walk across the bridge

Even if you never drink coffee or tea, this is a fascinating place. Located in the atmospheric old warehouse section known as Butler's Wharf, the museum tells the 350-year history of two of the world's most important commodities, tea and coffee, and displays Edward Bramah's stunning collection of tea and coffee artifacts. The Tea and Coffee Room offers, of course, tea and coffee. The small retail shop sells the Bramah teas and other related products, including lovely teapots, teacups, and coffeepots.

TELEPHONE: 020 7378 0222
FAX: 020 7378 0219
EMAIL: e.bramah@virgin.net
INTERNET: www.bramahmuseum.co.uk
CREDIT CARDS: AE, MC, V
OPEN: Daily 10 A.M.–6 P.M.

BRITISH MUSEUM SHOP (33)
Great Russell Street, WC1 (see map page 96)
Tube: Holborn, Russell Square, Tottenham Court Road

The British Museum has three separate shops selling unique gifts. The bookshop is a standout.

TELEPHONE: 020 7580 1788 (recorded information)
Gift Shop: 020 7323 8175
Bookshop: 020 7323 8587
Children's Shop: 020 7323 8828/9
EMAIL: sales@bmco.co.uk (catalog sales)
INTERNET: www.british-museum.ac.uk
CREDIT CARDS: AE, MC, V
OPEN: Mon–Sat 9:30 A.M.–5:30 P.M., Sun 11:30 A.M.–6:30 P.M.

BUCKINGHAM PALACE: THE QUEEN'S GALLERY AND SHOP and THE ROYAL MEWS SHOP
Buckingham Palace Road, SW1 (see map page 124)
Tube: Victoria, St. James's Park

THE QUEEN'S GALLERY AND SHOP (10)

It used to be open only during the summer, which is when Buckingham Palace is open to visitors, but the royals are smart enough to know they have a cash cow here, so now you can spend money 362 days of the year in their Gallery Shop. The shop is very well done and has a tasteful selection of regal gifts that run the gamut from pens and playing cards marked with the Buckingham Palace insignia to china teacups and countless goodies way under £10. I like the Victorian lavender sachets, the packets of fudge wrapped in a palace box with a red tassel on top, the little bags of hot toddy mix, and the exceptional variety of note cards, including boxed editions of Prince Charles's watercolors. There is even a bench for nonshoppers.

NOTE: Tours of Buckingham Palace take place daily 9:30 A.M.–4:15 P.M. during August and September, when the royal family is on holiday. Admission is around £11. Tickets are on sale from 9 A.M. daily at the ticket office on Constitution Hill. To avoid the excruciating queue, book ahead. You can do this using your credit card and telephoning 020 7321 2233.

The Changing of the Guard takes place daily at 11:30 A.M. from April 1 until July 1, and on alternate days thereafter. There is no charge for this.

THE ROYAL MEWS SHOP (12)

Please try to work your sight-seeing schedule to coincide with a time the Royal Mews are open. These are the working stables and garages that house the perfectly groomed horses and magnificent coaches and gilt-trimmed carriages you see in every royal procession. For my money, this is one of the must-sees for every London visitor. The Royal Mews are open Mon–Thur noon–3:30 P.M.; in the summer when Buckingham Palace is open, they are open Mon–Thur 10:30 A.M.–4 P.M.; they are closed for all royal occasions and in June during Ascot Week. The shop sells mugs, key chains, and other touristy items—the real draw is the mews themselves.

TELEPHONE: 020 7839 1377 (this is the number for Buckingham Palace; your call will be referred, but probably not to the queen or Prince Phillip)

FAX: 020 7930 9625

EMAIL: information@royalcollection.org.uk

INTERNET: www.royal.gov.uk

CREDIT CARDS: AE, MC, V

OPEN: *Queen's Gallery and Shop:* Daily 10 A.M.–5 P.M., closed Good Friday, December 25–26; *Royal Mews Shop:* Daily 9:30 A.M.–5 P.M.; open only to ticket bearers for the Royal Mews

COURTAULD GALLERY SHOP (54)
Somerset House, The Strand (down from the Hotel Strand Continental), WC2 (see map page 96)
Tube: Charing Cross, Aldwych

The Courtauld Gallery collection was founded in 1931 by industrialist and art patron Samuel Courtauld, and it features many of the most important Impressionist and Postimpressionist works in London. The small gift shop carries posters, stationery, cards, and books based on this and other collections.

TELEPHONE: 020 7873 2579

FAX: 020 7873 2417

INTERNET: www.courtauld.ac.uk

CREDIT CARDS: MC, V

OPEN: Mon–Sat 10 A.M.–6 P.M., Sun noon–6 P.M.

DESIGN MUSEUM SHOP (12)
Butler's Wharf, 28 Shad Thames Street, SE1 (see map page 182)
Tube: Tower Hill

The Design Museum is devoted to the study of architectural, interior, and furniture design and how they have changed the way we live. The shop has a good selection of designer articles, many related to the current exhibition.

NOTE: In order to get to the Design Museum and the Bramah Tea & Coffee Museum, walk along Shad Thames Street, which runs through Butler's Wharf. When it was built in 1871, it was the largest wharf along the River Thames. In 1984, largely thanks to the insight of Sir Terence Conran, the area slowly started to redevelop. It now consists of his restaurants (expensive), boutiques, art galleries, pubs and wine bars, and the usual sandwich shops.

TELEPHONE: 020 7403 6933

INTERNET: www.designmuseum.org

CREDIT CARDS: AE, MC, V

OPEN: Mon–Fri 11:30 A.M.–6 P.M., Sat–Sun 10:30 A.M.–6 P.M.

IMPERIAL WAR MUSEUM SHOP (17)
Lambeth Road, SE1 (see map page 182)
Tube: Lambeth North, Southwark, Waterloo

The national museum of twentieth-century warfare and Britain's memorial to the two world wars is housed in a former asylum that was once known as Bedlam. Some of it is dull, but not the re-creation of World War I trenches, "London's Blitz Experience," or the exhibition on espionage. The shop sells model airplanes any boy would love.

TELEPHONE: 020 7416 5320
EMAIL: mail@iwm.org.uk
INTERNET: www.iwm.org.uk
CREDIT CARDS: MC, V
OPEN: Daily 10 A.M.–6 P.M.

KENSINGTON PALACE SHOP (35)
Kensington Gardens, W8 (see map page 66)
Tube: High Street Kensington, Queensway

Kensington Palace will forever be remembered as the last home of Diana, Princess of Wales. The recently redone State Apartments, once the home of William and Mary and the birthplace of Queen Victoria, can be viewed on a special tour that includes the Royal Ceremonial Dress Collection, including dresses worn by the present queen, but none of Princess Diana's. After your visit, stop by the Orangerie for a light lunch or tea and a pastry.

TELEPHONE: 020 7937 9561
INTERNET: www.hrp.org.uk
CREDIT CARDS: MC, V
OPEN: Palace daily 10 A.M.–4 P.M., shop daily 10 A.M.–5 P.M.

LONDON TRANSPORT MUSEUM SHOP (51)
The Piazza, Covent Garden, WC2 (see map page 96)
Tube: Covent Garden

The museum, housed in part of the old Victorian Flower Market in Covent Garden, tells the story of London's public transportation system, from the first horse and buggy to the latest space-age marvel. Kids adore it. They can sit in the driver's seat of a red double-decker bus or a tube train. The gift shop is super; it has loads of reproductions of the famous London Transport posters, plus all sorts of other fun things, including "Mind the Gap" paraphernalia that ranges from a pencil or a mug to boxer shorts with the Mind the Gap logo properly positioned for emphasis.

TELEPHONE: 020 7379 6344
INTERNET: www.ltmuseum.co.uk
CREDIT CARDS: MC, V
OPEN: Daily 10 A.M.–6 P.M., last admission to museum 5:15 P.M.

MUSEUM OF LONDON SHOP (10)
150 London Wall, EC2 (see map page 176)
Tube: Barbican, St. Paul's

The museum was built in the mid-seventies on the site of a Roman fort. The exhibits tell the story of London and Londoners from prehistoric times to the present. An illuminated model recounts the story of the Great Fire of London, complete with smoke and crackling noises. The shop has the typical postcards, replicas, and gifty stuff.

TELEPHONE: 020 7600 3699

INTERNET: www.museumoflondon.org.uk

CREDIT CARDS: MC, V

OPEN: Mon–Sat 10 A.M.–5:50 P.M., Sun and bank holidays noon–5:50 P.M.

NATIONAL GALLERY MUSEUM SHOP (58)
Trafalgar Square, WC2 (see map page 96)
Tube: Charing Cross, Leicester Square

The National Gallery has more than two thousand paintings covering all the leading European schools from the thirteenth to the early twentieth centuries. There are two shops, one by the main entrance and a larger one in the Sainsbury Wing. Besides the usual posters and books, keep your eye out for their line of scarves, ceramic tiles, amusing T-shirts, and regal velvet slippers. The shop in the Education Centre has a wealth of toys, books, and activity guides designed to help children learn about art.

TELEPHONE: 020 7747 2537, 020 7747 2870 (mail order)

FAX: 020 7747 5951

INTERNET: www.nationalgallery.co.uk

CREDIT CARDS: AE, MC, V

OPEN: Daily 10 A.M.–6 P.M., Wed until 9 P.M.

NATURAL HISTORY MUSEUM SHOP (13)
Cromwell Road, SW7 (see map page 154)
Tube: South Kensington (take Museums exit)

The Natural History Museum was the Visitor Attraction of the Year in 1998. I am not surprised, if sheer numbers are the guiding measure of popularity. When I was there, the queue of excited young people waiting to get in to see an exhibition on bugs stretched for three blocks down Cromwell Road.

You can go to the shops without paying to go to the museum. To do this, drop by the reception area, sign in, and wear the sticker that identifies you as a shopper only. Free entrance to the museum is between 4:30 and 5:30 P.M. on weekdays and 5 and 5:30 P.M. on weekends, but in that short time span, I don't know what you would be able to see. In addition to the gift and book shops, near the exit of the dinosaur exhibit in Gallery 21 is a Dino-store featuring everything you can imagine with a dinosaur motif, and a plethora of information about these prehistoric beasts. Your children will adore this shop . . . just a warning.

TELEPHONE: 020 7938 9062 (gift shop), 020 7938 9022 (bookshop)
INTERNET: www.nhm.ac.uk
CREDIT CARDS: AE, MC, V
OPEN: Mon–Sat 10 A.M.–5:30 P.M., Sun 11 A.M.–5:50 P.M.

ROYAL ACADEMY OF ARTS SHOP (50)
Burlington House, Piccadilly, W1 (see map page 54)
Tube: Piccadilly Circus, Green Park

Popular changing exhibits here do inspire crowds and long lines. The best time to avoid the crush is early Sunday or Monday mornings. Most of the merchandise in their shop is geared toward whatever blockbuster show is on.

TELEPHONE: 020 7300 5757
FAX: 020 7300 5882
EMAIL: mailorder@royalacademy.org.uk
INTERNET: www.royalacademy.org.uk
CREDIT CARDS: AE, DC, MC, V
OPEN: Daily 10 A.M.–5:45 P.M.

ROYAL OPERA HOUSE GIFT SHOP (51)
Covent Garden, WC2 (see map page 96)
Tube: Covent Garden

The new Royal Opera House is magnificent. Don't miss taking one of the three daily tours, even if you don't like opera. The shop is as impressive as all the rest, and an absolute must for opera buffs.

TELEPHONE: 020 7212 9331
FAX: 020 7212 9256
EMAIL: shop@roh.org.uk
INTERNET: www.royaloperahouse.org
CREDIT CARDS: AE, MC, V
OPEN: Mon–Sat 10 A.M.–7:30 P.M.

ST. PAUL'S CATHEDRAL GIFT SHOP (13)
St. Paul's Church Yard, EC4 (see map page 176)
Tube: St. Paul's

Set in the arched basement of St. Paul's Cathedral, this large gift shop is definitely worthwhile. The selection covers everything from key rings to illustrated books, church memorabilia, and British-made goods. It is all in good taste—even the key rings aren't corny. Enter on the side if you don't want to pay to tour the cathedral. Bonus: it has one of the best public bathrooms in London and places to sit for your nonshopping tagalongs. There's also a restaurant and café, but I recommend timing your visit to include lunch at the Place Below, in the crypt at St. Mary-le-bow Church on Cheapside in the City, EC2 (see *Great Eats London*).

TELEPHONE & FAX: 020 7329 2029
INTERNET: www.stpaulsshop.co.uk

CREDIT CARDS: AE, MC, V

OPEN: Mon–Sat 9 A.M.–5 P.M., Sun 10:30 A.M.–5 P.M.

SCIENCE MUSEUM SHOP (10)
Exhibition Road, SW7 (see map page 154)
Tube: South Kensington (take the Museums exit)

The Science Museum packs five floors full of discoveries and inventions, with explanations about how things work. The many hands-on exhibits and an IMAX cinema make it a paradise for children of all ages. The bookstore is no exception.

TELEPHONE: 020 7938 8187

EMAIL: sciencemuseum@nmsi.ac.uk

INTERNET: www.sciencemuseum.org.uk

CREDIT CARDS: AE, MC, V

OPEN: Daily 10 A.M.–6 P.M.

TATE BRITAIN SHOP (36)
Millbank, SW1 (see map page 124)
Tube: Pimlico

The Tate is well loved for its collections of modern international and British art. Not to be missed are the Turner paintings in the Clore Gallery extension. In May 2000 the contemporary art moved to the new Tate Modern, housed in the old Bankside Power Station across the River Thames. The Millbank building is now called the Tate Britain. The gift shop is very good, featuring loads of gift books, boxes of stationery, and posters of their exhibitions. My favorite purchases are their umbrellas inspired by Monet, Miró, Matisse, and Braque.

TELEPHONE: 020 7887 8876

CREDIT CARDS: AE, MC, V

OPEN: Daily 10 A.M.–5:40 P.M.

TATE MODERN SHOP (1)
25 Sumner Street, Bankside, SE1 (see map page 182)
Tube: Southwark

The Tate Modern is Britain's new museum of modern art. Hailed by critics as "The Cathedral of Cool," the £134 million building was transformed from a power station (originally built by Sir Giles Gilbert Scott, architect of Liverpool's Anglican Cathedral and the designer of the famed red telephone booth) into a stunning space displaying international modern art from 1900 to the present day. The mammoth structure is opposite the River Thames from St. Paul's Cathedral and is a must-see for any London visitor. The gift shop has a fabulous selection of art books with a wonderful section devoted to children.

TELEPHONE: 020 7887 8000

EMAIL: information@tate.org.uk

INTERNET: www.tate.org.uk

CREDIT CARDS: AE, DC, MC, V

OPEN: Sun–Thur 10 A.M.–5:50 P.M., Fri–Sat 10 A.M.–9:50 P.M.

TOWER OF LONDON SHOP (15)
Tower Hill, EC3 (see map page 176)
Tube: Tower Hill

The Tower of London has been a castle, a palace, and a prison. Now it is a favorite tourist destination. One of the biggest attractions is the Crown Jewels, and while you may never wear the real thing, you can buy replicas of some of the pieces in the gift shop.

TELEPHONE: 020 7709 0765

CREDIT CARDS: AE, MC, V

OPEN: Nov–Feb Mon–Sat 10 A.M.–4 P.M., Sun 9 A.M.–5 P.M.; Mar–Oct Mon–Sat 9 A.M.–5 P.M., Sun 10 A.M.–5 P.M.

VICTORIA AND ALBERT MUSEUM SHOP AND
CRAFTS COUNCIL SHOP (12)
Cromwell Road, SW7 (see map page 154)
Tube: South Kensington (take the Museums exit)

The Victoria and Albert has the world's largest collection of decorative, fine, and applied arts, as well as the national sculpture collection. Its galleries cover seven miles and attract more than a million visitors a year. The gift shop keeps pace. It is the best in London, especially the handmade items from Britain's leading craft artists. At Christmastime, the selection is especially appealing.

TELEPHONE: 020 7938 8438

FAX: 020 7938 8623

INTERNET: www.vam.ac.uk

CREDIT CARDS: AE, MC, V

OPEN: Daily 10 A.M.–5:30 P.M., Wed until 10 P.M.

Shops by Type

Vintage Clothing

Glossary

America and Britain are two great nations divided by a common language.

—*George Bernard Shaw*

English	American
A	
all-in	all-inclusive
anorak	hooded jacket (parka)
B	
bank holiday	legal holiday
bath	bathtub
bathroom	a room with a bathtub in it
bedsit or bed-sitter	studio or one-room apartment
bespoke	custom-made clothing
bill	check (restaurant)
bin	trash can
bobby	police officer
bonnet (car)	car hood
book (*v.*)	to reserve
boot	car trunk
braces	suspenders
briefs	jockey shorts
brolly or bumbershoot	umbrella
C	
call (*v.*)	visit, as in pay a visit or call into a shop
caravan	trailer, mobile home
car park	parking lot
carriage	railroad car
cash point machine	ATM
chemist	pharmacist
chemist shop	drugstore, pharmacy
cinema	movie theater
coach	bus for long trips
cot crib	baby crib
cotton	thread
cotton wool	absorbent cotton
cupboard	closet
D	
dear	expensive
dinner jacket	tuxedo
directory inquiries	telephone information

diversion	detour
double	hotel room with double bed
dress circle	mezzanine/loge
dressing gown	bathrobe
dual carriageway	divided highway
dungarees	overalls

E

earthwire/earth	grounded plug
eiderdown	comforter
engaged	busy
en suite	hotel room with private toilet, shower, and/or bathtub
estate car	station wagon

F

face flannel	washcloth
fancy (v.)	to desire something
filling station	gas station
first floor	second floor
flat	apartment
flex	electric cord
fly over	overpass
fortnight	two weeks

G

gallery (theatre)	balcony
gangway	aisle
ground floor	first floor

H

hair grip	bobby pin
hair slide	barrette
handbag	purse
hardware	housewares
high street	main street
hire (v.)	to rent (as in rent a car)
holiday	vacation

I

ironmonger	hardware store

J

jersey	heavy sweater
jumble sale	used clothing sale, as in rummage
jumper/pullover	cardigan sweater

K

knickers	underpants

L

ladder	pantyhose run
let (v.)	to lease, rent
lie in, have a lie in (v.)	to sleep in

lift	elevator
loo	toilet
lorry	truck
lower ground floor	below street level, basement level

M

mackintosh	raincoat
mate	pal
mobile	cell phone
motorway	freeway

N

nappy	diaper
naught	zero
net curtain	sheer curtains

O

off-license/wine merchant	retail liquor store
off the peg	ready-made
one-off	onetime event or happening
over the moon	to be delighted

P

pants	shorts (men's underwear)
parcel	package
partner	live-in boyfriend or girlfriend
pavement/footpath	sidewalk
personal call	person-to-person telephone call
petrol	gasoline
phone box or call box	telephone booth
plaster	Band Aid
point, power point	outlet, socket
polo neck	turtleneck shirt
post	mail
post code	zip code
pram	baby buggy
public school	private school
purse	a woman's wallet
push chair	stroller
push out the boat	spend beyond the limit

Q

queue	waiting line
quid	slang for one British pound

R

reception (hotel)	front desk, lobby
return ticket	round-trip ticket
ring (v.)	to telephone
roundabout	traffic circle
rubber	eraser

S

saloon car	sedan
schedule	the same meaning, but pronounced "shed-ule"
self-catering	accommodation with kitchen
self-drive	car rental
sellotape	Scotch tape
service flats	apartment hotel
single ticket	one-way ticket
stalls	orchestra seats in the theater
subway	underground passageway
suspender belt	garter belt
suspenders	garters
swimming costume	bathing suit
swing a cat ("You couldn't swing a cat in here")	a saying for describing the size of a room

T

tailback	bumper-to-bumper automobile gridlock
telly	television
tights	panty hose
torch	flashlight
trainers	sneakers, athletic shoes (e.g., Nikes)
treble (room)	hotel room with three single beds
trolley	cart (at the airport, or in the supermarket)
trousers	pants, slacks

V

VAT (value-added tax)	sales tax
vest	old man's undershirt

W

waistcoat	vest
wardrobe	closet
water closet (WC)	toilet
wellies	waterproof boots, galoshes
windscreen	windshield

Z

zebra crossing	pedestrian crossing
zed (letter)	pronunciation of the letter z

Index of Accommodations

Hotels with Apartments and/or Kitchenettes

Index of Shops

Readers' Comments

While every effort has been made to provide accurate information in this edition of *Great Sleeps London,* the publisher and author cannot be held responsible for changes in any of the listings due to rate increases, inflation, currency fluctuations, the passage of time, management changes, or any losses thereby caused. The publisher and author also cannot be held responsible for the experiences of readers while traveling.

Great Sleeps London is updated and revised on a regular basis. If you find a change before I do, or make an important discovery you want to pass along, please send me a note stating the name and address of the hotel or shop, the name of the people you dealt with, the date of your visit, and a description of your findings. As the hundreds of readers who have written to me know, your letters are very important to me; I investigate every complaint and pass on every compliment you send me, and I read and personally answer every letter. Because of this, I do not provide an email address, since the volume of mail it would generate would make it impossible to personally reply to each message. I hope you will understand and still take a few minutes to drop me an old-fashioned letter telling me about your Great Sleeps in London. Thank you in advance for taking the time to write.

Send your comments to Sandra A. Gustafson's *Great Sleeps London,* c/o Chronicle Books, 85 Second Street, Sixth Floor, San Francisco, CA 94105.

For more about all of the books in the Great Eats/Great Sleeps series, and for updates as I travel, please visit www.greateatsandsleeps.com.